Issues of Justice:
Social Sources
and Religious Meanings

Roger D. Hatch
and
Warren R. Copeland
Coeditors

■ ■

Issues of Justice:
Social Sources
and Religious Meanings

■ MERCER ■

ISBN 0-86554-304-6

Issues of Justice:
Social Sources and Religious Meanings
Copyright © 1988
Mercer University Press
Macon, Georgia 31207
Printed in the United States of America
▪▪

The paper used in this publication meets
the minimum requirements of American National Standard
for Information Sciences—Permanence of Paper
for Printed Library Materials, ANSI Z39.48-1984.
▪▪

Library of Congress Cataloging-in-Publication Data

Issues of justice: social sources and religious meanings
Roger D. Hatch and Warren R. Copeland, coeditors.

350pp. 6x9″ (16x23cm.)
Includes bibliographies.
ISBN 0-86554-304-6 (alk. paper)
1. Social ethics. 2. Christian ethics—United States.
I. Hatch, Roger D. II. Copeland, Warren R.
HM216.I84   1988   88-8594
170—dc19   CIP

Contents

PREFACE

"What's the use? Every direction we turn we hit stone walls. Maybe it's time for us to face facts, move out to Eastbrook with all the other young professionals, and start enjoying life." With these words Scott articulated the gnawing sense of a dream fading. The immediate cause of this outburst was kindergarten at Lincoln School. Chris, their five-year-old, had gone off to her first day of school with great anticipation. A seasoned veteran of bedtime reading, "Sesame Street," two years of nursery school, and two parents who encouraged her ideas and questions—she expected school to be fun. It was not. At the first parents' conference, Chris's teacher welcomed Scott and Karen with glowing words about their bright daughter but quickly turned to talk of her other students. Children just were not ready for school the way they used to be before the neighborhood changed. At least, she sighed, it was only two more years until her retirement. Besides, she had never been taught how to deal with children of such different backgrounds—cultural, racial, economic, and family.

Once Chris was identified as a reader, she began to bring home little yellow books with silly animals saying words that all rhymed—"Sam, I am." Actually, soon Chris came dragging them home, and in the morning she wanted to stay in bed because her stomach hurt. So Scott and Karen made an appointment to see the principal, whereupon they were told of the difficulties of working with the other children and their parents. The lecture concluded with the suggestion: "Perhaps you folks really belong out in Eastbrook where Chris would be with children like herself and get the kind of education you seem to want." Yet, as Scott and Karen thought about that comment later, they agreed that Eastbrook did not offer the education they wanted. Eastbrook did not celebrate black history month with pictures of great African kings and queens and dramas about Frederick Douglass and Sojourner Truth. At Eastbrook Chris could not have felt LaWanda's braided hair or tasted the funny snack Pedro's mother brought on his birthday.

Louise and Fred live around the corner from Scott and Karen. Since the school district has a voluntary transfer program to improve racial balance, they do not have to move in order for their daughter to attend Eastbrook. Nevertheless, as Dawn approaches school age, they do face a difficult choice. If Dawn attends Eastbrook, her classmates will be academically stimulating, teacher morale will be much higher than at Lincoln, and the library shelves will be full of computer software. However, she will also be an oddity at Eastbrook, one of only two or three nonwhite children in her class. Some days she will be a pet, other days a threat. Eastbrook children have never heard of black history month, great African kings and queens, or Frederick Douglass and Sojourner Truth. Their skin is white, their hair is straight, and their snacks are both. Louise and Fred know that sending Dawn to Eastbrook runs the risk of undermining her sense of self, let alone pride in her heritage, but she probably will learn more math and grammar there.

Ten years ago, sitting in a sociology class together, Karen and Scott had promised themselves that they would not accept a society divided by race, that they would not perpetuate the system that resulted in their growing up in nearly all-white suburbs. Sitting together in an Afro-American history course at about the same time, Fred and Louise pledged to each other that their commitment to an integrated society would not keep them from making sure their children knew their own history. Can these two couples keep their promises to themselves? What do they need to know or decide in order to choose the best school for Chris and Dawn?

In the discipline of ethics, these stories are known as case studies. At this point, readers generally are invited to put themselves in the place of the people involved and determine what they would do. On an immediate personal level, the choice here seems to be between academic excellence and racial awareness. But is that the choice? Perhaps Lincoln is not as weak academically as it seems or it can be enriched with a little effort. Then again, perhaps with strong support from their homes, Chris and Dawn can become academically successful in spite of Lincoln. Perhaps Eastbrook can be opened up racially or Chris's and Dawn's parents can expose them to minority culture at home. If not, if there is a real choice that has to be made, then they shall have to decide whether academic achievement or cultural awareness is the more important value.

This is what a case study usually presents to readers: a difficult choice that individuals must make that raises significant questions of both fact and value. Yet in this particular case a voice within us may say: "This is stupid; people should not have to choose between intellectual development and racial awareness for their children." If so, we may have gained a first insight into what these four parents are now learning the hard way, namely, that the inequalities of race and class are so deeply embedded in our social order that even persons with every good intention cannot escape their effects. What we may well have here is a matter not of individual choice but rather of social choice.

If so, the questions we need to ask may be somewhat different. Why is our social order organized so that black and white students usually do not go to school together, so that the majority white schools generally have stronger academic programs than majority black schools, and so that violence often results from attempts to change these facts? How do other social institutions—such as the housing and job markets, political boundaries, or school-aid formulas—operate so as to reinforce segregated schools? What would it take to change this social order, both in terms of policy (full employment, scattered-site public housing in the suburbs, school funding mechanisms, et cetera) and in terms of associations (Parents for Integrated Education, a revitalized NAACP, a reform caucus in the Democratic party, et cetera)? Finally, do we still even believe in the value of integration or know how it is different from assimilation or mere desegregation?

When we ask such questions, we discover that these two couples face an issue of social ethics. So does a teacher who discovers that her student has missed class half of the time for the last month because his family was burned out of their home and all eight of them are living in two motel rooms. We also can include the high school students who raise money to feed starving children in Africa and the couples who are committed to equality in their marriage. Add the young man who would like to breathe clean air and even the child who wakes up crying from nightmares of nuclear war. All face the same truth: individual acts may save a few victims or provide a sense of defiance, but the social order merely churns out new victims and bigger challenges. Something deeper and broader must change—the social order itself.

The authors of this volume include teachers of Scotts and Karens and Louises and Freds. In various contexts inside and outside of academia, we raise basic social issues to the consciousness of our students. A few of them could care less. Many, perhaps most, find them interesting topics of study but not serious challenges to action. Yet a good number want, even pledge, to do something about poverty, racism, pollution, or sexism. Too often, however, like Scott and Louise, they find their efforts exciting but also lonely and discouraging. As Karens and Freds of an earlier generation, we also share in their joy and in their disappointment and frustration. One purpose of this book is to present analyses of these issues that are adequate to the complex character of our world. By so doing, we hope that we and our students—and many others who share our experiences—will see these issues in a new light that enables new action. In other words, readers should be able to return to questions of personal and social choice (in situations such as that facing Scott and Karen and Louise and Fred) with new resources for undertaking positive social change.

Religious Social Ethics

While of different ages, all of the authors came to some level of maturity during a period marked by major movements against such social ills as racism, poverty, war, environmental destruction, and sexism. In a variety of ways, all of us have been involved in one or more of these movements and have been shaped fundamentally by that involvement. Yet we usually were strange participants, seeking broader understandings and more fundamental rationales. As such, we were a bit too intellectual for many of the activists. As might be expected, we also generally were too concerned with action for most academics.

For nearly all of us, this marginality—being both too intellectual and too activist—was nurtured by our study of ethics and society at the Divinity School of the University of Chicago. But there it was celebrated as the unification of peculiar forms of thought—Aristotle, Hannah Arendt, John Dewey, and Alfred North Whitehead—with particular forms of action—voluntary associations and democratic social change. Since those days, some of us have added liberation theology and more radical social analyses to our resources. However, regardless of which resources we depend upon, all of us use them to do what we call religious social ethics.

Ethics is about making choices; its function is to reflect critically about what choices we should make. At its fullest, it finds completion in actual choices made about alternative courses of possible action. The intention of this book is to introduce readers to critical thought about some important choices we must make if we are to do justice. This justice—which is the basic purpose of social ethics—seems simple enough as a concept. In fact, the authors of this volume would narrow the meaning of that concept to something like "unity in diversity." Yet, to have any real idea of what that means amid the complexity of marginality in Thailand or economic policy in the United States requires considerable analysis. That is what the chapters that follow seek to accomplish. Once we have looked for justice in the complicated world around us, we shall return to the question of its general character much more able to specify its meaning.

To complicate matters further, this is an introduction to *social* ethics. The choices with which we shall deal involve basic issues of our social order such as sexism, poverty, environmental destruction, and war. To emphasize the social character of these issues is not to suggest they do not affect individuals, as millions of battered women, unemployed black youth, undernourished poor children, refugees from combat zones, and sufferers of pollution-fed emphysema know all too well. Neither does it imply that specific action by particular human beings will not be required to deal with these issues. What it does mean is that these issues are rooted in the very structure of our social institutions and that it will take changes in those social structures themselves in order to deal with them. This helps explain why some issues do not appear here. For instance, biomedical ethics usually centers on issues confronted by individuals or small groups of professionals rather than society as a whole. This stress on the social order also helps explain the focus upon the public and structural elements of each issue that is considered.

This is a volume about ethics and more specifically social ethics, yet our focus is most specifically upon *religious* social ethics. We take questions about the quality of our social order generally and about the nature and possible practice of justice in that social order in particular to be central to religion. Historically, religious institutions and traditions, certainly in the West, have had something to say about the nature and the importance of social justice. Theologically, the question of social justice is finally the question of the ultimate terms for human fulfillment, and religion is about that ultimacy. Thus, on both historical and theological grounds, social justice is a central religious question.

The Status of Social Justice

The confusion and frustration in which we and our students and other kindred souls find ourselves these days closely parallels the status of social justice itself. At least in the United States, even to speak of social justice is to date oneself. "We tried that, and it did not work," some people will tell you. At present, those who consider social justice a vain goal seem to have not only the political momentum but also all of the new ideas. It is becoming increasingly clear that this is true in part because advocates of social justice are confused in both thought and action. The authors of this volume argue in various ways that one basic reason for this confusion is that social justice too often has been reduced to seeking after private preferences.

This drive for private preferences is most obvious in what is being called by some the emerging "greed society." In this society, citizens are only asked to think about whether they personally are faring better. Many decry the emergence of such a greed society with moral indignation and look back nostalgically to a time when people were involved in movements for social justice. Yet critics of this naked appeal to self-interest need to reflect a bit on what has become of those movements that have been the heart and soul of our recent efforts at social justice in the United States.

The civil rights movement sought to end segregation and made great strides toward doing so. In the process, it discovered an institutional racism deeply embedded in our social order. The considerable achievement of ending legal segregation was not accompanied by a dismantling of this institutional racism. As a result, the majority of blacks were unable to take advantage of new opportunities, meaning their relative status actually has deteriorated during the past decade. At the same time as the reality of institutional racism came into view, the need to develop black power led blacks to reaffirm black unity. Confronted by the simultaneous challenges of institutional racism and rising black consciousness, one institution after another found it much easier to recognize a black caucus than to come to terms with its own racism. This led a bishop's assistant of one large church body to explain loudly to his fellow white church leaders that his organization had no problem with racism anymore because it had recognized and funded a black caucus. The assumption, consciously or unconsciously, seemed to be that if blacks were given a small piece of the pie, it would not be necessary to consider further the nature of the whole pie. A public issue cutting right through the entire social order was reduced to the private interest of blacks. A similar story could be written about the women's movement, the environmental movement, the peace movement, or the war on poverty. Sexism was reduced to women's caucuses, and poverty, environmental destruction, and war to lobbies or special-interest groups.

At times these groups may have become implicated in this reduction of public issues to private interests because they believed they could gain more from acting as interest groups than as advocates of a public issue. For instance, many universities that were unable or unwilling to address the systematic racism of their curricula, student life, or employment practices were quite willing to provide black culture houses and counselors to minority students. Who can blame black students for taking what they could get? At least they could use the funds to bring a speaker to campus to speak to their situation or to finance a tutoring program or just to support and encourage each other. These are all good causes. The problem lies with white institutions that use them as excuses to escape their own racism.

Moreover, if these basic issues are to be faced, the interest groups that resulted from these issues, such as black and women's caucuses, are essential to the expression of different traditions and perspectives. Certainly women can lay legitimate claim to a deeper understanding of the pain caused by sexism than can men. Similarly, blacks, the poor, Vietnam veterans, and environmentalists can claim unique insights. These groups are not about to abandon an issue that so deeply involves them personally just because it no longer is in the news. Peter Paris has remarked about this problem in relation to black churches. He describes the dual responsibility these churches have carried—to build up the race and to change the nation. Moreover, he suggests that there has been a sort of "rhythm of relevance" for when each of these purposes was more possible. Recent times have not been a good season for changing the nation, so all of these various groups have been forced to focus on their own equivalent of "building up the race."

Yet, if we are to come to terms with environmental destruction, for example, the Sierra Club must be seen not as one more interest group but rather as one articulation of the public's interest in environmental integrity. The same is true of the National Organization of Women on sexism, the National Association for the Advancement of Colored People on racism, SANE on war and peace, and the National Welfare Rights Organization on poverty.

As already suggested, institutions, including universities and churches, are deeply implicated in the reduction of public issues to private interests. It simply was easier than thinking and acting in the terms necessary to come to grips with the issues. Yet more conservative forces jumped at the opportunity provided by this reduction to turn their backs on these issues. Regardless of where we place the blame, the confusion is now widespread in our political life. When politicians of the left, such as Jesse Jackson, talk of a rainbow coalition, it sounds all too much like a collection of quite different interests rather than an interweaving of a range of issues important to the society at large. Centrist politicians, such as Walter Mondale, appear tied to so many disparate interests as to be unable to move in the direction of the public interest. Politicians of the right, such as Ronald Reagan, are able to dismiss most of the critical public issues of our day as narrow special interests. What all three share is the reduction in contemporary American life of public issues to private interests.

We propose, instead, to argue for social justice in this volume. The authors will address issues as *public*, embedded in the social order we all share and thus of importance to us all. While we certainly shall take note of the differential impact of that social order—such that some fare much better than others—and of the unique interest particular groups have shown in various issues, we shall assume and at the same time show that these are issues for the public at large. We also shall articulate public principles upon which to judge and act on these issues. The questions before us are not just matters of who gets which piece of the action but also whether it is worth having a piece of that particular action. These are questions of public value, not just private possession. Finally, our investigations will begin in the public debates and will seek to refine, extend, and provoke further debate rather than end it. They will be successful if they encourage readers to enter into public life with new understanding and new energy.

ACKNOWLEDGMENTS

This volume was first conceived at a meeting of the Social Ethics Seminar. Both editors and all of the authors of this volume are members of that organization. It is within that context, both at formal meetings and in informal discussions, that most of the ideas in this volume first saw the light of day.

While we are grateful to all of the members of the Seminar for both intellectual stimulation and personal support, we must express our particular thanks to Alan Anderson. For the two of us, the Seminar began in Alan's living room when we were graduate students and he was our teacher. What set Alan apart as a teacher and makes him such a superb colleague is his consistent pressure on us to develop our own best ideas rather than merely repeat his. It is this spirit that we now see embodied in institutional form in this Social Ethics Seminar itself.

Warren Copeland is grateful to the Faculty Research Fund Board of Wittenberg University for its generous support and genuine interest in this project. For stimulation and refuge, he thanks Clara, Scott, and Karen; if we are lucky, the various parts of four lives complement each other.

Roger Hatch thanks Marcia R. Sawyer for her encouragement and insights and the Department of Religion of Central Michigan University for its assistance and support in the preparation of the manuscript.

Finally, we are glad that our skills complement each other so well and that, at the end of this project, we still remain friends.

Warren R. Copeland
Wittenberg University

■■

Introduction

■■ What could be more boring and obscure reading than a discussion of ethical method? Yet we run the danger of not really understanding what an author is doing if we do not ask why a particular analysis is developed in the way it is. This is especially true when the topics are as common as the daily newspaper yet as complex as our social order. In part two of this volume we offer nine analyses of basic issues in our common life. It is hoped that references to the specific reading we shall do will keep our thinking sufficiently concrete and relatively interesting. Do these nine analyses share a common approach? Do they take up similar materials, make comparable claims, and base those claims on similar principles? Certainly these nine analyses are extremely diverse both in subject matter and approach. We believe, however, that they take up these quite different topics in manners enough alike to be termed a common method, especially in contrast to some alternative methods typical of contemporary religious social ethics.

For the authors of this volume religious social ethics begins and ends with issues—not theological concepts, personal values, or the suffering of a particular group of people, but issues. The impetus to action and thought is the experience of an issue cutting across our life together as human beings. The standard by which an ethical analysis is judged is its capacity to inform action on the issue at hand. Let us begin thinking about the nine chapters in part two by discussing the issue-oriented method used in them under five topics: the location of the issue, the importance of historical context, the role of dimension or perspective, the nature of principles, and the status of claims made. In each case I shall use illustrations at length from those chapters.

The Location of the Issue

For the authors of this volume, the issues discussed here at least are located in the social order.[1] The institutions of our society are organized in ways that deny our common humanity in some very basic ways—by race, sex, income, or citizenship, or by relative access to energy, information, or capital. When such denials occur, social ethical issues arise. Social order and institutions seem like such abstract and distant concepts, the kind only sociologists understand. We are not referring here to such abstractions but rather to the lived reality we all know quite well. When almost any American visits a new community, she assumes that it will have a poor part of town and a rich part. We all expect secretaries and nurses to be women and plumbers and electricians to be men. Every high school student learns that it is hard to get a job without education and skills. Anyone who lives downwind from a steel mill understands quite well that there is a trade-off between making steel and clean air. This is our social order. It dramatically shapes even the most personal aspects of our lives. It makes us laugh and cry. We see it deny both our own humanity and that of our fellow human beings. We want it to be just.

Some people locate the issues taken up in the following chapters in persons' psychological makeup or in cultural values. While the authors agree that these are important aspects of these issues, the issues actually reside in the social structure itself. We often wish that this were not true and hope that if we change our personal life-style or our cultural symbols, the issues will disappear. Such kinds of change are terribly important, but their success in addressing issues of social justice can only be measured by what does or does not change in the social order itself. We cannot escape. This is our social order; we have no other one. These issues will continue to deny our common humanity until that social order is changed.

Sexism and racism have often been analyzed in terms of the psychological makeup of whites and men or blacks and women or in terms of the

---

[1]Alan B. Anderson, "The Search for Method in Social Ethics," in W. Widick Schroeder and Gibson Winter, eds., *Belief and Ethics* (Chicago: Center for the Scientific Study of Religion, 1978) 107-28, argues for the subject matter of social ethics being issues in the social order.

dominance of white and male cultural symbols and the subordination of black and female ones. Clearly these aspects of the issue are significant. However, Roger Hatch and Mary Pellauer locate the issues of racism and sexism in the social order, seeing the psychological and cultural elements of these issues as dimensions of how the patterns of social institutions shape every corner of our lives. For example, Hatch discusses the various institutional forms racism has taken (slavery, Jim Crow, and the metropolitan color line), yet it has always been institutionalized. But perhaps the best single example is the manner in which Pellauer deals with rape. Obviously rape is the violent act of one person against another and as such draws us both to the psychological profile of the perpetrator and to the psychological damage to the victim. Yet, Pellauer helps us see this violent act as but one dimension of a complex of social institutional practices that both makes the act more likely and handicaps our response when it occurs. All of the psychotherapy in the world will not change that basic structure of sexism, a social structure.

In Capo's hands, even the flash and style of television news becomes a matter of the social order. Media—especially television news—is important because of its growing function in the social order. The issue for Capo certainly is not ratings. However, neither is it the trustworthiness of the news, as is the case with most ethical analyses of the news media. Rather, the central question is how news can facilitate the interchange essential to a democratic social order. Perhaps most interesting is how this focus brings matters of style and symbols back under consideration, but now in terms of how they short-circuit or facilitate such interchange. Similarly, objectivity, truth, freedom, and social responsibility are not dismissed as principles of news but instead are reinterpreted with a view to what each means if the central purpose is to initiate and extend democratic interchange. In the final analysis, the ethical significance of the news media rests on its place in the social order.

Livezey points out that peace too often is seen as a problem of human relationships or inadequate theory. However, he focuses upon policy, upon changing the direction of institutions so as to make peace a realistic value. Indeed, his entire analysis stresses actual structures of poverty, freedom, political interests, and military capacity and how they can be understood and shifted to support peace. According to Engel, the force that drives tropical deforestation is a set of ''mutually reinforcing technological, social, economic, political, and cultural factors''—in other words, a social order committed to modern development. Even Srisang's essentially cultural analysis takes as a beginning point poverty and marginalization. The problem of the Thai people, and especially of the Isan region, is how the Thai social order is organized. Srisang's retelling of the religious myth of the Isan is directed toward reconstituting that social order.

When we turn to domestic issues other than television news, the centrality of the social order is obvious. Copeland tells us that the primary discovery of our social-reform tradition is that poverty is a problem of our social order, not simply of personal failure. Usually appearing as a resource or technology debate, energy emerges here as a basic problem of social organization both in terms of how energy is distributed and in terms of how it is to be controlled. Similarly, economic policy is not just a question of the effects of a few shifts in policy here and there, but is a question of the structure of the economic order itself.

It may seem redundant, but these authors all believe that religious *social* ethics is about the *social* order. In fact, more than one inquiry into social ethics ends as an exercise in values clarification, personal growth, or cultural insight. The following essays do not intend to do so. If they help readers think some new ideas, reach new levels of personal resolve, or create new cultural symbols, so much the better. Yet, we are convinced that if none of this changes the social order itself, then the issues will remain. The institutions through which we live will continue to deny our common humanity.

The Importance of Historical Context

Nearly all scholars claim that history is important; most include a little history when they write. Often it is less than clear why history is important to the task at hand. Social ethics assumes history, assumes that human action makes a difference. Real novelty and innovation do occur in public life, in unprecedented ways and with unpredictable results. New issues arise, and old issues take on whole new shapes as the result of human initiatives. If history were not like this, ethics would not be about human choice but rather about coping with inevitable forces: natural, economic, technological, social, or divine. Indeed, some ethics finally implies just such a coping function, but not the following essays. They describe an exciting and messy view of history as a drama of human activity that does in fact change the course of events. Such a view of history does not just add a little color or texture to ethical analysis. It is essential to the very meaning of our work. This historical drama shapes our inquiries in two apparently contradictory ways.

We human beings are products of our world, of the social forces acting upon us. That is why it is an ethical issue when the social order denies our humanity. It cuts off human possibilities. Yet the present order has been formed by history, by past actions. Often identifiable acts have produced results that have interacted with the results of other actions in an interlocking social order with real power to shape lives. The following essays are not in the least naive about the power of these social forces. While some of the issues have emerged fairly recently, others have persisted for generations despite attacks by social movements and shifts in technological, social, and even theological forces. In the process, they have taken different shapes. If we are to understand the often brutal realities that shape our lives, we had better study how they came to be. Remembering that these brutal forces are themselves the result of human action, much of it well intentioned, should give us some hope that our action can make a difference and some pause that the results of our own action may be problematic.

Yet humans act as well as being acted upon. History is not just the account of the formation and inevitable culmination of blind forces. It is also the account of the actions of human beings who have dreams and learn lessons. This is especially significant to social ethicists because we study the failures of human society, those areas where humanity is denied. Yet it is generally the case that we are not the first to do so. Moreover, just because certain persons or groups failed to end war, poverty, sexism, or racism does not mean they did not hold noble purposes or gain helpful insights. Not to study history or to study it only from the perspective of the winners is to cut ourselves off from those sources of purpose and insight. The general view of history as the account of human acts helps us see it as both the source of the issue and as a resource for coming to terms with it.

A good illustration of these two aspects of the historical context is Hatch's discussion of the changing institutional forms of racism in the United States from slavery through Jim Crow to the metropolitan color line. Slavery was not inevitable; it was the result of a particular set of human choices. Once enacted, however, it set in motion social forces that have dramatically shaped people's lives right down to the present. In the process, other human choices changed the form racism took, for good or ill. Implied throughout Hatch's telling of this story is the idea that we cannot understand the dynamics of institutional racism today if we do not recognize its roots in the slavery and discrimination of the past. History is a problem. Yet history also allows us to join with Booker T. Washington and W. E. B. DuBois as they grapple with the Jim Crow of their day. In doing this, we not only come to appreciate the value of their struggle, but we also gain some insight from their analysis of the issue. Not to do so would impoverish our efforts to come to terms with the racism they changed but could not defeat. History is a resource.

Copeland's account of the history of the energy issue highlights this same double significance of history quite straightforwardly. The history of fuels is not in fact about natural resources. It is the story of human discovery and invention and the evolution of human institutions based on the resulting technology. This comes to us in the form of the facts of energy use, technological capability, and supplies of various fuels. In fact, these stand for a whole complex of social structures—from the housing and auto industries to universities researching fusion reactors—that cannot be changed easily or quickly without significant human pain. History shapes the problem. On the other hand, over a brief period of time—compared to issues such as peace or sexism—humans have tried to cope with the problem of less energy supply than demand. In the process, they have gained considerable insight into the human stake in an apparently technical issue. To proceed blind to these insights is to handicap ourselves. History is a resource.

On the international front, when Livezey describes alternative theories of U.S. foreign policy, they appear not as abstract, timeless concepts but rather as views that emerged at particular times in U.S. history, articulated by particular persons to fit specific situations. As a result, they take on the form of both a fixed reality shaping the present possibilities for our foreign policy and as interesting views of relations among nations that become resources for proposing a constructive direction for present policy. Similarly, neither the reigning ideology of modernization nor the two ethics that oppose it are abstractions for Engel. The former developed over time into the theme of our social order, and the latter are attached to actual people and associations in his telling. Certainly any new ethic has much to learn from the insights and shortcomings of these people and associations that embody the two ethics. This twofold sense of history takes on a more dramatic form in Srisang's account of Thailand. History has brought the Thai people to their present condition of poverty, marginality, and lack of freedom. Yet it is precisely that history that, by Srisang's account, provides the mythic resources for salvation. He does not look outside the history of the Thai people for help, but rather peers back into their faint past in order to gain vision for the future.

On the domestic side, Copeland's histories of poverty and economic policy deal with each as a public issue rather than a social fact. In the case of poverty, the result is an account of the discovery of poverty as a social rather than personal problem and of the successes and failures of various attempts to eradicate it. In the case of economic policy, he recounts the emergence of the various basic approaches to economic policy that we now encounter in the policy debate. In neither case is much attention paid to the sheer reality of poverty or to shifts in the nature of the economy itself. Yet the implication of the two stories are that poverty and economic policy are enduring issues that have just not gone away. Pellauer's discussion of the changing contours of the distinction between man's world and woman's place illustrates the shifting form of a stubborn fact of our social order. Yet when Pellauer looks for confirmation of her multidimensional analysis of sexism, she turns to a similar analysis by Elizabeth Cady Stanton. Stanton's movement a century ago failed to end sexism, but it did change its form and in the process gained profound insights into its nature. Capo reaches much further back in the history of the West to identify the intellectual roots of the accepted principles of journalistic ethics. Yet he also sees them as having emerged at specific times in the recent history of U.S. media as journalists took their stance in relation to particular events.

Perhaps it is the influence of Whitehead over these authors that has led to their use of history in these ways. He argued that we must take account of the sheer facticity of the past as it shapes and limits contemporary choices while always maintaining the power of human purpose to mold and integrate that facticity in creative ways.[2] Human initiative is real, and its results are enduring. In any event, these authors certainly see history as both limitation and resource for action. The humanity-denying character of the social order we have inherited seems all too inevitable, making of us all behavioralists who despair over the environment that shapes us. Yet in that same past, we catch glimpses of predecessors who have refused to accept the apparently inevitable and who in the process both bent the course of

---

[2]Alfred North Whitehead, *Adventure of Ideas* (New York: Free Press, 1967) 63-68, contains a discussion of this dual reality in relation to freedom.

human events in more humane directions and articulated even more creative visions that stand as resources for our own action. As both problem and as resource, history underlines the importance of human choice—and thus of ethics.

The Role of Dimension or Perspective

For the authors of this volume, reality is neither singular nor flat. Dorothy Emmet describes morality in similar fashion, using the metaphor of a prism: "Ideally moral judgment might be a white light showing clearly what action would be best in any situation. But just as light coming through a prism is refracted into a spectrum of different colours, so our moral thinking shows us a range of different features, and attention can fasten now on one and now on another."[3] Each of the following chapters displays such a moral spectrum. In some, it is referred to as dimensions of the issue, in others as positions, theories, perspectives, or principles. In each case, the author recognizes that the issue can be seen from more than one vantage point and can look quite different to different viewers. The implications we draw from this prismatic analysis are at least two. First, each dimension has integrity and thus deserves respect. They are not just straw men set up to be knocked down by the one true position. Second, in part because of the integrity of the various dimensions or perspectives, these analyses push toward some sense of comprehensiveness, some way of preserving the insights gained from each vantage point.

In her discussion of rape, Pellauer shows that it falls primarily within one of the six dimensions of sexism she has identified: "violence to women and the violation of our physical integrity." It is helpful to name it for what it is and to liken it to and distinguish it from other practices that fall within this dimension. Clarity is served by focusing on this band of the spectrum. However, an even richer understanding of rape results from then seeing the relation of violence to the other dimensions of the issue. For instance, the fact that most police officers and physicians are men adds immeasurably to our difficulty in handling rape with sensitivity and appropriate anger. Each dimension does have its special insights to add to a full understanding of the issue. Yet analyses that center exclusively on any one dimension miss the importance of the others and the complexity of the

---

[3]Dorothy Emmet, *The Moral Prism* (New York: St. Martin's Press, 1979) 1.

whole. It is because of this very complexity that Pellauer concludes that adequate intellectual inquiry into sexism must be interdisciplinary. In a similar manner, adequate political action must be based in a coalition of persons and groups that feel an urgency about the various dimensions.

When Copeland presents four representative views of poverty, he too is recognizing the complexity of that issue. At first glance, it is a quite different sort of complexity. Each of these views purports to be a holistic interpretation of the issue. The persons holding these views consider their positions contradictory to those who hold other views. Indeed, they often claim that the reason poverty is such a problem is that one of the alternative views has been too prevalent in policy making. Friedman places the blame on programs that limit individual freedom; Moynihan points to individualism as the culprit. What we learn from Copeland's analysis is that these various views involve assumptions about what it means to be human that shape their entire description and prescription. Then, like Pellauer, Copeland proceeds to pull the spectrum back together by arguing that a fully human understanding of poverty includes the best insights of each of the four views considered.

Having discussed isolationism, liberal interventionism, political realism, and liberal supranationalism as four theories of American foreign policy that have had their day in the sun and yet still (in somewhat revised forms) have advocates, Livezey does not dismiss them. Rather, he credits them with reflecting the experience and values of the United States faithfully enough so that in somewhat changed formulations they attract adherents today. He therefore proposes respectfully to borrow from each in constructing his own view, which he defends in part on the basis that it comprehends the best values reflected in the other four. Each of the two environmental ethics identified by Engel not only is based on important insights but also has resulted in significant achievements. He proceeds to construct his own ethic not by negating these two but by drawing upon their strengths. While the religious dimension of the crisis of the Thai people surely dominates Srisang's thinking, the social and political dimensions of that crisis are what drive him back into the religious myth of the people. In the process of recovering this mythic past, he not only adds a new perspective to political debate within Thailand but also increases our range of perspectives by relativizing our own cultural assumptions.

The three perspectives on economic policy identified by Copeland are, by his account, finally rooted in some basic ethical commitments that reflect important elements in human existence. Thus, when he attempts to construct his own interpretation of economic policy, he draws on the valid insights of the others. Similarly, Hatch describes three broad positions on racism—dilemma, indictment, and transformationist. Each has its own view of the practice of racism and how that relates to American ideals and values and its own religious roots. Given the integrity of these broad positions and the fact that all three are right about racism in some very fundamental ways, any adequate position must draw on all three and unite proponents of each.

The case of energy differs somewhat. Copeland contends that an important dimension, social equity, has been missing from the debate between pastoral romantics and industrial romantics. With the addition of this dimension, he tries to move both this and the fairness discussions forward by seeking some common ground among the contending perspectives that will allow some action to occur on the energy issue itself.

The most interesting aspect of Capo's treatment of four principles of journalistic ethics is the way in which he is able to treat them so concretely by examining how they measured up to a single event: Watergate. Indeed, his argument is that the television news media failed to tell that story as accurately as they might have if they had been guided by his principle of democratic interchange drawn from John Dewey.

In every case, these analyses assume that an issue can be seen in more than one way, that each way has much to be said for it, and that a fuller understanding of the issue can be had by taking these various views seriously. They tend to do this in two quite different fashions, one emphasizing dimensions of the issue and the other identifying perspectives on the issue. Those who emphasize dimensions probably do so in order to bring greater empirical adequacy to the ethical analysis, to include the widest range of facts.[4] Those who discuss perspectives probably do so in order to identify greater ethical depth to apparently factual descriptions, to make clear that facts are always presented within a framework of interpretation.[5] Crucial

---

[4]George W. Pickering, "The Task of Social Ethics," in Schroeder and Winter, *Belief and Ethics,* develops a rationale for the dimensional approach to racism.

[5]If this influence is to be traced back to Aristotle, the best source is *The Politics of Aristotle,* ed. and trans. Ernest Barker (1946; rpt., New York: Oxford University Press, 1962). A much more proximate source is Richard McKeon, *Freedom and History* (New York: Noonday Press, 1952). The authors were even more directly influenced by W. Alvin Pitcher: see, for instance, his "Radically Different Approaches to Foreign Policy," *Chicago Theological Seminary Register* 50 (April 1960): 22-26.

here is that each approach shares in the recognition that the issue is central. These are not simply so many interesting views on a common topic. Rather, they are dimensions of an issue or perspectives on an issue that denies our common humanity.

It is well worth noting, however, that all of this pluralism is resolved in somewhat different ways. In the case of some issues, the author argues for a comprehensive position that somehow moves beyond while taking account of the dimensions or perspectives that have been considered. Hatch on racism, Livezey on peace, Srisang on Thailand, Copeland on poverty, Capo on media, and Copeland on economic policy all proceed in this way, each in their own fashion. Pellauer on sexism and Copeland on energy find comprehensiveness in a somewhat different way. Instead of proposing one particular dimension or perspective somehow merging the best of the rest, they simply bring the dimensions or perspectives into interaction with one another to achieve inclusive views of the issues. While the first approach seeks greater integration than the second one does, both retain the healthiest respect for different points of view.

The Nature of Principles

By their emphasis on historical content and perspective, these essays add both texture and dimension to what are often flat, one-dimensional topics. In the process, they dramatically diverge from interpretations of racism or peace, sexism or poverty in terms of a simple battle of interest groups. This divergence becomes most clear when the essays take a constructive turn. For these authors, religious social ethics does not begin with theology, as is often the case with other approaches. Nevertheless, when these authors begin to advocate a particular approach, they appeal to principles, sometimes explicitly and directly, and other times by assumption and inference.

In every case, these principles seek a sort of comprehensive pluralism, an inclusiveness that does not homogenize perspectives. Perhaps this can be attributed to the influence of Alfred North Whitehead, whose definition of the good is the greatest possible harmonizing of the richest possible diversity.[6] Some of these authors would rebel at that suggestion, but the fact remains that the principles they propose include perspectives rather than

---

[6]Whitehead, *Adventure of Ideas*, 252-65, discusses this principle of harmonizing diversity in terms of beauty.

exclude them, seek connections as well as divergences. In the preface to this volume, we described the view of justice shared by the authors as "unity in diversity." We can specify in considerable detail just what unity in diversity means by referring to the principles that will emerge in the following analyses.

As Livezey turns to the task of proposing ways of taking peace seriously, he begins by recognizing that each of the four theories of the proper role of the U.S. in the world that he has discussed reflects deeply held values. Borrowing from each, he proposes ten commandments for U.S. foreign policy that seek peace while recognizing and enhancing the rival values of security, prosperity, governmental accountability, individual freedom, ecological conservation, and world community. In principle, he seeks a pluralistic comprehensiveness. In practice, he believes that the U.S. can best achieve this by following more faithfully its own democratic values. The results are policy proposals that seek to encourage pluralism, democracy, and dialogue on an interdependent globe.

In John Dewey, Capo finds the principle of democratic interchange, which Capo believes can help us rethink the value of network television news. This principle aims at a community of discourse that draws different views into dialogue. This dialogue can create the substance out of which organized, articulate publics emerge. In this way, television news actually could facilitate democratic participation rather than substituting for it or simply commenting cynically upon it. The principle of democratic interchange does not negate the principles of objectivity, truth, freedom, and social responsibility. Rather, it places them in a new context where they are judged by whether or not they facilitate "learning from joint experience with others how to enrich one's own understanding of things and to increase one's insight into the values to be found in living together in the human scene." By its very character and by how it functions in relation to other principles, democratic interchange seeks not authority and homogeneity but rather participation and dialogue.

Engel turns to the democratic ideal for principles to be used in constructing an environmental ethic. He finds in these principles the possibility of encompassing both human and nonhuman reality, both social and environmental justice. The resulting ethic respects the integrity of all parts of reality while recognizing their interdependence. The religious myth to which Srisang turns for help in addressing the problem of contemporary Thailand emphasizes, by his account, both common humanity and mutual respect. Certainly his own purpose is to find in the traditional faith of his people inspiration for a political and economic system that includes the Isan people in Thai society rather than marginalizing them, as is presently the case.

Pellauer does not identify her principles with any particular thinker, yet what we have said indeed applies to her principles. The six dimensions of sexism are for her internally related and cumulative. As a result, sexism is an interlocking system that allows for no simple solutions. Clearly, adequate action must proceed on a variety of fronts, while recognizing the connections with the other dimensions both intellectually and through political coalition. Hatch finally takes his stand within what he calls the transformationist approach to racism precisely because it seeks to take account of the most valid aspects of the other two alternatives—dilemma and indictment. In order to do so, however, the transformationist approach must project a vision of a U.S. society that does not now exist, one in which black Americans are both included and respected at the same time. Such a society would be marked by exactly the kind of pluralistic comprehensiveness we have been talking about.

Copeland finds comparable principles in Hannah Arendt and process thought, which he applies in various ways to the controversies over poverty, energy, and economic policy. By showing the particularly human problem caused by poverty, Arendt's portrayal of the human condition provides grounds for Copeland to propose antipoverty efforts that seek to undergird and stimulate human initiative and interaction. In the case of energy, Copeland uses the principle that the world is essentially plural and social to propose grounds for substantive dialogue and action that respects, protects, and even expands the spectrum of difference in areas where debate has become sterile and actors paralyzed. Finally, he argues that, by recognizing that all of our ideologies are rooted in legitimate aspects of what it means to be human, we can shift discussions of economic policy to a full consideration of the principles underlying ideological differences without remaining mired in endless ideological warfare.

Some principles divide and differentiate. By doing so, they make differences clear and highlight the uniqueness of various points of view. Sadly, they may also ignore connections and therefore make dialogue difficult. Other principles unify. In the process they usually stress commonality, emphasizing what different perspectives share. Too often individuality and uniqueness are blended out of existence in this unification. Throughout these essays the authors struggle to identify principles that allow interconnection and dialogue while respecting difference. All equally reject sheer isolated individuality and authoritarian unification. Whether by referring to the complex but interconnected nature of a social issue, aspects of the liberal originating religious visions, or particular authorities such as Dewey, Whitehead, and Arendt, these authors are all casting about for principles of comprehensive pluralism. When they find and use these principles, the result is to shift the discussion of each of the social issues without simply imposing authoritative prescriptions and often without settling very much in any final and authoritative fashion.

Status of Claims

As I suggested earlier, the method embodied in the following essays centers on issues. The measure of their success, then, is the issue. Whatever final authority they claim arises from their capacity to articulate the issue in such a manner as to make action on it more possible. Thus the authors return to the public arena in the end, having added new insights that shift the focus of discussion and action in creative directions. In sum, these essays seek a public authority based solely on their capacity to persuade actors that some new way of viewing an issue can assist in addressing it. When particular religious traditions or theologians are used, it is assumed that the insight gained must be tested in public.[7] When the moral situation or values of specific people are considered, it is for the purpose of enlightening public perception. When the experience of particular disadvantaged groups is discussed, it is assumed that these groups should rightfully take their place in the public. The test finally is whether what has been expressed assists in correcting the flaw in our social order that an issue represents.

This search for the pragmatic value of social ethics is well represented in Copeland's analysis of economic policy. Having taken us to the high ground of full self-transcendence where liberty, equality, and community support one another, he brings us back down to earth. It is in actual human societies where empirical inquiry is required in order to identify which of

---

[7]John Dewey, *The Public and Its Problems* (New York: Henry Holt, 1927), is an extended argument for the necessary public character of such claims, as well as for the difficulty of sustaining such a public.

The discussion that follows has much in common with the distinction Hannah Arendt makes between public and social. See, for instance, *The Human Condition* (Chicago: University of Chicago Press, 1958) 28-33. Franklin I. Gamwell, *Beyond Preference* (Chicago: University of Chicago Press, 1984), makes the philosophical case both for this distinction and for the possibility of principled judgments.

the three has been overemphasized and which underemphasized. More-over, it is in the actual political economy of the United States where pol-icies must be evaluated in terms of their potential for fully supporting human liberty, equality, and community. At that level, Copeland's description of the current situation stands as one among many, and it rises or falls ac-cording to its persuasive power. He has set some new terms for that dis-cussion, but they begin—not end—debate.

Srisang's essay is heavily influenced by liberation thought. This influ-ence is in no significant contradiction with the general method of these es-says because both approaches finally return to the historical location for confirmation. By Srisang's account, the test is whether he has helped poor people regain their "identity, dignity, and power to be and act." This would allow them to participate in a dialogue that presupposes freedom and hu-man dignity. Thus he places his own inquiry back into the public life of Thailand, where its measure is whether it inspires action to address the marginality of the Isan people.

Pellauer claims no special authority for ethicists and states clearly that social ethics is no substitute for social movements. The authority of the six-dimensional model of sexism she proposes is whether it stimulates dis-covery and investigation, makes possible a holistic view of the issue, and encourages a full range of activities to deal with sexism. She tests its ca-pacity to do so by applying it to a couple of particular aspects of the issue of rape and family life. Whether or not it works depends on whether it pro-duces new insight into the complexity of sexism. Similarly, Hatch makes no claims that the transformationist approach to racism is more rational, more Christian, or more American. Rather, he asks the reader to consider whether this view does not understand racism in a manner that pays greater attention to its complex mix of ideals, values, and practices and thus holds greater promise of inspiring adequate action against it.

Livezey explicitly states that his purpose is pragmatic and claims that his proposals for taking peace seriously are more likely to command public support over the next twenty years than any of the other alternatives. Rec-ognizing that his analysis is but one that must stand on its persuasive ca-pacity, he also encourages others to state their own views as a way to generate some public discourse with new depth and breadth about peace as a value. Clearly Engel is in search of an ethic that takes account of the political aspect of the ecological issue. His claim is that his democratic en-vironmental ethic provides the basis for thinking and acting on the most inclusive forms of justice. In the final analysis, he must appeal to the very publics he seeks to recognize on the basis that his view of the issue is more adequate than those presently advocated.

Capo quotes Dewey quite a bit. However, he is not satisfied simply to do so and to construct a principle for judging news based on it. Rather, he proceeds to test his principle by looking at a particular instance—Watergate—where TV news sought to play a constructive social role. Capo's principle is of value inasmuch as it provides some guidance for the actual practice of reporting. In the case of poverty, Copeland hopes that his statement of the full human meaning of poverty can enlighten future public consideration of that subject. In the case of energy, he claims to propose ways to proceed while respecting the values of disparate groups. In both cases, as with economic policy, the final measure of the fruitfulness of the analyses lies in the capacity to restate the issues in ways that make adequate action more possible.

Obviously, these authors are intellectuals who are very interested in ideas and concepts. Yet, precisely because they locate their issues in the social order, understand history as limit and resource, recognize the importance of perspective, and appeal to principles that are essentially public, any claims they make about the value of their work must be pragmatic. As pragmatic claims, they must persuade the reader to see the social order somewhat differently so that the full character of an issue becomes clearer. The hope is that if this intellectual task has been performed well, it can inspire us to get about the political task of changing the social order in such a way as to address the issues at hand.

Intellectual Context

All of the essays in the second part of this volume claim to be examples of religious social ethics. Yet there is precious little reference in them to theology or to God or to churches. We are left, then, with the question of just how they are *religious* social ethics. The five essays in the first part of this volume, although rich and diverse, all address the question of how religion and the social order are related. In the context of this volume, this means that they help us understand just how religion is at work in the ethical analyses that follow. Before proceeding to that overriding issue, it is important to recognize the particular function of each of these five essays.

George Pickering sets the context within which social ethics currently must operate. He does so by tracing the historic relation between religion and the social order in the American context. He begins with the story of how sectarian religion was drawn into a public dialogue on moral purpose, which itself became the religious center of American life. He then shows how the rise of corporate capitalism in the social order brought with it a new public religion with peculiarly revivalistic overtones—the Protestant Ethic. When critical issues in this capitalist social order reached proportions that no longer could be ignored, the Protestant Ethic itself came under fire from a mixture of the social gospel and critical social science. However, since that time, social science has bought the cloak of scientific objectivity at the price of its critical capacity, which formerly had been supplied by religious ideals. The result is a contemporary social science that justifies rather than criticizes the social order and that relegates religion to the irrational sphere of private life. It is within this context that contemporary social ethicists work.

The purpose of Robin Lovin's essay is to place the basic approach of the following issue analyses within the world of theological ethics. He does so by identifying five types of theological ethics in terms of how they relate religion to the social order: the ethics of sectarianism, of diverse tasks, of natural law, of process philosophy, and of realism. He dismisses the ethics of sectarianism and of special tasks as resources for reforming the social order because they share a fundamental pessimism about life outside of the religious community. He begins a dialogue of strengths and weaknesses between natural law and realism, with process philosophy as a sort of middle term most closely associated with natural law. In the end, realism's dynamic suspicion of any human creation provides a helpful limit to the tendency of natural law to invest too much meaning in social structures. On the other hand, natural law offers positive values to an otherwise cynical or escapist realism. Just how process philosophy fits into this dialogue is left for Lois Livezey's later essay to clarify.

Franklin I. Gamwell's essay is addressed most directly to the question of the relation between religion and the social order. He argues that inasmuch as the social activist values or sees one social practice as better than another, she is, implicitly at least, affirming God as the ultimate measure of such value. Thus public ideals imply theism. On the other hand, if God includes all of life, then the theist must be concerned with both public and private life. Thus theism implies public ideals. In the midst of this argument, Gamwell makes certain claims about the nature of both religion and the social order that we shall investigate further in a bit.

In a sense, Lois Gehr Livezey extends and specifies Gamwell's argument in terms of a source that the two of them and, to varying degrees, most of the authors of the chapters share—process thought. She first contends that Alfred North Whitehead's metaphysics describes all reality as inherently both private and public, individual and communal. She then discusses Whitehead's interpretation of justice under three headings: goods, rights, and virtues. By her telling, Whitehead describes the public good in some detail when he discusses the characteristics of civilization. In the name of Whitehead's doctrine of relativity, Livezey turns process thought's usual rejection of absolute individual rights into the affirmation of the right of association. The virtues necessary to the common good are assemblage (thought), mutual persuasion (action), and world loyalty (passion). This discussion is much more specific and suggestive than anything that has appeared previously from process thinkers on the subject of justice. Livezey concludes with a much more typical process discussion of the mutual relation between God and world and of the power of God as persuasion, which she expresses in the image of God as Holy Advocate.

As Peter Paris characterizes it, his purpose is practical, not theological. The general problem is how to bring justice to a moral community. More specifically, it is how to break down the parochialism that he finds typical of social groups from family to nation and to replace it with a unity that respects differences. Drawing upon Tillich, Paris concludes that in principle the answer is the moral imperative, the claim to common humanity. In practice, groups seem reluctant to recognize this claim, except as the oppressed demand inclusion on a common moral basis. Paris concludes that Christianity has the proper imperative of universal love but remains too parochial, not practicing enough what it preaches.

A Constructive Argument

Pickering creates the historical context and Lovin the theological one; Gamwell and Livezey provide a theological rationale grounded in process thought; and Paris returns us to the problems of practice. Yet, aside from these separate functions, these five essays taken together also constitute an argument about the relation of religion and the social order that goes something like this:

1. Value, and thus religion, is an inherent aspect of the social order;
2. In the light of religion, the social order is problematic;
3. The social order needs the insights and passion of religion if it is to be just; and
4. Religion must be embodied in the social order to be actual.

Once we have expanded upon this argument, we shall find that it is just such an understanding of the relation between religion and the social order that lies at the base of the analyses of social issues to follow.

1. Value, and thus religion,
   is an inherent aspect of the social order.

According to Pickering's narrative, this is precisely what was assumed from the founding of the American republic through the baptism of corporate capitalism by the Protestant Ethic to the reformist critics of the Protestant Ethic. Sadly, it is what contemporary social science has sacrificed in order to be scientific. According to Lovin, it is the recognition of this reality that makes the ethics of natural law, process, and realism relevant to social reform. For Paris, all human relations have a moral quality, so all human communities (social order, in our terms) are moral communities. To be human is to be able to know oneself; knowing oneself requires locating oneself in relation to others and the totality of things. So Gamwell concludes that humans are necessarily religious. It follows that the social order must be also. Livezey is more direct. For Whitehead, all reality has a subjective aim; purpose is integral to all existence. In the case of humans, civilization means the enhancement of positive purposes in the social order. In theological terms, God and the world are integrally related to one another. In their various ways, all five authors contend that religion is an inherent and fundamental aspect of the social order itself.

2. In the light of religion,
   the social order is problematic.

At a minimum, corporate capitalism poses some social and moral issues that, in Pickering's opinion, need investigation. More critically, he suggests that, by accepting the established social order and relegating religion to the private sphere, contemporary social science ignores basic problems in our social order. For Lovin, the strength of realists is their very capacity to see the shortcomings of the status quo, a necessary function of social ethics. Paris describes the parochialism and self-interest of social groups at great length. Twentieth-century Western society is marked by the dominance of economic and technological ideals that Gamwell believes are at great variance with the mutual enhancement of individuals called for by his theistic religion. He fears that the result could be ''unprecedented waste and destruction.'' Livezey says this is the context of Whitehead's cultural analysis. He sought some philosophical ground to affirm religious purpose amid an increasingly mechanistic and hostile social order. In each case, one function of religion is to raise questions about what the social order does to human meaning and purpose. In this sense, religion is necessarily critical, and our social order is found wanting.

3. The social order needs the insight and passion of religion if it is to be just.

This is the constructive conclusion of Pickering's essay. By pushing religion into the private realm, contemporary social science is unable to study and evaluate ideals as both hindrances and helps in furthering justice in the social order. Social change requires both the critical stance and the positive ideals that faith provides, according to Lovin. The corrective Paris proposes for the parochialism he decries is the moral imperative, which is religiously grounded. Gamwell argues that in the modern age human institutions have become so massive and complex and the possibilities and dangers of human action so obvious that atheism as to social purposes, which is typical of established liberalism, poses great danger. The net result is that we are unable to consider the human purposes of a social order that now dominates our lives. Livezey says that Whitehead agrees. In response, he offers the insights into the purposes our social order should serve encompassed in his description of civilization and the passion of social criticism and of loyalty to the world as it might be, which he considers the essence of religion. In each case, religion is a source for a just response to the problems in the social order. However, it also can be part of the problem or can fail to be practiced at all.

4. Religion must be embodied in the social order to be actual.

While not his main story here, Pickering concludes that alongside the failure of social science lies the failure of social ethics to perform its descriptive task. Similarly, Lovin states that theology raises problems of choice and action. In line with the practical purpose of his essay, Paris concludes that it is not enough to love the idea of justice; we must develop the institutions and cultivate the habits that put this idea into practice.

Gamwell states the same point in terms of the love of God. If we are to love God, and if God is related to all that is, then we must love the social order, which is such an increasingly important part of the world. Again the thesis reaches its fullest expression in Livezey's summary of Whitehead. Ideals must be embodied in concrete events or they remain merely potential. In terms of the relation between God and the world, this means that God also must be embodied in the world in order to be actual. Yet it is of the very nature of God to seek even greater embodiment of ideals and to persuade us to join in that task. Religion as world loyalty means seeking to make actual the world that might be. In every case, our authors recognize that religion, of necessity, calls for action in the social order.

Each of the five essays contributes to this common argument in its own way. It is because it reaches its highest statement in Livezey that we have taken up her discussion last at each step in the argument. Nonetheless, each author makes a contribution to this account of the relation between religion and the social order. As we return to the question of how this understanding is mirrored in the issue analyses, we return first to the question of the method common to those analyses. This is particularly appropriate because Pickering, Livezey, and Paris make comments directly related to ethical method.

One reading of Pickering's history is that it is an extended plea for an ethical method that integrates description of issues in the social order and attention to ideas. Surely it is just that characteristic of the issue analyses to follow that sets them apart from both most social science and most religious ethics. Livezey's description of assemblage as attention to the concrete realities of a social order sharpened by the recognition of issues of injustice in that social order seems but another way of summarizing the approach those issue analyses have in common. Finally, Paris describes the function of social ethics as clarifying the nature of moral conflicts that arise within a community and pointing the direction for their resolution. Taking into account the value he places upon diversity, this constitutes almost a general outline of how the social issues will be handled. The conflict will be described, various dimensions of or perspectives on it will be examined, and some constructive resolution will be proposed.

Religious Social Ethics

The question that remains is in what way the issue analyses are religious social ethics. The answer proposed is that they are religious social ethics in the sense suggested by the four theses about the relation between religion and the social order we have drawn from the following five essays.

1. Value, and thus religion,
is an inherent aspect of the social order.

To use Gamwell's language, the issue analyses to follow assume that the social order, like all human experience, is value laden and thus implicitly religious. The authors do not turn to some theological source to find out what is religious about war, racism, sexism, or poverty. Rather, they assume that an issue of basic social justice is inherently a religious issue. When persons support or deny the color line, they are in part practicing religion. When persons advocate or propose tropical deforestation, they are making a religious statement. When these authors begin with an issue in the social order rather than scripture or theological writings, they still understand themselves to be beginning with religious substances. When they examine the dimensions of or perspectives upon such an issue, they mean to be exploring further the religious contours of that social order.

2. In the light of religion,
the social order is problematic.

The ethics of sectarianism or diverse tasks might say that the social order is evil. These authors of the issue analyses, however, see both damnation and hope. That is why history is both a problem and a resource for them. If Lovin is right that social change needs the critical capacity of realism, there is plenty of that in the essays on social issues. Racism, sexism, and poverty persist over generations in spite of all efforts to oppose them. One part of the world arms for the next, and last, war while another suffers in hunger and powerlessness. Tropical forests disappear while poverty grows, and our media seems incapable of generating genuine public dialogue about either. Yet, in one case after another, the problematic character of the social order is revealed at a much deeper level. Just what is the relationship between American ideals and racism, poverty, sexism, war, or environmental destruction? Indeed, just what are our ideals in the first place? What is there about the basic vision of those who oppose these injustices that prevents them from confronting them effectively? In sum, while the simple recognition that our social order is unjust in some way initiates these analyses, they soon bring under investigation the very ideals that justify those injustices or fail to challenge them adequately.

3. The social order needs the insights and passion of religion if it is to be just.

This is the point at which what we usually think of as theology enters into the issue analyses. Sometimes the appeal is to figures such as Dewey, Whitehead, or Arendt. In other cases, the insights of a particular movement or community, such as the civil rights movement, the myths of Isan, or the American democratic tradition, are cited. In yet other instances, some constructive thought about comprehensive justice or the human condition appears. Whatever the source,[8] the purpose is the same—somehow to draw upon past or present religious insight in order to rethink an issue in our social order. These authors are convinced that the resultant reformulation of the issue will advance the cause of justice. However, these analyses are not just intellectual exercises. Rather, they assume and articulate a passion for justice that Pellauer, near the end of her analysis, quite rightly identifies as religious. These authors may respect diverse points of view and reason about purposes, but they are not cold and objective about the need for justice in our social order.

4. Religion must be embodied in the social order to be actual.

The religious passion for justice just described drives every one of the issue analyses finally back into the actual struggles for justice in our social order. The final purpose of the analyses of energy or economics is to produce better energy and economic policy. Engel, Pellauer, and Livezey finally address voluntary organizations fighting environmental destruction, sexism, or war. As suggested earlier in this introduction, all of these analyses are ultimately intended as contributions to actual efforts for justice, not simply as contributions to an intellectual discipline. The test of adequacy is finally the issue in the social order, not some abstract theological debate. To be actual, the religious commitment to social justice must be practiced in struggle, if not in policy. It must be embodied in some form and to some extent.

---

[8]Other sources than those used in these analyses would certainly be appropriate. However, while any resource should be a genuine representation of its source—e.g., good biblical scholarship—its value to social ethics rests on how much insight it brings to the matter of justice that is at issue.

Social Ethics and Social Justice

In the preface to this volume, we saw how the sense of frustration and confusion experienced by two young couples in regard to racism was mirrored in the search for social justice. The final question before us in this discussion of method is whether the methodological commitments described here hold promise for helping us rethink our efforts toward social justice. In the preface, we suggested that our basic problem was the reduction of an issue to an interest. How then do the chapters in part two illustrate a method that refuses to reduce an issue to an interest?

First, interests are held by individuals or groups; issues cut across the entire social order. For Hatch, racism is not just a concern of blacks. Rather, everyone in the social order has a stake in these issues—as well as in the issues of peace, environmental integrity, justice in the Third World, or television news media. In most cases the stake we all share involves self-interest, even for the apparent winners. Men may be emotional cripples because of the macho expectations of sexist society; military conflict may damage national security. The winners may pay a heavy price for winning. Yet, in the end these issue analyses contend that we all lose humanly in some way. Each of us has a human interest in justice that goes beyond any apparent immediate self-interest. Locating the issue in the social order itself makes that harder to ignore.

Second, interests are immediate and constantly changing; issues persist over time. Lobby groups representing interests come and go quickly and even more rapidly as the relative power of various interests shifts. The effective politician in government, or a church bureaucracy, or a corporation is the one who can tell which interests are on the rise and which on the decline. Issues, on the other hand, are perennial, so much so that we sometimes begin to think we shall have them with us always. For this reason history, both as the tale of how these issues became so imbedded in our social order and as a record of how others have thought and acted to end them, has much greater significance for issues than for interests.

Third, interests are one-dimensional; issues have perspectives. There may be complexities about the who and why of interests, and most of us enjoy reading or hearing journalists discuss who has what at stake in this or that piece of legislation or election battle. Yet we all know that sooner or later interests have to do with who is going to gain money, power, or fame. There is but one dimension to the picture. Issues, as we shall see, are not so flat. Even to understand what is at stake, let alone who and how, requires a prism. This is because issues appeal to more than one dimension of our lives, not just simple self-interest. As a result different aspects of human life, different conceptions of justice, or different spheres of human experience appear as perspectives on the issue at hand or dimensions of it that must be recognized as legitimate.

Fourth, interests require principles of either unity or pluralism; issues require principles that merge both pluralism and comprehensiveness. Since interests are held by individuals or groups, the alternatives seem to be that one individual or group dominates, thus realizing that interest, or that all individuals and groups keep each other at bay, creating a sort of balance of power. The latter is what often passes for pluralism in the contemporary scene. The essays in part two propose principles that are different from these standard views in two ways. First, the pluralism is deeper, including interests but moving beyond them to differences in valuation, in understandings of justice, or in views of what it means to be human. Second, there is an assumption that this deeper pluralism must be truly dialogical, precisely because the various perspectives are implicated in each other. They are variously described as internally related, interrelated values, or dimensions of human experience—all of which imply some sort of dialogical comprehensiveness to these pluralistic principles.

Finally, none of the issue analyses claims to advance the interests of a person or group as its primary purpose. In fact, the poor will benefit from an end to poverty, blacks from an end to racism, the people of Isan from an end to their marginality, and women from an end to sexism. Yet the primary claim in each case is that all members of the social order will gain from the removal of some denial of our common humanity. These issue inquiries seek first and foremost to serve justice, not interest. And in the final analysis, they appeal to the reader to do justice rather than advance interests.

The essays in part two are in search of social justice—social justice that recognizes that certain basic issues cut across our social order, denying that we are humans who share it; that knows the history of these issues; that respects the various perspectives on these issues; that is rooted in principles both pluralistic and comprehensive; and that calls us to public action. This is not history or social science as we have come to know them. Discussions of justice are more familiar as an aspect of religious ethics, yet there will be little, if any, appeal to the sources of authority typical of religious ethics, such as Scripture or theology. Rather, religion will remain an aspect of the social issue itself, and the final authority will remain practice—what will advance social justice. The following five essays will help us understand the historical and theological context and the philosophical and theological grounding assumed in those issue analyses that will follow. In the process, we shall come to see just how those nine essays on social issues are exercises in religious social ethics.

Both the social sources and the religious meanings for social ethics that follow have now been introduced. This has been done by referring often to what is to come. While necessary to setting a specific context, these references may be hard to follow without having read all of the essays. For this reason, the reader should return to the preface and the introduction to read them with new meaning in light of the entire volume. For now, it is time to move on from these preliminaries to consider some religious meanings for social ethics.

Part One

..

Intellectual Context:
Religion and the Social Order

George W. Pickering
University of Detroit

..

Social Ethics
in the American Context

■ ■ When Supreme Court Justice William O. Douglas wrote in 1951, "We are a religious people whose institutions presuppose the existence of a supreme being,"[1] there was no social science within which it would have been a statement subject to examination as a possibly true (or false) proposition, and there was very little theology that could accept it as a meaningful sentence either. The social sciences might have been willing to do opinion surveys to find out how many people actually believed such a statement. They might even have offered some explanation of how such "sentiments" functioned in the social system. But they were incapable of sustaining a disciplined inquiry into the truth or falsity of such a proposition. Theologians, on the other hand, especially theologians of the various Protestant persuasions, were inclined to treat such statements as idolatry pure and simple, as attempts to appropriate the mantle of the divine to cover the ambiguities and imperfections of things human.

During the previous two centuries, both the religious grounding of the idea of the public welfare and the institutional reality of the dialogue of moral principles had been lost. In this essay, I will suggest how this occurred, what the negative consequences have been, and how we might find ways to take up the issues of our common life.

---

[1]*Zorach v. Clausen* 343 U.S. 313 (1951).

Social ethics is the critical appraisal of both the content and the consequences of the various religious ethics that have been proposed and followed. Social ethics asks of religious ethics, "What does it contribute to the public welfare?" It would be difficult to overestimate the importance of this question for understanding American (or any other) culture. Religious ethics has historically played a major but not necessarily constructive role in shaping the behavior of individuals and groups. It has also been a major but not necessarily dominant factor in the development of institutions and in the identification of public issues in American life.

Ever since the Declaration of Independence, *religious ethics* has been a broad term that encompasses much more than the teachings of the churches. The Republic was established on the proposition that the government and all other institutions, including the churches, should be evaluated by their contributions to the "public welfare"; the public welfare consisted in the promotion and protection of equal rights, personal liberties, and the pursuit of happiness.

As a part of this new understanding, church and state were separated. Far from depriving the churches of any role in forming the national conscience, however, it was under the system of religious liberty that the churches emerged as legitimated voices for the moral direction of society. They were not, to be sure, the only legitimated voices of public conscience. They were joined by reformist groups of all sorts and by the developing social sciences. The price that all had to pay was to speak on public matters in the voice of citizens and convince their fellow citizens that their advice was for the good of all.

Social ethics is both a product of and a corrective for a religiously pluralistic society insofar as it inquires into the actual and probable empirical conditions under which a variety of ethical principles are proposed and the actual and probable consequences that flow from their interaction. The primary concern of social ethics is public issues, the ways in which they take shape in our midst and the way diverse ethical principles become part of the public issues themselves. The aim is to evaluate ethical principles in terms of their public functions while also providing reasonable grounds for evaluating public issues and proposals for their resolution. Each of the chapters in this book is an essay in social ethics.

The Protestant Ethic and the Spirit of American Capitalism

To understand the role of social ethics today, it is helpful to have a sense of American history and to see how religious and moral ideas have interacted with political and economic developments in times past. The idea of a natural law that is both accessible to all and harmonious with revealed religions has been a recurring theme in American thinking about ethics and society.

Benjamin Wright, surveying the thought of the earliest Puritans in America, concluded: "The concept of natural law has never been more completely absorbed in that of divine law than in this first generation of New Englanders" (Wright 1931, 15). By the early eighteenth century, the Reverend John Barnard proclaimed in a sermon that "this voice of Nature is the Voice of God"; but he did not leave the argument there. Since human beings are the apex of nature, he also claimed, "Thus tis that the *vox populi est vox Dei*" (the voice of the people is the voice of God) (Wright 1931, 44).

A generation later, Thomas Jefferson carried this line of thought one step further when he said, "The God who gave us life gave us liberty at the same time" (Wright 1931, 86). For Jefferson and his contemporaries, this idea that the people had God-given rights was a revolutionary, even if unsystematic, idea. For them it was a lure to creativity, and only slave-holders have actually rebelled against living under the framework that they created from this insight.

In addition to the expansion of the American population after the 1790s, two transformations permanently altered the way Americans would think about their public welfare: a transformation in their religion and in their economy. The conjunction of these two transformations gave rise to the now-famous Protestant Ethic. In America at least, the Protestant Ethic *was* the Spirit of Capitalism, and a refurbished doctrine of natural law was invoked to defend and explain the proposition that the voice of the market was the voice of God.

In 1789 the framers of the Constitution set out "to form a more perfect union, establish Justice, insure domestic tranquility, provide for the common defense, promote the general Welfare, and secure the Blessings of Liberty to ourselves and our Posterity." Economic growth was not among the stated purposes even though merchants and rural landholders provided national leadership then.

Yet in 1776 Adam Smith had written *The Wealth of Nations,* a book that might as well have been called the Capitalist Manifesto, for it preached a revolutionary doctrine. First, it assumed that the *increase* of wealth was and should be the overriding concern for any national economic policy, although this had never been the explicit and systematic goal of any economic policy. Second, Smith argued that a "System of Natural Liberty" was the best way to achieve this end. Others had spoken of liberty before, but Smith had in mind the free pursuit of preference (which he called "interest"). He claimed that if people were allowed to pursue their own private interests, the outcome of these efforts would result, as if coordinated by an invisible hand, in the common good—the increase of national wealth—although each person was actually thinking only of his or her own gain.

While these ideas were not written into the Constitution, they were woven into the fabric of the American economy during the first half of the nineteenth century when "merchant capitalism" was the order of the day. John Jacob Astor was the most successful of the merchant capitalists. When he died at mid-century, his estate amounted to some twenty million dollars. Millionaire was still a new term, and the *New York Sun* estimated that there were perhaps twenty-five millionaires in New York in 1847, though none even came close to Astor's twenty million. These were fortunes amassed through the direct ownership and management of family enterprises.

While merchant capitalists still exist today, Astor's death more or less marked the end of the merchant-capitalist era that had done so much to vindicate the ideas of Adam Smith. Not only had national wealth begun to increase on a regular basis, so had the income of the average person. The expectation of economic growth had become a driving force as much in individual lives as in the life of the nation.

In the 1850s, however, a new dimension was added to the economy without benefit of any grand theory or manifesto. This dimension was to change the scale on which wealth could be pursued, secured, and invested. It would remake the very social order of American life, altering not only the way business was done but also transforming the way life was lived and opportunities were distributed in the American republic.

The Corporation

This new dimension was corporate organization. Although in the 1850s corporate organization seemed like little more than a logical extension of merchant capitalism, within a very short period of time it had opened a whole new era, one of which we are still part.

Textile firms were the largest manufacturers established during the merchant-capitalist era; yet in the 1850s, after more than a quarter century of operation, only forty-one of them were capitalized at more than $250,000. The newer railroads, however, were already capitalized in the millions. By 1859 total investment in railroads had topped one billion dollars.

Building railroads provided much more than transportation. It also stimulated the formation of a national capital market, expansion of a national market in stocks and bonds, new methods of corporate finance, increased efficiency of mails, development of the Western Union system, and the emergence of a large-scale construction industry. With these, the base was laid for national marketing, the rise of a credit system, and ultimately mass marketing of goods at the retail level. Combined with the discovery of high-grade anthracite in Pennsylvania in the 1830s, thus making high-temperature heat processes feasible, these developments provided the prerequisites for mass production, first in oil, tobacco, and grain in the 1860s, then in metal-making industries by the 1870s (Chandler 1977, 79-121).

The upshot was the creation of industrial corporations that became leaders in the economy and that were capital intensive, energy intensive, manager intensive, and oriented to mass production. Andrew Carnegie's Edgar Thompson Works turned out 3,000 tons of steel a day in 1900. Only fifty years before, 3,000 tons of steel was the *annual* output of a first-class steel mill. By the 1890s Carnegie's enterprise was producing profits in excess of $20 million a year, the equal of Astor's lifetime fortune. Between 1850 and 1880, the capital invested in manufacturing increased by more than 400 percent, but the bulk no longer was invested in merchant-capitalist enterprises. The new order of the day was corporate capitalism, in which "the visible hand of management replaced what Adam Smith referred to as the invisible hand of market forces" (Chandler 1977, 1).

The social consequences of this change in economic organization appeared rapidly. Along with the growth of capital investment and productive output came the creation of three new social classes: the modern industrial wage-earning class, the modern corporate managerial class and, closely allied to them, the new professional and scientific class. The first was initially more numerous and noticeable. Between 1850 and 1880, wage earners increased from 958,100 to 2,732,600, and they worked for increasingly large firms. In spite of the depressions of the 1870s, wages paid out increased 300 percent between 1850 and 1880 while the number of wage earners only increased 185 percent. Thus labor shared in some of the economic growth (Hacker 1940, Appendix A).

This expansion and concentration of the wage-earning class spurred rapid urbanization after the Civil War. Chicago—with 30,000 inhabitants in 1850, 300,000 by 1870, 1,000,000 by 1900, and 3,000,000 by 1920—was paradigmatic of the development of industrial cities under the impact of corporate capitalism.

In 1790 the U.S. had a population of four million, most located in small towns and rural areas. By 1840 the population had risen to seventeen million, but only eleven percent was urban. By 1870 the population tide had shifted. Out of thirty-eight million, ten million were urban dwellers. Between 1860 and 1870 urban population increased faster than rural for the first time in American history—and therein lay the future. By 1920 the census showed a population of almost 106,000,000, a majority of whom lived in urban areas.

A new social world had taken shape, and it spread from coast to coast. It was a world predominantly industrial in its economic base, corporate in its organization of productive resources, urban in its concentration of population, and "secular" in its civic conventions. Calvin Coolidge stated the obvious when he said in the 1920s, "The business of America is business."

This new social world had not developed in a moral vacuum. The dominant strands of religious understanding had become entwined with economic growth as both the result and the vindication of "true religion." This symbiosis of religion and economics came to be known as the "Protestant Ethic" because of its origins, but its adherents were not limited to Protestants.

Religious Revivalism

It would be impossible to overestimate the influence of religious revivalism as an active force in the making of the Protestant Ethic. Given the other-worldly orientation of revivalism, with its emphasis on being saved from the snares and delusions of this world, it may seem an unlikely ally of economic growth and all the materialistic connotations that go with it. Theologically, revivalism was (and is) other-worldly, but psychologically, revivalism was (and is) the ultimate in individualism. The idea of the individual facing the void of eternity unless the call to conversion should come, the individual as the object of a cosmic decision, placed the individual at the center of the dramas of history and religion and the experience of being saved at the center of the individual's life.

Religion, like success, had become something that one either had or did not have, something the individual could get or lose. "Conversion" was the decisive standard for having or not having religion, and this emphasis contributed several major unintended characteristics to the experience of life in America. It put a premium on *change* and became the deepest model for what real change should be, that is, change of heart, of preoccupation, of awareness, and of feeling in the lives of individuals. Such conversion was thought to be the only morally authentic source for other important changes.

This emphasis on individual conversion fostered the idea that the most important issues of this life were subject to immediate and sudden change. It provided an emotionally charged orientation toward the future as the sphere of human fulfillment. The "world" became a foil in the drama of the individual's life and salvation. The "world" was a series of enemies and temptations, on the one hand, and opportunities for witness and blessing, on the other hand. These enemies, temptations, and opportunities, however, also lay within the individual. Responsibility was understood as a missionary enterprise, paternalistic perhaps but also "selfless" because revivalistic responsibility was possible only when the ordinary passions of the self had been subjected to the divine will.

Revivalism promoted an ethic of active submission to a higher will, a higher law. It was a striving, not a complacent submission. It gave the individual authority to act. That authority emanated from the experience of being saved. Ordinary experience was suspect because it was unconverted; being saved seemed to provide its own assurance and certainty. The experience of conversion and its attendant certainty became the evangelical Protestant version of infallibility in matters of faith and morals. Uncertainty came to be associated with a lack of faith, a problem of character, a sign of unreliability.

Because of its emphasis on experience, revivalism has often been called anti-intellectual. Yet revivalism everywhere gave rise to schools and colleges that were intended to represent converted reason in its battle with unconverted reason. For the revivalist, the conflict was not between faith and reason, it was between converted and unconverted reason. Converted reason was committed to producing "moral results."

This individualistic emphasis on moral results led to a preoccupation with questions of technique and management at the expense of more substantive questions and to a virtual obsession with the components of personality and the dynamics of commitment. The desired moral result was commitment, a commitment to "more"—more control of the self and its opportunities.

Clerical Economics

Early on, this religious ethic was assimilated into a theory of economics called "clerical economics" because its leading exponents were clergy. If conversion freed the individual from the bondage of sin, then it also set the individual free to pursue whatever opportunities and preferences presented themselves. Indeed, it virtually commissioned the individual to pursue the vigorous life of self-assertion in the name of missionary responsibility. Revivalistic activism was the sacramental union of the Protestant Ethic and the Spirit of Capitalism.

The religious emphasis on the regeneration of the individual and the economic emphasis on growth flowed from distinct sources, yet they flowed together in ways that transformed the face of both religion and economics and with them the concept of public welfare. The Reverend John McVicker of Columbia University was one of the first to propound the new synthesis of religion and economics. In 1825 he proposed that the study of economics "demonstrates the necessary connection that subsists between national virtue, national interest, and national happiness. . . . What religion condemns as contrary to duty and virtue, Political Economy proves to be equally opposed to the peace, good order, and permanent prosperity of the community" (quoted in Bryson 1932, 311).

The Reverend Francis Wayland, president of Brown University, wrote both an *Elements of Moral Science* and an *Elements of Political Economy*, both of which were widely used as textbooks in American colleges throughout the nineteenth century. He preached the same message in both books: "The laws which govern economic life are laws of God and must not, nay cannot, be tampered with" (quoted in May [1949] 1963, 15).

From the perspective of this clerical school of economics, the public welfare was best served by private property, no charity except to those afflicted by nature, no government interferences in the economy, no unions of wage earners. These were as much the laws of God as they were the principles of sound economics. One chose salvation or fell into condemnation in the workplace quite as much as one did at the camp meeting. Indeed, one's performance in the economy became a measure of one's character. Hard work was a sign of good character, and hard work paid off. Poverty therefore was a sign of moral deficiency.

From the beginning there was a nationalistic element in clerical economics. In addition, by the end of the Civil War the individualistic Protestant Ethic had become the centerpiece of a triumphalist nationalism. Respectable mainstream Protestants believed with Edward Beecher, "Now that God has smitten slavery unto death, he has opened the way for the redemption of the whole system" (quoted in Hopkins 1940, 9). If the war had been the Cross of the American Way, the nation had risen triumphant and cleansed, awaiting its glory and further splendor.

Responses

This melding of revivalistic religion, moralistic economics, and chauvinistic nationalism ensconced a social ethic at serious variance with American life as it came to be dominated by industrial capitalism and its attendant social transformations. For a few, this social ethic had to be reassessed. For most, however, it was merely a matter of damning the realities and shifting the strategies in the pursuit and proclamation of the Protestant Ethic, largely unreconstructed.

Russell H. Conwell, who advocated a "gospel of wealth," was a case in point. In his hands, the old orthodoxy of the Protestant Ethic became a vibrant gospel of Christian capitalist individualism—no inner tensions, no doubts allowed, a pietism of moral development through material success. Conwell's gospel was aimed at those who had not yet achieved wealth, and his "good news" was that anyone who had the moral fiber for it could get rich.

Andrew Carnegie, on the other hand, spoke on behalf of those who had been thrust into the burden of riches. Carnegie agonized over the relation of the individual to the disposition of wealth in the service of some wider social good. His answer was philanthropy to the community, the private provision of public goods.

Bishop William Lawrence discovered and occupied the high moral and religious ground from which both Carnegie's and Conwell's gospels of wealth could be harmonized with the orthodox language of the Protestant Ethic. "In the long run," he proclaimed, "it is only to the man of morality that wealth comes. We believe in the harmony of God's universe. We know that it is only by working along His laws natural and spiritual that we can work with efficiency. . . . Godliness is in league with riches. . . . Material prosperity is helping to make the national character sweeter, more joyous, more unselfish, more Christlike'' (quoted in Pauck 1967, 277).

Not only was the business of America business, but under the gospel of wealth the religion of America was business, too. The Protestant Ethic *was* the Spirit of Capitalism. So, once again, as with the earliest Puritans, the concept of natural law had been completely absorbed into that of divine law, only this time divine law had been completely subordinated to secular hopes for material prosperity. Indeed, everything had been subordinated to that. The Puritan dream of a city set upon a hill that would be a beacon to all the nations had been transmuted into the dream of making it big and then doing good, a dream that was beginning to come true for some with magnetic force in the late nineteenth century. It was, however, also a dream that was taking an uncertain institutional shape to which attention would have to be paid.

From the Protestant Ethic and the Spirit of Capitalism to the Civic Credo and the Spirit of Privatism

In the last quarter of the nineteenth century, a major shift was under way in the institutional basis for the public welfare, and this was accompanied by a series of efforts to reconsider the intellectual content of the idea of the public welfare. Since the Protestant Ethic and the Spirit of Capitalism provided the prevailing intellectual content for the idea of the public welfare, any such reconsiderations involved religion as well as economics and politics. But ever since the revolution of 1776, religion in America involved much more than the churches and their teachings. It involved the Republic itself, which was based in the promise to respect and enhance the God-given rights, personal liberties, and pursuit of happiness that belonged to the people. Purely secular reconstructions of the public welfare, therefore, were as culturally undesirable as they were intellectually misconceived.

There was, however, no clear or obvious route to religious reconstruction under the impact of the increasingly urban, industrial, and corporate social order. The situation was truly problematic, and a problematic situation had little attraction in a revivalistic culture that placed a premium on certainty. Such intellectual change as did occur, therefore, was accomplished through a series of partial but systematic assertions, each aiming to supplant not only the Protestant Ethic but its air of superior certainty as well. Since reconstructions of the Protestant Ethic and the Spirit of Capitalism took on an immediate appearance of attacks on the American Way of Life, the Christian religion, and the most productive economy in the world, most of the criticisms of the social order were mounted in the name of democracy or Christianity, with heavy nationalistic overtones. This was not simply a matter of rhetorical strategy; most of the critics of American society in the late nineteenth century were as excited about the possibilities for a Christian democratic America as the defenders of the status quo were convinced that America was already Christian and democratic.

America was a "Protestant culture" in some sense, but the Protestant churches were in as much ferment as the rest of the society. Little wonder that A. M. Schlesinger called those years "A Critical Period in American Religion, 1875–1900," shaped by "two great challenges to organized religion, the one to its system of thought, the other to its social program." For a significant group of thinkers at the time, however, these were not two separate problems but rather one complex set of issues: how to understand the emerging social order and the altered place of the individual within it in terms of the prospects for justice in the community. This was a problem for the churches, to be sure, but not for them alone.

The Rise of the Social Sciences

The increasing prominence and specialization of the sciences was yet another of the social changes that were taking place. Although it was hardly perceived at the time, this change was destined to have a transformative effect on the national structure of classes. By becoming closely allied with corporate industrialism, the sciences made a distinctive contribution to the making of a professional-managerial-scientific class. As "science" increasingly became identified with "competence," concern about the state of the society had become an aspiration to develop a science of society.

It was, however, unclear what the scope, methods, and standards should be for a "science of society." The American Social Science Association (ASSA), which existed from 1865 until 1909, was composed of persons committed to the pursuit of such questions and to the promotion of scientific studies of society and its problems. Twenty years after the founding of the ASSA, Frank Sanborn reflected on its purposes: "To learn patiently what *is*—and to promote diligently what *should* be—this is the double duty of all the social sciences" (Bernard [1943] 1965, 545, 559).

The initial purpose of the ASSA was to keep both normative and empirical concerns unified in a common inquiry; but early on, normative and empirical concerns became polarized rather than complementary. The creation of a science seemed incompatible with the direct pursuit of social reform. The acquisition of objective knowledge seemed incompatible with a commitment to the active pursuit of a wider justice. The construction of a theory of society seemed incompatible with the creation of professional practices aimed at human betterment.

These polarities led to the association's dissolution and set the development of American social science on a path that it has followed ever since. In 1870 the National Prison Association broke away and cast its lot with the direct pursuit of institutional reform. In 1874 the National Conference on Charities and Corrections broke away and cast its lot with the development of professional practices. In 1884 the American Historical Association broke away and cast its lot with the acquisition of objective knowledge. The development in 1885 of the American Economic Association, in 1888 of the American Statistical Association, in 1889 of the American Academy of Social and Political Science, in 1903 of the American Sociological Society, and in 1905 of the American Sociological Association completed the dismantling of the original vision of an American Social Science Association in which "facts" and "values" could be systematically examined in their natural relations with each other.

The proliferation of "disciplines" was in keeping with the increasing specialization that has marked the development of all sciences. It appeared that the exclusion of all concerns regarding the purposes for which such knowledge would be used was also in keeping with the development of other sciences as well. In an effort to escape the stultifying association with clerical economics and "moral science" in the manner of Francis Wayland, the social sciences, by 1900, were dedicated to the proposition that an analytical science of society, social relations, and economics could be independent of evaluative concerns. Thus in the midst of one of the most dramatic, rapid, and multidimensional social upheavals in the history of social change, social sciences were born committed to finding value-free universals to account for the value-laden particularities of the American experience.

The result, however, was anything but a "value-free" science of society. Instead there developed a science that relied on and promoted uninspected values and purposes that it claimed were in principle irrational and beyond the scope of any rational discipline. It was a high price to pay just to avoid either espousing or confronting the Protestant Ethic and the Spirit of Capitalism. In effect, however, it placed social science at the uncritical service of both, thus adding the prestige of science to their already considerable social and cultural power. At the same time, this strategy of excluding questions of principle from the possibilities of rational discipline declared the problem of defining the public welfare outside the bounds of rational discourse, subject only to the competitions for power.

The full implications of this division of intellectual labor were not immediately apparent. Indeed, even after a century of living with them, they are still not commonly apparent—especially to those who labor most devotedly in the fields thus defined. The strict methodological separation of social science from the problems of social ethics seemed at first to be a reasonable division of labor that left both fields free to develop in a complementary tension with each other. In fact, though, it has led to the dominance of uninspected values in social science, to the exclusion of social ethics from the domain of rational disciplines, and to the acceptance of a radical and irrational subjectivism in matters pertaining to the public welfare.

Richard T. Ely

In the 1880s the movement for the development of a social science had been closely allied and sometimes identified with the movement for a Social Gospel. Richard T. Ely, a leader in the founding of the American Economic Association, was a man stirred by both of these impulses. Interest in both social science and the Social Gospel had been stimulated by the specter of class conflict that had begun to erupt in the 1870s. The depression of 1873 had been followed by lingering and severe unemployment, militant agitation for labor unions, and talk of Marxist socialism. When most of the railroads east of the Mississippi announced a ten-percent reduction of wages in 1877, it "precipitated the most destructive labor battle in American history." As Henry May described it, "Trains were halted; troops fought with angry mobs; bloodshed and fire mounted in Baltimore, Pittsburgh and other railroad centers. Spokesmen of religion were forced, like editors and professors, to answer the question why, in the home of Christian progress, desperate men were refusing well-meant advice, defying authority, organizing and battling with the determination of despair" (May [1949] 1963, 91-92). This was what people called "the Social Question."

In response, Ely wrote: "It is doubtful if history records any more rapid social movement than the ominous separation of the American people into two nations," that is, labor and capital. In helping frame the founding principles for the American Economic Association, he wrote: "The conflict of labor and capital has brought into prominence a vast number of social problems, whose solution requires united efforts, each in its own sphere, of the church, of state, and of science" (quoted in Abell 1962, 60, 69). Although he spoke of a Christian economics in his early writings, as time went by he came to think of the science of economics more as a means for policy, Christian altruism as providing the ends for policy, and the state as the instrument of policy. In the long run, that is what he meant by "each in its own sphere." It was a vision of a scientifically aided, professionally administered, Christian society.

The social sciences thus had returned to the age-old premise that a society required a common core of religious beliefs and moral values if it was going to function as a unified community. For Ely, this was not much of a problem because he assumed that "Christianity" provided such a core and that, even though the churches were divided as to its meaning, the state could still be unified under its aegis.

Albion Small

Albion Small, on the other hand, believed just as strongly as Ely that a society needed a common core of religious beliefs and moral values, but he believed that the Christian churches would have to change considerably in order to provide it. For him, religion was the central and unresolved issue of American life, and everything depended on a unifying resolution of that issue. "In the apparent conflict between self-interest and collective welfare, the religious motive exerts a most powerful influence in securing social or altruistic conduct" (quoted in Vidich and Lyman 1985, 180).

Small had resigned as president of Colby College in 1892 to become the founder of the nation's first department of sociology at the University of Chicago. As he approached the creation of sociology as a discipline, Marx was the challenge, the corporation was the problem, and religion was the key to progress with justice.

Small believed that corporate capitalism could be both useful and justified as long as it was based in the proposition "that men are more important than capital, and that all political and legal and economic practices must be held accountable to that principle" (Vidich and Lyman 1985, 183).

As he viewed the society, however, corporate capitalism was not grounded in that principle: *"Capital, as it is legally established in modern industrial countries, is bound to answer to the charge of having acquired legal rights which public policy cannot permanently concede"* (Vidich and Lyman 1985, 184).

Even this was a religious issue in Small's understanding of it:

In one aspect a corporation is a deathless superpersonal selfishness vested by the state with superpersonal powers. This monster is commissioned by the state to exercise its superpersonal powers within the society of plain persons. Thus we have unconsciously converted our property system from a protection of similar natural persons against one another, into a licensing system of supernatural persons. . . . The invention is not, and cannot come to, good, unless the society of plain persons can either endow the corporation with souls, with soul's liabilities, or create and operate in its own interest an adequate superpersonal control of the superpersonal enginery of corporations. (Vidich and Lyman 1985, 185)

Either way, providing souls for the corporation or public controls over it required religiously inspired vision. *"A church which has no positive attitude, no definite policy toward the group of problems thus indicated, can scarcely hope to impress men whose lives pivot upon these problems as dealing with anything very close to reality"* (Vidich and Lyman 1985, 185). Small addressed this warning to a church group, well aware that the actual churches had no definite policy toward such issues.

This remained an unresolved problem in Small's theory of American society. Neither the churches nor the generalized American values seemed to be up to the task of providing unified moral direction for the community at large. In 1914 Small had surveyed selected leaders in American institutional life on the question, "What is Americanism?" The result had not indicated any very strong common core of beliefs and values.

Small himself had a vision for American society, and his analysis depended materially on that vision's being realized even though his analysis provided no grounds for it.

My own Pillar of Fire and Pillar of Cloud, in this wandering toward the Kingdom, is a vision of *the American Religion*. . . . Its work is dedication to an ideal of life in which each shall give his best to all others, and receive his best from all the others in promoting a method of life in which our dealings with one another, from the most trivial individual act to the most momentous public policy, shall do all that is possible toward realizing the most and the highest of which each and all of us are capable. . . . I do not know of anything short of *The American Religion* which can be more than a settlement of preliminaries to the genuinizing of our lives. (Vidich and Lyman 1985, 191)

Social coherence, it seemed, had to wait for religious conversion on a national scale even though social analysis gave no reason to suppose it was likely to happen. And so too did social justice have to wait. While Small's prose had an optimistic glow about it, his message was not encouraging.

Franklin H. Giddings

Small's contemporary at Columbia University, Franklin H. Giddings, held and promoted a much more secular and much less troubled view of American society and of the role that sociology could play in the resolution of its conflicts. Giddings solved the problem of social coherence by building it into human nature, and he disposed of the problem of social justice by attributing its progress to scientifically informed managerial intervention in the ongoing evolution of society.

It was human nature, Giddings taught, to have a "consciousness of kind" and to engage in "voluntary associations" based on that consciousness. Consequently, the inequalities of industrial society were not necessarily a problem. Liberty and equality would emerge out of the wise management of opportunities afforded by the evolutionary process, but they were not immediate political principles. They awaited the development of the "social personality," and that awaited "the reconciliation of clashing interests among individuals, classes, and races" (Vidich and Lyman 1985, 106).

Giddings was cautious in his approach to social change. His notion of consciousness of kind translated into a theory of "reference groups" through which individuals identified themselves personally and located themselves socially. To understand society, therefore, it was essential to understand the reference groups that existed and the extent to which individuals identified with them.

For this, one needed attitude- and opinion-survey methods and techniques. Accordingly, Giddings and his colleagues at Columbia emphasized statistical surveys. As Vidich and Lyman (1985, 110) explain: "Using the knowledge so gained to index the consciousness of kind, they could then chart the degree of consensus in society and advise policy makers on the consequences of any proposed reform programs. By combining the statistical study of consensus with predictions about the effects of public policies, the Columbia sociologists laid their claim to participate in the management of a rational social order."

Giddings combined his advocacy of statistical precision with a very plastic procedure for cost-benefit analysis. "There can be no social gain that does not entail somewhere, on the whole community or on a class, the breakup of long established relations, interests, and occupations, and the necessity of a more or less difficult readjustment" (Vidich and Lyman 1985, 115).

For every gain, somebody had to lose. Vidich and Lyman (1985, 15) summarize the position this way: "Giddings' sociology supplied both a remedy to and a sociodicy for the specifics of the Social Question. Capitalism, urbanization, the depopulation of the countryside, and the creation of wage labor were all evidence of progress. And the price was paid by those least able to bear it—the lazy, improvident, unintelligent, nonadaptive sectors of the population." Giddings was no social Darwinist, however. Those who paid the price for social progress should be cared for through scientifically managed social-welfare policies. The general orientation was quite clear, though: social problems were the price of social progress.

Giddings thought of his science as an instrument for extending democracy, indeed for creating a democratic empire. "Only when the democratic empire has compassed the uttermost parts of the world will there be that perfect understanding among men which is necessary for the growth of moral kinship. Only in the spiritual brotherhood of that secular republic, created by blood and iron not less than by thought and love, will the kingdom of heaven be established on earth" (Vidich and Lyman 1985, 119).

Giddings thus offered a positivist science—apparently objective because of its dedication to statistical techniques and methods—in the service of perfecting an already evolving and potentially global society. It was a quantifiable vision, and the fact that it was quantifiable drew attention away from any critical assessment of its normative content. By the 1920s it was the "Giddings Men" who were giving leadership in the definition and institutionalization of American social and behavioral science.

The Pittsburgh survey was an early effort to develop the statistical-survey method and to display its usefulness for understanding community problems and framing rational solutions to them. Conducted between 1907 and 1909, the Pittsburgh survey was followed by many more community surveys around the country, and—whether it helped to solve any of Pittsburgh's problems or not—thereafter no social problem was considered to be understood and ready for concerted action until there were statistical charts and graphs portraying the psychosocial demography of the situation and the probable consequences of alternative courses of action.

Major philanthropies were attracted to the Giddings version of social science. As Vidich and Lyman (1985, 132) point out: "Whereas both Christian Socialists and secular radicals emphasized the *Redistribution* of wealth, Rockefeller, Carnegie and other industrial giants, guided by the plutocratic version of the Social Gospel, considered its *rational management* to be appropriate expression of their special calling to holy stewardship." The Giddings view of society coincided with this view of wealth. For Giddings, rational management of social resources, not their redistribution, was the goal of wise policy. "Central to his outlook was a belief in the inherent social, cultural, and moral propriety of the American system of government and economy, coupled with an assurance that the human problems of an industrial civilization could be solved by piecemeal applications of government-sponsored social science" (Vidich and Lyman 1985, 135-36).

The revivalist emphasis on management, technique, and the dynamics of personality had been transposed into the new social and secular key. Conversion—the development of the social personality—was to be wrought by the social process itself. What appeared to be social conflict was but a moment in the larger process of change, a social cost for social progress. A new version of natural law was in the making, the natural law of social development.

Talcott Parsons

Talcott Parsons put forth an economic theory of the social system in which the progressive nationalism of the Giddings school could be legitimized through inclusion in universalistic and necessitarian categories. Parsons proposed that "net money advantage" was the link between personal motives and institutional realities: "Between certain alternatives, choice will be made in such a way as to maximize net money advantages to the actor, or to the social unit on behalf of which he acts" (Vidich and Lyman 1985, 83). From there Parsons elaborated a theory of a self-equilibrating social system that accounted for everything from personality to culture, economics, politics, and religion. This social system was characterized by a "universalistic achievement pattern" or, in short, a work ethic. Everything was adjusted to that. "The state in such a system, it may be remarked, tends to be regarded as any other collectivity, justified only in terms of its service to value goal-achievement. It may very well be, then, that the problem of institutionalizing collective responsibility is one of the most serious points of strain in such a social system" (Vidich and Lyman 1985, 48 n. 6).

America might have its problems or "strains" but, in Parsons's view, it stood at the top of the evolutionary process. "Socio-cultural evolution, like organic evolution, has proceeded by differentiation from simple to progressively more complex forms" (Vidich and Lyman 1985, 78). His examples of "socio-cultural evolution," however, were taken from twentieth-century peoples whom anthropologists had studied, and his evolutionary scheme completely abstracted them from their actual history. As Vidich and Lyman (1985, 79) point out, "Parsons presents an orderly evolutionary scheme that disconnects social processes from the actual history of colonialism, imperialism, and the natives' responses to them."

Events had lost any intrinsic meaning; they served only to illustrate various states of the social system. Determining the public welfare, which the founders of the Republic considered the highest work of politics, had been reduced to "the problem of institutionalizing collective responsibility." As such, it was a "strain." Only the "system" was real. The abstract concept of a self-equilibrating system had been substituted for the concrete idea of a self-governing people with names, addresses, personal biographies, social opportunities, political purposes, shared histories, and a possibly reasoned sense of their own importance in the larger scheme of things.

Ironically, this theory was put forth as if it were a defense of democracy! Its message was that the system works and that the more people worked, the better the system worked. Making the system work better became the high calling of sociology. "Functional" became the value-free code word for "good." Since the "Judeo-Christian heritage" and market capitalism were already built into the system, there were not any fundamental problems about the purposes to be pursued, only questions about the most effective means. America was on the right track.

Parsons had answered the question that had caused Comte to begin his sociological investigations in the first place: "Why is Europe the scene, and why is the white race the agent, of the highest civilization?'' Comte considered that ''the most important sociological inquiry that presents it-self'' (Vidich and Lyman 1985, 17 n. 1). Parsons had expanded ''Europe'' to ''the West'' and found the answer in good luck and hard work, the good luck of having a useful heritage that not only justified but inspired hard work. Parsons had provided a secularized and polysyllabic reassertion of the Protestant Ethic, now understood as the Judeo-Christian heritage, and the Spirit of Capitalism, now justified as a self-regulating system.

Parsons, of course, did not state his conclusions in just this way. When combined with his theory of sociocultural evolution, his theory of the so-cial system presented Western democratic societies as the ultimate in so-cial differentiation and complexity, the leaders of sociocultural evolution, the most important actors in contemporary world history by right of their evolutionary status, the representative embodiment of the natural law of evolution.

The Question of Social Justice

Sociology had traversed a long and tortuous road from the Social Question to the Social System, from the perception that something was wrong to the assurance that all was well—or would be in the long run, given some hard work—without ever having directly confronted the question of social justice. It had reached for whatever ideals were at hand; but it had excluded the rational examination of those ideals from the purview of its discipline, and it had engaged in no criticism of those ideals except in terms of their feasibility. As far as one can tell, most sociologists sincerely be-lieved that their science would be of service to a democratic society, but, in the terms of their science, that was an irrational commitment that they could not defend.

Yet, like every other contender for public influence, social scientists have had to address as well as analyze the common moral concerns of the American people and say what they think they can contribute to the public welfare. The only clear answer they have been able to give is that they can protect society from meaningful criticism and help it implement such pol-icies as those in authority say they want.

These two intended contributions to the public welfare are not unre-lated. The combination of Parsonian functionalism and the positivistic sta-tistical studies of various problems has the immediate effect of casting the knowledge of social problems in a context that also justifies them. They become problems to be solved by experts. In this view, all political issues become irrational issues that would better be left to the experts. After all, the American creed of democratic humanitarianism is already embedded in the culture and its institutions and will pay off for everyone in the long run under the ministrations of majoritarian, consensual strategies. Time and the normal functioning of institutions will solve all the problems that can be solved. The system works best if each person or group tends to its own business and works hard. Problems are caused by irrational hopes or fears or by attempts to impose private purposes on the system as a whole. The harms incidental to the pursuit of the greatest good for the greatest number can be managed if people will just maintain an atmosphere of civic calm. If they won't, the police stand ready to impose it.

This is the Civic Credo, which by mid-century stood as the successor to the old Protestant Ethic. The only public purpose that came within the purview of the Civic Credo was to see that as many private purposes as possible could be achieved. That is why I call it the Civic Credo and the Spirit of Privatism. The social sciences, as they had developed in America, were a major contributor to its articulation and rational justification. Where the Protestant Ethic and the Spirit of Capitalism had had the force of religion, the Civic Credo and the Spirit of Privatism had the support of both science *and* religion. There were other ideas around, but these had the force of orthodoxy.

Beyond the Civic Credo:
Social Science and Social Ethics

Thus far I have tried to show how social science—which began as a quest for critical knowledge of the social order, its conflicts, and inequalities, to aid in the pursuit of a wider justice—came to "function" as the protector of society from meaningful criticism. As defenders of the Civic Credo, the social sciences found their usefulness as management tools in government and business. Probably the most extensive use of the social sciences is in the curricula of M.B.A. programs, business schools generally, and various public-administration and public-policy centers. From there, the social sciences have found an institutional home wherever there is something to be administered. "Management" had become a "science."

Having invented themselves as experts and laid claim to the highest form of secular authority in a modern society (that is, competence), social scientists have yet to learn how to speak in the voice of citizens. Like the clerical economists in the nineteenth century, they still think that their expertise gives their ideas some right to rule and exempts them from the burden of being persuasive. By virtue of their methods and uninspected values, they are more at home in the hierarchical world of corporate organization, where purposes are already institutionalized, than they are in the open political arena, where purposes have to be discussed, debated, defended, revised, and ultimately decided.

It is not necessary, and it would not be wise, to assume that the purposes of groups and individuals are the only, or even the universally decisive, determinants of human events, but it is pure folly to leave them altogether out of any account of human action and human communities. The ideas that people hold about the goods to be achieved in this life enter materially into the course of human events, and it makes no sense to maintain that these ideas are in principle any more subjective and arbitrary than any other ideas.

The role of ideas is as much an empirical question as the role of "net money advantage" or "selfishness," both of which are ideas themselves. People act on ideas that they believe to be true. The role these ideas play in the actions of groups and individuals and in the events of their lives may well depend to some degree on whether or not those ideas are true—true in general, true in the way they are believed, true in the sense of leading to the results people expect. That is, there are many situations about which we want to know and in which empirical questions cannot be treated fully without also entertaining normative questions.

For instance, many people may believe that blacks are inferior to whites. But we cannot give an adequate description of the role played by that idea without also having to come to terms with the question of whether that idea is true—true in general, true in the way it was believed, or true as a guide to proper action. If this idea is not true, then in some important respects, those who act on it will be committing an injustice.

Yet American social science has developed on the basis that empirical knowledge of the society could be generated without having to deal with this normative side of things; that the role of ideas could be studied without asking whether they were true; and therefore that human action could be studied without asking whether it was just. Maybe it is possible to do this in a limited and provisional way, but the course of American social science seems to be living proof that this self-imposed limitation cannot serve as the basis for a whole science of society. It leaves too much of social, political, and religious life outside its purview, and the result is not a value-free but a subservient social science, dominated by unexamined purposes and unable to see the trees for the forest.

Rather than include substantive moral and religious problems within the scope of the inquiry, orthodox social scientists have developed a high-minded disdain for the intrusion of explicitly ethical concerns into the quest for social understanding. Writing about "ethnic stratification," Tomatsu Shibutani and Kian Kwan provide a pure type for the defense of orthodoxy in which all normative concerns are relegated to a vile form of "irrationalism":

> Ironically, one of the major barriers to a better comprehension of these phenomena is the indignation of the investigators. Social scientists are human beings, and their emotional reactions to the injustices they see make difficult the cultivation of a detached standpoint. Men who are angry often look for a responsible agent to blame, and this search for culprits often vitiates research. There was a time when other obnoxious phenomena were explained in terms of malevolence; earthquakes and diseases have been attributed to the machinations of personal enemies. Other scientists seem to have overcome the animistic approach, but still it persists in the social sciences. When difficulties are perceived in moral terms, there is a tendency to explain events by imputing vicious motives to those who are held responsible. Furthermore, moral indignation often blinds the student to many facts that would otherwise be obvious. All too often deeds regarded as reprehensible are assumed to be fundamentally different from those that are approved, and the moral dichotomy often prevents one from recognizing that both may be manifestations of the same social process. (Shibutani and Kwan 1965, 14-15)

Instead of approaching the social order as morally and intellectually serious but unfinished business, the discipline went for total explanations that would supposedly avoid the need for justification or at least come prior to it. This idea inspired the positivists just as much as it did the systems theorists. Statistical positivistic techniques for data gathering were promoted as providing all the data that counted in the universe defined by the research project. Positivism promised to provide a total explanation of the *parts*.

On the other hand, functionalist systems theory, as with Parsons, approached the social order as if it were somehow a *whole* that could be understood as exemplifying universal laws of development to which its participants were forever adjusting. For the positivists, the "world" consisted of data that, once known, could be exploited for any purpose it could serve. For the systems theorist, the "world" consisted of highly structured behavior patterns that could be exploited for any purpose they would serve.

Advocates of functionalist systems theory identified Marxism as their chief rival, as well they might. Nonetheless, both suffered from the same faults. Each viewed the social order as an identifiable system subject to universal laws. Each discounted the ultimate importance of political life and the dialogue of moral principles that is its organizing center. Each also discounted the moral and intellectual seriousness of religious orientation in the human condition. Each focused on the structurally conditioned aspects of human behavior and explained them as exemplifications of universal laws while neglecting the purposive aspects of human action and the particularistic aspects of human histories. Consequently, both ended up believing that fundamental issues could be settled once and for all and that thereafter only problems of management would remain in the community at large. Politics is absorbed into administration; whatever cannot be managed is deviant.

It is interesting that both Adam Smith and Karl Marx shared a common misconception. Both believed that once the economic system was working at full capacity for the good of all, then society would experience a diminished need for political life. Perhaps they can be excused for having believed this since each of them wrote before the truly phenomenal productivity of modern economics was unleashed. But neither the followers of Marx nor American social scientists, who follow so much in the footsteps of Adam Smith, can be excused so lightly. They have lived in times of sustained economic expansion, and they have seen that the increase in social resources is accompanied not only by an increased demand to participate in the political life of the society but also by an increase in the options actually available for the pursuit of the public welfare.

Economic structures and conditions enter as a factor in all human situations, but poverty is much more deterministic than affluence because poverty restricts and affluence expands the choices that actually can and have to be made both by individuals and by the people as such. These choices have to be made by the people as individuals and as a whole, that is, politically. There is no "system" that makes them. Citizens make these choices on the basis of whatever ideas persuade them as true if they have access to the political process. Otherwise, "power figures" make these choices on the basis of what they believe they can get away with.

What we need is a social science that can examine and identify the reasonable differences that arise in the process of identifying the public welfare, an argumentative rather than a dogmatic social science, a social science that takes normative concerns as seriously as it does empirical ones, one that does not forbid itself from asking whether people really do have rights and what it would take to protect and enhance them. In short, we need a social science that does not reject the task of social ethics as American social science did at the turn of the century, at great cost to our self-understanding as a people.

What is at stake here is not just a narrowly academic question about how best to do social science or a merely technical question about the place of social ethics in the current lineup of academic disciplines. What is at stake is our ability to give reasonable, critical, and informed accounts of ourselves as a people who have generated significant issues in our own common life and in our interaction with the other peoples who share this globe. If our own public welfare depends on the promotion and protection of equal rights, personal liberties, and the pursuit of happiness, then so does the broader public welfare in terms of which we are but one people among others.

Intellectual honesty as well as political wisdom requires that we face up to the full implications of the issues that we have generated in our common life. The full implications are contained in the observation that there are reasonable differences among us with regard to the actual content of what should count as the public welfare. Critical and informed accounts of ourselves, therefore, will include the problematic character of those reasonable differences. This means taking the dialogue of moral principles with utter seriousness, not as abstract, subjective, irrational, ideological commitments to be explained away by something more basic such as "the social system" or "class conflict."

Benjamin Franklin is supposed to have said that "time is the stuff that life is made up of." That is true, but time is never empty; it is filled with issues that have to be resolved one way or another. The question is what role moral, metaphysical, and religious principles will play—along with systemic and circumstantial factors—in the making, the identification, and the resolution of those issues. Time may be the stuff that life is made of, but issues are the things that make time human and that make timeliness a matter of some importance in human affairs.

Facing up to the full implications of the issues that we have generated in our common life begins, then, with a focus on those issues as the truly ultimate matters so far as this life is concerned. Metaphysical propositions, religious affirmations, and theological doctrines all find their truth and creativity finally tested by their capacity to contribute to the identification, explanation, and resolution of the issues of this life. We have seen how *some* metaphysical propositions, religious affirmations, and theological doctrines both contributed explicitly to the making of the Protestant Ethic and the Spirit of Capitalism and gave rise to a world whose institutional reach exceeded the grasp of its major ideas. We also have seen how, in reaction to this, a social science developed that, therefore, attempted to exclude any direct or positive contribution from *all* metaphysical propositions, religious affirmations, and theological doctrines. This social science too was confronted with issues that exceeded the grasp of its ideas, but what is even worse, it held ideas that denied the importance of any issues it could not "manage." I have called these ideas the Civic Credo and the Spirit of Privatism to indicate that this attempt to exclude fundamental questions from social science did not succeed. It only drove them underground. To face the full implications of the issues that we have generated in our common life requires a new approach to the integration of normative and empirical concerns, an approach in which issues are at the center of attention and in which the metaphysical, religious, and theological dimensions and components of those issues are treated explicitly.

The essays in this book give some idea of what would be involved in, and what we could expect from, a social science that accepted the task of social ethics as an integral part of the quest for social understanding.

Reference List

Abell, Aaron I.

1962 *The Urban Impact on American Protestantism, 1865-1900*. Hamden and London: Archon.

Bernard, L. L. and Jessie Bernard

[1943] 1965 *Origins of American Sociology: The Social Science Movement in the United States*. New York: Thomas Y. Crowell; Russell and Russell.

Bryson, Gladys

1932 "The Emergence of the Social Sciences from Moral Philosophy." *International Journal of Ethics* 42 (April): 304-23.

Chandler, Alfred D., Jr.

1977 *The Visible Hand: The Managerial Revolution in American Business*. Cambridge MA and London: The Belknap Press of Harvard University Press.

Hacker, Louis M.

[1940] 1947 *The Triumph of American Capitalism: The Development of Forces in American History to the End of the Nineteenth Century*. New York: Simon and Schuster; Columbia University Press.

Hopkins, Charles H.

1940 *The Rise of the Social Gospel in American Protestantism, 1865-1900*. New Haven: Yale University Press.

May, Henry F.

[1949] 1963 *Protestant Churches and Industrial America*. New York: Harper & Brothers; Octagon Books.

Pauck, Wilhelm

1967 *The Heritage of the Reformation*. Glencoe IL: The Free Press.

Schlesinger, A. M.

1932 "A Critical Period in American Religion, 1875-1900." *Proceedings of the Massachusetts Historical Society* (June): 523-47.

Shibutani, Tomatsu and Kian W. Kwan

1965 *Ethnic Stratification*. New York: Macmillan Company.

Vidich, Arthur J. and Stanford M. Lyman

    1985 *American Sociology: Worldly Rejections of Religion and Their Directions*. New Haven and London: Yale University Press.

Wright, Benjamin F.

    1931 *American Interpretations of Natural Law*. Cambridge: Harvard University Press.

Robin W. Lovin
University of Chicago
Divinity School

▪ ▪

Theological Foundations for Social Ethics

▪ ▪ In a Midwestern community, Jewish parents object to the public high school choir's singing Christmas songs at the downtown holiday festival. A women's group tells a state legislature that to limit a woman's choices on abortion amounts to imposing someone else's religious beliefs on her. A conservative Protestant church in a Southern city establishes a "Christian academy" for parents who are angered by desegregation in the public schools. A coalition of church leaders demands better services for low-income neighborhoods in a major city, while young men in a rural religious community refuse to register for the draft. These incidents and many others like them are pointed reminders that religious groups and religious ideas play an important part in social ethics. The problem can be stated abstractly under a variety of labels: church and state, freedom of religion, faith and works, belief and action. All of the formulations point to an underlying theological issue: how to relate the absolute demands of religious faith to the requirements of life in a society. It is a problem that becomes especially pointed when persons of many different faiths participate together in public decision making.

Although a thinking person who has faith and who lives in society is inevitably involved in both theology and social ethics, these two concerns are never identical. Nor can theology relate to social ethics as philosophy often does, simply as a tool for an analytical task. Contemporary Anglo-American philosophy, particularly, often understands itself to be a way of thinking about language, a way of making sense of the discourse that goes on in social ethics without being a direct influence on the ethical choices themselves. Other types of philosophy try to explain the presuppositions of choice and action of any sort. Here again, the goal is to understand what persons and groups are doing when they make ethical choices. Philosophy can question choices that seem logically inconsistent or identify explanations that are incoherent, but it need not—and today it often does not—bring its own understanding of human nature and the purposes of human life to bear on decisions in social ethics.

Theology is different. Theology is reflection on the beliefs and traditions of a particular religious community. Of course, theology is not restricted to repeating uncritically what Catholics, Lutherans, Methodists, or Mennonites have believed and taught. Fundamental theology tries to express these beliefs as truths about human life in general, restating a particular faith in ways that allow those of other faiths—or of no faith—to recognize the reality of the theological teaching in their own experience. Nevertheless, the theologian is always committed to a body of ideas, specific things believed to be true about human life, with implications for human choice. The theologian is never simply an analyst of other ideas.

This distinct subject matter of theology raises critical issues when problems of choice and action are concerned. Communities of faith typically have their own ideas about the way of life that is appropriate for someone who shares their beliefs. While they may try, as the New Testament says, to live for aims "such as all count honorable,"[1] few would be satisfied to say that the life of faith is no more than a matter of generally recognized good behavior. On the other hand, if the requirements of faith are truly the commandments of God, it is hard to see why anyone should be excused from living up to them. So the theologian—and, indeed, any thinking person of faith—is always caught up in deciding not just what is true and what is false, but what is particular to the believing community and what is universal.

How you answer this theological question immediately affects your decisions in social ethics. If you believe that the most important moral standards of your faith are requirements of mutual love and self-restraint that clearly apply only to believers, you will be primarily concerned to make choices that leave you free to live your own life with those who share your faith. Therefore, you may have little interest in the standards of behavior

[1]Rom. 12:17.

that the laws impose on other people. By contrast, if you think your faith articulates in a clear and compelling way moral standards that are essential for a good society, you will want—as far as possible—to adopt laws and set expectations that impose these standards on everyone. If you find yourself upholding standards that most people will not accept, you must decide whether to withdraw and fight only for the right to live out your beliefs, or to engage in a long struggle to transform society's standards so that they are more nearly in line with the requirements of your faith.

Religious attitudes toward social action, then, range from a sharp separation of questions of faith from questions of public action to a position that identifies religious action with social transformation. Between these extremes there are many patterns of interaction that are important for religious social ethics. In this chapter we will examine five types that have emerged in the development of contemporary Christianity. Other religious groups no doubt would give evidence of similar patterns, but we cannot claim that these are the only patterns or that every religion must exhibit all of them. The types are generalizations from history.[2] Still, they show us ways to relate faith and ethics that will aid our understanding of the arguments we will meet in religious social ethics (including the arguments in this volume), and they suggest ways to keep the relationship between faith and social ethics constructive.

A Community Set Apart:
The Social Ethics of Sectarianism

Perhaps the most straightforward way of understanding the distinction between religious faith and the wider community owes its origin to radical Protestant communities that emerged during the Reformation era. These groups, which survive in modern denominations such as the Mennonites or the Church of the Brethren, are characterized by stringent scrutiny of adult candidates for membership and may require or encourage their mem-

---

[2]In this way, the patterns we describe here are like the "ideal types" used by Max Weber to clarify ideas in sociology. They are abstractions from what people actually have said and written, not hypothetical constructions of what people might believe. However, it is unlikely that any single person in history fits the "typical" description exactly. The types or patterns described here also owe much to the specific types used by H. Richard Niebuhr in his study of the relationships between Christianity and culture. See Max Weber, *Economy and Society* (Berkeley: University of California Press, 1978) 4-22. See also H. Richard Niebuhr, *Christ and Culture* (New York: Harper & Row, 1951).

bers not to participate in certain forms of public activity such as military service, social insurance, or public education. The rigorous requirements for membership, the emphasis on self-sufficiency, and the distrust of the organizations of the wider society reflect an underlying conviction that the institutions that are successful and appeal to large numbers of persons are fundamentally flawed; hence the only way to express one's faith is to separate oneself from them as far as possible.[3]

Members of these sectarian groups understand the rigorous self-discipline that this separation requires. They do not expect that many persons will accept their way of life. They recognize that religious institutions are under constant pressure to offer a more inviting compromise with the ways of the world. Nevertheless, they insist that from the beginning, Christianity has been about the radical choice that Jesus offered between his way of life and the ways of the society in which he lived. They call for those who can do so to discard their illusions about social progress and values in public life in order to recognize the power of violence and coercion, especially military violence, by which modern societies maintain themselves. John Howard Yoder's *The Politics of Jesus*[4] offers a contemporary statement of this position, based both on biblical study and modern political thought.

It would seem that the sectarians' position cannot be a social ethic at all, since their witness is their refusal to participate in society's organized violence. More precisely, their social ethic is the ethic of their community, for it is only among believers that the relations of love, justice, and mutual respect can be maintained. The community rests on a strong sense of identity derived from the biblical story of Jesus' rejection by the world in which he lived. Sectarian Christians also recall brutal persecutions that occurred when their pacifist convictions brought them into conflict with the military aims of the nations in which they lived. On the basis of Scripture and their own experience, these communities do not expect a following, or even a very widespread understanding, of their position.

---

[3]Early Christian monks also expressed their faith in separation from society, but as monastic orders became a regular part of the church, they reconceived their mission not as a separation from the rest of humanity but as a special vocation within the wider Christian community. Separate communities of faith have been less common in Judaism; however, the Essenes, who lived in isolated settlements near the Dead Sea from at least the second century B.C.E., are an important example.

[4]John Howard Yoder, *The Politics of Jesus* (Grand Rapids: Eerdmans, 1972).

Limiting social ethics to the community of faith, of course, means that it is rather difficult for sectarians to press moral claims against the wider society. Sectarian communities may vigorously pursue their legal rights to private schools or to exemption from military service in countries where the public law recognizes those rights, but they have no basis on which to make general claims about what their rights ought to be if the necessary arrangements for their community are not accepted by the law. In such cases, the sectarian communities usually will accept persecution with the same equanimity that they accept their exemptions in a more tolerant society.

This reluctance to press their own case in public argument is not the result of passivity or a false humility among sectarians. It follows from their conviction that a shared faith is the only truly meaningful ground for human action. In a public forum, many persons will neither understand nor accept those arguments, and the forum itself—the law court or the public-school auditorium, for example—may simply exclude the religious argument. Under those circumstances, the sectarian has no illusions that the positions the religious community shares can be made persuasive, or even made clear, to a wider audience. This does not entirely exclude the determined sectarian from a role in public debate. Simply to collect information and make it available helps to keep an issue alive and allows others who share the concern for their own reasons to frame their own arguments for action. The Seventh-Day Adventists, for example, publish a magazine called *Liberty*, which presents information on religious freedom around the world to a large audience. Keeping that problem before the public is perhaps the best defense the Adventist community has against the persecutions that have often disrupted their life together.

In recent years, however, a Roman Catholic form of this social ethic has found a more activist stance, paradoxically by radicalizing the criticism of society. What the Europeans call "political theology" (it also figures prominently in Latin American "liberation theology") begins with a thoroughgoing critique of the exploitation, waste of resources, and self-deception that characterize life in industrialized and bureaucratized societies. Such pervasive distortion penetrates even the churches and absorbs them into a culture of passive consumerism. The only escape from this is the resolute movement of Christians to take responsibility for their own lives in a "basic community" church that gives them a place to see themselves clearly and to relate to one another without falsehood.[5] The basic community church does not withdraw from the impossibly corrupt society that surrounds it. Instead, it becomes a center for social criticism, drawing on the best resources for analysis available—principally, its advocates suggest, Marxist economics and social theory. The basic community church thus becomes a center for activity that may issue in a genuine social revolution.

A Working Relationship:
The Social Ethics of Diverse Tasks

Sectarian Christians see their relationship to the wider society as a whole. Membership in Christian community comprehensively determines what they may do and what they must avoid in the world where the rest of humanity lives. Other theologians begin their social ethics with the recognition that the lives of individual Christians are always involved with others in business relationships, in shared space with neighbors who must make decisions about the civic community, or at least in establishing a police power strong enough to restrain those who would otherwise prey on everyone, Christian and non-Christian alike. The distinction between the community of faith and the wider society is real; there are obligations of mutual love and of support prevailing in the community that it would be unrealistic to expect from those outside. Still, say those writers who insist on a working relationship, the Christian must depend on society in important ways, and the Christian may appropriately participate in deciding questions of justice, enforcing order, and defending the society against its enemies.

Historically, this has been a typically Protestant way of thinking. Martin Luther sharply distinguished the sphere of the church from the sphere of secular authority. Christians participate in both, adjusting their actions to the particular requirements of each. The Christian who must forgive and forbear in the church may take up the soldier's sword or the hangman's noose in society, for these murderous tasks are essential for the security and happiness of the whole people.[6] Modern writers usually have thought that the Reformers distinguished the two realms a bit too sharply, but the

---

[5]Johannes Metz, *The Emergent Church* (Philadelphia: Fortress Press, 1981).

[6]Martin Luther, "Secular Authority: To What Extent It May Be Obeyed," in John Dillenberger, ed., *Martin Luther* (Garden City: Anchor Books, 1961).

basic pattern of two independent, yet functionally related, centers of authority remains. Emil Brunner suggested that the relationships established by God are apparent in recurrent patterns of human life that all societies follow. Five interdependent "orders of creation"—church, state, family, labor, and culture—remain constant in human history, and disorder inevitably follows when their functions are confused or when one of them tries to dominate the rest.[7] The constitutional principle of separation of church and state, so important to religious life in the United States, owes its origin to many sources—including nonreligious statesmen who simply wanted to eliminate religion from public life altogether—but the continuing power of the principle is no doubt due largely to the work of Protestant groups (Congregationalists, Baptists, Presbyterians, Lutherans, and others) who had theological reasons to support the separation that the Constitution required.

The implications that churches have drawn from this working relationship between the diverse orders of society often have been rather conservative. The notion of a public order that must impose by force a minimal morality that falls far short of what we might follow voluntarily in the community of faith lends itself to the conclusion that any order we have is probably better than the anarchy that may ensue if we tamper with the system.

What gives this theology a powerful social impact in the contemporary world is its stress on the diversity of functions that make up human society. It is not enough simply to impose order on a nation; the order must be one that preserves church, state, family, labor, and culture as distinct centers of social creativity. Totalitarian systems that attempt to regulate all phases of life by the state or the party may provide order, but they do not respect the diversity of tasks that is important to this theological account of the good society. Karl Barth stressed the different tasks of church and state as an argument against the Hitler regime's attempt to enlist the churches in its glorification of Germanic culture.[8] Dietrich Bonhoeffer, who ultimately died in a Nazi concentration camp, insisted in his *Ethics* that those who claim to know the command of God must demonstrate it concretely in the

---

[7]Emil Brunner, *The Divine Imperative* (Philadelphia: Westminster Press, 1947).

[8]Karl Barth, "Church and State," in *Community, State, and Church* (Gloucester MA: Peter Smith, 1968).

"divine mandates" of work, family, state, and church.[9] The work of Barth, Brunner, and Bonhoeffer is particularly important whenever a society is under pressure to sacrifice all human relationships to a single social program.

A Pattern of Purposes:
The Social Ethics of Natural Law

A third way of understanding the relationship between society and the community of faith is to consider the different purposes each serves. When these are properly identified, church and society are still distinct, but their relationship is complementary, not competitive. The society provides an order in which persons pursue temporal goals. They develop their capacities through education; they provide for their physical safety and security in their possessions; they contribute their energies and talents toward the creation of material wealth and cultural goods that everyone can share. The community of faith, by contrast, is primarily concerned with eternal goals. The believer's relationship to God is what is decisive for faith, however important the mundane concerns of daily life may be.

So faith and society serve quite different goals, but these two systems are not separated from one another, nor is their relationship merely functional. Properly understood, the temporal goals of society serve the more important eternal goals of faith. The goods of peace and security, the supply of human material needs and the protections of families and cultural resources are obviously important goals, worth pursuing on their own terms, but when they are achieved, they also create conditions under which persons can more freely develop their relationships to God.[10]

Characteristically, then, this third way of thinking about faith in relation to society sees the goals of faith and those of society arranged in hierarchical order. Temporal activity has a distinctively subordinate place, but properly pursued it contributes to the achievement of spiritual goals. What this hierarchical relationship means in practical terms, however, is that persons in the community of faith can take action in society quite seriously, and they can pursue society's goals of order, security, and prosperity on society's own terms. One need not ask whether others in society

---

[9]Dietrich Bonhoeffer, *Ethics* (New York: Macmillan, 1965).

[10]Jacques Maritain, *Integral Humanism* (South Bend: University of Notre Dame Press, 1973). See especially the appendix on "The Structure of Social Action."

share the faith in order to work with them on practical matters. They may be quite indifferent to the higher spiritual aims, or they may be committed to a quite different understanding of their relationship to God. Those are important issues in the spiritual ordering of life, but when it comes to working for justice or peace, those issues need not divide the society.

Clearly, this way of thinking about the relationship between faith and society presupposes an extensive system of goals that all persons pursue and that all, upon reflection, can recognize and agree to honor. The requirements of justice, for example, must be set by some facts about human nature and human needs; and while systems of justice may vary in detail from nation to nation, the basic obligations they impose must be universal. Decisions about justice are not matters of historical accident, nor does each society simply decide for itself what it will call just. Rather, the universal features that a good society must have are established by a *natural law*, which expresses requirements for a good human life that are independent of history and culture.

This line of thinking originated with Aristotle and the later Stoic philosophers, who sought to identify a core of shared moral principles that united the diverse peoples and customs of the ancient world.[11] Natural law took systematic theological form in the work of Thomas Aquinas, who renewed the study of Aristotle in the medieval church. Ever since, natural law has been an important element in Roman Catholic moral theology. Protestants, generally suspicious of legalistic moral rules, for a long time avoided the formulations of natural law introduced by Aquinas, but recent years have brought a new appreciation of the limits and constraints that reality imposes on all human creativity. As Dietrich Bonhoeffer put it, ''At least it seems possible to infer with certainty that in social life there are laws more powerful than anything that may claim to dominate them, and that it is therefore not only wrong but unwise to disregard them. We can understand from this why Aristotelian-Thomist ethics made wisdom one of the cardinal virtues.''[12]

The basic form of the natural-law inquiry has always been a rational exploration of the limits that nature imposes on human activity and the pat-

---

[11]For a history of natural-law ideas, see A. P. d'Entreves, *Natural Law*, 2d ed. (London: Hutchinson, 1970).

[12]Dietrich Bonhoeffer, *Letters and Papers from Prison* (New York: Macmillan, 1971) 10.

terns that human life takes on when it develops according to plan. Rational inquiry today, of course, is considerably more complex than it was in the prescientific era, and many forms of modern science explicitly deny that the search for patterns and goals in human life that characterized the older natural law can be scientific. Nonetheless, one finds many contemporary religious ethicists, Protestant and Catholic, upholding that same respect for a rational inquiry into the conditions of human life that was found in Thomistic moral theology. For such writers, as we will see, a study of the problem of poverty or of race relations cannot proceed on the basis of moral judgment alone. A careful study of economic science, or of sociology, also is required; and the truths that these investigations discover about the conditions of human life are presumed to be consistent with theological truths, however much the premises of science and theology may differ. Religious social ethics, then, concerns itself with the facts and theories about social life for the same reason that natural-law theory has always attended to the conditions of the temporal good: the good achieved for human life in society prepares the way for the spiritual achievements that are the distinctive concern of theology. In sum, the life of faith cannot flourish without the material conditions that sustain the life of the body and the social community.

Moral theologians seek the good of society, confident that the patterns that serve the good and the natural laws that set the conditions for its achievement are themselves part of a larger pattern that sets human beings and their life in society in a right relationship to God. Because the life of society has more than a merely functional relationship to the life of faith, understanding and improving social life becomes an expression of faith, but also an inquiry in which the faithful can learn from all persons, of whatever convictions, who take the tasks of society seriously and approach them honestly.

The Reality of the Ideal:
The Social Ethics of Process Philosophy

The patterns of relationship we have examined so far stress the differences between the goals and values of the religious community and those of the wider society. Sectarian groups and those who carefully observe the distinctive tasks of different "orders" or "mandates" hold Christian values that cannot be put into practice in society as a whole. For although natural-law theorists stress the cooperation of all persons in the rational pursuit of social goals, the Roman Catholic thinkers who have developed natural law most fully as a system of religious ethics continue to stress the difference between temporal good, which can be pursued in society, and eternal good, which concerns a person's relationship to God.

One way of thinking about social ethics has largely avoided this dichotomy between religion and society. The "process philosophy" of Alfred North Whitehead and Charles Hartshorne emphasizes a theistic dimension implicit in every ideal or goal.[13] (Franklin Gamwell's essay in this volume treats this issue in more detail.) Process philosophy systematized a creative era in American thought, represented by William James, Josiah Royce, C. S. Peirce, and others who usually are identified as "pragmatists." These philosophers stressed the importance of religious ideals in human history and human aspirations, and they did not distinguish sharply between theological and philosophical inquiries. For those who take this point of view, the important distinction is not between religious insights and the values of society, but between the ideal and the present state of affairs. Reality is a process of change, not an eternal relationship between things as they are; so a proper appreciation of reality includes an understanding of the directions of change and of the divine totality within which all particular changes take place.

When process thought is applied to ethics, it leads to a comprehensive view of the problems of social choice and social change. Participation in the social process can never be reduced to a sort of market transaction in which the individual meets purely personal needs. To have a social life is to share a set of ideals with others, and thus, from the process point of view, to share with them in a religious community. Process thought thus clearly provides a foundation for participation in social ethics. It is less clear that it provides a critical perspective for choosing between the different social ideals that may be available at any given time. Critics charge that the affirmations of change and the conviction that all reality ultimately finds a place in God leads to an optimistic readiness to overlook evil and destructive tendencies in some social movements. We know from process thought that choice is important. We are less sure what sorts of choices we ought to make.

------

[13]See, for example, Alfred North Whitehead, *Process and Reality* (New York: Macmillan, 1929), and Charles Hartshorne, *A Natural Theology for Our Time* (LaSalle IL: Open Court Press, 1967). A good contemporary statement of process thought in theology is John B. Cobb, *The Structure of Christian Existence* (Philadelphia: Westminster Press, 1967).

Nevertheless, process thought precludes choices that exalt one community at the expense of others or treat some persons as though their values and choices were expendable. Since every value points in the end to its source in a universal, divine reality, every value choice is implicitly critical of partial and limited perspectives on reality. To defend a way of organizing society or understanding the world, it is not enough to demonstrate that it conforms to the requirements of Christian tradition or vindicates the historical purposes of a nation or ethnic group. Only the whole scope of evolutionary development and human history provides a context large enough to validate a particular choice. In practical terms, this means that process thought, like natural-law theory, establishes a community of discourse in which everyone may participate and in which information from a wide range of scientific and historical studies is relevant. Concerning this point, social ethicists trained in the quite different traditions of Roman Catholic moral theology and American liberal Protestantism come together.

The result, particularly in recent religious social ethics in America, has been a careful attention to social science and a method that begins by establishing carefully the facts that surround the issue in dispute. At the same time, religious social ethics avoids commitment to a single social-science perspective in which to seek all truth. The religious social ethicist often follows a pattern suggested by Warren Copeland's essay on economic policy. Copeland sets out a variety of social-science perspectives and examines each one to discover its fundamental presuppositions. It is the basic values and the vision of the good human life in each of the theories, not its technical details or the accuracy of its predictions, that interest us most. In addition to the values implicit in social science, religious social ethics also is concerned with the direct examination of codes of ethics or standards of conduct that govern business transactions, professional practices, and public service. Here, as in James Capo's essay on ethics in television news, the task is to relate specific standards of conduct to the values that are held in our society at large and, if possible, to values that prevail in human societies generally. Hence, Capo explores "the correspondence between the maxims of press responsibility and the mythologies that undergird American life and belief."

Social ethics need not always make a complete statement about reality. When we look at a careful theological reflection on social conditions or an exploration of the values that shape a social group, we cannot always determine whether the writer is influenced by some tradition of natural law, by process thought or, indeed, by some other system that teaches us to take all reasoned approaches to the human condition seriously. It is not even necessary that the writer be able to identify these influences for himself or herself. What is important is the incorporation of scientific and historical information into an open inquiry that seeks patterns of human fulfillment in the life we all share together. Process thought reminds us that although the theological premises of that inquiry often remain unspoken, they always are important.

Transcendence and Transformation:
The Social Ethics of Realism

An approach to social ethics based on process thought presupposes an intricate relationship between the goals and needs of individuals, the requirements of society, and the overall course of change in the history of the universe. Where events lack this neatness, as events often do, process thought must insist that the disorder is only apparent and that in the long run the harmony between the individual and the universal prevails. An alternative approach avoids sweeping generalizations about human life and insists instead on critical examination of each historical situation, without preconceptions. If process thought tries to conceive of reality as a whole, our fifth approach marks a more circumscribed kind of realism. This realism turns a suspicious gaze on every attempt to speak about values and social structures in universal terms. It calls our attention to points at which values conflict, as for example when our obligation to tell the truth conflicts with the obligation not to injure other persons or cause them unnecessary pain. Realism above all reminds us that our own ideas are always subject to change, that what we think is natural often is nothing more than what we are used to seeing. Among Protestant theologians, Reinhold Niebuhr particularly insisted on this.[14] He might find a pleasing irony in having his point confirmed by Mary Pellauer's exposure of the unquestioned sex-role stereotypes that prevailed in his own family life. The realist introduces a note of caution and a reminder of historical change into all attempts at ethical generalization.

---

[14]Reinhold Niebuhr, *Christian Realism and Political Problems* (New York: Scribner's, 1953).

Such realism leads to a critical perspective on the values a society or a group professes at any specific time. The realist will want to know whether these principles are lived out consistently, whether they have unhappy consequences the society prefers not to notice, and whether these commitments really are as permanent as they seem. Often this perspective results from an experience of the contradictions and hidden negations in a society's values. Some of the most effective realists in recent American history have been members of minority groups, who have lived with the unspoken exceptions to our society's commitments to equality and democracy. The "dilemma," "indictment," and "transformationist" positions that Roger Hatch identifies among interpreters of American racism are all variations on this theme of critical realism, although the "transformationist" interpreters probably express the realist insights most consistently. Still another group of realists can be found among those who work in professions where outmoded codes of conduct simply no longer fit the conditions of present practice. When that happens, as James Capo suggests it has happened in the news media, people find themselves expressing devotion to values such as "truthfulness" that still seem noble but that really give them no guidance in deciding what to do.

Of course, these perceptions may lead to nothing more than cynicism, to a denial that values have any meaning at all. The realist, by contrast, tries to preserve a sense of value and moral obligation by pointing to the limits within which each traditional system is valid. Moral insights are discredited, says the realist, only when we try to generalize them beyond their real applicability. We preserve morality, paradoxically, by confining it within its limitations.

Thus, while the natural-law writer seeks permanent patterns that govern all human life and the "orders of creation" theorist tries to define an invariant relationship between the diverse elements of society, the realist concentrates on history, on the different social patterns that unfold in historical change, and on the new moral insights that become possible even as some of the old truths have to be retired. This does not require a denial of persistent moral realities, but the realist suspects that we are more likely to be led astray by believing in permanence than by being attentive to change. John Bennett says, "The Catholic emphasis on natural law has much to commend it. . . . There is a moral order that we know something about apart from Christian faith, even though this knowledge is more likely to be distorted than the Catholic moralist admits.''[15] Similarly, the realist acknowledges the process theologian's requirement that we think about values in a universal context. However, the realist finds it more important to point out that we always fail to achieve that universality than to articulate it as an ideal.

The realist is skeptical of human moral achievements but also is hopeful for social transformation. Knowing that none of our patterns in life is truly permanent, necessary, and unchanging, the realist knows that it always is possible to find a new way to do justice or to meet human needs. In contrast to the conservative observers who are reluctant to risk what has been achieved in the mere hope of a society that could be somewhat more just and somewhat more caring, the realist knows that our achievements already are at risk all of the time anyway. Realists suspect that the achievements we have will prove in the end less perfect than we think them to be, and they count heavily on incremental changes that promise a little more justice or a little less suffering, for these are the changes that make the greatest difference in individual persons' lives. For the same reason, realists reject utopian thinking. Just as it is a mistake to think that our present practices and concepts will not change and cannot be improved, it is also a mistake to think that at some point in the process of transformation we will come to a place where all flaws are eliminated and further changes are unnecessary.

Realism, then, is a social philosophy of freedom. This freedom is not the political freedom to choose one's leaders and to follow one's own plans, but a more fundamental freedom to envision alternatives to the given conditions of life and to live beyond the constraints that history happens to have placed upon us. No matter how serene and unchanging our surroundings, or how sternly we have been taught to accept our limitations, we know that something else is possible, and those possibilities define our situation quite as much as the bare realities with which we begin.

Such realism fits well with the Protestant conception of God, who always transcends any system of theology that we try to impose on divine reality. It accords, too, with Protestantism's historic rejection of legalistic moral systems that try to bind the individual conscience. When such a faith in a transcendent God and in human self-transcendence confronts the ques-

---

[15]John C. Bennett, *Christian Ethics and Social Policy* (New York: Scribner's, 1946) 39-40.

tion of faith and society, it will not establish some single pattern to relate them. It will insist that we see each existing situation as it really is, but it also will remind us that the reality we observe is perpetually changing. Thus this faith holds us accountable for the transformations we can envision and enact.

Conclusion

The five ways of relating faith and society we have examined here are ideal types or patterns. Probably no one thinks in just one of these patterns all of the time. Confronted with the demands of action and the compromises that real events impose, we may borrow ideas from several of the types to construct what seems a workable and faithful response to the circumstances. The issue-oriented essays in this collection, however, do suggest some generalizations about the five types and their relevance to social ethics and social change.

First, it seems difficult to make use of a sectarian pattern or a pattern that stresses the diversity of the "orders" in social life to guide practical efforts for change within the existing framework of society. This is not because these patterns simply offer religion's blessings on the way things happen to be. Indeed, both the sectarian writers and the "orders of creation" writers are sharply critical of worldly standards and actions. The problem is that they are so pessimistic about life outside of the communities of faith that they can envision no measures that would significantly improve it. The same problem comes up in a different form in the political and liberation theologies that adopt the sharp distinction between the "base community" and the social order. Only a revolutionary change that sweeps away the old order entirely can make a real difference. The efforts at incremental change that occupy the social ethics of the realists are dismissed by these more radical thinkers as palliatives that create an illusion of progress without affecting the real sources of the problem.

This is not to say that radical or conservative forms of this sharp distinction between faith and society have no social ethics at all. In their insistence on preserving the freedom and integrity of the church in the midst of a corrupt world, they create an important center of meaning and value for those who suffer most from the injustices of society. In times of persecution under totalitarian governments, when other forms of action are limited indeed, this preservation of the community of faith may be a most important form of social action. For those whose goal is social transformation, however, these first two patterns provide little guidance.

By contrast, the realist insistence that society is constantly transformed by the imaginative visions of those who are not bound too closely to the status quo seems to be the most effective reinforcement for social ethics as a discipline for social change. In its critical approach to all existing values, seeking out pretentions and inconsistencies in the way society is organized, realism loosens our allegiance to existing rules and powers and frees us to envision new ways of living together. The importance of realism in the struggle for racial justice is apparent. It no doubt will play an important role in overcoming sex-role stereotypes and in developing new and more humane patterns of economic life as well.

Realism's witness to human freedom from the existing conditions of life cannot, however, be the whole of a social ethic. Unless this freedom is to drift away into the utopian idealism that the realists themselves have criticized, realism eventually must take responsibility for spelling out new norms and patterns that will meet our current needs for justice and order in society. Of course, these norms themselves are subject to change and criticism, but we must run the risk of choosing and upholding them as more adequate to our present situation than what has gone before or than other alternatives we can imagine.

That is where the enduring usefulness of the natural law and of process thought becomes apparent. To sustain a process of social change, we need some explicit commitments to goals and standards that seem to apply very widely. Only by attention to the values we hold, as well as having a critical eye for our own illusions, can the community of faith join with others in formulating norms and building the knowledge by which such values can be realized in fact. A rational inquiry that discloses what persons need first to achieve a just and secure life together and then to relate themselves appropriately to God remains an important guide for social ethics, despite the valid realist warnings against overestimating our conclusions.

Annotated Bibliography

Coleman, John A. *An American Strategic Theology.* New York: Paulist Press, 1982. Coleman continues the tradition of Catholic social thought exemplified by John Courtney Murray and applies its insights to contemporary problems in social ethics.

Fuchs, Josef. *Christian Ethics in a Secular Arena.* Washington: Georgetown University Press, 1984, and *Natural Law.* New York: Sheed and Ward, 1965. Fuchs presents the theory and contemporary applications of the natural-law tradition in Catholic moral theology.

Gustafson, James M. *Protestant and Roman Catholic Ethics.* Chicago: University of Chicago Press, 1978. Gustafson explains the major differences between two important forms of Christian ethics. This is a general study of theological ethics, but it clarifies many important issues specific to religious social ethics.

Hauerwas, Stanley. *A Community of Character.* Notre Dame: University of Notre Dame Press, 1981. Hauerwas is a leading Protestant social ethicist writing today. His work combines theological reflection on important social problems with a special emphasis on the role of the church in shaping moral consciousness and moral choices.

Murray, John Courtney. *We Hold These Truths: Catholic Reflections on the American Proposition.* New York: Sheed and Ward, 1960. Murray offers an understanding of American political culture in the light of Catholic social thought. Some of the ideas in this book also played a part in Murray's work on the Declaration on Religious Liberty at Vatican Council II.

Niebuhr, H. Richard. *Christ and Culture.* New York: Harper & Row, 1951. Nearly forty years later, Niebuhr's study still provides an important framework for organizing and comparing Christian theological understandings of society.

Niebuhr, Reinhold. *The Nature and Destiny of Man.* 2 vols. New York: Charles Scribner's Sons, 1943, and *The Essential Reinhold Niebuhr.* Ed. Robert McAfee Brown. New Haven: Yale University Press, 1985. Niebuhr's *Nature and Destiny,* written at the beginning of World War II, remains the classic summary of Protestant Christian social thought in the twentieth century. The collection edited by Brown provides ready access to many of Niebuhr's important essays.

Franklin I. Gamwell
University of Chicago
Divinity School

..

Theism and Public Ideals

Introduction

■ ■ Philosophical issues are unavoidable in religious social ethics. This does not mean all studies in the field should or can include an explicit address of such issues. It does mean, however, that philosophical commitments are implied in all social-ethical commitments, so that religious social ethics that does not at some point attend to such matters explicitly always does so implicitly. The relevant philosophical issues include questions about religion, questions about social ethics, and questions about the relationship between the two. This essay will focus upon the relationship between religion and social ethics, although something will have to be said about each of them independently in order to permit a discussion regarding their relationship. More precisely, I will seek to address the question: Is there a religious basis for public (that is, social and political) ideals?

Until the modern period, most of Western civilization answered this question affirmatively. The classical Greek, Hebrew and Jewish, Christian, and Islamic traditions generally were in agreement that social and political life properly takes its bearings in some sense from transcendent or ultimate reality. Since the premodern West was largely informed by these traditions, it was, on the whole, characterized by this conviction. There were exceptions to this general rule. Western civilization has never been without people who considered themselves irreligious and who nonetheless found some basis upon which to affirm social and political ideals. On the other hand, some within the Western religious traditions believed that public ideals were inconsistent with their faith, so the withdrawal from (or at least indifference toward) the social order was religiously required. But these exceptions do not gainsay that the premodern West voted over-whelmingly in favor of a religious basis for social and political life.

The modern West stands in contrast. It is true that the nature of mo-dernity has been and continues to be the subject of extensive scholarly in-quiry and debate. Nonetheless, there is widespread agreement that the distinctive characteristics of this period include the relatively pervasive af-firmation (in theory and practice) of human autonomy, where this means that the standards for belief and action are, at least in principle, critically chosen by each individual. Autonomy, then, is distinguished from heter-onomy by virtue of which standards of truth and goodness are set author-itatively by inherited religious, cultural, or institutional orders. Some have argued further that the increasing affirmation of autonomy has meant the increasing "secularization" of human life, where this means that life is divorced from the influence of religious meanings (see Berger). The merit of this argument depends in part upon what the term *religion* is taken to include. Still, it is clear that the modern period has witnessed the increas-ing denial of religion in something like the traditional sense exhibited in Jewish, Christian, or Islamic communities. I have in mind the traditional claim that the world and our lives within it have their source and end in a transcendent or divine reality. If this affirmation is called theism, then at least theistic religion has become widely unconvincing in the modern pe-riod, and a theistic basis for public ideals is widely denied. This specific relation between religion and public commitment is my subject. In other words, I shall construe the question about a religious basis for public life to mean: Is there a theistic basis for social and political ideals?

Even after this reformulation, however, the question is not entirely clear. For it is apparent that there are two different ways in which the issue might be posed. On the one hand, this might be a question raised by people who are committed to public ideals and who are asking whether there is any implicit theistic conviction in their commitment. On the other hand, it might be a question raised by people who understand themselves to be theists and who are asking whether there are any implicit public ideals in their theistic conviction. One might also imagine a third group of people who understand themselves as both publicly and theistically committed but who seek greater clarity about the relationship or relationships, if any, between these two commitments. Analytically, however, this last interpretation of the question is nothing other than the sum of the first two—that is, (1) does a commitment to public ideals imply a theistic conviction? and (2) does a theistic conviction imply a commitment to public ideals? Accordingly, I shall proceed by addressing these two questions in turn. Still, I shall try to suggest that people in the third group at least have the right commitments, because public ideals do imply theism and theism does imply certain social commitments. In the nature of the case, the argument here must be programmatic in character, that is, suggestive of a line of thought that would require considerably more comprehensive presentation in order to be fully convincing. Nonetheless, I intend that there be sufficient argument to show that the program is at least worth pursuing.

Public Ideals Imply Theism

In asking first whether the commitment to public ideals implies a theistic conviction, some preliminary considerations will prove instructive. To begin with, there is the undeniable empirical fact that many of the most sincere and admirable advocates of public ideals have been and are explicitly atheists or, at least, nontheists. Any cursory review of those to whom we have looked as public leaders in the causes of, say, civil rights, world peace, or environmental integrity will reveal men and women without self-conscious theistic affirmations. Arthur Schlesinger, Jr. once said of Reinhold Niebuhr: "No man has had as much influence as a preacher in this generation; no preacher has had as much influence in the secular world" (Schlesinger 149). If Niebuhr himself was clearly a theist, it is equally clear that many whom he influenced in the secular world, and who became as committed as he to liberal realist ideals, did not share his profound religious faith, so that Morton White could speak of the powerful company of "atheists for Niebuhr" (White 117).

This empirical fact should be considered not because it argues against all supposed relations between public commitment and theistic conviction, but rather because it helps to clarify the sense in which the question at hand may be usefully asked. Based on my examples, it is evident that public commitment does not entail an *explicit* or self-conscious theism. Nonetheless, that conclusion leaves open whether public commitment entails an *implicit* theistic conviction. An empirical investigation of what social activists *say* they believe is irrelevant, for what now is at stake is the meaning of a public commitment and what it implies. At least insofar as we seek to construct our own beliefs, what people *do* think about theism is of less significance than what they *ought* to think about theism. Only the former can be settled by an empirical investigation of their explicit beliefs, and the latter, which has to do with the implications of their public commitment, will be true whether they think so or not.

There are, of course, some who find fault with the claim that people who explicitly or self-consciously deny theism might be implicitly committed to it. The assertion that people are in some sense "anonymous theists" is criticized as a kind of religious imperialism that presumes to know more about other people than they know about themselves and, therefore, is unjust to their sincerity and their freedom of belief. In my judgment, however, this charge gains whatever force it seems to have precisely because of a failure to distinguish between explicit and implicit convictions. One questions the sincerity of others only by charging that what they *say* are their convictions are not in fact what they *explicitly* believe. Further, one is unjust to others' freedom of belief only when one denies them an equal right to draw their own explicit conclusions and to act upon them in speech and deed. But it is thoroughly consistent with a full respect for sincerity and freedom of belief to say that someone is implicitly committed to claims that he or she does not explicitly recognize and to seek to persuade him or her of that fact. This is indeed a claim to know what another does not know, but so is every case in which one person holds that another person's explicit beliefs are false. If this be imperialism, then anti-imperialism can only be the absurd position that all explicit beliefs are equally valid. To the contrary, if a person affirms X and denies Y, when in truth X implies Y, there is no credible alternative to saying that he or she is implicitly committed to convictions not explicitly held. Moreover, the relevant democratic or anti-imperialistic requirement is not the refusal to challenge explicit beliefs but the insistence that only reason and evidence will settle the issue, so that one never claims dogmatic finality but remains open to persuasion even as one seeks to persuade.

It is equally important in the present context to realize that one who affirms divine reality has no alternative except to say that explicit atheists are "anonymous" or implicit theists. This follows if we mean by the divine a reality that transcends the world because it necessarily relates to all other things as both their source and their end, so that to be anything at all is necessarily to be related to this all-encompassing transcendent. If there is a reality without which there could not be anything at all, then every affirmation that something exists implicitly affirms the divine. More specifically, if there is One without whom we could not be at all, then this is One who relates to us in everything we do, so that every understanding of ourselves must be an implicit witness to the divine. Accordingly, those who understand themselves to be publicly committed must be implicitly committed to theism. Conversely, were theists to concur that one might understand one's life without an implicit theistic conviction, they would concede that the God in whom they believe is not the transcendent source and end of the world as such, and therefore not really divine at all.

But if theism can be true only if any and every understanding of ourselves implies the divine reality, there is an important consequence for religious social ethics. The convictions advanced by theists as the basis for public ideals must themselves be publicly assessable or verifiable. This claim, one should note, is widely denied in contemporary and traditional theology. In one fashion or another, it has been said that the truth of theism is only revealed through special historical events (for example, the Exodus or the event of Jesus the Christ), so that theistic claims are verifiable only by those who are placed or who place themselves within a confessional relation to that special revelation. But if God is the One with whom we always are engaged, so that theism is implicit in any self-understanding, then the experience of God is universal and the knowledge of God open to any individuals who can so much as ask the question of how their lives should be understood. God is, as some theologians say, generally revealed, and special revelation cannot be other than a disclosure of what is available to human existence generally. I hold, in other words, that the solely confessional view of theism also is an implicit denial that God is the source and end of all the world. Moreover, it is this solely confessional claim regarding theistic belief that merits, for theists, the charge of imperialism in public life. Insofar as this claim provides the basis for public ideals, confessional theists advance public purposes of which nontheists have no genuine grounds to be persuaded, and theists may probably be indicted for attempting to impose a confessional vision of the common good.

I conclude, then, that theism can be true only if all social activists implicitly affirm it and if the truth of theism and whatever it does or does not require for the public world is open to anyone who asks about the proper understanding of human life. But this conclusion is contingent upon the premise "*if* theism is true," and the first form of the question about theism and social ethics is whether the commitment to public ideals does indeed imply that truth. It now is time to turn from preliminary considerations to the question itself. As I have noted, there have been and are many social activists who answer no and, further, there have been and are many philosophers and political theorists who argue likewise. Indeed, this probably has been the dominant reply given by ethical and political philosophy in the West within the last century. Thinkers otherwise as diverse as Karl Marx, John Dewey, Jean-Paul Sartre, Martin Heidegger, Hannah Arendt, and John Rawls are, if I read them rightly, agreed about this: the appropriate public ideals do not imply theism.

I am persuaded, however, that the putative logical independence of moral and political ideals from theism is fallacious, because the claim that human life has any worth at all implies a transcendent reality in the sense already described. Accordingly, I hold that all atheistic ideals fail to justify or defend successfully the ideals for human action that they advocate precisely insofar as they deny the dependence of human worth upon the divine reality. I cannot here attend to the various arguments of atheistic ethical philosophers and, therefore, cannot do more than assert my judgment that they fail. But I should, at least briefly, suggest the line of thought through which the positive claim that I have made—namely, that human worth implies theism—might itself be defended.

I already have mentioned in passing that human life is a kind of existence that, whatever else it may involve, includes a capacity to understand itself. Indeed, it is solely because of this capacity that the present question regarding the proper understanding of ourselves in relation to public ideals and theistic claims might arise. But just because humans understand themselves, they simultaneously must understand in some sense all other things that do or might exist. For to know oneself as this particular individual is simultaneously to know that one is different from all other things. Thus, the human capacity for self-understanding necessarily is the capacity to think about existence as such—and in this broad sense one might say that to be human is necessarily to be a philosopher. With a slight turn of focus, one may say that human existence is perforce religious, in the broad sense that self-understanding necessarily relates the self to or locates it within the totality of all things of which one is a part.

Assume, then, that a proper self-understanding includes an affirmation of our own worth in a sense that permits us to distinguish better and worse alternatives for human action. Since self-understanding occurs only in relation to all things, it follows that the importance of our action must be understandable in relation to an evaluation of all things. To this it might be objected that one may understand existence as such without an evaluation of the totality. One might assert, for instance, that human action is properly evaluated only in relation to, or insofar as it contributes to, future human existence. With this assertion one is, in a narrow sense of the term, a *humanist*. But to say that importance relates only to human existence is to deny worth to everything else, and to say that nothing else is important *is* an evaluation of all other things. Evaluative conclusions, in other words, always imply evaluative comparisons, so that the worth of human action implies a comprehensive evaluation by virtue of which human action is compared to the worth of all other things.

If this is so, then we are within sight of the theistic conviction. For an evaluation of the totality implies a reality in accord with which the importance of all things is properly measured, and this measure can only be constituted by a comprehensive reality of which all things are parts or within which all things are included. To be sure, this claim will be vigorously rejected by many, and I can here only refer the reader to some of the parties to the debate (see, for example, Dewey 1934; Gewirth; Brummer; Hartshorne 1937, 1974; Ogden). But I hold that a comprehensive evaluation implies a comprehensive reality, and this reality is, by definition, transcendent to the world because everything else in the world is a part of it.

Thus humanism, in the narrow sense I previously mentioned, cannot be true because it inconsistently claims that a comprehensive evaluation is constituted by a reality—future human existence—that is not comprehensive. Moreover, the same inconsistency is found within any assertion that some reality within the world is the basis of worth. To the contrary, evaluation implies a cosmic unity of all things, so that all things derive whatever worth they may enjoy from their inclusion within this divine totality. If human action truly makes a difference, this is measured by the difference it makes to the all-encompassing One. In saying this, I do no more than rephrase the argument presented by, among others, Reinhold Niebuhr. A human being, wrote Niebuhr, "stands outside of himself and his world, making both himself and the world an object of his contemplation. This higher dimension of freedom is the source of all religion. It forces human beings to relate their actions in the last resort to the totality of things conceived as a realm of meaning" (Niebuhr 1942, 44). Accordingly, any sense of worth at all—and, mutatis mutandis, any ethics at all—is at least implicitly theistic.

Of course, none of this means that humans always explicitly evaluate their actions in accord with a theistic ideal. On the contrary, as Niebuhr above all has made clear to us, humans may falsely take some reality within the world to represent their total end (see Niebuhr 1941-1943; 1944). Some people, for instance, may assert that the only measure of importance is their own interest or those of some limited "interest group" to which they belong. The practical consequence of this view is that social and political order is understood as those relationships emergent from the conflict of individual interests or interest groups, and the implication is that coercive power is the only relevant social and political capacity. Although Thomas Hobbes might be cited as an advocate of this view, it does not claim many explicit contemporary adherents in its baldest, or Hobbesian, form. Nonetheless, those who advance a tempered version of this position are legion. I refer to the view that our public world is simply an arena in which individuals pursuing their own preferences interact, in competition or cooperation, such that there is no genuine common good. In fact, the only ethical constraints upon the pursuit of one's own perferences are the equal rights of others to pursue theirs. I suggest that something very like this defines the political philosophy of what I call established political liberalism, that is, liberalism as it is understood by most liberals and as it has come to be widely influential in American political history. So understood, the tradition of established political liberalism may be traced to John Locke and John Stuart Mill. Also, it is related to the pervasive American affirmation that society's most general purpose is to maximize those economic resources with which individuals may pursue their diverse preferences. In any event, it is precisely the claim that human life is properly a matter of satisfying preferences that constitutes the atheistic compromise in established liberalism. Sheer preference is a choice without a transcendent measure of human importance; on the contrary, the affirmation of sheer preference implicitly asserts that human choice is its own measure of worth.

There are, to be sure, contemporary atheists who are decidedly critical of established liberalism and who advance a full and robust vision of the common good. Just because such liberalism is established, these critics generally are those who call for reform of the social order—or revolution—in the name of socialist or communitarian ideals. Expressions of this position may range from the reformed liberalism of John Dewey to the more radical assertions in some forms of Marxism. In the absence of theism, however, the importance of one's action can only be measured by the reformed social order or ideal state of affairs that is envisioned. Since this state of affairs is not a reality at all so long as it remains unrealized, one's sense of worth depends upon the promise that it will be achieved—upon the conviction that the good society is more or less historically inevitable. Nor will it help to say that action is worthwhile if there is only progress toward the ideal, because the approximation itself has worth solely by virtue of the ideal envisioned. Insofar as there is an effective denial of theism, in other words, there is a tendency toward false optimism with respect to the socialist or communitarian ideal. Generally speaking, of course, events sooner or later reveal false optimism for what it is. At that point, such idealists may become increasingly cynical about the public world and increasingly given to coercive or violent means in the quest for reform. Something like this appears to have been the case with many who joined student movements in this country in the early 1960s and became explicit advocates of violence in the later 1960s. In practice, then, reformers often turn into cynics who are difficult to distinguish from those who hold that one's own interest is the only important thing.

On the other hand, it is not necessary that reformers be false optimists or become cynical. Since these possibilities result from the effective denial of theism, there also is the possibility that reformers will be realistic in their commitments. This will occur insofar as the conviction is entertained that human worth, as the importance of all things, is properly measured by contribution to the divine reality.

Theism Implies Public Ideals

If that preceding argument can be sustained, then we may insist that a commitment to public ideals includes an implicit theistic affirmation. But it is not immediately apparent that the converse also is true, that theism requires public commitments. After all, the argument presented sought to suggest no more—although, to be sure, no less—than the divine source for any worth that human action may have. Without further deliberation, we cannot be sure that the worth that the divine measure requires of human action includes public purposes. Thus, we must now turn to the second way in which the question about theism and social ethics might be posed, namely, does theism imply a commitment to public ideals?

As I mentioned in passing at the outset of this essay, there is a significant tradition in Western religion that has tended to answer this question in the negative. According to the New Testament scholar John Knox, for instance, there is no social ethic in the writings of the early Christian community. In Knox's view, this absence does not mean that all social ethics are contradictory to the Christian faith but instead betrays the early community's anticipation of a coming "eschaton" or end to the world, so that changing the given social order seemed irrelevant to the divine Kingdom. More broadly speaking, wherever religious faith has become other-worldly in a sense that competes with the ultimate significance of this-worldly affairs, it has focused its moral imperatives upon relationships within the community of faith and/or upon the private integrity of the individual. Christian monasticism and, perhaps even more so, Christian mysticism have often markedly illustrated this tendency. It also has been said that something of this tradition is in part responsible for the tendency in more "conservative" American Christianity to focus religious sensibility upon personal growth and family or intimate relationships—in short, upon private as opposed to public life.

But if authentic theism has the character I claimed, then this tradition tending to exclude public commitment must be rejected. Since the divine reality is properly understood as the totally inclusive reality, then commitments to this reality imply commitment to the world. This point was once made by Charles Hartshorne in commenting upon the New Testament commandment "Thou shalt love the Lord your God with all your heart and all your soul and all your mind and all your strength, and your neighbor as yourself." If one loves God with *all* of one's being, Hartshorne asked, what remains with which to love one's neighbor and oneself? Clearly nothing remains; so the commandment is sensible only if love of God *is* love of neighbor and self because the divine reality is inclusive of both. Similarly, Alfred North Whitehead once wrote that "religion is world-loyalty" (Whitehead 1926, 60), intending thereby no repudiation of theism but, on the contrary, the assertion of what loyalty to the divine reality includes. If love of God is a love for all the world, then theism does imply a commitment to public life, since the relationships of the social and political order are thoroughly a part of the world.

It also follows that theism implies a commitment to all nonhuman creatures because the natural environment, in its multiplicity of forms, also is included within the divine. Accordingly, the theistic affirmation sets the terms for an ecological concern that appreciates the natural environment not only in its importance to human existence but also as important in itself. World loyalty, then, is loyalty to the character of all relationships within the world and an intent to promote, insofar as it falls to us, relationships that enhance rather than destroy the creatures or individuals related. To maximize the difference that our actions make to God is to maximize the extent to which we promote relationships within the world that are mutually enriching.

It is evident, of course, that our freedom to influence the world is fragmentary; the character of many relationships within it is beyond our power to affect significantly. Also, among those matters that do wait in some measure upon us, we must make choices; we are powerless to attend to them all simultaneously. In principle, then, the relationships that have greatest claim upon our attention are those where our action has the greatest contribution to make to the enhancement of individuals. To some, this principle may seem to argue for a focus upon private life after all. It is in our family and intimate relationships, the argument runs, that we have the most power to enrich others. But that conclusion has been reached too quickly. It may be, generally speaking, that private relationships are those in which we have the greatest opportunity to be good for a single other individual. But it also may be true that the maximal good for any individual involves the diversity of relationships that only public life can offer and, in any event, that private relationships will be impoverished (indeed, probably impossible) without some attention by at least some people to the public order. Moreover, our public action, by its very character, affects far more individuals, even if each of them to a lesser extent. With respect to any given individual at any given time and place, then, the only conclusion available in principle is that appropriate attention to private relationships, on the one hand, and public relationships, on the other, depends upon the state of affairs in question.

Whatever may have been or is the case in other times and places, there is a special claim addressed to us in the twentieth-century West by the public order. I mentioned earlier that modernity is characterized by the pervasive affirmation of human autonomy, understood in contrast to the heteronomy of inherited religious, cultural, or institutional orders. Human belief and action have become increasingly subject to standards that are critically chosen by each individual. One principal consequence of this affirmation has been the recognition that our public order is not simply established by inheritance but is a human creation that is constantly open to change. Moreover, John Dewey argued convincingly some fifty years ago that social change in the modern age has created a "new era of human relationships.'' He referred to the effect that the revolution in modern empirical science (itself an expression of autonomy) and the application of science in modern technology have had upon institutional or public life. Briefly stated, institutions have become so massive and the web of institutional interaction has become so extensive and complex that the lives of individuals in Western societies are influenced far beyond any previous era by the social and political order of which they are a part (see Dewey 1954). Modern life, Dewey concluded, has become dominantly corporate.

Some three decades later, C. Wright Mills made much the same point (as have many others) when he distinguished between private troubles and public issues and insisted that all too often troubles in our lives that we take to be private in origin are the consequence of issues within a public order that is unprecedented in scope. Neither Mills nor Dewey gave as much attention to the international as they did to the domestic order, but it is not difficult to extend the general analysis. As the scientific/technological/industrial revolution has created a new era of human relationships nationally, it has simultaneously magnified—in something like a quantum measure—the effect of our institutional activities upon the rest of the world. I take the line of thought that Dewey and Mills articulated to be essentially correct—especially so as the century nears its completion. It is precisely because of the massive influence of the institutional order on vast numbers of human lives that I take authentic theistic commitment—that is, a love of mutually enriching relationships in the world—to entail in our time and place a special attention to our public life.

This conclusion is all the more apparent when we make explicit a further implication of what already has been said. The same revolution that has made modern life dominantly corporate also has opened the social and political order to new possibilities of human creation and change. As I have noted, the modern affirmation of autonomy itself implies such possibilities. Nonetheless, conditions may severely constrain the extent to which association can be purposively designed or reconstituted. This is so when the sheer biological necessities of human life demand most of the attention of most individuals and/or the means of communication are sufficiently limited and sufficiently slow to restrain extensive self-conscious interaction. In fact, however, the affirmation of autonomy has become increasingly pervasive more or less simultaneously with, and in part because of, scientific/technological/industrial achievements that have greatly expanded the matters open to human choice, including the limits of our public life. Far more people—indeed, in Western society, potentially all people—have been or could be assured of the biological necessities with far less tax upon their purposes. At the same time, and as a result of the same processes, communication has been so escalated as to open self-conscious association on a scale unimagined by earlier societies. Indeed, to say that modern life has become dominantly corporate and to say that this new era presents unprecedented possibilities of human association are two ways of saying the same thing. It is this situation, in which public life is both so powerful and so open to human purpose, that makes commitment to the One who includes all things a commitment to public ideals.

Of course, to say that the opportunities for public purposes are unprecedented is not necessarily to say that human purpose has been or is being well-exercised. That corporate life becomes dominant does not automatically yield the mutual enhancement of individuals that is the theistic telos of relationships within the world. To the contrary, there is increasing evidence that twentieth-century Western society has been constituted by the pursuit of economic and technological ideals whose continued public supremacy presents the condition for or the threat of unprecedented waste and destruction: in exploitation of the natural environment, in the debasement of the many by the few, in the escalation of potential warfare to virtually unthinkable proportions, and in the increasingly banal attachment of even the most advantaged to economic rewards rather than enriched human community. Again, it is my judgment that established political liberalism, which, roughly speaking, understands the social or institutional order to be in service to the satisfaction of diverse individual preferences, remains the most effective or influential political understanding in contemporary America. If it is true, as I suggested earlier, that the established liberal affirmation of preferences is a denial of theism, then one might also say that our public life is compromised in significant measure by implicit or explicit ideals that are atheistic in character. Moreover, this incongruence between the actual character of our corporate life and its possibilities adds urgency to the public claim upon our theistic commitment.

Conclusion

I said at the outset that there are people who understand themselves as both theists and social activists and ask for clarity about the relations between the two. I also said that these people at least have the right commitments, and I now hope that some of the reasons for saying this have been suggested. The pursuit of public ideals does imply a theistic commitment and, especially now, theism implies a commitment to public ideals. Of course, the fact that *theism* implies public purposes also defines, at least in the most general sense, *which* public ideals we ought to pursue—namely, those that direct us maximally toward a public order of relationships through which individuals are mutually enhanced. On the other hand, the fact that public commitment implies theism reflects the divine source of that worth or commitment in our lives, without which we could have no commitments at all. In our love of the world, we love the One from whom we come and to whom we all go and thereby enjoy, in the words of Whitehead, "a quality of mind steady in its reliance that fine action is treasured in the nature of things" (Whitehead 1961, 274).

Reference List

Berger, Peter

    1967 *The Sacred Canopy: Elements of a Sociological Theory of Religion.* Garden City NJ: Doubleday & Company, Inc.

Brummer, Vincent

    1982 *Theology and Philosophical Inquiry.* Philadelphia: Westminster Press.

Dewey, John

    1934 *A Common Faith.* New Haven: Yale University Press.

    1954 *The Public and Its Problems.* Chicago: Swallow Press. Original publication: 1927.

Gewirth, Alan

    1978 *Reason and Morality.* Chicago: University of Chicago Press.

Hartshorne, Charles

    1937 *Beyond Humanism.* Lincoln: University of Nebraska Press.

    1974 "Beyond Enlightened Self-Interest." *Ethics* 84:3 (April 1974): 201-16.

Mills, C. Wright

    1959 *The Sociological Imagination.* New York: Oxford University Press.

Niebuhr, Reinhold

  1941-1943 *The Nature and Destiny of Man.* 2 vols. New York: Charles Scribner's Sons.

    1942 "Religion and Action." Ruth Nada Anshen, ed. *Science and Man.* New York: Harcourt, Brace & Company.

    1944 *The Children of Light and the Children of Darkness.* New York: Charles Scribner's Sons.

Ogden, Schubert M.

    1966 *The Reality of God and Other Essays.* New York: Harper & Row.

Schlesinger, Arthur, Jr.

1956 "Reinhold Niebuhr's Role in American Political Thought and Life." Charles W. Kegley and Robert W. Bretall, eds. *Reinhold Niebuhr: His Religious, Social, and Political Thought*. New York: Macmillan Company.

White, Morton

1959 *Religion, Politics, and the Higher Learning*. Cambridge: Harvard University Press.

Whitehead, Alfred North

1926 *Religion in the Making*. New York: Macmillan Company.

1961 *Adventures of Ideas*. New York: Free Press. Original publication: 1933.

Lois Gehr Livezey
Princeton Theological
Seminary

..

Goods, Rights, and Virtues: Toward an Interpretation of Justice in Process Thought

■ ■ This essay explores Alfred North Whitehead's contribution to philosophical and theological theories of justice, focusing on his discussion of the common good, human rights, and virtue. The central thesis is twofold. One: Whitehead's reinterpretation of the nature of experience seeks to make a persuasive case for the recovery of a public world in the face of the modern privatization of experience: ontologically, epistemologically, ethically, politically, and religiously. Hannah Arendt calls it "world-alienation."[1] In other words, Whitehead's philosophy sets the terms for an argument to establish the ontological possibility and intelligibility of public-regarding moral principles of human action. It is also a theological argument, borrowing from the centrality of the doctrine of God and the world for this theory of action. Two: However, it is Whitehead's interpretation of "civilization" that is decisive for moral action and judgment, for it is his concept of civilization that gives priority and specificity to public-regarding moral principles.

---

[1]Hannah Arendt, *The Human Condition* (Chicago: University of Chicago Press, 1958) 248-57.

A Common World to Think About:
The Philosophical Grounds
for Public-Regarding Moral Principles

In *Adventures of Ideas* and other writings on the nature, development, and problems of "civilization," Alfred North Whitehead traced the modern problem of human action to the collapse of the foundation for public-regarding moral principles: "Instead of dwelling on the brotherhood of man, we are now directed to procure the extermination of the unfit" (*AI* 36).[2] Indeed, I contend that Whitehead's own philosophical efforts were directed, in large part, to disclosing the inadequacies of theories contributing to the devaluation of the public realm (Descartes, Kant, Locke, and so forth) and to developing a constructive argument for, as he once put it, a "common world to think about" (*SMW* 84).

Whitehead developed this argument through a reinterpretation of the nature of experience, cast in terms of the analysis of "actual entities" as "the final real things of which the world is made up" (*PR* 18). It was the priority of actual entities in Whitehead's philosophy that led me initially to focus on human action as the most concrete and fundamental reality of our humanity and the locus of "reasons"—moral and otherwise—in a Whiteheadian analysis of human experience. Whitehead's analysis of actual entities and so of human action is organized in terms of the distinction and correlation of *private* and *public* ("subjective immediacy" and "objective immortality"). Two characteristics of his argument should be noted at the outset. First, contra Hannah Arendt, "public" and "private" are aspects of every action; they do not refer to distinct categories of action.[3] Second, "public" and "private" are mutually implicative notions. The public world is a component in the internal constitution of every action, and private experience is the "self-enjoyment of being one among many"

---

[2]The following abbreviations of titles and editions of Whitehead's works have been used throughout this essay. Page references of these works have been placed in parentheses immediately after the citation.

   AI   *Adventures of Ideas*. New York: Free Press, 1967
   MT   *Modes of Thought*. New York: G. P. Putnam's Sons, 1958
   PR   *Process and Reality: An Essay in Cosmology*, Corrected Edition. Edited by David Ray Griffin and Donald R. Sherburne. New York: Free Press, 1978
   RM   *Religion in the Making*. Cleveland: World Publishing Company, 1960
   SMW   *Science and the Modern World*. New York: New American Library, 1978

[3]Arendt, *The Human Condition*.

(*PR* 145). Let me say a bit more about the nature of action in Whitehead's analysis.

Human action in its public aspect: "objective immortality"

In Whitehead's philosophy, the nature of a thing consists in its relations with other things. The most general statement of this fact is the principle of relativity: "It belongs to the nature of a 'being' that it is a potential for every 'becoming' '' (category of explanation iv). This principle must be taken together with the principle of process: "Its 'being' is constituted by its 'becoming' '' (category of explanation ix).

Whitehead's special concern, however, is the relations between things that are actual; these are the subject of his theory of "objective immortality." Objectification "refers to the particular mode in which the potentiality of one actual entity is realized in another actual entity" (category of explanation viii). In this way, the past becomes a component and a condition in the becoming, or concrescence, of present action. Every action is "a mode of . . . housing the world" (*PR* 80). The world becomes a "common world" in that it is exemplified in the constitution of every actual entity or action (*PR* 7, 148). This objectification of the world in action establishes both the solidarity and the intelligibility of the world. The dictum of modern epistemology, that "apart from the experiences of subjects there is nothing," does not, in this view, exclude the public world from its scope (*PR* 167). In thus establishing the possibility of a "common world to think about," Whitehead establishes grounds for public discourse and common action and so makes the world potentially a matter of mutual responsibility.

The other side of the coin of objective immortality is the self-transcendence inherent in action. Every action has consequences that establish a context of possibilities and limitations (conditions) for future actions. In a word, action is power. Yet we do not understand the nature of power until we consider that power is inherent in receptivity as well as agency. Appealing to Plato, Whitehead argues that "the essence of being is to be implicated in causal action on other beings"—both as "the agent in action and the recipient of action" (*AI* 120). Power is fundamentally characterized by mutuality.[4] Indeed, in process thought, the essence of power—di-

---

[4]See Bernard M. Loomer, "Two Conceptions of Power," *Process Studies* 6:1 (Spring 1976): 5-32, for the distinction between "unilateral" and "relational" power.

vine and human—is that it is community-creating, sustaining, and transforming—or destroying. Power is grounded in the fact that our actions issue in a network, a web of relationships, and so make a difference in the world, for better or worse. It is the nature of power to form associations.

Human action in its private aspect: "subjective immediacy"

In Whitehead's philosophy, the ultimate principle characterizing actuality is the principle of creativity "by which the many, which are the universe disjunctively, become the one actual occasion, which is the universe conjunctively, . . . creating a novel entity other than the entities given in disjunction. . . . The many become one, and are increased by one" (*PR* 21).

"Creativity" and "process" are notions that refer to the actualization of actual entities or action. Action is an act of self-creation, although it is not an act of creation ex nihilo. Rather, it is constituted by the prehensions of other actualities and possibilities; it is conditioned and composite in character.

Whitehead's concept of freedom is an essential dimension of his interpretation of creativity. Action "is internally determined and is externally free" (categorical obligation ix). This concept of freedom is a complex one. The decisive element of the creative act is the subjective aim. The subjective aim, by virtue of its autonomy and its teleology, establishes the voluntariness and purposiveness requisite to moral action.[5] But freedom encompasses more than voluntariness and purposiveness. The "decision" that constitutes the freedom of the creative act is "always imaginative in its origin" (*PR* 245); it is the capacity for the introduction of novelty and so of transformation. And it is integrative, even artistic, in its conclusion, synthesizing its world of actualities and possibilities in a "final modification of emotion, appreciation, and purpose" (*PR* 28).

The purposive character of action is closely related to the valuative character of action. The subjective aim is an aim at some value or importance. The notion of importance is fundamental in Whitehead's thought: "The generic aim of process is the attainment of importance" (*MT* 16). It

---

[5]See Alan Gewirth, *Reason and Morality* (Chicago: University of Chicago Press, 1978) 21-42.

is the aim at importance both in "the immediate present and the relevant future" (*PR* 27). In this view, the creative act is the realization of some determinate value. Thus the world is not a world of "bare facts" but a world of value-laden facts, each exemplifying some intrinsic (for itself) and transcendent (for others) importance. The fact that value is intrinsic to action provides a reason, in the nature of things, for self-respect and (together with the doctrine of a common world) for mutual respect, which in turn establishes the grounds for the formulation of a theory of individual rights.

In view of the criticism of process ethics for its "indeterminateness" (Henry Clark) and its "lack of anchorage" (Max Stackhouse),[6] I want to emphasize that Whitehead's doctrine of internal relations and the doctrine of the actualization of potentiality in the creative act *describe* individuality; they do not dissolve it. His theory of concrescence—defined in terms of creativity, valuation, and the aim at importance, and freedom or "decision"—represents exactly an effort to explain how an integrally related, dynamic world issues into a plurality of definite, determinate individuals.

In this section, I have sought to establish two basic claims:

One: Whitehead's analysis of actual entities provides the basic framework for an interpretation of human action. By virtue of his theory of "one type of actual entities," Whitehead's description of the nature of actual entities illumines the nature of human action and the most general character of human possibilities and limitations.

Whitehead's description of action seeks to give intellectual justification to an individuality that is not solipsistic (or world-alienated) and to a commonality that is not uniformity. The individuality of action consists in its particular standpoint or "social location" in the actual world, its synthesis of the world of actualities and potentialities, and its "self-enjoyment of being one among many." Such an experience of being one among many is, of course, the very definition of the polis in Greek tradition.

The commonality expressed in action is twofold. It refers to the common world; the concept of solidarity expresses the fact that all actions have in common the public world, the consequences of past actions, which they share. And it refers to a common nature, "the common fact of value-ex-

---

[6]Henry W. Clark, "Process Thought and Justice," in John B. Cobb, Jr. and W. Widick Schroeder, eds., *Process Philosophy and Social Thought* (Chicago: Center for the Scientific Study of Religion, 1981) 132-40; Max L. Stackhouse, "The Perils of Process: A Response to Sturm," ibid., 103-12.

perience" (*MT* 151). The concept of valuation expresses that what all actions have in common is that each one is unique in the world. To be sure,
both aspects of commonality are constitutive of every actual becoming—
the one as objective datum, the other as subjective form.

Two: Whitehead's philosophy provides the first step in the constructive recovery of public-regarding moral principles. The principle of relativity (namely, that "every item of the universe, including all the other
actual entities, is a constituent in the constitution of any one actual entity"
[*PR* 148]) and the category of subjective intensity (namely, that the subjective aim is a double aim at importance in "the immediate present and
the relevant future" [*PR* 27]) establish the grounds or reasons for a "common world to think about." It is in the constitution of action that the
world appears—as it is, as it might yet be. In this internal relation of the
public world to human action lies the ontological possibility of public-regarding moral principles.

Toward an Interpretation of Justice
in Process Thought

In the development of a theory of justice in process thought, systematic
philosophy is necessary, but it is not sufficient. As I noted above, an analysis of the essential nature of human action is grounded in the system of
general principles that characterizes all actualities. But, Whitehead argues, there is not one type of perfection: "Each society has its own type
of perfection" (*AT* 291). Therefore, the search for moral principles requires a social analysis.

In other words, while it is true to say that, in process thought, all action
is constituted by the publicity of others and contributes to the public world,
the normative importance of that public contribution and its specific character is not a matter of ontological determination. Whitehead speaks to this
point in his discussion of peace in *Adventures of Ideas:* "It is in the nature
of the present that it should thus transcend itself by reason of the immanence in it of the 'other.' But there is *no necessity as to the scale of emphasis* that this fact of nature should receive. *It belongs to the civilization
of consciousness, to magnify the large sweep of harmony*" (*AI* 291, my
italics).

In Whitehead's writings, then, "civilization" is decisive for the interpretation of the moral significance of human action, and it is so in two ways.
It transforms the question of ontological possibility into one of moral re-

sponsibility; and it gives further specification to the general principles of morality that guide the human venture. Thus it is Whitehead's analysis of the concept of "civilization" to which we now turn for our bearings on the nature and significance of the common or public good(s), human rights, and the values or virtues.

The public good: the morality of truth, beauty, art, adventure, and peace

Morality, in Whitehead's view, seeks the maximization of importance (*MT* 19). It has a threefold reference: "Everything has some value for itself, for others, and for the whole" (*MT* 151). Morality, in this view (most of the time), is primarily concerned with maximizing importance in the public world: "The effect of the present on the future is the business of morals" (*AI* 269). This is true in the double respect of its bearing on the importance of individuals and on the unity of the social order as a whole. Thus the two most general principles of morality are the principles of the generality of harmony and the importance of the individual (*AI* 292).

In *Adventures of Ideas,* Whitehead gives further specificity to that importance that morality seeks to maximize. He defines the good at which individuals and societies aim in terms of five essential qualities of "civilization": truth, beauty, art, adventure, and peace. In other words, the concept of civilization, as defined by these five qualities, answers the question of *to what end* with respect to human action and association. Art is that human capacity for valuation that is grounded in freedom and characterized by consciousness, spontaneity, purposiveness, discipline, and joy. It aims at beauty and truth. Beauty has to do with the internal relations of the various components of experience; it is the interweaving of many feelings into one complex pattern exemplifying harmony and intensity. Beauty refers to the intrinsic importance of individuality. Truth is the conformity of this activity of valuation to the breadth and depth of the actual world from which it emerges, including our common or shared history as well as the reality of God. In a world essentially characterized by process, the aim at truthful beauty requires adventure—the quest for new perfections and so the possibility of self- and world-transformation, and peace—the gift of self-transcendence. Whitehead sums it up in saying of art that it "heightens the sense of humanity" (*AI* 271).

The complex and interrelated notions of truth, beauty, art, adventure, and peace specify the essentially and distinctively human meaning of importance. It is a cliché of Whiteheadian analysis that art is concerned with the enjoyment of the present in its immediacy, as distinct from morality, which is concerned with the efficacy of the present in the future or public world. In my view, art and morality do not differ with respect to the character of the importance sought. In contrast to art, however, morality emphasizes the public effect of the importance sought. It requires a "goodness"-impact statement, so to speak; for "goodness," in Whiteheadianese, refers to the character of the public world, insofar as it is beautiful (*AI* 268).

Perhaps one could say that civilization, thus defined, constitutes the public or common good that is the principle of human action, morally and politically speaking. But the notion of a common good is not a simple matter in a pluralistic, relativistic, dynamic world such as Whitehead describes. Earlier, I referred to the double nature of our common humanity: the common world of the past and the common nature of value-experience. In light of this analysis, I contend that "the common good" expresses the sense of responsibility, at once individual and social, for the world and the nature we have in common. The good of action, required of all, is one that maximizes the importance of the common world (the generality of harmony) and that maximizes the common capacities for valuation (the importance of the individual). The distinction is not a dichotomy because the importance of one is dependent upon the importance of the other.

If the moral "imperative" to maximize importance requires the maximization of truth, beauty, art, adventure, and peace, what might that mean? I'll consider these aspects in terms of their public significance: truth is the adequate *re-presentation* of the public world (especially with respect to the depths of the reality of God and the world), so as to reveal its significance. Beauty is the adequate *appreciation* of the public world in terms of the integration of diversity into some intrinsic importance. Art, the very capacity for free and purposeful action itself, is the contribution of *complex finite value to the harmony* of the public world. Adventure is the relevant *transformation* of the public world. And peace is *faith* in the public world, that "fine action [that] is treasured in the nature of things" (*AI* 274).

As a matter of constructive interpretation, I propose that a Whiteheadian theory of the common good has both aggregative and distributive aspects. The first claim doubtlessly needs no argument. The overwhelming tendency (of Whiteheadians and critics alike) is to interpret Whitehead's ethics in purely aggregative terms, which his own definition of morality as the maximization of importance surely supports. But there is also a distributive principle implicit in Whitehead's description of the moral principles of individual importance and general harmony. Such a distributive principle is implicit in Whitehead's appeal to the commonalities of human nature. It has something of the character of Gewirth's "equality of generic rights," which "requires of every agent that he accord to his recipients the same rights to freedom and well-being that he necessarily claims for himself."[7] Thus the maximization of importance can reasonably be interpreted to include a principle of universalizability (*for all*). Such a distributive principle also seems to follow from the realities of a shared world and the requirements of the principle of the generality of harmony.

Human rights and human nature: Whitehead's interpretation of freedom

The freedom of the self-creating non-communal individual is his personal and private possession. . . . The civil rights, which guarantee his freedom of expression in all the dimensions of his life, are consonant with this view of the self.[8]

In "Theology in the American Grain," Bernard Loomer summarizes and rejects an interpretation of selfhood and freedom that, he rightly notes, Western theories of human rights have largely taken for granted. He then develops a process interpretation of selfhood and freedom as emergent from and for the sake of relationships. But Loomer never returns to the question of what view of rights would be consonant with his radically reconstructed doctrine of individuality. One could suppose that, having disposed of this "self-creating non-communal individual," he is content to dispose of the correlative notion of civil rights as well. Like Loomer, most process theologians have been silent on the subject of rights, or passing references suggest that they take for granted the classical liberal concept of human rights, despite shaking its foundations.[9] Douglas Sturm is an exception to the rule; he has developed an argument for the place of human rights within a

---

[7]Alan Gewirth, "The Basis and Content of Human Rights," in J. Roland Pennock and John W. Chapman, eds., *Human Rights* Nomos 23 (New York and London: New York University Press, 1981) 119-47.

[8]Bernard M. Loomer, "Theology in the American Grain," in Cobb and Schroeder, *Process Philosophy and Social Thought*, 149.

[9]W. Widick Schroeder, "Structure and Context in Process Political Theory: A Constructive Formulation," ibid., 63-80.

"communitarian" politics, that is, a politics characterized by the priority of the common good.[10]

Quite by contrast, the history of "this growth of the idea of the essential rights of human beings, arising from their sheer humanity" (*AI* 13), forms the basic thematic structure of Whitehead's historical analysis of civilization in *Adventures of Ideas,* which culminates in the "paradigm shift" in the presuppositions of political theory and practice, the shift from slavery to freedom. Moreover, it is the interpretation of human rights that is at stake in the threat to democracy—and so to "civilization"—and that seems to have occasioned the book.

In spite of the importance of this topic, Whitehead's discussion is by no means systematic. Yet it is illustrative of important dimensions of moral principle and social justice.

One aspect of his argument, which I will not go into here, is his very interesting discussion of natural law as "immanent" yet evolving. It suggests some important modifications of traditional arguments for essential human rights, without abandoning their "natural" foundation. A second aspect is the question of what bearing Whitehead's reinterpretation of human experience has on the theory of human rights in process thought. Third, Whitehead's discussion of "custom" and "contract" locates human rights as a problem of the social order. And finally there is the matter of the transcendent reference; for, in the last analysis, Whitehead's appeal with respect to human rights is neither to the laws of nature nor to the customs and contracts of society but to the "wisdom" that is God: "Progress consists in modifying the laws of nature so that the Republic on Earth may conform to that society to be discerned ideally by the divination of Wisdom" (*AI* 42).

The relevance of Whitehead's interpretation of experience for a theory of human rights is complex. I can only mention a couple of aspects, illustratively. In view of the criticism of process thought on this point, let me say again that, as I read him, Whitehead's theory of human action is a revaluation of individuality, not a devaluation of it. His doctrine of human rights is grounded in distinctive human capacities for valuation and purposiveness and, specifically, in the capacities for truth, beauty, art, adventure, and peace. The concept of rights suggests the obligation of the

---

[10]Douglas Sturm, "Process Thought and Political Theory: Implications of a Principle of Internal Relations," ibid., 98.

society to acknowledge, protect, and promote these capacities and purposes for "civilization" in individuals and throughout the social order. Such capacities and purposes can only be realized through the exercise of freedom. Apart from the fundamental reality of the freedom of action, as described earlier, it would be meaningless to speak of rights and duties. On the other hand, Whitehead displays an interesting ambivalence with respect to the importance of the freedom of thought for the sake of "civilization" in the definition of human rights and responsibilities. For, just as he concludes this discussion, he introduces his criticism of what he calls the "literary treatment" of freedom (*AI* 65-67) and argues for due consideration of basic life needs and economic conditions in any deliberations concerning freedom, rights, and duties.

The principle of relativity sets the stage for the rejection of the concept of "absolute individuals with absolute rights" (*AI* 63), but Whitehead does not settle the question of what the relative or social character of rights is. Yet he offers a clue to the implications of this sociality for human rights in his account of the development of the concept of freedom. The turning point, according to Whitehead's version of the story, comes with St. Paul: "It is interesting to speculate on the analogies and differences between the deaths of Socrates and of Paul. Both were martyrs. Socrates died because his speculative opinions were held to be subversive of the communal life. . . . Unfortunately for Paul, as he journeyed he left behind him organized groups, indulging in activities uncoordinated with any purposes of the state" (*AI* 54-55). Note that while Paul may not have died for his thoughts, it is the distinctive character of the "freedom of corporate action" to be the outcome of thought rather than custom or habit. Moreover, this freedom seems to be distinguished by the public-regarding character of its purposes and ideas. Thus Whitehead enlarges on his interpretation of Paul's significance with reference to the Roman Emperor Trajan's response to those Christian churches organized by Paul: "He [Trajan] is even unconcerned with their organization into groups, so long as no overt action emerges affronting the traditional association of the state with religion" (*AI* 55).

In his analysis of "civilization," then, Whitehead develops an interpretation of human freedom as essentially political. Whitehead does not develop this line of argument. But it seems to me that the sociality of human nature provides the basis on which to formulate a theory of human rights related to the creation and nurture of relationships, that is, rights of association. In other words, a Whiteheadian doctrine of human rights should be cast in terms of claims upon the social order for the protection and promotion of human capacities essential to the initiation, preservation, and transformation of relationships.

Another perspective on the significance of the sociality of the nature of things emerges in Whitehead's discussion of "custom"—the inherited modes of order—and "contract"—the spontaneity of freedom—in their bearing on the notion of human rights (*AI* 63ff.). Again, there is the dialectic of relativity and creativity, inheritance and innovation, immanence and transcendence. There is an inalienable social (communal) definition in every theory and practice of human rights. Nevertheless, the introduction of thought—"a standpoint of generality"—into the habits of a community is the difference between society as such and "civilization."

Virtue: the morality of character in process thought

In process thought, the generality of harmony and the importance of the individual represent the good at which human action aims (or ought to). I have suggested that truth, beauty, art, adventure, and peace constitute a further specification of the good. One could argue that these five qualities of civilization are more like virtues than goods. In Whitehead, the search for clear distinctions is almost always a fruitless search. However, I have reserved the category of "virtue" for those aspects of human life that have something of the nature of *habit* and are of such *importance* that, Whitehead says of them, the worth of life may be judged by their presence or absence. Specifically, Whitehead states that the life of a human being receives its worth or value (a) "from the way in which unrealized ideals shape its purposes" (*MT* 37-38); (b) by virtue of its "liability to persuasion" (*AI* 83); (c) when "it has merged its individual claim with that of the objective universe," which Whitehead calls the religion of "world-loyalty" (*RM* 59). Thus virtue, at least public virtue, in process thought has to do with the interrelated virtues of thought, action, and passion appropriate to citizenship. The virtue of thought is assemblage; the virtue of action is mutual persuasion; and the virtue of passion is world-loyalty.[11]

---

[11]William A. Simpson has suggested to me that it would be appropriate to Whitehead as well as contemporary philosophical ethics to include a discussion of technology and its impact on virtue. This is an intriguing suggestion, and I intend to explore it in further writing.

a. Assemblage

At a conference in Chicago on "Liberation in Process Thought and the Black Experience" in 1985, Henry Young argued that process theologians have largely ignored the social crisis created by both classical and modernist philosophies and so have developed an alternative metaphysics unhinged from an adequate social analysis (and consequently are complicitous in the perpetuation of these injustices). Variations on this theme echoed throughout the conference.

This is a serious question for process theology, and no Whiteheadian interpretation of justice can evade it. Moreover, process theologians have lent credence to this critique. Whitehead's own writings were mostly social analyses of one sort or another: science, religion, education, sociology—laced with philosophical speculation (only *Process and Reality* is pure systematic philosophy). But contemporary process theologians are another matter. Loomer says, for example: "I think that a theology of relations can include the positive values of theologies of liberation *without being committed to specific analyses* of racism, sexism, or economic functioning."[12]

In my view, Whitehead's notion of assemblage is a mode of taking the social order seriously, empirically and philosophically, within process thought. In *Modes of Thought,* Whitehead distinguishes two modes of philosophy: the one is "systematization" or systematic philosophy, which is "the criticism of generality from the specialism of science" (*MT* 4); this is a matter for experts. The other is "assemblage," which is the "survey of society from the standpoint of generality" (*AI* 97). Whitehead describes this latter mode as a philosophic habit that is "the very essence of civilization" (*MT* 4) and of citizenship in a democratic society (*AI* 98). In this aspect, then, philosophy is not the task of specialists but of citizens. "It is our business—philosophers, students, and practical men—to recreate and reenact a vision of the world, . . . a properly concrete philosophy [whose function lies] in guiding the purposes of mankind" (*AI* 99).

In *Adventures of Ideas* the standpoint of generality is lodged firmly in empirical, historical inquiry. Here, assemblage requires "a survey of possibilities and their comparison with actualities . . . [in which] *the fact, the theory, the alternatives, and the ideal, are weighed together*" (*AI* 98, my

---

[12]Loomer, "Theology in the American Grain," 147, my italics.

italics). According to this reading, assemblage is not a transcendent principle of criticism, abstract vis-à-vis any concrete particular situation. Rather, it maintains its foothold in particularity—in analyses of actual situations or problems, in competing interpretations and alternative solutions, in the appreciation of the variety of actual values or standpoints, in the articulation of relevant ideals. Here, Whitehead argues that the philosophic mode of thought appropriate to morality requires a "standpoint of generality," informed by history, appreciative of diversity, and "undaunted by novelty" (*AI* 97-98).

Lest this view be cast off as mere pluralism or relativism, it should be reiterated that, for Whitehead, the concept of "civilization" (defined in terms of the qualities of truth, beauty, art, adventure, and peace) offers a clarification and specification of this standpoint of generality with respect to the unrealized ideals, the type of perfection relevant to our essentially yet distinctively human experience.

But something more is needed: a principle to interpret the values and structures that constitute and organize the actual world of our life together, including the good and evil there exemplified. Indeed, the ideals of civilization can only be given concrete meaning and their relevance tested in the context of the public world. Now the obvious fact is that the actual or public world is characterized by various forms of injustice, or by ordering principles that obscure, distort, and deny the essential fact that we have our world—and our humanity—in common. And assemblage, that standpoint of generality that weighs together facts, theories, alternatives, and ideals, must take its empirical cue, its ground of relevance, from the actual injustice of the world, so that it may be the bearer of "some imaginative novelty, relevant yet transcending traditional ways" (*FR* 66).

Thus I propose that assemblage, that philosophic habit requisite to democratic citizenship, itself requires clarification and specification by "the issue" at stake in the situation. Assemblage, thus defined, provides process thought with the social analysis requisite to social ethics, moral judgment, and the struggle for justice and peace.

b. The politics of mutual persuasion

In mutual persuasion, the public realm becomes subject to public discourse. The philosopher-king gives way to the citizens. The politics of mutual persuasion emerges from and is shaped by the publicity, plurality, and purposiveness of human action. The first refers to the community-creating and -destroying power of action, discussed elsewhere in this essay.

The public consequences of action make the question of power a political problem.

The second refers to that elemental experience of being one among many. A corollary of plurality, so understood, is that the political significance of persuasion rests not only on the possibilities of mutuality and even harmony but also upon the inevitabilities of conflict. The principle of persuasion presupposes that the world is constituted by different standpoints, perspectives, and purposes, that "strife is at least as real a fact in the world as Harmony" (*AI* 32). Thus to speak of the creation of the world as "the victory of persuasion over force" is not an appeal to some pre-established harmony but an imperative for the nonviolent resolution of conflict on the grounds that violence, domination, and degradation cannot transform or transmute conflict into a creative and enduring generality of harmony, the public good. Thus for Whitehead, who was not a pacifist, the politics of persuasion and the resort to force are antithetical: "The recourse to force, however unavoidable, is a disclosure of the failure of civilization" (*AI* 83).

The purposiveness of action liberates the principle of persuasion from the classical liberal emphasis on the priority of process by raising the question of "to what end?" In other words, persuasion is not just a process of conflict resolution. Its raison d'être is those ideals, noble or base, whose realization in this or that occasion or group of occasions creates, preserves, transforms, or destroys the world. In mutual persuasion, then, a public world is created that rests not only on the instinctual or emotional basis of community but on thought, the imaginative consideration of relevant ideals (assemblage). Thought, in turn, transforms the emotional basis of community into love of the world.

Voluntary associations are primary examples of the principle of persuasion, by Whitehead's own definition. Not long ago I was asked what mode of social organization is implicit in the worldview of process thought. I named the public-regarding independent or voluntary associations (the churches, the abolitionist and suffrage groups, Southern Christian Leadership Conference, National Organization for Women, Amnesty International) that have, in this country and elsewhere, throughout our history, provided the organization of social criticism, the definition of moral purpose and vision, and the advocacy of and impetus to democratic modes of changing the world.

c. The religion of world-loyalty

The beginning of civilized or rational religion is, according to White-head, a "sense of criticism" of the structures and faiths of the social order. Religion, in this view, is preeminently "the gadfly of civilization" (*AI* 11) or, more aptly, "at once gadflies irritating and beacons luring" (*AI* 18). It is this basic insight that leads Whitehead to his famous dictum that "religion is what the individual does with his solitariness" (*RM* 47). The solitariness at the heart of religion does not mean that religion is strictly a private matter. What our individual does with his or her solitariness is to think, which is character-forming and -transforming, to be sure; for "as we think, we live" (*MT* 87). However, the significance of solitariness, in this context, is its contribution to social criticism and world-loyalty. Its hallmark is the standpoint of generality, clothed with the lure, the passion, for the general good. Thus this religion of world-loyalty is characterized not by a preoccupation with self-preservation but by a self-transcending valuation for others and for the whole, the love of humankind and all creatures. And, here as elsewhere, the standpoint of generality and the introduction of novelty "traffic together," for the religion of world-loyalty requires a loyalty not to the world as it is but to the world as it might be. Hence the relevance of solitariness vis-à-vis the immediate environment, and the ever-present element of tragedy. Whitehead puts the matter succinctly in the contrast between "world-consciousness" and "social-consciousness." It is the difference between the religion of world-loyalty and the religion of "me and my friends"—each with the morals of its kind.

Ultimately, of course, the interpretation of religion as world-loyalty brings us to our final topic, the doctrine of God and the world that underlies and undergirds the interpretation of goods, rights, and virtues.

God and the World:
The Theistic Foundation of an Interpretation
of Justice in Process Thought

Ultimately, this vision of justice is grounded in the character and the relation of God and the world.

God and the world:
mutual immanence and mutual transcendence

God and the world share the character of mutual immanence and mutual transcendence, creativity, and valuation.

(a) "Mutual immanence" refers to the fact that God and this temporal world are internally, essentially related to one another. "God with us" means in part that we have the world in common. The objective immortality of the world in God is constituted by the consequent nature of God: God's objectification of the world in the subjective immediacy of God-self—in *truth*. The objective immortality of God in the world is constituted by the superjective nature of God, the causal efficacy of God in the world—in *love*: the world is in God and God is in the world (*PR* 348). The consequent nature of God answers at once the problem of loss and the question of a truth that transcends relativity. Also, because God experiences the world in its suffering and joy, process theology has rejected the doctrine of divine impassibility in favor of a doctrine of divine suffering and joy in solidarity with the world.

(b) "Mutual transcendence" refers to the fact that God and the temporal world are internally determined as well as internally related. The freedom of God is expressed in the primordial envisagement of the realm of potentiality, which is unconditioned. It is expressed, also, in the consequent nature of God. The first phase of God's consequent nature is a conformal feeling of the world; that is, God feels the world as it is. But in its more complex phases, the consequent nature involves the integration of the divine physical feelings of the world with the divine conceptual valuation of possibility. The subjective forms of these complex, integrative phases issue in God's judgment: "The consequent nature of God is his judgment on the world. He saves the world as it passes into the immediacy of his own life. It is the judgment of tenderness which loses nothing that can be saved" (*PR* 346). It is an act of divine decisions regarding the relative importance of the actual world in God. Finally, with respect to the superjective initiation of a temporal subjective aim, the freedom of God is the freedom of purpose and passion, the freedom of introducing relevant novelty, and the urge for its realization in the concrescent occasion.

(c) Third, God and the world share the character of creativity, of "order entering upon novelty." Whitehead's doctrine of the consequent nature of God means that God "shares with every new creation its actual world; and the concrescent creature is objectified in God as a novel element in God's objectification of that actual world" (*PR* 345). But the significance of God's creativity is not limited to the subjective immediacy of the divine experience. Through the initial subjective aim, the primordial nature of God conditions, though it does not determine, the creativity of every temporal act (*PR* 108). In this way, otherwise unrealized possibilities gain an ordered relevance to concrescence. Whitehead calls this aspect of God's superjective nature "the particular providence for particular occasions" (*PR* 351). It is the adventure of God in the adventure of the world. The point that I want to emphasize here is the imagination of God. When I think of God (à la Whitehead), I envision One who is not only the paradigm of suffering love, but One who is incredibly imaginative in the face of what we do and who perseveringly "confronts what is actual in [the world] with what is possible for it" (*RM* 153). By virtue of God's vision, we may yet not perish but change the world.

(d) God and the world share the character of valuation. Indeed, nowhere is God more crucial to Whitehead's philosophical system than in connection with the question of value and the aim at importance.[13] In *Religion in the Making*, Whitehead speaks of God as "the valuation of the world" (*RM* 152), and this is so in several respects: the primordial nature of God is an unconditioned conceptual valuation of the realm of possibilities; the consequent nature of God is the valuation of the realm of actualities, in judgment and in reconciliation, in light of the primordial vision of what might have been and might yet be; the superjective nature is the aim of God at the attainment of value in the world. In the togetherness of the primordial, consequent, and superjective dimensions of Godself, the absolute standard of valuation is the love of the world: "God is that element in virtue of which our purposes extend beyond values for ourselves to values for others, . . . that element in virtue of which the attainment of such a value for others transforms itself into value for ourselves" (*RM* 151-52).

Justice and the power of God in the world

The foregoing discussion of mutual immanence and mutual transcendence has important relevance for the question of the power of God as well. Whitehead's theory of actual entities establishes that no actuality can be absolutely other-determining, other-determined, or absolutely self-determining (in the sense of requiring nothing but itself in order to exist). This argument for the irreducible plurality of powers and freedoms has

---

[13]Robert Coburn argues that while Whitehead's philosophy does not require God for strictly systematic or empirical reasons, his argument regarding the axiological character of explanation does make cogent a doctrine of God. See Robert Craig Coburn, "The Concept of God and the Metaphysical Theory of A. N. Whitehead" (B.D. thesis, University of Chicago Divinity School, 1954).

meant the rejection of divine omnipotence in process theology. God and the world limit each other, because all things are self-creating in some respect and all things set limits or conditions for future others; thus all power, including God's power, limits and is limited by the presence of others. Yet the language of "limitation" may be inapt, given the meaning of power in process thought.[14]

What difference does it make to speak of power in terms of the reciprocity of receiving and giving? What difference does it make to speak of power in terms of persuasion rather than coercion? We have seen that God shares rather than abrogates our solidarity and our plurality. But God is absolutely unique by virtue of the perfection of the divine experience of the actual world and the divine vision of and passion for the good. Perhaps we should speak of God in terms of the perfection rather than the limitation of power. Nevertheless, the repudiation of classical doctrines of divine omnipotence delegitimates the appeal to omnipotence or providence to justify the status quo or to trivialize worldly evil. This, in turn, opens up the space of human action in a radical way. With respect to the struggle for justice, there is a great deal of difference between viewing sexism, racism, poverty, or war as "inevitable," a fate to be suffered (in Calvin's terms, "our lot"), and viewing them as problems to be solved—without mitigating the complexity or the intransigence of evil.

Furthermore, whatever may be the case with respect to divine capacities for coercion, persuasion is the normative expression of power. This paradigm of persuasion constitutes a radical rejection of power as domination/subordination and a fundamental critique of violence. Indeed, Whitehead is persistently and specifically critical of antidemocratic doctrines of the relation of God and the world, of the theologies of "a Divine Despot and a slavish Universe, each with the morals of its kind" (*AI* 26, 36). In its place, the concept of God as the lure to the creation of world-community represents a radical call to action in a world turning conflict not into complex harmony but into holocaust.

Let me conclude with the following reflection on the power of God in the world. Whitehead rejects the concept of God as Holy Warrior—the God who parts the sea and closes it over Pharaoh and his army, who flattens

---

[14]I am grateful to Matthew Johnson of the Divinity School of the University of Chicago for raising this issue in a conversation at the conference on "Liberation in Process Thought and the Black Experience," Chicago, 8-9 November 1985.

Jericho and orders the genocide of the Canaanites—in favor of the concept of God as Holy Poet, harmonizing the harmonies and discords. The limitations of this symbolism notwithstanding, we should not dismiss this symbolization of God the Holy Poet too quickly. According to G. Ernest Wright, the significance of warrior language for God is its affirmation of the *political* significance of the relation of God and the world.[15] But God the Poet need not be interpreted as apolitical God-language. We have only to remember the significance of poetry and song in every struggle for justice from the days of Moses and Miriam through the slave songs of this nation's beginnings to the civil rights, peace, and feminist movements of our own era. The concept of God as One whose vision of new possibilities and passion for their realization inspires (and so empowers) us—this concept of God as the ground of *imagination toward transformation*—is "not nothing" in a world so paralyzed by hopelessness, perishing in its loss of vision.[16]

My own view is that Whiteheadians can and should say more: God is a unity of (1) *suffering* with the reality of injustice and violence in the world—in which consists true divine understanding of and judgment on our world (the consequent nature); (2) *vision* of new and alternative possibilities for the world (the primordial nature); and (3) *passionate persuasion* for the transformation of the world, passion for justice and peace, constitutive of the world as the initial aim of every creative act (the superjective nature). This unity of suffering, vision, and passionate persuasion is the perfection of advocacy. Thus I propose the concept of God as Holy Advocate, calling us and indeed empowering us to advocacy for justice and peace in our time.

---

[15]G. Ernest Wright, *The Old Testament and Theology* (New York: Harper & Row, 1969) 145.

[16]See Charles H. Reynolds, "Somatic Ethics: Joy and Adventure in the Embodied Moral Life," in David Ray Griffin and Thomas J. J. Altizer, eds., *John Cobb's Theology in Process* (Philadelphia: Westminster Press, 1977) 116-32, for an argument regarding God as Ideal Participant, attentive to these imaginative and passionate aspects of Whitehead's idea of God; also, for a biblical perspective on the importance of imagination and passion, see Walter Brueggemann, *The Prophetic Imagination* (Philadelphia: Fortress Press, 1978).

Peter J. Paris
Princeton
Theological Seminary

..

Expanding and Enhancing Moral Communities: The Task of Christian Social Ethics

■ ■ The problem this essay addresses is the possibility of expanding and enhancing moral communities not to promote any imperial enterprise but to increase justice for all concerned. Assuming that this objective is desirable, we must identify the necessary conditions that make it possible. In other words, assuming a vast plurality of moral communities in our nation and world, and assuming a general abhorrence for all forms of imperial hegemony that too often have attended such expansion in the past, my aim in this essay is to discern the way in which justice can be achieved, enhanced, and preserved in the expansion of moral communities. I believe that this subject constitutes the most important ethical problem confronting the modern world, namely, how conflictual moral communities can achieve unity with justice for all concerned. It is the problem implied by the existing conflicts among the first, second, and third worlds; between rich and poor; men and women; black and white; Christianity and other religions; majority and minority groups wherever they are found. In brief, the primary locus of this problem is moral conflict as expressed in the many and varied structural inequalities caused by racism, sexism, poverty, and all other forms of human subordination.

This inquiry focuses on whether or not moral communities have a natural impulse to foster the good of other groups in an unselfish way, on the capacity of moral groups to do justice toward other moral groups. In this essay I will demonstrate how traditional family and tribal communities, along with most voluntary associations, are necessarily resistant to this project. Then I will discuss the conditions necessary to enable one moral community to embrace other communities in just ways. Following a brief assessment of the resources within Christianity that could contribute to the resolution of this problem, I will point to two contemporary institutions that illustrate the resolution I advocate. But first let me outline my method in Christian social ethics.

Christian Social Ethics as a Practical Science

The quality of human relationships constitutes the moral dimension of human life and, hence, the subject matter of social ethics. Morality pertains to the activity of doing the good and becoming good. Knowledge of morality for the sake of enhancing its quality is the aim of social ethics. In other words, knowing what humans can do for the sake of enhancing the good and becoming good is the whole of ethical inquiry.[1]

The breadth of moral relationships is considerable, ranging minimally from the encounter of two persons to the ever-increasing complexity of relations in familial, tribal, national, and international communities. In fact, the condition of plurality is a sine qua non for moral relations. Human relationships, however, are not limited to face-to-face encounters. They can be indirect, as in the case of an officer transmitting orders to a subordinate or a pilot releasing bombs over a prearranged target area. In any case, all human relationships are moral relations because they exhibit a certain quality, and consequently every human community is a moral community. Also, a correlation exists between the size and/or power of the community and its capacity for either moral greatness or its contrary. Accordingly, the nation-state is the highest moral force presently available because it legislates morality and determines the fundamental conditions under which individual citizens and groups of citizens can hold, express, pursue, and promote their interests, beliefs, ideas, aims, and purposes. Thus the subject matter of ethical inquiry must include the whole range of human associations—family, religious, social, professional, political.[2]

---

[1] It was Aristotle who first classified ethics as a practical science.

[2] My view of social ethics is similar to Aristotle's understanding of *Politics*, which for him was the master science of human action. See his *Nicomachean Ethics*, bk. 1, chs. 1-2.

In addition to plurality, a second condition necessary for moral relationships is freedom, which is expressed in the activities of deliberation and choice.[3] Moral agents must have the opportunity to choose among alternative modes of action. Where there is no choice, there can be no moral action. Persons cannot be held responsible for activities undertaken by compulsion. Choice implies freedom; namely, every action could have been other than it was.

The occasion for ethical inquiry arises whenever the moral consensus of a community has been disrupted either from within or from without. The function of social ethics is to clarify the nature of the moral conflict with a view toward finding its resolution. This is no simple task since the resolution of any moral conflict implies not only rigorous analysis of all the relevant facts and their relation to one another but also a moral assessment of those facts in accordance with some acknowledged criteria.[4] Thus ethical inquiry arises out of some actual moral conflict (that is, a set of facts as a starting point) and aims at resolving that conflict so as to enhance the quality of moral life. In brief, social ethics is a practical inquiry for two reasons: (a) because human action is its subject matter and improved action is its goal and (b) because practical reasoning is a more appropriate method for studying human action than scientific reason because of the variability of the subject matter due to freedom.

Now in this essay we are concerned about Christian social ethics. How does the qualifier "Christian" affect the nature of social ethics? First, the qualifier "Christian" refers to an additional factor in social ethics indicated by the question, "What has Christianity to say about the quality of human relationships?" I assume that Christianity has a contribution to make to the resolution of our problem and thus I seek its recognizable form both in thought and in practice.

Constraints against Expanding Moral Communities

Those who possess imperialistic aspirations view the problem of expanding moral communities solely as one of strategy since the ethical is-

---

[3]Aristotle's explication of efficient causation constitutes one of his major contributions to ethical inquiry. See *Nicomachean Ethics,* bk. 3.

[4]These criteria are many and varied, as evidenced by the numerous schools of ethical thought in our day, such as utilitarianism, naturalism, teleology, deontology, relativism, and pragmatism, to mention only a few. For a concise and detailed analysis of these schools, see William K. Frankena, *Ethics* (Englewood Cliffs NJ: Prentice-Hall, 1963); Richard T. Nolan and Frank G. Kirkpatrick, *Living Issues in Ethics* (Belmont CA: Wadsworth, 1982).

sues are not problematic for them. Rather, they consider their own needs, interests, projects, and philosophy of life as normative and those of all others are relativized accordingly. In fact, more often than not, they view other communities only as possible or actual means to their desired ends. Further, they are prone to rationalize their assumed position of privilege by viewing all others as needing the salvific relationship they seek to establish or to maintain. Unfortunately, the expansion of Christianity via the nineteenth-century Western missionary movement was closely tied to the imperial motive of extending Western civilization by means of commerce and colonialism.[5]

Cultural pluralists are suspicious of all intentional efforts to expand moral communities, on the historical grounds that such expansion has often implied some measure of moral hegemony on the part of the one seeking to extend itself. Assuming the moral integrity of every moral community and the lack of a commonly accepted cosmology in this post-Enlightenment period, the notion of expanding moral communities in any just way is considered unworkable by one of our most prominent moral philosophers, Alasdair MacIntyre.[6] Similarly, although many Christian ethicists—especially relationists, contextualists, and dispositionists like H. Richard Niebuhr, James Gustafson, and Stanley Hauerwas—strongly affirm pluralism, their fear of moral and religious hegemony restrains them from attending to the task of constructing just relations among diverse communities.[7] Consequently, they focus their attention on the moral integrity of groups and the way in which moral problems can be resolved ideally by attending to the dynamics of relations, contexts, and character.

---

[5]Contemporary revisionist scholars of African Christianity have provided more than enough evidence to support this judgment. Some of the most prominent of these are: J. F. A. Ajayi, *Christian Missions in Nigeria, 1841-1891: The Making of a New Elite* (Evanston IL: Northwestern University Press, 1969); Lamin Sanneh, *West African Christianity: The Religious Impact* (New York: Orbis, 1983); Adrian Hastings, *A History of African Christianity, 1950-1975* (Cambridge: Cambridge University Press, 1982); E. A. Ayandele, *The Missionary Impact in Modern Nigeria, 1842-1914: A Political and Social Analysis* (London: Longman's, 1966).

[6]This viewpoint permeates Alasdair MacIntyre's book, *After Virtue* (Notre Dame: University of Notre Dame Press, 1981).

[7]See H. Richard Niebuhr, *Radical Monotheism and Western Culture* (New York: Harper & Row, 1960); James M. Gustafson, *Christian Ethics and the Community* (Philadelphia: Pilgrim, 1971); Stanley Hauerwas, *The Peaceable Kingdom: A Primer in Christian Ethics* (Notre Dame: University of Notre Dame Press, 1983).

Now I contend that moral community is expanded justly whenever moral conflicts between moral communities are resolved to the mutual satisfaction of all concerned. For example, the successful outcome of the recent civil rights struggle in this country under the leadership of Martin Luther King, Jr. has had such an effect, and the ongoing struggle, it is hoped, will improve on that outcome. Thus the expansion of moral community does not necessarily imply an imperialistic invasion of other communities, nor does it necessarily threaten the values implicit in cultural pluralism. As will become clear presently, human communities have no natural impulse to expand themselves in a morally just way, that is, in acts of pure altruism toward others outside their own kin or tribe. Notwithstanding the fact that individuals frequently have given up their lives for the sake of others, we have little knowledge of groups acting unselfishly for the welfare of others. In fact, social scientists generally agree that pure altruism is contrary to human nature, which is fundamentally self-interested in all of its activities.[8] Nevertheless, I contend that such occurrences do happen from time to time with enduring effects. But their appearance and preservation necessitate strong desires, concentrated struggle, effective strategies, and the most careful deliberation. In short, just relationships between groups require the exercise of political wisdom at its best.

The Evolutionary Development of Moral Communities

It is widely thought that the family constitutes the primary locus for moral community because of its priority in the order of biological and social development. Traditionally, the family was held together by strong

---

[8] According to the sociologist Sister Marie Augusta Neal, except for August Comte and Pitirim Sorokin, sociologists had given virtually no attention to the issue of altruism until the sociobiologist Edward O. Wilson published his book, *Sociobiology: A New Synthesis* (Cambridge: Harvard University Press, 1975), arguing for a genetically grounded selfishness in human nature. Since then the discourse in social science has been carried on largely by social psychologists. See Sister Marie Augusta Neal, "Commitment to Altruism in Sociological Analysis," *Sociological Analysis* 43 (1982): 1-22. In the area of theological ethics, Reinhold Niebuhr's negative statement on the capacity of social groups to do justice is explicitly set forth in his *Moral Man and Immoral Society* (New York: Charles Scribner's, 1932). In 1974 Garrett Hardin published an essay entitled "Living on a Life Boat," *Bioscience* 24:10 (October 1974): 561-68, which launched a major discussion of lifeboat ethics and triage in relation to world famine. That discussion culminated in a special issue of *Soundings: An Interdisciplinary Journal* 59:1 (Spring 1976) entitled, "World Famine and Lifeboat Ethics."

natural bonds of belonging, such as soil, blood, race, language, and patriarchal rule.[9] Not only was the integrity of the family highly valued by all its members, but it was assumed that each of them would have defended with his or her life the family's honor against all external threats.

Families tended to extend themselves into wider spheres, where they were readily recognized and respected as "extended families." Such extensions constituted the substance of ethnic or tribal communities. Like families, these latter groups represented wider social expressions of natural instincts and vitalities, evidenced by their overriding interest in self-preservation and advancement. In this respect, their instincts and vitalities could be viewed as analogous to those of the herd. Accordingly, they clustered together for security and worked cooperatively for the group's survival and well-being. Thus in this evolutionary process "familial consciousness" was enlarged by "tribal consciousness," and consequently loyalty to soil, blood, race, and patriarchy was increased considerably. This provided the basis for the development of theories and practices of nationalism, racism, and sexism.

Few moral problems arose in either traditional families or tribal associations because individuals in both groups tended to exhibit a high degree of loyalty to the prevailing norms and customs that characterized each. Occasionally, however, such problems did arise, sometimes in the form of power struggles but more frequently caused by one or more members who had assimilated some new experience from outside the familiar environs and sought to gain validation of that experience by the family or tribe. The resultant disharmony always evidenced itself in two conflicting parties: (a) the one (usually the larger whole) strongly resisting the new experience as a threat and (b) the other seeking sufficient change in the group such that it might accommodate itself to the new experience. In the ensuing struggle, the bearers of the new experience risked expulsion from their group while the latter sought to preserve the status quo by reacting against the threat in a posture of self-defense. Traditionally, such moral conflicts were hastily corrected by the leadership, drawing upon the coercive powers of its authority. Those who failed to comply with the dictates of that authority

---

[9]In his perceptive analysis of myths of origin, Paul Tillich has demonstrated the importance of those natural bonds such as soil, blood, and social group and the threat they present to freedom. See his "The Presuppositions of Political Romanticism," in *The Socialist Decision*, trans. Franklin Sherman (New York: Harper & Row, 1977) 13ff.

were viewed as betrayers of the tradition and could, as a last resort, be severed from the community's life-preserving resources.

Industrialism, technology, and urbanism severely disrupted traditional family and tribal cohesion. Uprootedness from the soil and separation from blood relatives caused urban dwellers to find substitutes for these natural affinities. Consequently, the "social group"[10] has emerged today in such varying forms as professional associations, social clubs, labor unions, political parties, and religious communities, to mention only a few. As we will see, even the nation-state can be viewed as a social group. Social groups are specialized secondary expressions of the natural dynamics inherent in families and tribes. While membership in the latter is determined by natural conditions of entitlement (that is, birth, blood, territory), membership in the modern social group is based on the reciprocity of individual choice and the group's approval.[11] Like their natural counterparts, these social groups are oriented toward activities that serve the primary needs of their members. In other words, their chief objective is to maintain and promote a more pleasant and secure life for their members. Like families and tribes, social groups also demand a high measure of conformity from their members. Hence, each social group tends to exhibit one opinion and one interest. In fact, social groups tend to discourage diverse opinions and interests because they consider them threats to their unity.

Like families and tribal associations, modern social groups are incurably parochial. Even their public interests exhibit a certain parochialism in the sense that they are not totally altruistic. Their natural tendency is to spurn outsiders, although their lack of self-sufficiency forces them into various functional relationships with different peoples. Trade in goods and services usually comprises the nature of these functional relations. Frequently, however, an unintentional by-product of these functional rela-

---

[10]For a detailed discussion of the concept "social," see Hannah Arendt, *The Human Condition* (Chicago: University of Chicago Press, 1958) 38ff. I agree with Arendt's view that the social realm threatens the integrity of both the private and public realms by giving private matters high public visibility.

[11]I have included all voluntary associations in the category "social group." James Luther Adams defines "voluntary associations" as groups that occupy the space between family and state, both of which he views as natural communities. See his "The Voluntary Principle in the Forming of American Religion," in Elwyn A. Smith, ed., *The Religion of the Republic* (Philadelphia: Fortress, 1971). See also various essays in D. B. Robertson, ed., *Voluntary Associations: A Study of Groups in Free Societies* (Richmond: John Knox Press, 1966).

tions is the mutual exchange of various cultural values, which constitutes one of the principal ways by which social groups absorb alien values.

Characteristically, families, tribal associations, and social groups possess minimal capacity for integrating outside elements, whether they be persons, ideas, or values. They all tend to view outsiders with varying degrees of suspicion, distrust, and hostility. Their self-protective herd instinct causes them to relate in the following ways to those outside their group: (a) *coexistence:* establishing physical and social distance from the other, based on an attitude of distrust, as evidenced by the need for continuous surveillance of the other's activities or (b) *domination:* establishing and maintaining a position of control over the other by some combination of physical force, psychological warfare, economic dependency, or political hegemony. Thus coexistence inevitably leads to some type of cold war, and the domination of humans implies some form of resistance. Hence, neither contributes anything to harmony and peace.

Clearly, these ways of relating to the outsider presuppose the condition of hostility, which negates all efforts aimed at creating wider moral communities capable of integrating larger amounts of diversity in a just form. Since much of the modern world's associational life is characterized by the ethos of these social groups, and since these social groups are not naturally disposed toward uniting with others solely for the good of the other, our present age represents no significant advance in moral relations in spite of the immense developments in almost every other dimension of our cultural life.

Expanding Moral Communities

As mentioned above, conflicting moral values provide the occasion for ethical inquiry. Since most of our associational life is rooted in the natural instincts of self-preservation and self-enhancement, and since our social groups are characteristically impervious to the admission of alien elements into their respective domains, *the basic problem of our time is how we can break out of our parochialism and expand our moral communities for the sake of justice.*

Unlike those whose primary interest is the preservation of small communities, mine is a passion for the creation of communities capable of including as much quantitative diversity as possible.[12] Although it appears

---

[12]Here I disagree with Aristotle and Arendt, both of whom believed that viable moral communities necessitated limitation to city-states and small towns, respectively.

that no natural impulse motivates us toward the formation of such wider communities, neither does any natural condition prevent us from doing so. On the contrary, humans have the unique capacity to transcend every natural impulse and to envision and create new communities that are regulated not by natural needs and desires but by the goal of preserving and promoting our common humanity. Hence, the end is a human construct, namely, a better world. Further, humans actualize themselves as humans only as they exercise their capacity for establishing moral communities in which diverse peoples can associate with dignity, self-respect, independence, and peace. In such communities, freedom, equality, and liberty are not abstract principles but are the actual conditions of experience. Those who choose to remain in bondage to the entitlements derived either from their place of origin or from some other natural condition such as gender, race, religion, or nation fail to actualize their human potentialities. Like the lower animals, they merely participate in the biological cycle of life, procreation, acquisition, and death. Consequently, the meaning of their lives is integrally tied to their acquisitions.

Since social groups resist plurality and do not encourage freedom—the two primary conditions for moral relationships—it follows that social groups have a limited capability for effecting the kind of moral expansion sought. That is to say, no social group can evolve naturally into a wider moral community in spite of its capacity either to absorb alien cultural values incidentally through exchange relationships or its ability to integrate foreign peoples into its group by conquest and/or propaganda.

The wider moral communities sought are brought into being by humans thinking and acting cooperatively to effect a more inclusive world. This problem cannot be resolved in the realm of thought but, rather, in the sphere of action. Neither can the resolution be a certain fixed formula that needs simply to be applied to particular situations. Instead, it is a moral problem that can only be resolved by humans committed to a lifetime of acting cooperatively for the sake of our common humanity. This involves maintaining the conditions under which our common world can endure and flourish.

Since our natural instincts oppose such a community, how then does it arise? The answer to that question rests on a basic presupposition, namely, that the natural powers of resistance have been broken. In other words, loyalty to soil, blood, race, and patriarchy must be overcome before any moral advance is possible. Tillich answered this question in principle by arguing that the so-called myth of origin is broken by the unconditional demand experienced by humans as their essential nature whenever they encounter the moral imperative. In Tillich's view, this moral demand is the root of all prophetic thought in the sphere of religion and of all liberal, democratic, and socialist thought in the realm of politics.[13]

> Now a person experiences an unconditional demand only from another person. The demand becomes concrete in the "I-Thou" encounter. The content of the demand is therefore that the "thou" be accorded the same dignity as the "I"; this is the dignity of being free, of being the bearer of the fulfillment implied in the origin. This recognition of the equal dignity of the "Thou" and the "I" is justice.[14]

Tillich rightly perceived the necessity of giving ontological status to the claim of justice. The unconditional character of the moral imperative points to its ontological nature. The human significance of the moral imperative is that we will become persons only by treating others as persons.[15] But Tillich's discussion of the moral imperative is thoroughly formal in its ontological status and is ambiguous in its historical content. Further, for Tillich, moral relations occur in "I-Thou" encounters and are limited therefore to the self-constituting activity of the individual person: "Morality is the function of life in which the centered self constitutes itself as a person."[16]

Tillich argues that persons encounter the moral imperative whenever they meet a "thou" who demands justice in being treated as a subject. Similarly, I argue that the parochialism of social groups is broken in principle by the demand of outside groups for justice. Such a demand is always based on the experience of injustice. Those who initiate the claim are the sufferers of the injustice and consequently they alone are the bearers of constructive social change. Religiously, they have been viewed as proph-

---

[13]Tillich, *The Socialist Decision*, 5.

[14]Ibid., 6.

[15]Paul Tillich, *Systematic Theology*, vol. 3 (Chicago: University of Chicago Press, 1963) 38-50.

[16]Ibid., 38. Although I understand morality and justice to be broader than Tillich does, I do not disagree with his view of the moral imperative and its function in forming persons. More specifically, I applaud the unity of acting and becoming that attends Tillich's description of the moral act.

ets when they identify with the in-group's traditions and appeal to those traditions as the authoritative source for their claim. When the bearers of social change stand outside those traditions they are bent on changing, they are rightly labeled revolutionaries. In either case, their demands are always empirically based, and they struggle for their dignity and freedom.

Since every group has a center of cohesion rooted in either conventional or legal authority, each group necessarily expresses some form of justice. In fact, some argue that the social group's form is determined by its understanding of justice.[17] Since social groups exist for themselves, and since they are oriented to the well-being of their own members, on what basis then would an outside group bring a claim of justice? In other words, the rightful claims of justice imply a common moral realm. Enemies do not appeal to one another for justice. They can only appeal to some other community of moral belonging. Apart from such a reality, enemies must remain polarized and constantly on the brink of war. Accordingly, two types of moral struggles seem to present themselves: (a) an outside group psychologically and sociologically identifying with the traditions of the insiders and feeling unjustly segregated or discriminated against appeals to those same traditions as the source of appeal for its moral claim[18]; (b) an outside group that shares no common traditions with the insiders and consequently can appeal to no moral consensus. The outside group must then do one of two things: (1) appeal to some moral community apart from that of the insiders in the hope that they might be persuaded to exercise various forms of pressure (for example, economic, diplomatic, et cetera) as means of forcing the insiders to agree to negotiate change[19] or (2) prepare for the inevitability of war.

Unlike social groups, oppressed people embody an impulse for universality that is expressed in their claim for justice. Their discontent with the particularity of their condition stimulates them to struggle for justice,

---

[17]This appears to be Tillich's view (see *Systematic Theology*, 3:79). This also is Aristotle's view of justice as law and its function in the constitutions of states.

[18]This has been the practice of all civil rights struggles, including those of black Americans, women, trade unions, lesbians, and gay men, to mention only a few. Often the early stages of these struggles involve amendments to the constitution of the state or to the administrative laws in various jurisdictions: for example, Civil Rights Acts of 1964 and 1965 and the 1986 Gay Rights Bill in New York City.

[19]The contemporary struggle for the liberation of black South Africans is a good example of this method.

that is, equality within a wider humanity. Every prophetic and revolutionary group presses such a claim.

Moral Agency for Effecting Wider Moral Communities

The primary condition for effecting wider moral communities is the
ready availability of various groups of people suffering from differing forms
of injustice and struggling to gain adequate moral support for their claims,
which are basically moral, religious, and political. These people struggle
continuously for their humanity in worlds where structures and principles
of subordination and exclusion make gender, race, class, nationality, and
religion the material cause of inequality in social condition, political participation, civil liberty, economic opportunity, and group advancement.
Like all people, the oppressed also seek freedom, equality, liberty, and the
pursuit of happiness—not as ideas but as real experiences.

How do we know whether the claims of injustice are true, and why
should we respond in any positive way to them? As indicated above, every
claim for justice is an empirical claim, and consequently the content of the
claim is available to any who might wish to undertake their own independent investigation.

The question, "Why should we respond in any positive way to such
claims?" raises a more basic question, namely, that of the moral capacity
to make such a response. Those who do not have the capacity to respond
positively could hardly ask the question. The modern world, unfortunately, is largely deficient in the moral capacity to respond positively to
such demands for the following reasons: (a) we find ourselves in bondage
to the ethos and dictates of parochial social groups that control our lives
both personally and collectively; (b) we find ourselves in bondage to a cultural ethos in which thinking and acting are shaped by values of the ruling
technological paradigm in our social order. These values Gibson Winter
names as "progress, development, evolution, power as domination, freedom as autonomy"[20]; (c) we find ourselves in bondage to a philosophical
and theological idealism that aims at setting forth universal ideas and principles far removed from historical embodiment. Thus parochialism, utilitarianism, and idealism constitute major societal constraints against the
formation of wider moral communities. But these conditions can be over-

---

[20]Gibson Winter, *Liberating Creation: Foundations of Religious Social Ethics* (New
York: Crossroads, 1981) 102.

come when adequate commitment to such an end exists. Such an achievement is evidenced in the United Nations Organization, which represents the kind of moral construct humans can design when they choose to do so.

Is Christianity in any way removed from the criticism I have made of social groups? The answer is both yes and no. Negatively, the parochialism of churches has been evidenced in numerous ways: by declaring certain spaces, groups, and occasions sacred and therefore unchangeable; by affirming given sociopolitical power structures; by referring to the churches metaphorically as families. But there is also a sense in which Christianity contains certain resources for the solution to our problem, namely, its vision of a universal humanity inclusive of all races, classes, and nations. Clearly the churches have not worked hard enough to institutionalize this ideal, which is practical to a much greater degree than our theologies and practices would lead us to believe. On the one hand, the Roman Catholic Church has done much in this regard even though it has been severely constrained by its strong centralized system of ecclesiastical control, which implies the church's aim of representing the unity of the church in its own particularity. On the other hand, the Protestant recognition of the ambiguity of Christian experience and the need for creating unity within the apparent disunity has led to the formation of the World Council of Churches. Many have extolled the virtues of the World Council of Churches, but none has spoken more aptly of its practical significance than Paul Tillich, who wrote: "In practical terms it is able to heal divisions which have become historically obsolete, to replace confessional fanaticism by interconfessional co-operation, to conquer denominational provincialism, and to produce a new vision of the unity of all churches in their foundation."[21]

Nevertheless, the parochialism of most Protestant churches leads to views of moral and religious self-sufficiency that prevent them from considering the good of others and from seeking opportunities for cooperative work. Unfortunately, inter-religious dialogue and cooperation based on the value of mutual respect has little visibility in our day. Respect for diverse moral communities and the desire for mutual friendship between and among them, together with sensitive and appropriate responses to the claims of oppressed peoples for justice, are the products of religious and moral train-

---

[21]Tillich, *Systematic Theology,* 3:171.

ing. That training must be undertaken by institutions that embody the virtues that I have advocated. It is not enough to love diversity as an idea or even to promote it as a tangent since neither changes anything. Rather, we must seek to cultivate the personal and institutional habits necessary for creating unity while preserving diversity. I remain hopeful that this quest could become for us a way of life.

Part Two
..

Public Issues:
Justice in the Social Order

Mary Pellauer
The Commission
for Women, ELCA

■■

Understanding Sexism

■ ■ Sexism is not an easy issue to come to grips with, emotionally, morally, politically, or intellectually. It can be painful and confusing. Sexism is sometimes difficult even to notice in our personal reactions or social institutions. We take its operations so much for granted that even we who are feminists, after years of experience in the movement, may stumble upon some new patch of sexism. Second, American habits of individualism add to the difficulties of perceiving this issue. It is easy to believe that attitudes or behaviors are the unique product of one's own individual wishes, desires, background, or aims. Sexism may be readily passed off as a function of a personal idiosyncrasy or as a personal failure. We who are women thus are led to blame ourselves for our institutional fate, and others may discount the invidious patterns that are created by the separate behaviors and actions of so many individuals acting one at a time. Furthermore, it is not easy to change one's ways or grapple with institutional or personal solutions. It is a long and difficult journey from the belief that this is the way things are or must be to the perception that these arrangements are wrong and can be changed.

In addition, the functioning of sexism itself is complicated. After forty years in the earlier women's rights movement, Elizabeth Cady Stanton asserted that this social reform was the most complicated ever to dawn in human history. It was so complicated, she thought, because in the very areas of life in which one expected to find the most solidarity between the sexes (the family and religion), one found instead the worst opposition. Indeed, sexism seems even more complicated today than in Stanton's time. The earlier women's rights advocates fought for the right to be included in institutions such as politics or education. Today most of their battles have been won. However, the war itself seems to go on and in far subtler terms than a hundred years ago.

Feminism also is complicated. The very language in which we talk about our cause has its intricacies. Is "feminism" the same as "women's liberation"? When we add radical feminism, socialist feminism, and others, varieties of feminism seem to proliferate. Nor is it obvious that certain of our slogans, which communicate so much within the movement, are as meaningful to listeners who have not been initiated. "The personal is the political," for example, sometimes stymies people with long experience in other social movements. "Our bodies/our selves" similarly may require translation, as does other language about sexism or male chauvinism or patriarchy or misogyny or women's issues, depending on the predilections of the speaker. Do these all mean the same thing? It is not always clear how different feminist programs and priorities fit together. Gender-inclusive language, childcare centers, rape hotlines, and programs for displaced homemakers sometimes seem to be in very different political worlds.

To understand painful and complex matters is difficult in itself. To understand an issue such as sexism, which presupposes a social grasp of the world, runs against the tide in a culture that exalts the individual. To understand matters of injustice that have become less clear, more elusive, and subtle over the span of a hundred years greatly burdens a person struggling with the issues. How is the ordinary woman or man to come to grips with such matters?

The social ethicist comes to such questions with no special insight or resourcefulness that might resolve them magically, as though with a wand in the hands of a fairy godmother. Nor does working in such a field insure greater moral wisdom or virtue for its practitioners than is possessed by other persons. There is no privileged position outside the fray of ordinary conflicts and interests, beyond the pangs and frustrations of everyday struggles. The social ethicist working on sexism does not have a grasp of what is "really" involved, which is a shortcoming that feminists in other fields or in political efforts have.

As a field of intellectual inquiry, social ethics shares much with many other academic fields. Insofar as it involves social analysis, it borrows from endeavors of the social sciences. It differs from them, though, because social ethics' normative and prescriptive aims are as important as its analytical and and descriptive aims. The subject matter of social ethics is justice. This means that social ethics involves social and political movements for change. As a result, social ethics naturally shares the controversial quality of these movements, while bringing to bear various academic tools of research and thought that are germane to current issues.

Social ethics is helpful, however, because it offers the opportunity to crystallize and to focus so much of what usually is left unsaid about our patterns of life together. It offers an opportunity to explore a tradition of discussion and action about our community's future for those who are concerned about its moral dimensions (and not everyone is). Furthermore, by concentrating upon issues of justice, social ethics provides us with the opportunity to view in the round, "holistically" (as feminists might say), questions that frequently are taken up in fragmented and piecemeal fashion.

I shall first propose a way to understand sexism in a complex, multidimensional fashion. This multidimensional model is helpful in reaching for a measure of comprehensive theoretical clarity that does not deny or oversimplify the pain and confusion of this struggle; in providing a social rather than an individualistic perspective; and in guiding action toward justice. I shall illustrate some of the advantages of this framework with the example of rape and sexual assault. Second, the dynamic historical nature of sexism—its changes over time—requires some clarification so our understanding and action can assume their most effective shapes. Third, comparing sexism with racism may highlight some specific features or particular dimensions of sexism. Last, I shall suggest some of the implications of this perspective for justice on this issue.

A Complex, Multidimensional View of Sexism[1]

Sexism as it operates in the U.S. social order[2] is constituted by six complex, dynamic, internally related, and cumulative dimensions. (We shall return to those qualifiers in a few pages.) These are:

---

[1]While there are many colleagues, past and present, to whom I shall acknowledge debts in citations and other references in this essay, several have contributed most directly to this draft. For more than a decade, Lois Gehr Livezey has ably discussed with me the merits and demerits of the view proposed here. Ethicists Beverly Wildung Harrison and Barbara

1. *"It's a man's world,"* but *"woman's place is in the home."* These two folk sayings point to a recurrent feature of our social life in the area of the relationship of the home to the world and the division of the sexes between them. The feminist slogan, "the personal is the political," targets this relationship between home and world or between the private and public aspects of our social life. The private realm of home, family, and childcare is where women belong. It is that part of life for which we are uniquely suited or primarily responsible. The public world—the world of work, politics, history, and highly visible leadership—belongs to men. Or so the folk sayings, and social structures out of which the folk axioms grew, assert.

A brief historical note is in order. Earlier forms of man's world/woman's place in the West relied upon de jure restrictions to exclude women from the world—that is, primarily from politics and religion. In earlier eras, work was not outside the family household. This traditional, preindustrial form of the first dimension I shall call "patriarchy."

With industrialization, economic production shifted out of the home into factories or other places of business. Thus men became "breadwin-

---

Andolsen have both made important remarks on previous versions of this essay.

Intellectual antecedents of this perspective are principally two. A contemporary multidimensional view of racism in the work of a colleague in social ethics has been important in clarifying for me various ways of viewing social issues (see George W. Pickering, 1978). It is an open question among feminists whether analogies between racism and sexism clarify or obscure either or both issues. I suggest that an explicitly multidimensional approach can be helpful precisely on this count; see the discussion in section three of the paper.

This proposal also is akin to at least one effort in the tradition of feminist theory. Elizabeth Cady Stanton, frequently characterized as the most influential theorist of the last women's rights movement, advocated a complex and multidimensional perspective on her struggle. She spoke of a "four-fold bondage" in family, politics, society, and religion, "so many cords twisted tightly together, strong for one purpose." She added, "To my mind, if we had at first bravely untwisted all the strands of this four-fold cord which bound us, and demanded equality in the whole round of the circle, while perhaps we should have had a harder battle to fight, it would have been more effective and far shorter." (See Elizabeth Cady Stanton, "The Antagonism of Sex," Elizabeth Cady Stanton Papers, Folder 7, Library of Congress).

[2]Some of these features may also operate elsewhere. However, I am not proposing essential characteristics of sexism, but empirical and historical ones. If these six dimensions operate in other societies, that is to be determined by ordinary investigation. For a discussion of crucial similarities across cultures, see Michelle Zimbalist Rosaldo, "Woman, Culture, and Society: A Theoretical Overview," in *Woman, Culture, and Society,* ed. Michelle Zimbalist Rosaldo and Louise Lamphere (Palo Alto: Stanford University Press, 1974) 17-42.

ners'' in exclusive ways they had not formerly been. Many women followed their traditional tasks into the world of the factory; others did not. Thus, in one historian's phrase, the roles of women in the early nineteenth century split into those of "the lady and the mill girl."

The lady did not work in the world of salaried labor; she was destined, in Veblen's phrase, for conspicuous consumption. The structure of sexism inhabited by the lady I shall call "pedestalism." The mill girl, on the other hand, worked outside the home until marriage, when she was expected to quit (or was terminated) in order to tend to her primary responsibilities of home and family.

Many mill girls did not leave their jobs, of course. They created a slightly different pattern than either patriarchy or pedestalism, one that today is the recurrent pattern of most women's lives. Today more and more married women and especially married women with children are employed in the salaried labor force outside the home. I call our current structure "women's two roles." Most women today have two jobs—one paid, outside the home, and one unpaid, inside the home. (See further discussion in section two below.) However, elements of the two earlier forms of man's world/woman's place remain with us, particularly when we distinguish between women or different classes, races, and geographical sections of the country.

There are important corollaries to "man's world/woman's place." The isolation and privatization of women is the most important of these. The competition of women with each other for men is a function of woman's place. Assigning love a more important place in the lives of women than of men highlights the centrality of the private realm in the life prospects of women. Training women as though maternity, childcare, and housework will be the fundamental work of their lives clearly follows from woman's place. Subordination also contributes to maintaining man's world/woman's place by the sheer physical distance between workplace and home. Certain strands of consumerism similarly contribute to isolating women from each other; every home its own laundry, for example. The gross lack of childcare centers or the resistance to parental work leave at the birth or illness of children also may be seen as a factor keeping women in their place.

But the structures of the public world have a specific dynamism of their own, to which we now turn.

2. *The denial to women of equal access to high-quality public institutions that minister to basic life needs and that distribute power, wealth,*

and cultural goods. Virtually no examples of economic parity between the sexes exist. Women's salaries in the world of paid work are not quite two-thirds those of men. The average full-time female worker earns fifty-nine percent of the salary of the average male worker. Some economists speak of a dual labor market that channels women into low-level positions (secretarial, switchboard, nursing) and men into higher-level slots.

Salary and occupational differentials between the sexes combine to make women disproportionately unemployed and poor. The quality of institutions such as welfare and social security thus is directly relevant to large numbers of women, and the general decline in the quality of service of major institutions such as health care also bears its relevance to sexism.

Whether wealth and power are directly related to each other is an open question. But so far as women are concerned, we have neither in comparison with men. Few women are represented in the top levels of organizations, upper management of corporations, or the administration of schools. Nor do women's artistic, intellectual, or volunteer efforts fare better in gleaning tangible social rewards. When we scrutinize chains of institutional command, women are concentrated in the lower levels, receiving and executing policies rather than making them.

Nor are the symbolic goods of the culture equally apportioned. Images of women portrayed in media of all sorts tend to reinforce stereotypes of the sexes. Neither the producers nor the content of art and literature, as in science, have adequately represented the experience of half the human race. Schools, which convey the cultural heritage to rising generations, follow the familiar patterns.

In the world of large-scale social institutions, factors of class and race intersect with gender. Hence we note with regard to salaries and wealth that white men are at the top of the scale, followed by black men, then white women and, last of all, black women. Alternatively, we need to notice that the class status of women (which tends to follow the class status of husbands or fathers) complicates matters. While women form half the "upper" (and all other) classes, they rarely exercise the power of the men in their class. Similarly, poor women of nonwhite or non-English-speaking sectors of society fall prey to double or triple jeopardy.

3. *The denial to women of ordinary status within society.* Status, social honor, prestige, and value go overwhelmingly to male individuals and male efforts in our society. The devaluing of women's selves, work, and personality traits is seen most clearly in the straightforward comparisons

of better and worse, superior and inferior, but there are other modes of "extra-ordinary" status. Tokenism and the false exaltation of the pedestal are also ways to deny women ordinary status. We also may speak of women's relative status—that is, assigning status to women on the basis of the relevant male affiliated with them, such as husband or father (the president's wife, Rembrandt's mother). This dimension includes all notions, implicit or explicit, that assign to males the status of the norm from which females deviate.

4. *The debasement of women's psychic or existential life.* Women internalize sexist expectations about the nature of the world and the roles of the sexes, about their own possibilities, history, behavior, and self-image. (So, of course, do men; but the degree to which the inflation of one's existential life is a distortion or debasement is beyond the scope of this essay.) Given that power, wealth, and status are aligned with men and not with women, it is not surprising that women suffer wounds to self-esteem and self-concept. Nor is it surprising that women are overrepresented among those who seek emotional care or therapy. Women's socialization into the expressive and emotive roles has made the exploration of this dimension a strength of the present women's movement, which has targeted, with lucidity and perceptiveness, female self-images as passive victims.

5. *Violence to women and the violation of their physical integrity.* The specific facts of reproduction and sexuality, together with the vulnerability of women's bodies relative to those of men, open the door to a wide variety of distortive practices regarding "our bodies/our selves." Directly assaultive violence to women clearly belongs here: rape and sexual assault, battering of women, sexual abuse of children by adults. Less dramatic but no less important violations of women may be seen in other social practices related to women's bodies: lack of contraception that is both safe and effective, lack of abortion rights for all women, sterilization abuse, the overuse of radical mastectomy and hysterectomy, inflexible and expensive hospital systems of childbirth. Similarly violative are parts of the social order that single out women's sexuality, such as the use of female sexuality in advertising or pornography, the misunderstandings of our sexual functioning that persist from an era before Masters and Johnson, the cosmetics industry, sexual harassment on the job. There also is reason to suspect that certain health hazards in industry may affect women in discriminatory ways. Sexism in health-care systems, whether in research

or delivery, also is related in a major way to the perpetuation of violence and violation.

6. *The rationalization of all the above.* This refers to any argument, assumption, or conclusion that makes any of the above seem right, good, natural, unchangeable, inevitable, taken-for-granted, or divinely ordained. The scale of sophistication varies widely here, from the elaborate scientific theories of a Freud or the theological writings of a Karl Barth to the crude misogyny of a Norman Mailer. Similarly, there are folk sayings that distill sexist wisdom. "You can't thread a moving needle," for example, asserts that rape is impossible.

This complex, multidimensional view of sexism, I stress, is *a* model for understanding what women are up against in our society, what feminists are struggling to rectify. Furthermore, it is a model that aims to garner the widest range of empirical evidence within itself so as to sketch the comprehensive nature of sexism in our society. Sexism is a *systemic* problem. I am proposing a *multidimensional* model so that comprehensiveness does not sacrifice specificity and concreteness.

At the beginning of this section, I indicated that these six dimensions were complex, dynamic, internally related, and cumulative. It is time to explain that series of qualifications. By *complex* I mean that sexism is not a simple, single, or homogeneous phenomenon. Rather, it is a whole made up of complicatedly interrelated parts. Now any one of these dimensions by itself is a problem worthy of attention and rectification in its own right. To say that they are complex and *internally related* means that when any single dimension of these six is present, one or more of the others is likely to be present as well. When two or more of these dimensions are present in a given situation, they are mutually reinforcing. Finally, when these structural components of sexism are stacked on top of each other, the weight of injustice, the human burden, increases proportionately. They are, in other words, *cumulative* in impact. We will illustrate further the complex, internally related, and cumulative character of this model with the example of rape in the next few pages.

What of the *dynamic* character of sexism? Up to this point, in fact, our description has been fairly static. It is as though we mentally "froze" the social order in place at a given time so as to separate out its component parts related to injustice to women. As such, it is a kind of mental ideal, a mental summation, helpful in disentangling the constituent parts of sexism from one another and setting us about exploring their relationships to each other and to the whole. But the static nature of the model should not mislead us into believing that sexism itself is static or that it has always assumed the forms in which we live at present. On the contrary, sexism is dynamic. It has changed over time, assuming different configurations in different historical periods. The dynamic processes of sexism are most readily grasped when we look at previous forms of dimension one, man's world/woman's place, over the course of American history. To this we shall return in section two.

The purpose of this multidimensional model is to stimulate discovery and investigation. The model itself does not prejudge the particular, specific complex of factors that are most relevant to any concrete situation or institution. It does, however, suggest lines of inquiry and attention for activists or researchers in specific situations.[3] Nor does the model claim that any one of these factors is more basic than the rest, although feminists may have convictions or arguments about which are more fundamental in our time or earlier ages. For example, feminists convinced of the shaping character of economic structures concentrate their energies upon dimension two, believing that capitalism or the means of production determine the other dimensions of sexism. Others, convinced of the shaping character of symbols, images, and ideas, concentrate upon issues of language, culture, and attitudes as those elements that determine the other dimensions of sexism. This multidimensional model does not take a stand upon such conflicts within the feminist movement, but it does assert that, whichever funda-

---

[3]For example, feminists involved with higher education might proceed in the following way. Colleges and universities are institutions that fall primarily into dimension number two; they are among the agencies that minister to basic life needs (insofar as knowledge is a basic life need) and that distribute power, wealth, and cultural goods. The curricular program is the basic structure within the school that accomplishes these ends. Feminists concerned may therefore undertake a diagnostic review of the curriculum's substance, both in itself and with regard to the impact of the curriculum upon the other five dimensions.

But the comparison itself is only one facet of any higher educational institution. The composition by gender of the faculty, student body, administration, board of directors, clerical and maintenance staff, and the relations between these bodies are directly relevant to questions concerning the distribution of power, wealth, and cultural goods *within* the institution.

There are, in addition, important questions to be posed concerning the interface between any particular school and other social institutions that surround it: what vocational patterns its graduates pursue, its "external" relations with (for example) police, medical facilities, government officials, the patterns of family life in which it is embedded, and so forth.

mental convictions one works from, attention must be given to all six of these dimensions in order to be adequate to the full scope of sexism.

Let us illustrate the model of sexism more fully by examining one of its aspects. Violence against women, dimension five of the model, provides us with a case study of the interlocking mechanisms of sexism in our society and indicates the complexities needed in any program for justice for women. Rape (or sexual assault) is a particularly urgent aspect of the many kinds of violence and violation to which women are subjected in a sexist society.

Rape claims a quarter of a million victims annually, if we use only the legal definitions of this crime.[4] The rape victim is, first, a victim of violence. The rape victim, however, has more to contend with than just the brute trauma of the act itself, with its immediate physical and psychic effects.[5] The woman sexually assaulted is all too well aware of the general rationalizations of rape: that rape is impossible or that the victim is to blame. "She must have been asking for it"; "What were you doing there, anyway?" "You can't thread a moving needle." (These rationalizations, dimension six, may be internalized by her in complicated ways, and do contribute to the psychic effects, dimension four.) In many subcultures she may experience a further status decline (dimension three) from her already devalued status as a woman, for she is now "damaged goods." This may engender further consequences in terms of her chances for marriage (dimension one). The sense of shame or dishonor, in any case, precipitates further psychic effects (dimension four).

---

[4]This probably is an underestimate. If we notice the uncertainties and controversies regarding the defining, reporting, and study of rape, we may well go through the six dimensions in another direction, as it were. Since in only one or two places does the law include the possibility that a husband may rape his wife, we encounter directly the sanctity of the marriage and family system under current conditions, which assume that by entering marriage a wife has granted sexual consent in perpetuity to a husband. This fact points to the interlocking of curious notions of woman's sexuality (dimension five) with man's world/ woman's place (dimension one) via the legal system (dimension two). The many problems of the underreporting of rape and the judgments made by police of "unfounded" rape charges may be viewed via the intersections of other dimensions.

[5]It is central to note that it is only in the last decade that rape victims, like battered women, have been studied empirically. "Rape trauma syndrome," which simply describes the aftermath of the rape on the victim, is a new concept in the criminological, psychological, medical, and ethical worlds, a fact that tells us a great deal about our high-quality public institutions and the cultural goods that they purvey.

The resounding silence about rape and sexual assault in most of our schools, places of work, churches, media, and the political order makes it even more difficult for a rape victim to come to grips with her experience (interlocking dimensions two and four). She may lack even the most elementary information about this crime. If she seeks counseling, there are few places to which she may turn for sensitive and informed treatment other than rape-victim hotlines.[6] No one knows, in statistical terms, how influential the fear of rape may be in keeping women from venturing into certain neighborhoods or from venturing out at certain times of day. But we who are women know it in our bones and our stomachs. We should not underestimate the power of this fear of rape to keep us in our place (dimension one)—despite the fact that many women are raped right at home in what is alleged to be a safe place for us.

Furthermore, within both law-enforcement agencies and hospital emergency rooms, a good deal has changed with regard to the humane treatment of the rape victim. But it has changed erratically. One may still wonder how any individual rape victim will be treated. This is particularly true in light of the pitifully small funding and hiring of policewomen to work with rape victims. The miniscule record of rape convictions makes it unlikely that the victim will find it worth her while to push the case in light of the price she may have to pay.

The composition by sex of hospitals, police departments, district-attorney staffs, lawyers, and judges (and the substantive content of the training of these professionals in medical schools, police academies, and law schools) are all relevant to adequate programs about rape. Hence, the inequalities of access to high-quality public institutions (dimension two) affect what transpires with regard to violence against women.[7]

---

[6]On the other hand, "professional" help may not necessarily be what she needs, given the biases of certain psychoanalytic schools. Long-term studies of rape-trauma syndrome indicate that seeking support from friends, relatives, or other persons in a network of relationships is the most crucial factor in healing; it is the item that may mark the difference between recovery in a matter of months or a matter of *years*. Churches and seminaries should take particular note of this work. No one needs training in depth psychology or years of analysis before offering resources of support to the rape victim. Such findings also reinforce feminist discussions of networking and support as being among the critical factors in the women's movement. This point is echoed, I might point out, by sociologists who study battered women. They point out that the isolation of the battered woman may be among the crucial causative factors in battering.

[7]Similarly, we shall not go into the degree to which the multimillion-dollar pornography industry and soft porn in advertising, television, and movies contribute to a climate in

In this brief example we have not exhausted the full scope of rape and sexual assault as one strand of the operations of sexism. The point, however, is that in order to appreciate the ramifications of even this one item in the arsenal of sexism, we must explore its entwinement with the other aspects of the social system. For us to come to grips with programs adequate to cope with rape, we must reach for a view of the social system as broad as this. Sexism is an interlocking system that reaches across the whole range of our social order.

Specifying analytically distinct but practically interwoven sectors of its operation may help us grasp the full array of concrete activities required to eliminate rape or any other particular subsection of injustice to women. If we are able to put our fingers concretely on the many facets of the operations of sexism, we also may be able to specify ways in which feminists working on what seem to be distinguishable and disparate segments of the issue may in fact be working together. We must not become mesmerized by any particular strand of sexism so as to ignore others. If we understand the complex and multidimensional operations of sexism, then we can appreciate more fully the broad coalitions necessary to come to terms with it.

Home and Family

Sexism is also dynamic in nature. Its structures have changed significantly over time. There are many difficulties in illustrating these changes with regard to our previous example. Because of the uncertainties of reporting and recording rape, it is difficult to assess whether it is increasing or declining, even in the twentieth century when statistical records have been kept. Let us turn, therefore, to another major structural component of this model to indicate some of the historical changes important in understanding how sexism has operated and operates today in the United States.

Concerning the six-dimensional model, it might be objected that it is anachronistic to begin by asserting that "it's a man's world" but "woman's place is in the home." It is 1988, after all, not 1640; no one believes

---

which rape is likely to occur. For a fuller treatment of rape and sexual assault from the perspective of the feminist ethicist, we also would need to ask about histories, ethical treatises, or theological works that may provide resources and insights on this topic.

that anymore. There is something to be said for this objection, particularly if we agree to lay aside the right-wing backlash to the women's movement as somewhat unrepresentative of what most Americans believe today. But there are good reasons for thinking that this set of folk axioms still holds.

Let me illustrate the contemporary form of man's world/woman's place with remarks from a well-known twentieth-century theologian. It is perhaps not coincidental that these remarks come from the pages of a major women's magazine:

> Reinhold Niebuhr: What is significant about the modern intelligent woman and the present generation of college girls, though, is that they have determined that they are going to unite two vocations—a woman's biological vocation and the vocation dictated by their individual talents. . . . [T]his calls for a very rigorous procedure.
> Interviewer: I take it, then, that you believe that fatherhood doesn't hold the same position in the life of a man that motherhood holds in the life of a woman?
> Niebuhr: I'm quite sure it doesn't. I am married to a woman who spent a quarter of a century teaching in a woman's college. I know from my own experience and from the contact I have with her students that there is a very great difference between the biological role of the sexes. My wife and I used to have breakfast together. I'd go to my office and see students or write books. My wife had to get the children ready for school, provide for the lunch and do the housekeeping, in addition to her work as a professor. That is why I say combining the two vocations is very difficult.[8]

It is fascinating that Niebuhr believed that dressing the children, preparing meals, and doing housework were women's *biological* vocation. This perspective no doubt obscured the contingent nature of this division of labor in the Niebuhr household—and rationalized it, of course. Perhaps Niebuhr is not to be blamed overmuch for this, since I see little evidence that his colleagues organized their lives differently. Indeed, it is to Niebuhr's credit that he even noticed that his freedom from the daily chores of life at home contributed to his professional activities and detracted from those of his wife. The example is instructive precisely because it begins to articulate the burdens that fall upon women determined to "unite two vocations." It makes it perfectly clear why shared housework is such an im-

---

[8]"An Interview with Reinhold Niebuhr," conducted by John Cogley, *McCall's*, February 1966.

portant goal of the contemporary feminist. Niebuhr was precisely right: it is very difficult to do both by yourself.

Shared housework, however, is a privatized solution to a problem about the very relationship of public to private. It assumes the structures of sexism themselves as we currently experience them. Shared housework is a far cry from the proposals of earlier feminists (such as Charlotte Perkins Gilman) that we reorganize the private sphere itself. Communal dining facilities and socialized housecleaning, for example, would contribute to lessening the isolation and fragmentation that characterize our homes. Under current conditions, most apartment complexes amount to no more than one-family dwellings stacked on top of each other. They may provide communal laundry facilities or occasional communal recreation, but rarely do they free individual families from other "private" tasks.

Women's two roles, the contemporary variation of the relationship of home to work, represents an insistent tug upon women to reassume responsibility for the home. But the homes in which we live today are fundamentally different from the homes of the tradition. As countless historians and economists have pointed out, until about the end of the eighteenth century the home encompassed the whole range of human activity—except for politics and religion. Specifically, it encompassed economic work.

Before industrialization, the home was the workplace, the primary unit of economic production. Whole families labored there to ensure the survival of the family unit. Since work was located at home, it was not difficult for mothers or other family members to work productively while they watched over the children, many of whom also were working. Thus to exhort women to stay at home did not mean forbidding women from productive labor.

Industrialization, however, removed the production of goods from under the family roof. Many women of the nineteenth century, debarred from those public, salaried economic or political efforts, experienced their situations as enforced uselessness. Many thousands of these women poured their energies into the burgeoning voluntary associations of the period. Others embarked on the process of professionalizing the declining amount of domestic labor that remained at home, and the field of home economics was created. A host of magazines advised homemakers on the new standards expected in their field of work. The home was increasingly described as a "haven in a heartless world," to borrow Christopher Lasch's phrase. Supplying the emotional needs of the male members of the human family became a large portion of the female task.

Furthermore, just as for Niebuhr the rationalization for the family structure in which he lived was intimately tied to its description, so with the version of man's world/woman's place called "pedestalism." A new trend of thought proclaimed women to be too pure, chaste, fragile, or spiritual for the hugger-mugger of the economic and political life of the nation. These novel claims of women's moral and spiritual superiority stood the usual Western tradition on its head, for the arguments of preindustrial patriarchy insisted upon women's sinfulness and lack of rationality. Denied a direct role in politics, religion, or the production process, women were described as indirectly influential in the life of the nation. Motherhood was a central mode of that influence. "All that I am or ever hope to be I owe to my sainted mother," many statesmen and captains of industry were reported to have said. Ironically, these tributes to the power of motherhood coincided with a declining birthrate. Women were exhorted to stay home to concentrate more energy, concern, and talent on fewer children.[9]

The "true woman"—not just the ordinary woman—was described variously by her propagators in hundreds of sermons and articles. But one thing was clear: any woman working for a living or pursuing a public career sacrificed her claims on the ideal. Nonwhite women likewise were excluded. No one described the females enslaved on plantation fields as too pure and fragile to work.

Of course not all women wanted to stay home and, equally important, not all women could afford to stay home. Many women followed the displacement of the production of goods from the household into the new manufactures. By and large, during the nineteenth century, these women were young; they worked until they married, when they either quit or were terminated; hence, they were and are known as "mill girls." (But we might just as well know them as "serving girls," since at the turn of the century forty percent of the female labor force was employed in domestic and per-

---

[9]There are many studies of this romantic ideology. The best single study to date is Kathryn Kish Sklar, *Catherine Beecher: A Study in American Domesticity* (New York: W. W. Norton, 1976). But see also Barbara Welter, "The Cult of True Womanhood, 1820-1860," *American Quarterly* 18 (Summer 1966): 151-74. For a study of the ways in which the new ideology could be put to use by women of the period in voluntary associations, see Carroll Smith-Rosenberg, "Beauty, the Beast and the Militant Woman: A Case Study in Sex Roles and Social Stress in Jacksonian America," *American Quarterly* 23 (1971): 562-84.

sonal service.)[10] It was not until well into the twentieth century that large numbers of married women, and married women with children, returned to productive labor in the major institutions of the economy.

These women were not, however, the "college girls" of Niebuhr's comment. Women's two roles, the contemporary form of man's world/woman's place, was first and most vulnerably experienced by married working-class women of the last century. A journalist living in an industrial town in the late-nineteenth century reported that the experience gave her "another view of what the Industrial Revolution had done to women." What she saw was not unusual for the urban-industrial American life of poor women:

> In the cotton mills whole families worked together, mostly the same tasks and always the same hours. All worked, but when the whistles blew and the toilers poured out of the mills and hurried to their homes, what happened? The women of the mills went on working. They cooked and served meals, washed dishes, cleaned the house, tucked the children into bed, and after that sewed, mended or did a family washing. Eleven o'clock at night seemed the conventional hour for clothesline pulleys to begin creaking all over town. The men of the family were asleep by this time after an evening spent in smoking, drinking, talking union politics with cronies in barrooms or corner groceries, or placidly nodding at home over a newspaper. . . . [A] woman in the mills and at home worked an average of fourteen hours a day and had babies between times.[11]

Despite the changes in families due to the hard-won abolition of child labor, the extension of compulsory public schooling, and the eight-hour

---

[10]The complicated impact of both new forms of technology (machine production of goods) and new forms of human organization (corporate bureaucracies and the assembly line) on women's work cannot be fully treated here. In some fields (for example, the printer's trades) the introduction of machinery forced women out; in others (switchboards, typewriters), it did not. The two single biggest shifts of importance in women's wage labor are the shift away from domestic and personal service and the shift toward women's dominance of the white-collar clerical staffing of most major corporations. For the latter, see Margery Davies, "Woman's Place Is at the Typewriter," *Radical America* 8:4 (July-August 1974). The policies of labor unions in various fields are additionally complicating. See Heidi Hartmann, "Capitalism, Patriarchy, and Job Segregation by Sex," *Signs* 1:3, pt. 2 (Spring 1976 supplement).

[11]Rheta Childe Dorr, *A Woman of Fifty* (New York: Funk & Wagnalls, 1924), cited in *The American Woman: Who Was She?* ed. Anne Firor Scott (Englewood Cliffs NJ: Prentice-Hall, 1971) 19-20.

day, the home and housework patterns of these nineteenth-century families remained substantially intact. Among working couples in 1975, the average woman spent twenty-nine hours per week in family care, compared with nine hours for the average man. Despite much-touted labor-saving devices for the home, convenience foods, and the growth of the service-oriented sector of the economy, the amount of time spent in housework among working women has changed hardly any since the 1920s.

Since there unquestionably is less actual physical labor to be done in the home, how are we to understand the persistence of these tasks and expectations in the lives of women? Our expectations about the roles mothers are to play have expanded and diffused. Psychologists and child-development experts rush to advise women about their "relationships" to their children. It no longer is enough that children are clean, safe, and reasonably nourished. Nor are parents primarily concerned with the salvation of their offspring's immortal souls, as were Puritan parents. We now are held responsible for whether our young are neurotic or fulfilled human beings. These expectations about the proper roles of parents are more vague, more amorphous, less amenable to being concretely accomplished, and more conducive of guilt.

Man's world/woman's place, in other words, has dynamically shifted its contours over time. The structures I have called patriarchy, pedestalism, and women's two roles differ considerably from each other. Our current situation is complicated by the fact that remnants of the earlier forms still are with us. Further, the interaction between man's world/woman's place (dimension one), the major institutions of the economy (dimension two), and rationalizations for the system (dimension six) is complex and dynamic as well. It is difficult, for example, to assess the degree to which the ideology of Victorian womanhood merely extolled the status quo in its day or accelerated its expansion.

Without serious attention to the ways in which sexism has been in a process of dynamic historical change, contemporary understandings of the situations of women are truncated and crippled. When the family and home are under discussion, it is easy to assume that the structures we know are the same ones that have always been present—and to conclude, perhaps, that this is the way they always must be. The social ethicist seeking to clarify our contemporary moral debates and policy requires a historical perspective on such issues.

Sexism and Racism

Feminists frequently compare sexism and racism. The women's liberation movement, like its predecessor the woman suffrage movement, was in fact born in the struggles of women seeking racial justice in American life. In the last century, Susan B. Anthony spoke of "sex-slavery" to make the oppression of women as vivid as black slavery was to her audiences. In our day, feminists who wish to highlight the need for nonstereotyped language may use analogies to the black struggle. Calling an adult female a "girl," for example, is as degrading as calling an adult black male a "boy." Similarly, many of the same tactics were and are used by both groups—demonstrations and marches, legal remedies, or affirmative-action suits. "Sexism" itself probably was readily coined in the late 1960s because of the current use of "white racism."

But how similar are the two injustices? Are there aspects of sexism that are obscured by these analogies? Clarification on this score may be helpful to those advocating greater justice with regard to either racism or sexism. And some explicit comparisons are made possible by the multidimensional view of sexism suggested earlier in this paper.

Were we to factor racism into its various dimensions, a view of that issue would look formally very much like this view of sexism, especially in dimensions two through six. Blacks too are subject to different salary scales, certain kinds of occupational labeling, lack of ordinary status, existential debasement, specific forms of violence, and rationalizations for the system. On the other hand, blacks are not fifty percent of the North American population; they do not live on every street corner of every small town where there is human habitation. Women are half of every race, class, ethnic group, and geographical subsection of the social order. We are not closed off into geographically based ghettos, but into woman's place. (If we were to stretch our political language slightly, we might say that women are "segregated" into woman's place, but I am not convinced of the usefulness of this metaphor.) Practically speaking, the major differences between these two oppressions result from the varying operations of ghettoization and privatization. There are at least four substantive differences that it might help to note here.

First, the average white resident in an American suburb may never encounter black persons in such a way as to know them personally, let alone live on intimate terms. In contrast, everyone has a mother, and most people also have daughters, nieces, aunts, schoolmates, and so forth. The one injustice proceeds due to the disrespect and fear possible on the basis of geographical distance, the other on the basis of proximity, if not intimacy.

Second, within the enclaves of segregation, a black culture has arisen. Women, on the other hand, have few same-sex spaces in which to cultivate shared understandings, leadership, social institutions, arts, language. Black communities have at their disposal black churches—whose leadership was indispensable in the civil rights struggle. There are no women's churches in which we are the preachers, theologians, church officials. While there may indeed be a women's culture (perhaps even a women's language), it exists on rather more inchoate and intangible grounds than black culture.

Third, the large social institutions primarily responsible for their perpetuation are different. Real estate dealers, various banking practices, and municipal governments play a role in maintaining the ghetto, with or without slums. Marriage and the family and the advertising industry (which not only uses women's sexuality to sell its products, but directs much of its appeal to women as consumers rather than as producers) play important structural roles with regard to sexism.

Last, we may note that different forms of violence and violation cluster around these two massive social injustices. In black communities, arson, police brutality, race riots, and street violence in certain neighborhoods may be added to the earlier depredations of slavery and lynching as prominent forms of violence. The forms of violence and violation to which women are prey—rape and sexual assault, battering, sexual harassment on the job, and the whole array of odd practices with regard to women's reproductive functions—result from the physical and sexual differences between men and women.

Privatization also functions with regard to racism, but lacks the centrality that it has in the case of sexism. A white neighborhood experiencing its first black family may feel fragmented and atomized, each family in private fearing for its safety or for the financial investment in its home. It is the rare group of white neighborhood dwellers, one suspects, that self-consciously organizes itself either to resist what is perceived to be an encroachment of "them" *or* to resist its own fears and potentially violent impulses with calm. But while white flight from a neighborhood may be experienced as so many private responses in a chain reaction, it has its organized side, especially when residents are prey to panic-peddling on the part of real estate dealers or red-lining by banks. The privatization of white responses to racial issues plays a major role in perpetuating the composition of our cities by leading us to believe that racial separation is a "natural" or "automatic" response.

Black people, however, rarely are taken in by such tactics. Indeed, greater solidarity among black people may result. This is a rather different structure than the privatization of women built into man's world/woman's place. Because the structure of ghettoization creates black communities, black Americans return home after work, say in an integrated office or factory, to others who share their situations and perceptions. Sexism, on the other hand, runs through our homes and bedrooms, sometimes dividing the very space of our private world into "her" kitchen and "his" game room. Nor are black people enjoined, by biology as well as by cultural pressure, to marry whites, to find romantic fulfillment with the very group of persons who benefit from their oppressed positions.

It is important to emphasize the particularly painful place occupied in our society by black women. Black women are not able to escape the interstructuring of racism and sexism, for they experience both injustices at once in their persons. Black women are subject to both kinds of violence. Given the flight of quality public institutions from our metropolitan ghettos, they are least likely to find adequate resources for medical care, legal redress, or personal healing after being victimized by violence. Lowest on the income scale, disproportionately represented among the poor, black women have rarely experienced the form of sexism called "pedestalism." Indeed, misunderstandings between black women and white feminists are likely to occur just because of these different mechanisms of injustice. Indeed, black women frequently claim that they would like the luxury of being able to stay home to take care of the house and children. It is not unusual for black women to view the feminist movement as being in opposition to the struggle for racial justice.

Yet the differences between racism and sexism should not be exaggerated. The felt burdens of oppression, individual behaviors of internalized victimization, the pains of tokenism, strategies for enhancing self-esteem and assertiveness, and many rationalizations of both injustices run parallel in the two cases. But once again the possibility of clarifying the parallels and discontinuities between these two social issues is greatly enhanced by a self-consciously multidimensional approach. It provides us with means for the focused exploration of such questions and hence with a real practical payoff for coalition in the struggles against racism and sexism.

Implications for Justice

If the multidimensional view of sexism sketched and illustrated in this essay adequately indicates the problem we face, which is the injustice inherent in our social arrangements by gender, what might we say with regard to its counterpart, the justice we seek?

First, it requires systematic and comprehensive changes across the full sweep of our social order, taking into account the interlocking nature of the various dimensions of our lives together. Merely tinkering with the system as it stands will not be enough; no piecemeal, fragmentary programs will be adequate. I hope that the example of rape and sexual assault has brought this out clearly, but rape is only an example. I could as easily have appealed to broad ramifications of adequate daycare facilities, restructuring the nuclear family, equal pay, existential aspects of sex roles, the status or prestige of women and our work, or the theories and rationalizations by which sexism is perpetuated.

Second, just as the injustice we face is complex, so doing justice on the issue of sexism is inevitably complicated. No simple solutions or simple-minded suggestions will be adequate. Women of different socioeconomic classes and different races face structures of injustice that are not identical. Programmatic recommendations for facing these challenges need to take serious account of such variations in problems and needs, lest we create policies that rectify the injustice for some while exacerbating it for others.

Furthermore, not all six of these dimensions are amenable to legislative or public-policy solutions. It is difficult to see, for example, how shared housework or psychic debasement can be made appropriate matters of law or other formal structural determination. Such dimensions of injustice require other approaches. Assertiveness training and consciousness-raising groups are among the informal strategies the women's movement has employed to meet these dimensions of sexism. We must tend to our informal modes of change and transformation with devotion to our legal and structural efforts.

Just as the multidimensional model outlines the scope and the shape of the injustice on this issue, so it may function as a pointer toward sketching the contours of justice. To return to our six dimensions, justice on the issue of sexism requires:

1. Restructuring the relationships between the domains of home and work.

2. Equal access of women and men to high-quality public institutions that minister to basic life needs, and the equal distribution of power, wealth, and cultural goods.
3. Ordinary status for both women and men.
4. Equal existential burdens and joys for both sexes.
5. Stopping violence against women; respect for women's integrity as "our bodies/our selves."
6. The rationality of justice.

This multidimensional perspective thus is helpful in clarifying and analyzing the needs of justice. But at the same time, it is bare and somewhat sparse. We do not know what such a society would look like concretely or what experiences of life its members would encounter. Even to contemplate, in fantasy, a world that would not be structured into the pernicious patterns of home and work requires some imagination, some breaking away from our taken-for-granted patterns of thinking, talking, and acting. I suspect it requires a certain willingness to experiment with a variety of possible forms of family life, to be flexible enough to adapt our homes to varying needs at varying times.

In academic terms, an adequate view of this injustice and its counterpart of justice requires us to have an interdisciplinary perspective. The injustice involved stretches far beyond the compartmentalized views of knowledge institutionalized in school or university departments. This may be one reason that women's studies courses tend to be thematic or problem-oriented rather than bounded by disciplinary lines. But in this context, it ought to remind us especially that *ethics* itself must be an interdisciplinary field. If we are to be attentive to the actual contours of injustice in which we are embedded—which is what the shouting is about, after all—we need to stretch beyond the analysis of moral language or religious prescriptions into the domains of the social sciences—psychology, sociology, economics, history.

In political terms, such a perspective requires coalition building between groups working on programs directed against particular aspects of sexism. Frequently those who work on rape and those who work on childcare facilities or employment opportunities seem to be in different political worlds, with little or no communication or sense of division of labor. This can only be disastrous for the prospects of achieving greater justice for us all.

Similarly, if we feminists are serious in aiming toward justice for *all* women and not simply for white women or middle-class women, we need to attend to building bridges toward groups who struggle against racism or class inequalities. At the very least we need to be open to discussing these other social issues on their own terms and to exploring the ways in which sexism intertwines with them. Moreover, we need to be self-critical about our own biases, to explore honestly our prejudices, and to do the work required for our transformation. That there is both racism and classism in the women's movement is beyond doubt. There also is sexism in movements and groups aiming toward racial justice and economic justice. Without facing squarely these limitations to our own grasp of justice, while working wholeheartedly on our part of these issues, we run the risk of perpetuating other massive injustices in our society.

The pains and complexities of sexism make it difficult to understand; its dynamic adaptations to changing historical circumstances indicate how difficult it is to overcome. The enormity of a systemic injustice such as this, and the depth it reaches in our psyches, social structures, and history, may bring advocates of justice to despair and depression. But we have resources equal to these tasks collectively. "Sisterhood is powerful," the women's movement has said over and over again. Singly, we have little chance of remaking this unequal and unjust arrangement into a more equitable one. But together we have a chance. Indeed, the living opposition to sexism, in group associations, provides us with the possibility of action to transform sexism into justice. Living opposition to sexism provides us with the possibility of understanding the pernicious, massively patterned injustice for what it is. Indeed, without opposition to sexism there is no hope of understanding it at all.

Social ethics has its own contributions to make to the transformation of an unjust social order. Social ethics, however, is not a substitute for a social movement. The social ethicist with the good fortune to work at a time when there are viable movements for justice abroad, such as the women's movement, has more than one reason to be grateful. Movements for justice offer practitioners in this field an expanded horizon of inquiry and action. But with or without the expanded arenas for our work created by the women's movement, this field has specific responsibilities for identifying, investigating, articulating, and moving to transform social patterns of injustice embedded in our communal life.

Such efforts are not trivial or unimportant. Indeed, concerns about justice may be among the most important features of human existence. Justice is one of the depth structures of human life. Struggles for justice do not merely float along the surface of life; they plunge us into the most fundamental questions and conditions of being and meaning. Injustice violates human personality, distorts the terms of human community, and warps our relations to cosmos and being.[12]

To understand sexism does not require saints or geniuses. It requires only ordinary people, struggling together for justice, thinking together as we go about our own experience, searching for resources, including those of the depths of life, being honest about the pains and vulnerabilities as we go, and being creative about our options. These are capacities we always already have at our disposal in everyday life. As a poet says,

My heart is moved by all I cannot save:
so much has been destroyed

I have to cast my lot with those
who age after age, perversely,

with no extraordinary power,
reconstitute the world.[13]

---

[12]Feminists have made similar claims from the beginnings of our struggles, although little attention has been paid to such ideas. For instance, Mary Wollstonecraft, perhaps the first public advocate for women's rights, claimed that "God is Justice Itself." (See *A Vindication of the Rights of Woman* [1792; rpt., New York: W. W. Norton, 1967] 158.) Susan B. Anthony exhorted women to "pray by your actions," for she believed that God called us "to break every yoke and let the oppressed go free." (See Mary Pellauer, "The Religious Social Thought of Three Woman Suffrage Leaders: Towards a Tradition of Feminist Theology" [Ph.D. dissertation, University of Chicago Divinity School, 1980].) These foremothers' words echo in contemporary statements of feminist theologians: "Passion for justice, shared and embodied, is the form God takes among us in our time," says Beverly Wildung Harrison (*Making the Connections: Essays in Feminist Social Ethics,* ed. and with an introduction by Carol S. Robb [Boston: Beacon, 1985] 263).

[13]Adrienne Rich, "Natural Resources," in *The Dream of a Common Language: Poems, 1974-1977* (New York: W. W. Norton & Co., 1978) 67.

Further Reading

Andolsen, Barbara, Christine Gudorf, and Mary Pellauer, eds. *Woman's Consciousness, Woman's Conscience: A Reader in Feminist Ethics*. Minneapolis: Winston Press, 1985.

Baxandall, Rosalyn, Linda Gordon, and Susan Reverby, eds. *America's Working Women: A Documentary History, 1600 to the Present*. New York: Vintage, 1976.

Boston Women's Health Collective. *Our Bodies/Our Selves*. New York: Simon and Schuster, 1979.

Cott, Nancy. *The Bonds of Womanhood: "Woman's Sphere" in New England, 1780-1835*. New Haven: Yale University Press, 1977.

Daly, Mary. *Beyond God the Father: Toward a Philosophy of Women's Liberation*. Boston: Beacon, 1973.

_____. *Gyn/Ecology: The Metaethics of Radical Feminism*. Boston: Beacon, 1983.

Dreifus, Claudia, ed. *Seizing Our Bodies: The Politics of Women's Health*. New York: Vintage Books, 1977.

Fiorenza, Elizabeth Schussler. *In Memory of Her: A Feminist Theological Reconstruction of Christian Origins*. New York: Crossroads, 1983.

Gilligan, Carol. *In a Different Voice: Psychological Theory and Women's Development*. Cambridge: Harvard University Press, 1982.

Jagger, Alison M. and Paula Rothenberg Struhl, eds. *Feminist Frameworks: Alternative Theoretical Accounts of the Relations between Women and Men*. New York: McGraw-Hill, 1978.

Kessler-Harris, Alice. *Out to Work: A History of Wage-Earning Women in the United States*. New York: Oxford University Press, 1982.

Lerner, Gerda, ed. *Black Women in White America: A Documentary History*. New York: Pantheon, 1972.

Oakley, Ann. *Woman's Work: The Housewife, Past and Present*. New York: Vintage, 1976.

Rich, Adrienne. *On Lies, Secrets and Silences: Selected Prose, 1966-1978*. New York: W. W. Norton, 1979.

Ruddick, Sara and Pamela Daniels, eds. *Working It Out: 23 Women Writers, Artists, Scientists, and Scholars Talk about Their Lives and Work*. New York: Pantheon, 1977.

Ruether, Rosemary Radford. *Sexism and God-Talk: Toward a Feminist Theology*. Boston: Beacon, 1983.

Sargent, Alice G., ed. *Beyond Sex Roles*. New York: West Publishing Co., 1977.

Spretnak, Charlene, ed. *The Politics of Women's Spirituality: Essays on the Rise of Spiritual Power within the Feminist Movement*. Garden City NY: Anchor, 1982.

Starhawk. *The Spiral Dance: A Rebirth of the Ancient Religion of the Great Goddess*. San Francisco: Harper & Row, 1979.

Stellman, Jeanne Hager. *Woman's Work, Woman's Health: Myths and Realities*. New York: Pantheon, 1977.

Walker, Alice. *In Search of Our Mothers' Gardens: Womanist Prose*. New York: Harcourt Brace Jovanovich, 1983.

Roger D. Hatch
Central Michigan
University

■ ■

American Racism

■ ■ Busing, affirmative action, special minority set-aside programs, voting rights, equal opportunity, open housing, quotas, prejudice, discrimination—these are but a few of the specific ways the issue of racial justice has come before us in recent years. However, while these particular problems may be relatively new in public discussions, racism is not new. Each age has had its own set of specific terms to identify the various aspects of racial justice.

In fact, racism has been a constant element in American life. Over time there have been tremendous shifts in American economic, social, and political practices and policies. Yet American racism has persisted. Never has there been a time in American history when racism has not resulted in major economic, social, and political conflict, although often the conflict has been hidden from public view.

Three Institutional Forms

Despite the abundance of specific ways we have tried to identify and describe it, racism in American life has taken just three distinct institutional forms: slavery, Jim Crow, and the metropolitan color line. Slavery was an economic, social, and political arrangement that lasted for about two centuries in America. Shortly after slavery was abolished, American racism took a new institutional form—Jim Crow. This refers to the series of legal barriers to full equality and citizenship for black Americans, that is, the "separate but equal" segregation laws. This institutional form of

American racism was dismantled by the civil rights movement of the late 1950s and early 1960s.

However, even before Jim Crow was eliminated, a new institutional form of American racism had arisen—the metropolitan color line, often called "institutional racism." This relatively new form of American racism is not well understood. In part, this explains our current difficulty identifying and talking about the problem in public discussion. In clear distinction from Jim Crow, which consisted of a specific set of exclusionary laws and official rulings, institutional racism refers to the maze of formal and informal mechanisms that has continued to spread racism. We see its effects in such things as inner cities being inhabited principally by black people and other minorities, surrounded by a ring of suburbs composed principally of white people. Blacks and other minorities generally are subject to inferior schools, inferior public services, higher infant-mortality rates, unemployment rates that run two to three times as high as for whites in both good times and bad times, and underrepresentation at every level of the political process. However, all of these things are seen as the result of natural social, economic, or political processes rather than as the result of racism. All of this constitutes the metropolitan color line, the institutional form in which American racism presents itself to us today.

While slavery, Jim Crow, and the metropolitan color line are distinct institutional embodiments of racism, we err in terms of both thought and action if we focus only on their differences rather than their common features. Those who have opposed racism through the centuries and who have struggled to eliminate it from American life often have failed to distinguish between racism and a particular institutional form of it. Abolishing slavery did not abolish racism, just as eliminating Jim Crow did not eliminate it. Many people today believe that the civil rights movement was a failure because it did not eliminate racism. In fact, it did a positive thing by eliminating Jim Crow. At the same time, however, it did fail to deal with racism in the form of the metropolitan color line.

A Working Definition

Just what is it that we mean when we use the term *racism*? What common elements lie behind racism's three institutional forms? I find helpful this working definition, which has six dimensions.[1]

---

[1]George W. Pickering, "The Task of Social Ethics," in W. Widick Schroeder and Gibson Winter, eds., *Belief and Ethics* (Chicago: Center for the Scientific Study of Religion, 1978) 224.

1. *Separation* of the "races" geographically, socially, and institutionally.
2. *Subordination* of blacks and other "nonwhites" in terms of their access to:
   a. basic life needs,
   b. high-quality public institutions, and
   c. structures for political freedom and power.
3. *Denial of ordinary status* to "non-white" people.
4. *Fear and avoidance* on the part of both "whites" and "non-whites."
5. The expectation and presence of *violence,* which is understood to be legitimate under the circumstances.
6. The *rationalization* of all of these.

These dimensions are interrelated and reinforce each other. Where two or three are present, others are likely to be there. The first dimension, "separation," really sets the terms for all of the relationships and interactions between the races. In general, separation has led to "subordination." Most often, this is seen in terms of denial of equal access.

In the area of education, for example, at one time institutional separation meant that many local and state laws declared that white children and black children must attend separate schools. In 1954 the Supreme Court in *Brown v. Board of Education* said, "Separate education is inherently unequal." The Court agreed that, in education, separation leads to subordination. It leads to unwarranted feelings of superiority and inferiority and to establishing first-class and second-class schools. That form of separation was legislated institutional separation, or Jim Crow, which was abolished as a result of the civil rights movement. Currently, the separation of the races is based on housing patterns rather than restrictive legislation. However, this likewise has led to separate schools for white and black children and to the subordination of black children.

Separation and subordination convert black and other nonwhite people into "problems" for the rest of society. In the process, they stop being ordinary members of society and are seen as different. One result of such separation, subordination, and denial of ordinary status is the creation of a climate where people fear and avoid people of other races. This dynamic of fear and avoidance creates a "legitimate" expectation of violence. This violence can be turned either inward or outward, depending on the situation. Finally, separation, subordination, denial of ordinary status, fear and avoidance, and violence are thought to be part of particular economic arrangements (such as slavery or capitalism), part of class conflicts or differences, part of normal relations between any two groups, part of normal human tendencies, or part of natural inequalities. Thus these various dimensions of racism are rationalized, explained away.

History of Racism as a Public Issue

While racism has been a constant element in American life in its three institutional forms, only intermittently has it become a public political issue. In the last century, racism has been a public political issue for less than a score of years and right now is not so. Thus current debate, insofar as there is any, is about whether racism should be thought of as a public issue at all or whether it is simply a problem of personal attitudes and prejudices.

Following the Civil War, the 13th Amendment (1865) abolished slavery, the 14th Amendment (1868) provided equal protection under the law and full citizenship rights for black people, and the 15th Amendment (1870) affirmed the right of blacks to vote. Then a period of Reconstruction attempted to eliminate the effects of slavery and to provide for the needs of 3.5 million former slaves—"freedmen." This was a problem for which there was national and public responsibility, although most freedmen lived in the South. For the most part, national resources were allocated to what was understood as a regional problem. The Freedmen's Bureau set up by the federal government furnished supplies and medical services and established schools for freedmen, supervised contracts between freedmen and their new employers, managed confiscated or abandoned lands in the South, and organized freedmen's courts and boards of arbitration. Also attempting to aid freedmen were a variety of church-missionary associations. They provided food, clothing, and medical supplies right after the war and then turned their attention to education.

Reconstruction was fairly successful in dealing with some of the remnants of the system of slavery, but it was not successful in ridding the country of racism. Because the 1876 presidential election was inconclusive, the House of Representatives was forced to decide it. Early in 1877 Southern Democrats agreed to support Republican Rutherford B. Hayes for president rather than the Democrat Samuel J. Tilden in return for a pledge that Reconstruction laws would not be enforced. So North and South were reunited, but at the expense of blacks. Their separation and subordination in the American social order was the price paid for the "compromise." Reconstruction's promise to freedmen of forty acres and a mule slowly was replaced by the sharecropping system. Reconstruction's end also was the end of racism's being a public political issue. Not until the civil rights movement did racism again gain that status.

Because racism is not now under serious public discussion, and because it so rarely is, it may be helpful to identify the elements that came together to produce the civil rights movement, which sought to eliminate the Jim Crow system.

Booker T. Washington. Following the collapse of Reconstruction, the Jim Crow system—the "separate but equal" system—arose first through local custom and later was established by law. The central figure in this era following Reconstruction was Booker T. Washington. In an address to the Atlanta Exposition in 1895, he summed up the shift in thinking that had taken place since Reconstruction: "In all things purely social we can be as separate as the fingers, yet one as the hand in all things essential to mutual progress. . . . It is important and right that all privileges of the law be ours, but it is vastly more important that we be prepared for the exercises of these privileges."[2] Washington believed that by staying in the South, by obtaining a useful education, by holding a useful job, and by acquiring property black people ultimately could "earn" full citizenship rights. White good will, especially the good will of philanthropists and foundations, was crucial to pursuing these aims. Washington understood the problem of race to be the problem of black underdevelopment. Black people themselves were largely responsible for this. The major agents for change were to be schools, foundations, and the strivings of individual black persons. Compared to Reconstruction, this marked a retreat (1) from viewing the problem as a national problem to viewing it as a regional one; (2) from seeing it as a public or political problem to seeing it as a personal problem of black underdevelopment; and (3) from the use of national and public resources to the use of private philanthropy to solve the problem.

---

[2]Booker T. Washington, "The Atlanta Exposition Address, September—1895," from *Up from Slavery* (New York: Doubleday, Page and Co., 1901), as quoted in August Meier, Elliott Rudwick, and Francis L. Broderick, eds., *Black Protest Thought in the Twentieth Century,* 2d ed. (Indianapolis: Bobbs-Merrill, 1971) 6-7.

W. E. B. DuBois. In 1903 a young professor at Atlanta University, W. E. B. DuBois, published a slim volume, *The Souls of Black Folk.* In it he offered a critique of Booker T. Washington's approach, pointing to the "triple paradox" of Washington's career:

1. He is striving nobly to make Negro artisans business men and property-owners; but it is utterly impossible, under modern competitive methods, for workingmen and property-owners to defend their rights and exist without the right of suffrage.

2. He insists on thrift and self-respect, but at the same time counsels a silent submission to civic inferiority such as is bound to sap the manhood of any race in the long run.

3. He advocates common-school and industrial training, and depreciates institutions of higher learning; but neither the Negro common-schools, nor Tuskegee itself, could remain open a day were it not for teachers trained in Negro colleges, or trained by their graduates.[3]

Accordingly, DuBois called for three things: the right to vote, civic equality, and the education of youth according to ability. He stressed slavery and race prejudice, rather than black underdevelopment, as the causes of black people's plight. He concluded that individual black striving and self-help would do little in themselves unless they were joined by efforts on the part of the larger society. He wrote that Washington's doctrine "has tended to make the whites, North and South, shift the burden of the Negro problem to the Negro's shoulders and stand aside as critical and rather pessimistic spectators; when in fact the burden belongs to the nation, and the hands of none of us are clean if we bend not our energies to righting these great wrongs."[4] DuBois still understood the problem as a black problem, but now it was understood as being caused by whites, first by the institution of slavery and then by race prejudice. DuBois attempted to make race a public political issue again. Where Washington focused on black self-development, DuBois concentrated on protest to achieve his political aims and purposes. DuBois tried to unite the ideals of civil rights and self-respect, whereas Washington focused mainly on self-respect.

Early Civil Rights Organizations. For the next four decades, a variety of persons and organizations accepted (at least implicitly) DuBois's view

---

[3]W. E. B. DuBois, *The Souls of Black Folk* (1903; rpt., New York: Fawcett Books, 1961) 49.

[4]Ibid., 53.

of the problem of race as a black problem caused by whites. There were attempts to discover *how* whites were causing the problem and what strategies could be developed to combat it. For the NAACP, the problem was that whites had subverted the 14th and 15th Amendments; this they attempted to fight through the courts. DuBois was one of the major figures in the NAACP. For socialists and communists, the problem was that capitalists exploited labor, so they tried to organize black workers. A. Philip Randolph and his Brotherhood of Sleeping Car Porters were among the most successful organizers. For Marcus Garvey and other black nationalists, the problem was that blacks had no real place in this nation. Garvey and his many followers attempted to leave and go to Africa. For the Urban League, the problem was that blacks were an immigrant group to the Northern cities, so they tried to help integrate and assimilate them into a new way of life.

An American Dilemma. In 1944 a massive report on the problem of race in American life was published. *An American Dilemma: The Negro Problem and Modern Democracy*[5] was the result of a four-year study funded by the Carnegie Foundation and directed by Swedish social scientist Gunnar Myrdal. It was a public proclamation from the respectable, nonprotesting segment of society that America indeed had a racial problem. Nearly every aspect of the problem was detailed. This problem, the study said, was no small, isolated problem; it lay at the very heart of America and its value system. Central to the analysis of the problem was the notion of the American Creed, which includes such ideals as freedom, equality, and justice. The Creed described what Americans believe about their country. It also served as a standard of judgment for the racial problem: America and Americans should live up to the Creed. The dilemma referred to in the previously mentioned title is the conflict between the values in the American Creed and other more narrow values and practices. This is a conflict not so much between various groups of people but within individual persons and institutions. In short, when it came to racial justice, America and Americans were schizophrenic.

Myrdal saw an interdependence between all of the factors in the racial problem. He referred to this as the "principle of cumulation." For example, an increase in education often leads to better economic status, and

---

[5]Gunnar Myrdal, *An American Dilemma: The Negro Problem and Modern Democracy* (New York: Harper & Row, 1944).

this often leads to better housing and political representation. Thus by understanding racism as a single, unified problem with many interrelated factors, Myrdal provided the intellectual basis for a coalition of different groups working together for racial justice. Myrdal showed how these different groups actually were not competing. The work of one group supported the work of all the others. However, such a coalition of groups did not occur in a significant way until the civil rights movement.

The NAACP and Brown v. Board of Education. From its inception in 1907, the NAACP focused its energies on attacking Jim Crow through the court system. It set out to have the "separate but equal" notion overturned. By the late 1940s, it had won some important, but limited, legal battles. Then on 17 May 1954 the Supreme Court announced its ruling in *Brown v. Board of Education.* It declared invalid its 1896 ruling in *Plessy v. Ferguson,* which had established the "separate but equal" doctrine. In *Brown,* the Court declared that "separate is inherently unequal." The decision pertained specifically to educational institutions, but a wide application soon was sought.

The Civil Rights Movement

By the late 1950s, a loose coalition had been formed to bring about an end to all Jim Crow regulations and laws. This coalition was composed of the various protest organizations that had existed for several decades, along with some new ones such as the Southern Christian Leadership Conference and the Student Non-Violent Coordinating Committee; of some labor organizations; and of some church groups and white liberals. This loose coalition is referred to as the civil rights movement.

The issue for the movement was clearly understood as segregation. This was a black problem caused by whites through discriminatory legislation. The *Brown* decision provided the legal backing to the civil rights movement as it set out to challenge segregation laws. The attack was mounted on a variety of fronts: education, politics, housing, public accommodations, jobs, and many other areas of life. For the first time since Reconstruction nearly a century earlier, racial injustice was understood to be a national and public problem to be dealt with by national and public resources.

The chief strategy that emerged was nonviolent direct action: boycotts, sit-ins, and marches. In part this was due to the key role Martin Luther King, Jr. played in the movement. He had been thrust into the limelight as a result of his role in the Montgomery, Alabama, bus boycott in 1955 and 1956. On 1 December 1955, Rosa Parks, a black seamstress sitting at the front end of the segregated section at the back of the bus designated for blacks, was asked by the bus driver to give her seat to a white man who had just boarded, as was required by law. She refused and was arrested. The black community, led by King, decided to boycott the buses and find alternative means of transportation. The final result was the desegregation of buses.

Soon segregation laws were challenged in a variety of ways: sit-ins to desegregate public facilities (1960); "Freedom Rides" to desegregate public transportation (1961); marches, demonstrations, and boycotts to desegregate employment opportunities and all public accommodations (1962-1963). In August 1963 more than 250,000 people participated in the "March on Washington for Jobs and Freedom Now." This was followed by the passage of the Civil Rights Act of 1964, which desegregated public accommodations. In 1964 attention turned to voter registration, principally in the South. A campaign by King's Southern Christian Leadership Conference in Selma, Alabama, in 1965 succeeded in focusing national attention on the issue of voting rights for black Americans. Congress later that year passed the Voting Rights Act, which made illegal the discriminatory devices and practices that had prevented blacks from voting. Within fifteen years black voter registration had increased more than 400 percent.

In just a few years the civil rights movement had been successful in ridding the country of most Jim Crow laws. However, just as a century earlier the abolition of slavery had not meant an end to the problem of racism, so now the elimination of Jim Crow laws did not mark the end of the racial problem. This was because American racism already had assumed a new institutional form, which was the metropolitan color line.

During the period of the civil rights movement, racism in its Jim Crow form became a public political issue. What were the crucial elements that led to this? (a) A reasonably clear understanding of the problem as a public political issue of justice rather than a personal problem of white prejudice or black underdevelopment. In this case, it was DuBois's understanding of Jim Crow as a black problem caused by whites through restrictive legislation. (b) Some basis for getting diverse groups to work together. Myrdal, with his notion of the principle of cumulation, provided the intellectual grounds for coalition. (c) A legal foundation for challenging the Jim Crow segregation system. The NAACP provided this by bringing a series of court cases that culminated in *Brown v. Board of Education,* which declared segregated education illegal. (d) Effective tactics. Nonviolent direct action accomplished this. (e) Some basis for developing broad public support. Myrdal's notion of the American Creed allowed people to be "conservative" in supporting racial justice by supporting the basic American values of freedom, equality, and justice. Further, the beatings and jailings of nonviolent protestors did much to develop broad public sympathy and support.

Positions in the Public Debate

When racism in its Jim Crow form was a public political issue during the 1950s and 1960s, three broad positions emerged in the public debate. Each of these positions was linked with certain tactics or strategies for combating racism. An examination of these may prove helpful as we seek to understand racism in its form of the metropolitan color line. These positions are the dilemma, indictment, and transformation positions.

Dilemma. The dilemma position, taking its name from Myrdal's study, basically accepted the ideals of American culture and attempted to bring everyday practice into line with them. This position also often was called "liberal." Advocates of this position believed that, because of the American principles of freedom, equality, and justice, the racial problem had been solved in principle. What was needed was to bring practice in line with these good principles. Myrdal stated it clearly:

> From the point of view of the American Creed the status accorded the Negro in America represents nothing more and nothing less than a century-long lag of public morals. In principle the Negro problem was settled long ago; in practice the solution is not effectuated.[6]

People adopting the dilemma position could be either optimistic or pessimistic about the possibility of closing the gap between American ideals and American practice. Myrdal, for example, wrote:

> When looking back over the long manuscript, one main conclusion . . . is this: *that not since Reconstruction has there been more reason to anticipate fundamental changes in American race relations, changes which will involve a development toward the American ideals.*[7]

---

[6]Ibid., 24.

[7]Ibid., lxi.

Benjamin Mays, another advocate of the dilemma position, took a somewhat more pessimistic view. In 1971 he wrote: "No one can deny that the masses of Negroes are little if any better off than they were before 1955."[8]

Dilemma interpreters viewed American society as being, generally, a positive kind of reality. This was particularly true on the level of general values and ideals such as freedom, equality, and justice—the American Creed. These ideals were only partially embodied in everyday life, but they were "the cement in the structure of this great and disparate nation."[9] American society's practices, however, did not embody the American dream fully enough. The challenge, as Mays put it, was "to make the American dream a reality for every American."[10] But this need not involve an unthinking acceptance of the American dream. "It is not always easy for a black man to swear allegiance to the flag, but the American dream is embodied in that allegiance, and until it is repudiated one can still hope for and work toward the day when it becomes a reality."[11] Later, Mays wrote,[12]

> I do not know whether there is a solution to the Negro-white problem. . . .
> It seems to me, however, that we have no choice but to continue our efforts
> to make this country a decent place for all Americans. As Henry van Dyke
> says, in *The Other Wise Man*, "it is better to follow even the shadow of
> the best than to remain content with the worst."

What had to be done to establish a more just society was to reduce or remove the impediments to the full and effective functioning of the American Creed. Education and religion could attack narrow beliefs and values that were not in line with the American Creed, thus reducing internal impediments. Reforms in the legal, political, and economic arenas could reduce the external impediments to the American Creed. Such reforms were to be sought in a variety of nonviolent ways: demonstrations, political and economic pressure, lawsuits, sit-ins. Thus the activities of the NAACP, the Urban League, SCLC, and SNCC all served to promote the American Creed, as did the activities of churches and schools.

---

[8]Benjamin E. Mays, *Born to Rebel* (New York: Scribner's, 1971) 310.

[9]Myrdal, *An American Dilemma*, 3.

[10]Mays, *Born to Rebel*, viii.

[11]Ibid., 275.

[12]Ibid., 320.

Indictment. Advocates of a second widespread position did not understand the American racial problem to be the existence of a gap between American ideals and American practice, as in the dilemma position. Instead, the problem was understood to be the domination of American culture by a bankrupt set of ideals. American practice revealed the true ideals and values that operated in American society. For black Americans, and others, the result of the domination of American society by these bankrupt values was disastrous. Consequently, these values first needed to be indicted; then a new set of ideals and values needed to be introduced into society and embodied in practice. More recently, this basic position has become known as black power.

Malcolm X, one of the most forceful and articulate proponents of this position, saw America as a country that exploited blacks psychologically, spiritually, economically, and politically. "The black man in North America was mentally sick in his cooperative, sheeplike acceptance of the white man's culture."[13] At the root of the problem is a fraud, the lie that black people are inferior and white people superior. The truth of black people's true worth and true role in history has been hidden by a conspiracy down through the generations and by a continual brainwashing of blacks.[14] There has been no gradual progress. Malcolm said in 1965 that the black American

> doesn't see any progress that he has made since the Civil War. He sees not one iota of progress because, number one, if the Civil War had freed him, he wouldn't need civil-rights legislation today. If the Emancipation Proclamation, issued by that great shining liberal called Lincoln, had freed him, he wouldn't be singing "We Shall Overcome" today.[15]

Malcolm envisioned a society characterized by freedom, justice, and equality, where all people would have respect as human beings.[16] But bringing this about would involve radical change.

---

[13]Malcolm X (with the assistance of Alex Haley), *The Autobiography of Malcolm X* (New York: Grove Press, 1964) 312.

[14]Ibid., 54.

[15]Malcolm X, *Malcolm X Speaks: Selected Speeches and Statements* (New York: Merit, 1965) 141.

[16]Malcolm X, *Autobiography*, 272.

Since Western society is deteriorating, it has become overrun with immorality, and God is going to judge it, and destroy it. And the only way the black people caught up in this society can be saved is not to *integrate* into this corrupt society, but to *separate* from it, to a land of our *own*, where we can reform ourselves, lift up our moral standards, and try to be godly.[17]

These moral standards were not going to come from the American Creed or Christianity because Christianity was "the white man's religion."[18] The white man "has *twisted* his Christianity to keep his *foot* on our backs . . . to keep our eyes fixed on the pie in the sky and heaven in the hereafter . . . while *he* enjoys *his* heaven right *here* . . . on *this earth* . . . in *this life*."[19] For Malcolm, the antidote to white religion was a special religion for black people—the religion of the nation of Islam.[20] Islam was "the one religion that erases from its society the race problem."[21]

The steps to bringing about a society characterized by freedom, justice, and equality for all involved, first, exposing and indicting the bankruptcy of American society and American values as they existed. Next came separation and self-respect:

As other ethnic groups have done, let the black people wherever possible, however possible, patronize their own kind, hire their own kind, and start in those ways to build up the black race's ability to do for itself. One thing the white man can never give the black man is self-respect! The black man never can become independent and recognized as a human being who is truly equal with other human beings until he has what they have, and until he is doing for himself what others are doing for themselves.[22]

Transformation. The third position on American racism did not see American ideals and values as essentially good (dilemma) or as essentially bad (indictment). Instead, it saw a mixture of good and bad ideals and values. It argued that American society should be transformed by pursuing some of the best ideals and values and by eliminating or holding in check some of the worst.

---

[17]Ibid., 246.

[18]Ibid., 241.

[19]Ibid., 200-201.

[20]Ibid., 220.

[21]Ibid., 340.

[22]Ibid., 275.

While early in his public career he advocated the dilemma position, by the early 1960s Martin Luther King, Jr. advocated a transformation position. Other prominent advocates of this position included A. Philip Randolph and Bayard Rustin. King found in America two dominant and contradictory strains: a positive one (the democratic heritage) and a negative one (racism) that contradicted and qualified the positive one. Disagreeing with the dilemma position, he wrote, "For the good of America, it is necessary to refute the idea that the dominant ideology in our country even today is freedom and equality while racism is just an occasional departure from the norm on the part of a few bigoted extremists."[23] He examined influential American leaders such as George Washington, Thomas Jefferson, Patrick Henry, John Quincy Adams, John Calhoun, and Abraham Lincoln for their leadership in the area of racial justice. Like those holding the indictment position, he observed, "Virtually all of the Founding Fathers of our nation, . . . those whom we cherish as authentic heroes, were so enmeshed in the ethos of slavery and white supremacy that not one ever emerged with a clear, unambiguous stand on Negro rights."[24] He noted that the situation had not changed much since then. He concluded, "The racism of today is real, but the democratic spirit that has always faced it is equally real."[25] Thus while King found the current situation to be bad, as in the dilemma position, he did find within American ideals and values some basis for moving toward racial justice.

King wanted to construct a society based on "what is best in the American dream and . . . the most sacred values in our Judeo-Christian heritage."[26] For him this meant the ideals of brotherhood, democracy, community, freedom, and peace. Because all life is interrelated, "my personality can only be fulfilled in the context of community."[27] Integration was an essential part of this. In seeking integration, a black person not only was "winning rights for himself," he also was producing "substantial results for the nation."[28] "We will try to persuade with our words, but if our

---

[23]Martin Luther King, Jr., *Where Do We Go from Here? Chaos or Community* (New York: Harper & Row, 1967) 81.

[24]Ibid., 88.

[25]Ibid., 97.

[26]Martin Luther King, Jr., *Why We Can't Wait* (New York: Harper & Row, 1963) 94.

[27]Martin Luther King, Jr., *Stride toward Freedom* (New York: Harper & Row, 1958) 87.

[28]King, *Why We Can't Wait,* 152.

words fail, we will try to persuade with our acts."[29] King concluded that nonviolence was the ultimate form of persuasion. He advocated nonviolence because he thought it was "the only way to reestablish the broken community."[30]

Comparison of Positions

The dilemma position begins by examining American ideals and values, and on this basis proceeds to criticize American practice. The choices we face concern how to close the gap between ideals and practice. Any movement toward racial justice will be in small steps rather than in dramatic leaps. The dilemma position does not allow a serious examination of American ideals and values; it simply assumes they are good and should be pursued. The indictment and transformation positions, on the other hand, do allow for such an examination of American ideals and values. One conclusion is that the American Creed is excessively individualistic. This has led to an understanding of racism as an individual problem of white prejudice or black underdevelopment rather than being an institutional issue of justice for the entire society.

The indictment position begins by examining American practice and on the basis of this indicts American ideals and values. The choices we face concern how to replace the current bankrupt set of ideals and values operating in American society. But the indictment position can offer no real guidance on which other set of ideals and values to adopt or on how to go about adopting them. It calls, in effect, for mass conversion of American society. Further, because it holds that American practice has been uniformly bad, it fails to allow for the possibility that some good ideals and values may be present in American society.

The transformation position sees both good and bad ideals and values and good and bad practices present in American society. The choices we face concern which of these ideals and values we should emphasize (and criticize) and which practices we should emphasize (and criticize). This will be determined by an empirical investigation of the facts. The transformation position thus is more inclusive than either the dilemma or indictment interpretation and actually includes both of them. It requires both

---

[29]King, *Stride toward Freedom*, 193.
[30]Ibid., 196.

the identification of American ideals and values (dilemma) and the criticism of them based on American practice (indictment). Those holding the transformation position have been particularly critical of the excessive individualism in the American Creed and have seen this as a key obstacle to dealing effectively with racism in its various institutional forms. It hinders us from seeing problems as *social* problems of public policy and inclines us to see them simply as individual problems. Unlike the dilemma position, which believes racism already has been solved on the level of ideas and ideals, the transformation position believes racism is a problem requiring both thought and action. Those holding the transformation position, after examining the situation, do not see the American Creed as providing a sense of interrelatedness and community adequate to sustain the fundamental social change that is necessary if racism is to be addressed effectively. This is what must be created.

For all these positions, racism has important religious dimensions. Visions of what can be and of what ought to be have their sources in various religious traditions. Some of the steps they indicate we should take to establish racial justice involve religion. But deeper reasons exist for discussing religion and racism together.

Whether we affirm or deny racism, we must define the proper relationship of all human beings to each other. This "proper" relationship includes either equality or inequality. Doing this is a religious task because religion involves some idea of the way things really are or ought to be as well as our responses to it. This "proper" relationship of equality or inequality usually is justified by appealing to some ideas about how people ultimately become fulfilled as human beings.

Finally, the difficulty of sustained action against racism leads to questions about whether there is any kind of justice beyond this life, whether there is any meaning to American racism other than the tragic results so far, whether opposing racism is worth all the trouble. The only answers to these questions are religious.

The Contemporary Discussion

As indicated earlier, there is little discussion today of race as a *public* or social issue. By the time Martin Luther King, Jr. was assassinated in 1968, the coalition known as the civil rights movement had pretty well fallen apart. In part, this was due to the inability of racism's opponents to describe clearly and persuasively the workings of the metropolitan color line.

The Nixon administration (1969-1974) made a conscious choice to downplay racism as a public issue on the national political scene. It pursued a policy that it called "benign neglect." In dealing with congressionally mandated affirmative-action programs, the Nixon administration emphasized white women as much as possible rather than members of minority groups.

By the end of the 1970s, those who believed that racism was principally a private issue of white prejudice or black underdevelopment rather than a public issue of justice had won the day. Two events in 1978 symbolize this well. One was the publication by William Julius Wilson, a black sociologist at the University of Chicago, of *The Declining Significance of Race*.[31] In this highly debated book, Wilson argued that, in the economic arena, class was more important than race in determining black access to privilege and power. While the book presented a complex argument calling for increased federal government attention to the economic dimensions of racism, particularly as they affect the black underclass, the public at large and much of the academic world latched onto the book as evidence that governmental bodies no longer needed to deal with the problems of institutionalized racism.

The second event was the Supreme Court's decision in *Regents of the University of California v. Bakke*. Alan Bakke, a white student who hoped to be admitted to medical school, challenged an affirmative-action program at the University of California-Davis. The Supreme Court, in a 5-4 vote, ruled that this particular affirmative-action program was unconstitutional, although the Court believed there could be (and actually were) other affirmative-action programs that were constitutional. While this was a narrow and ambiguous ruling, it was taken by many to mean that institutions no longer actively needed to pursue affirmative-action programs.

Ronald Reagan's administration moved from neglect of racial justice by the federal government to direct opposition. Reagan initially opposed the extension of the most important achievement of the civil rights movement—the 1965 Voting Rights Act—and only reluctantly agreed to sign it. In the courts, his Justice Department promoted a variety of groups who opposed the existing civil rights laws. In his first few budgets, Reagan proposed drastic cuts in federal civil-rights-enforcement efforts and in those

---

[31]William Julius Wilson, *The Declining Significance of Race: Blacks and Changing American Institutions* (Chicago: University of Chicago Press, 1978).

social and economic programs aimed at minority groups. The U.S. Commission on Civil Rights objected to Reagan's first budget proposal in a lengthy and strongly worded document entitled *Civil Rights: A National, Not a Special Interest.*[32] Their objections, however, did not prevail, and most of the budget cuts were enacted.

During the two decades following Martin Luther King's assassination, many members of the civil-rights coalition lost interest or turned to other pursuits. Some, however, such as Andrew Young, entered the realm of electoral politics. Civil-rights organizations such as the NAACP, the National Urban League, and the Southern Christian Leadership Conference continued to exist and were joined by Operation PUSH, headed by Jesse Jackson.

Even these groups, though, found it difficult to pursue racism as a public political issue and turned largely inward to self-help or self-development programs. For example, the NAACP sponsored ACT-SO (Afro-Academic, Cultural, Technological, and Scientific Olympics), and Operation PUSH developed PUSH-EXCEL—both of which were programs designed to promote academic excellence among black students. Both the NAACP and Operation PUSH also attempted to increase job opportunities for black people by organizing the potential power of black consumers.

Jesse Jackson's presidential campaigns have been an exception to this turning inward. In a move reminiscent of the civil rights movement, Jackson attempted to create a "rainbow coalition" of the rejected, bringing together blacks, whites, Hispanics, American Indians, Asians, women, the young, the poor, and the old.

Yet by the late 1980s, study after study showed that the situation of black people in almost every area of American society was stagnating or actually getting worse. Black unemployment was nearly two and a half times as high as white unemployment. The gap between black and white median family incomes was increasing, not decreasing. The percentage of college students who were black was decreasing. Blacks only had about one-tenth of the political representation that would be expected based on their numbers in the population. And the overwhelming proportion of black children still attended all-black schools that were poorly funded.

---

[32]United States Commission on Civil Rights, *Civil Rights: A National, Not a Special Interest* (Washington: GPO, 1981).

What might it take for citizens to address problems such as these effectively? Based on the experience of the civil rights movement, I believe it will take four things. (a) *Some understanding of the metropolitan color line as a social problem* rather than simply as a problem that results from natural social, economic, or political processes or from the prejudice of individual white people. Such an understanding would imply that it is possible to change things through social action. (b) *Some basis for getting diverse groups to work together.* A multidimensional definition of racism, such as the one presented earlier, would do this on an intellectual level. In addition, this would need to be done on the organizational or political level. Jesse Jackson's attempt to form a "rainbow coalition" is one example. (c) *Effective tactics.* Just as in the civil rights movement, a variety of tactics would be called for, including: legal challenges to laws or public policies that sustain or promote racism; organized attempts to change public policies and institutional practices; and organizing the economic and political power of advocates of racial justice to pursue change.

(d) *Some basis for developing broad public support.* This is closely related to the first three requirements. In many ways, what is called for is mass education about racism as a social problem. I believe the dilemma and transformation positions have the most to offer here because they can point to things we already believe about "justice" and "equality" as part of the appeal, rather than having to call for the mass conversion of American society, as the indictment position does. Finally, I believe the transformation position provides the best basis for developing sustainable public support because it also would allow us to think about some of the ways that American ideals have been interwoven with or amenable to racist doctrines and practices. It would allow us to understand why past efforts to overcome various institutional forms of racism have been successful but have not been enough. While the transformation position does not lead to an optimistic view of American racism, it does allow hope.

Using a multidimensional understanding of racism, such as the one proposed earlier, would help us get some sense of whether our actions and the policies we advocate actually promote racial justice. Using it, we can see that creating racial justice means:

1. Eliminating or decreasing the separation of the "races" geographically, socially, and institutionally.
2. Eliminating or decreasing the subordination of "non-white" people in terms of their access to:

      a. basic life needs,
      b. high-quality public institutions, and
      c. structures for political freedom and power.
  3. Recognizing ''non-white'' people's ordinary status within the social order.
  4. Eliminating or decreasing the fear and avoidance on the part of both ''whites'' and ''non-whites.''
  5. Eliminating or decreasing the expectation and presence of violence.
  6. Eliminating or decreasing the rationalization of all of these.

Doing all of this is, of course, an immense task. But if individuals and groups can work together in sustained and systematic ways, some measure of racial justice can be achieved. Social problems call for social action.

Annotated Bibliography

The History of American Racism

DuBois, W. E. B. *The Souls of Black Folk*. Chicago: A. C. McClurg & Company, 1903. Various reprint editions are available. In this slim volume of essays, DuBois asserts "the problem of the Twentieth Century is the problem of the color line"; challenges the approach of Booker T. Washington, then *the* black leader; and describes what it means to be a black person in America.

Meier, August and Elliott Rudwick. *From Plantation to Ghetto*. Third edition. New York: Hill and Wang [1966], 1976. An "analytical, interpretive, and interdisciplinary history" of the major institutional forms of American racism.

Meier, August, Elliott Rudwick, and Francis L. Broderick, eds. *Black Protest Thought in the Twentieth Century*. Second edition. Indianapolis: Bobbs-Merrill [1965], 1971. A large collection of documents in which black Americans debate ways to combat American racism, with a focus on various organizations of protest.

Myrdal, Gunnar. *An American Dilemma*. New York: Harper & Row, 1942. A massive study of "the Negro problem and modern democracy" whose point of view became adopted by many in the civil rights movement.

Tussman, Joseph, ed. *The Supreme Court on Racial Discrimination*. New York: Oxford University Press, 1963. A useful selection of cases in eight areas: education, travel and dining, race and freedom of speech, the Japanese evacuation, discrimination and livelihood, restrictive covenants, juries, and voting.

The Civil Rights Movement

Anderson, Alan B. and George W. Pickering. *Confronting the Color Line*. Athens: University of Georgia Press, 1986. An examination of the coming apart of the national civil rights movement in Chicago in the mid- and late-1960s. An excellent complement to Morris's volume (below).

Collins, Sheila D. *The Rainbow Challenge: The Jackson Campaign and the Future of U.S. Politics*. New York: Monthly Review Press, 1986. An examination of Jackson's 1984 campaign for the presidential nomination of the Democratic party, set in the context of various U.S. movements for social change in the twentieth century.

Jackson, Jesse L. *Straight from the Heart*. Edited by Roger D. Hatch and Frank E. Watkins. Philadelphia: Fortress Press, 1987. A representative collection of Jackson's most important speeches and essays.

Malcolm X. *The Autobiography of Malcolm X*. With the assistance of Alex Haley. New York: Grove Press, 1964; and *Malcolm X Speaks: Selected Speeches and Statements*. New York: Merit, 1965. The best sources on the work and thought of Malcolm X.

Morris, Aldon D. *The Origins of the Civil Rights Movement: Black Communities Organizing for Social Change*. New York: Free Press, 1984. A thorough examination of the early years (1953-1963) of the civil rights movement.

Oates, Stephen B. *Let the Trumpet Sound: The Life of Martin Luther King, Jr*. New York: Harper & Row, 1982. A sensitive biography of King.

Washington, James Melvin, ed. *A Testament of Hope: The Essential Writings of Martin Luther King, Jr*. San Francisco: Harper & Row, 1986. The best collection of King's work available.

Williams, Juan. *Eyes on the Prize*. New York: Viking, 1987; and Carson, Clayborne et al., eds. *Eyes on the Prize: A Reader and Guide*. New York: Penguin, 1987. Companion volumes to the first year of the PBS television series on the civil rights movement.

Lowell W. Livezey
Princeton University

..

Social Ethics of War and Peace

■ ■ If peace were not a value, then war would not be a problem, action for peace would not be a responsibility, and foreign and military policy would not be matters for ethical reflection. But it is a value, both in the straightforward sense that nearly everyone does want it and in the more sophisticated sense that everyone should want it—because it is more humane, constructive, creative, civilized, even more efficient than war.

On the other hand, if peace were the only value, or if it clearly were the highest value, it would hardly require ethical reasoning, and it would be easy to achieve in practice because the reasons that people and nations fight would give way to the overriding considerations of peace. Since nothing would be "worth fighting for," conflicts either would be resolved nonviolently or conflicting parties would give in rather than go to war.

Peace is one value among many. This fact undermines the evangelical zeal of some peace advocates. It gives proponents of military strength rhetorical ammunition. It complicates the lives of responsible citizens. And it provides work for social ethicists. This fact presents the central problem not only for this essay but also for charting a responsible course for the United States in the international community.

The United States, by what it does or does not do in the international community, unavoidably affects the realization or loss of values other than peace. Such values include:

- the security from attack and political independence of many countries, including the United States itself

- the economic prosperity of many countries, including our own
- the accountability of governments to the people they govern
- the extension and enrichment of individual freedom in this and other countries
- the conservation of the ecosystem
- the increased sense of community among the world's people

There is, of course, disagreement about the relative importance of these values, about the degree to which the United States should seek to advance them, and about the means that should be employed. But few deny that security, prosperity, governmental accountability, individual freedom, ecological conservation, and world community *are values*—that they are conditions people both want and should want. And it will become clear as we proceed, if it is not already, that these values are inextricably linked to that of peace.

Social ethics is a disciplined way of thinking about how values like these might become reality and about how choices among them might be made when they cannot all be realized to the same extent at once. Since these social values can be realized only in the real world, social ethics examines them not only as abstract ideas but also as tangible choices about what a country, corporation, organization, or individual is going to do. For the most part, social ethics is concerned with choices about public policy, and it is in public policy that the possibilities of war and peace are shaped. Public policy, however, is constructed mainly in bits and pieces, not in grand choices between war and peace. It is the little choices—whether to intervene in Central America or to ratify a treaty on seabed mining or to build a more accurate nuclear missile—that shape the future, usually in ways that no one can predict.

Each of these choices depends in part on values, especially on the values of peace, prosperity, security, accountability, freedom, ecology, and community. But values do not give answers directly to policy questions. At first it may seem that those who value peace more than security or prosperity would be most likely to support disarmament and oppose military spending. Similarly, it may seem that those who are primarily devoted to ecological balance might be willing to discourage economic investment abroad even at the expense of future prosperity. But such choices are not as obvious as they seem, for they depend not only upon the values at stake but also upon

- *facts* of the situation—for example, how many weapons various countries already have or how fragile the ecological balance actually is, and
- *theories* of foreign policy—that is, explanations of what kind of military policy leads to peace or to war.

Among policymakers and the public, there is some dispute about the facts and about which theories best explain the causes and consequences of such common problems as war, dictatorship, and poverty. Citizens and organizations that advocate policies like disarmament and foreign aid not only affirm values but also depend upon facts and theories to justify their positions. This essay illustrates how facts, theories, and values can be integrated in a social-ethics analysis of the problem of war.

Detailed ethical analysis of particular choices requires a detailed review of the relevant facts. Some facts always are in dispute, and available information may be biased or inadequate, but the broad outline of the world situation is sufficiently clear and agreed upon for our introductory purposes here. Therefore, we shall proceed directly to a discussion of the four main theories that have guided U.S. foreign policy and continue to be followed by policymakers. Although these different theories recognize most of the same facts, they attribute different importance to different aspects of the world situation. Moreover, each theory assigns its own priorities to the various values at stake in any policy choice. So our purpose in this section will be to show how theories of foreign policy use facts and embody values as they make foreign policy, especially policies that affect the problem of war.

Finally, we shall consider how peace might be more effectively pursued. We shall do so as social ethicists; that is, we shall focus on alternatives for U.S. policy. We shall do so with due regard to the world situation (to the facts) and not attempt to engage in distortions or wishful thinking. We shall attempt to be explicit and honest about our theory of foreign policy, explaining why some facts are considered more crucial than others and how certain consequences—such as war or peace—are believed to result from some conditions or actions and not from others. Finally, we shall attempt to show how values other than peace would be affected by policies intended to enhance the likelihood of peace. We shall try to remember that it may not always be possible to promote all values equally, and if this is the case it is the ethicist's task at least to clarify the choices and possibly to recommend a solution. But we should also attempt creative definitions of policy so that different values can be pursued in concert. As Robert Gilpin wrote in the introduction to *War and Change in World Politics:*

> If peace were the ultimate goal of statecraft, then the solution to the problem of peaceful change would be easy. Peace may always be had by surrender to the aggressor state. The real task for the peaceful state is to seek a peace that protects and guarantees its vital interests and its concept of international morality.[1]

Theories of U.S. Foreign Policy[2]

In designing a foreign policy, it is extremely difficult to judge the consequences of particular actions and conditions. Or to put it another way, even if we know the priority goals—say, peace, prosperity, and freedom—it is difficult to know which actions will achieve them. One cause of this difficulty is the lack of relevant experience. There has been so little lasting peace that we must supplement limited experience with considerable speculation in order to describe the conditions that would make peace possible. Even the limited but crucial task of preventing nuclear war is made more difficult by the fact that nuclear wars never have occurred. As a result, we have no experience by which to judge how weapons perform or people behave under those nearly unimaginable circumstances.

Another factor is that with changing circumstances the experiences we do have are of questionable relevance. We know, for example, that Europe was mostly at peace for the century beginning with the Congress of Vienna (1815) and that during this time a "balance of power" was maintained among the major European states. But how similar is the world today to nineteenth-century Europe? Do the same circumstances now prevail that made the European balance possible one and a half centuries ago?

Even without a sufficient basis in experience, countries cannot avoid making judgments about the likely consequences of their actions. Even individuals and organizations that criticize foreign policy and call for change

---

[1]Robert Gilpin, *War and Change in World Politics* (New York: Cambridge University Press, 1981) 8.

[2]In this section I have made extensive use of Cecil V. Crabb, Jr., *Policy-Makers and Critics: Conflicting Theories of American Foreign Policy* (New York: Praeger Publishers, 1976), a book that is recommended for its much more thorough treatment of the subject than is possible in this essay. However, my analysis differs from Crabb's in some respects and should not be taken as a summary of his.

do so in the belief that different policies would produce better results. In the attempt to decide which policies are best by explaining and evaluating their consequences, *theories* of foreign policy are developed. In brief, a theory of foreign policy sets forth the goals and values it is possible and desirable for a country to achieve; the kind of national behavior (foreign policy and international conditions) conducive to those goals and values; and reasons why the proposed behavior and conditions can be expected to achieve the desired consequences.

In a pluralistic society like the United States, it is not surprising that citizens and policymakers disagree about which values are the highest, which goals are most important, and which policies would do most to achieve them. These disagreements are expressed in the conflicting theories that guide policymakers and critics. Four main theories have guided United States foreign policy and are still influential. The two oldest theories and the two that appear as opposite ends of the spectrum are *isolationism*—the view that America should avoid foreign involvement as much as possible—and *liberal interventionism*—the view that America should actively promote liberal (American) values abroad by a variety of means, including military force.

Two additional theories that have become important in the twentieth century are *political realism*—the view that the pursuit of national self-interest in a manner compatible with available power provides both a guide and a limit to foreign involvement—and *liberal supranationalism*—the view that transnational loyalties and institutions, especially laws, can govern the behavior of nations, limiting violence and increasing cooperation.

Each of these theories will be briefly described, followed by a brief look at the world situation from the standpoint of the theory.

Isolationism. For the first 150 years of national life, the United States was a profoundly isolationist country. Its policy was, as George Washington put it in his Farewell Address, to have "as little political connection (with foreign nations) as possible" and to "steer clear of permanent alliances with any portion of the foreign world."[3] This did not mean, however, that American policy was devoid of values. Rather, foreign entanglements were rejected precisely to secure and preserve the opportunity to develop the values for which the new republic had been founded:

---

[3]Quoted ibid., 1. Available in *The Writings* of George Washington from the original manuscript sources, 1745-1799 (Washington: GPO, 1940).

national independence, self-government, individual liberty, and economic progress. Participating in Europe's affairs not only would distract from the primary task of building a nation embodying these values, but would run the risk of corrupting the values themselves.

While some Americans believed their highest values should be adopted by the rest of the world, they sought to promote them only by the power of America's example. Even the First World War—justified to the public as "the war to end all war" and the war that would make the world "safe for democracy"—was viewed at the time as an exception to an otherwise unchangeable isolationist principle that was required by the unique events of the early twentieth century. Indeed, in the 1920s and 1930s America reverted to an isolationism as pure as ever. Isolationists affirmed a strong defense for the United States itself, and most affirmed the Monroe Doctrine of U.S. supremacy in the Western Hemisphere as essential to that security. But the defense policies were unilateral, required no alliances, and permitted no projection of power far from American shores.

As a result of World War II, the preeminence of the United States in world affairs, and the rise of global interdependence, the theory of isolationism has been greatly modified and limited. Few of its advocates propose complete withdrawal from world affairs. Nevertheless, the idea still is alive in various policy proposals, which have considerable support in government, citizens' organizations, and the general public.

Neoisolationists vary in their views of legitimate defense, though nearly all support a clear nuclear-deterrent capability and most support the NATO alliance (with the Europeans paying a bigger share). But especially since Vietnam and Watergate, the old isolationist argument has wider appeal: that foreign involvements undermine America's ability to achieve its best values at home. There is a widely shared fear that with growing military expenditures, concentration of ever-greater power in government, and the many frustrations of global relations, America no longer will be in control of her own destiny. In addition, there is the new isolationist belief that involvements abroad can undermine the American power of example and the good values the U.S. professes because of the tendency to be identified with dictatorships and aligned on the "wrong side" of revolutionary movements. Democracy, it is said, will be better off in the world if America stays home.

Liberal Interventionism. Although isolationism was the dominant American theory of foreign policy prior to World War II, there was also significant support for the view that the values the isolationists sought for America could not be secured for America alone. As the Century Group, an interventionist citizens organization in the 1930s, put it: "Democracy in North America could not long survive if totalitarians dominated the rest of the world."[4] In addition to the pragmatic judgment that isolationism would not secure American values at home, there also was a sense of moral responsibility to take these values to the rest of the world and the belief that America's "example" needed to be reinforced with tangible commitments abroad. "This nation of ours," wrote Secretary of State John Foster Dulles (for inscription in the wall of the Dulles Library of Princeton University), "is not merely a self-serving society but was founded with a mission to help build a world where liberty and justice would prevail."

The "liberal" values that provided the rationale for American intervention include national independence (Wilson's "self-determination"), self-government (preferably on the American or British model), individual liberty, free enterprise (capitalist or mixed-market economies), and more generally the belief in progress, science, and the perfectibility of the human institutions associated with "the American way of life."

The means of intervention have been quite diverse. Although direct military force is the most obvious and tangible, diplomatic pressure, economic sanctions and/or assistance, and even the role of unofficial parties at times have had significant impact. For example, in China around the turn of the century, American missionaries not only sought conversions to Christianity but also actively promoted social and political change. This was encouraged by the U.S. policy of "extraterritoriality" under which Americans charged with crimes in China would be tried in American courts.

Liberal interventionism came into its own, however, with World War II. As a leading isolationist, Senator Arthur H. Vandenberg, put it later, the Japanese attack on Pearl Harbor "ended isolationism for any realist."[5] Although nonmilitary forms of intervention still had a part, they were quickly overshadowed by the direct use of military force in World War II; in the policy of "containment" (of the Soviet Union) beginning in 1947; in the covert operations of the Central Intelligence Agency and the Special Forces beginning in the 1950s; and in the overt policy of "counterinsur-

---

[4]Crabb, *Policy-Makers and Critics*, 49.
[5]Ibid., 24.

gency'' initiated under President Kennedy and expanded during the Vietnam War. This period also brought increased nonmilitary efforts to promote the American way of life. The Marshall Plan, essential to the rapid reconstruction of Western Europe, reinforced the policy of containment while it made life a lot more pleasant for Europeans. The Peace Corps and the Alliance for Progress simultaneously contributed to the well-being of developing countries and complemented the counterinsurgency policies of the Kennedy and Johnson administrations.

Although isolationist sentiment has grown in the aftermath of Vietnam and Watergate, liberal interventionism is not dead. The nonmilitary version was enhanced in the early 1970s when, with the support of international human-rights advocates, laws were enacted requiring that foreign assistance and other economic ties favor countries with good records in political and civil rights and individual freedom. Although the Reagan administration does not support these laws, it still is required to implement them.

In the late 1970s and early 1980s, military intervention again received increasing public support. Increased economic and military aid to Central America has been advocated as a way to promote both national independence (from the Soviet Union) and the transition to democratic government. The Rapid Deployment Force, first announced by President Carter, is designed to intervene quickly in local conflicts where American values and interests are threatened. Military budgets under the Reagan administration have emphasized increasing U.S. ability to project power to all parts of the world.[6] Although both the Rapid Deployment Force and the Reagan military budget are seen by many as rather crass military opposition to the Soviet Union, the rationale for the opposition is that it will enable liberal values to prevail at home and abroad against the onslaught of totalitarianism that the Soviet Union is believed to promote.

From the liberal interventionist point of view, the relative military weakness of most of the world is what makes U.S. readiness to intervene so crucial. Although most countries of the developing and nonaligned world prefer freedom to totalitarianism and participate in the Western-oriented world-market economy, they would be helpless on their own in the face of Soviet military power. Thus the U.S. must be able to intervene to ensure that the freedom of these ''teeming masses'' will not be denied by Soviet

---

[6]Leslie Gelb, *New York Times*, 7 February 1982.

intervention. For this reason, U.S. military power must be sufficient not only to prevent a direct attack on our own territory and that of our formal allies but also to resist Soviet meddling in the affairs of others.

Political Realism. Every theory of foreign policy claims to be "realistic" in the literal sense of taking full account of the tangible realities of power and circumstance. But political realism is a school of thought that claims to take these realities more seriously and to avoid the temptation to let either ideals and generosity or pride and myopia obscure a clear view of what actually is possible. As a result, a country guided by political realism is supposed to achieve the full benefits of its power but will not get itself (and its neighbors) in trouble by pursuing objectives that are not in its best interest or that are beyond its capacity to achieve.

Political realism, often known by the German word *Realpolitik,* originally was associated with the ideas of Germany's Chancellor Bismark and the stable balance among Europe's major powers during his time, the nineteenth century. In the United States, the theory did not become a major part of the foreign-policy discussion until after World War II, when it was adapted to the new world situation by both scholars and diplomats, including George F. Kennan, Hans J. Morgenthau, and Henry A. Kissinger. They thought that realistic analysis and the prudent use of power could help the United States avoid the dangers inherent in isolationism and liberal interventionism and in the oscillation between the two that public opinion seemed to require.

Political realists are more likely to talk about "interests" than values, although the distinction is not an absolute one because an interest is what is good (or has value) for the country. Although in the United States interests have to be defined through the political process, realists believe that the main interests are so obvious and widely recognized that they should and will be pursued more or less consistently.

National security is the first and most crucial of these durable interests, and it in turn is closely associated with order and stability. For realists, power is exercised mainly in concert with others. Thus security typically depends upon orderliness in much of the world, not just the area around one's own territory. In the nineteenth century this mainly meant Continental Europe and England. Today it is taken, by different realists, to mean either the Atlantic community, the North Temperate Zone, or the whole world. In addition to stability on a regional basis, security also requires the prevention of a nuclear attack on the United States.

The second major persistent interest is the well-being of American society. Generally speaking, this is assumed to depend upon an international economic system favorable to trade, investment, and the purchase of raw materials. At the same time, a measure of self-sufficiency also is conducive to well-being. Realists may, for example, disagree about the priority between measures that would assure the external supply of oil and measures that would increase the energy self-sufficiency of the country. The well-being of society also depends upon a clean, balanced environment, a high level of cultural development, an optimal population size, and the preservation of democratic institutions—all of which have been sought by a combination of domestic and foreign policies.

Finally, it generally is assumed that America has an interest in a reasonably hospitable political environment abroad. This is not an affirmation of the "mission" to build a world of justice and liberty advocated by John Foster Dulles. Indeed, most political realists have little interest in the internal politics of other countries—how their governments treat their own people—except as this affects their attitude toward the United States. The promotion of international human rights in the Soviet Union or in Argentina is not a case advanced by political realists. Yet in some measure, and the measure is in dispute, internal politics do affect external relations. As a result, revolutionary change and the rise of leftist governments often are viewed by realists as contrary to American interests.

The balance of power is a central concept in the political-realist theory of international affairs. While "balance" does not require that power be equally shared, it must be decentralized, and the distribution must be stable. Thus political realists advocate "prudence in victory," illustrated by Henry Kissinger's counsel that Israel should not humiliate Egypt in the 1973 war. Political realists prefer that states prevent each other's expansion rather than escalate their power struggles at the expense of stability. This is illustrated by Kissinger's effort at strategic arms limitation talks (SALT), permitting the Soviet Union to attain rough equivalence with the U.S. rather than accept the destabilizing consequences of uncontrolled nuclear competition. In short, in this theory it is possible for a country to have too much power, or project power too far, for its own good. But, conversely, the failure to "balance" the power of an adversary also can lead to instability by providing an opportunity for aggression.

In the overall analysis, there is a rough balance of power between East and West, between NATO and the Warsaw Pact. But it is a precarious balance, one that could be upset by a breakthrough on either side in nuclear weaponry or by political change in regions where both the Soviet Union and the United States have interests (for example, if the Islamic revolution were to sweep across the Middle East). Political realists maintain that the best hope for peace is to try to consolidate and maintain the balance.

Balance of power is a concept that applies to major powers. This usually means strong military powers. So what of the small, poor, militarily weak countries where half of the world's people live? First, the needs, wishes, and interests of developing countries (except for China, because of its huge army) are not a major factor in the strategies of political realists. While these countries have to be heard at the United Nations and may need to be placated in return for the right to use their ports to buy their raw materials, they simply do not have enough power to count in the balance. Political realists, therefore, generally are not strong supporters of foreign assistance, are relatively unlikely to be concerned about local wars, and show relatively little interest in North-South politics.

Yet the weaker countries are not completely irrelevant, even from the perspective of political realism. Relations with them can be greatly beneficial to the more powerful countries, particularly if they exercise a measure of domination. Thus the relationships among major powers include certain ground rules about their relations with the rest of the world. In the purest form, the world is divided into "spheres of influence." For example, following World War II Eastern Europe was in the Soviet sphere of influence and Latin America was in the U.S. sphere. The rest of the world was more ambiguous, although the United States established itself militarily with a series of bases and alliances around the globe. It was, therefore, not expected that the Soviet Union would use military power to extend its influence in southern Asia, Africa, or Latin America. In this context, its recent role in Southeast Asia, Angola, Ethiopia, and Central America has been considered by realists to be expansionist and destabilizing.

However, this brings us to the final aspect of political realism to be considered: the view that the balance of power should reflect the realities of power (otherwise it will not be stable). Thus at the end of World War II the Soviet Union could project power overland to dominate Eastern Europe but not by sea to Southeast Asia or Africa. Thirty years later its "strategic reach," while still limited, is sufficient to support a measure of influence beyond Soviet borders. Thus, unless the U.S. and/or the countries of Africa and Asia themselves increase their military presence in these areas, political realism suggests that Soviet influence will increase. This is a destabilizing but inevitable adjustment to the increased relative power of one state within the system.

Liberal Supranationalism. Whereas political realists seek to reduce the status of liberal values in international relations, another group of theorists claims that these values should be expressed in the very structure of the international system and not simply in the goals of the states within the system. The heart of the idea is the rise of international law so that it will govern the behavior of states, preventing war and ensuring both security and freedom to sovereign states. Just as in the liberal democratic state, individuals were subject to the law, equal before the law, free and secure because of the law, and participants in making the law, so in the new world order states would participate freely, equally, and nonviolently in an international legal and political system. Moreover, while the states would be very diverse, and their right to govern themselves in diverse ways would be guaranteed (by the principle of sovereignty), the international system nevertheless would foster liberal values within the states as well. George F. Kennan, a "realist" critic of supranationalism, put the central idea succinctly: "It is the belief that it should be possible to suppress the chaotic and dangerous aspirations of governments in the international field by the acceptance of some system of legal rules and restraints."[7]

The purest expressions of supranationalism have been set forth by citizen organizations, especially the World Federalist organizations,[8] and by individual scholars such as Grenville Clark and Louis B. Sohn in *Introduction to World Peace through World Law.*[9] Unfettered by the immediate requirements of policy or by politically powerful opponents, in the 1940s and 1950s these organizations and individuals were able to contribute concepts of a new world order that then could be partially expressed in American policy. The most important example of this is the U.S. contribution to the design of the United Nations and American support for it during its first decade (1945-1955). The U.N. Charter pledged its members to "save

---

[7]George F. Kennan, *American Diplomacy* (Chicago: University of Chicago Press, 1951) 95.

[8]The principal national World Federalist organization now active in the United States is the World Federalist Association, Arlington, Virginia.

[9]Louis B. Sohn, *Introduction to World Peace through World Law* (Chicago: World Without War Publications, 1973).

succeeding generations from the scourge of war" by refraining from the use of force, "save in the common defense."[10] It guaranteed the sovereignty of states and provided for the "self-determination" of colonies and territories (that is, they were free to become sovereign states if they chose to do so). It also promised that member states would respect the fundamental rights and freedoms of their individual citizens, a pledge elaborated later in the Universal Declaration of Human Rights and a number of human-rights treaties. To ensure these promises, the United Nations founded a General Assembly, a Security Council, and a Secretariat to create and implement a detailed body of international law, requiring that states act in a manner consistent with their commitments under the Charter.

The classical liberal values of free enterprise and a market economy also guided American policymakers in constructing the international economic system following World War II. Both the International Monetary Fund and the World Bank (formally the International Bank for Reconstruction and Development) were designed to encourage international trade and investment with a minimum of government regulation. Moreover, these international financial institutions were designed and governed to favor countries whose domestic economies operated mainly on free-market principles.

Thus the United States and its allies, in a position of relative strength following World War II, were able to establish liberal values to a considerable degree in the new international political and economic institutions. But to establish values in the design and intent of institutions is not necessarily to realize them in practice. The major failure was the fact that, despite their commitments under the U.N. Charter, states did not refrain from the use of force. There have been more than 150 wars (defined as international military conflicts in which more than 1,000 people are killed) since the United Nations was formed. War may be "against the law," but neither the U.N. nor any other institution has the power to enforce the law. As a result, in America today there are many former federalists and disenchanted supporters of the United Nations who have concluded that one of the other theories, while second best, is needed to guide policy in the world as it actually is.

Nevertheless, the ideas of liberal supranationalists still have a part in the formation of United States foreign policy. First, the U.S. is, of course,

---

[10]United Nations Charter.

still a member of the U.N. even though there is little expectation that it will prevent war or help significantly to advance individual freedom. And to some administrations—most recently that of President Carter—the U.N. has been a positive expression of liberal values because it enabled militarily and economically weak states to participate on more or less equal terms with the more powerful. On the other hand, it was disturbing to liberals when an alliance of Third World countries used their equal status to get U.N. approval of a "New International Economic Order," which denied or distorted free-market principles.

Second, a new, somewhat more modest form of supranationalism emphasizes the creation and use of "functional" organizations. The European Economic Community, or "Common Market," is the most prominent example. While the EEC never was intended to regulate member states' use of force, it does limit their sovereignty over economic decisions in order to strengthen their economic power for their mutual benefit. At the global level, the World Health Organization, the Food and Agriculture Organization, the International Labour Organization, and many others serve important "functions" for the mutual benefit of their members. To make this possible, the members give up a little of their freedom of action (their sovereignty) by agreeing in advance to act in accordance with the agency's policy.

Supranationalism has not been very successful with respect to peace and security. However, its advocates point out that the rapid increase in international trade, travel, and communication, the global competition for scarce resources, and the universal problem of environmental decay all generate increased need for agencies to deal with these problems on a supranational basis. In the nuclear age, even a local war always involves the danger of escalation to a global level. Thus pragmatic necessity, rather than liberal ideals, may now provide the principal basis for supranationalism in world politics.

Taking Peace Seriously

Since nearly everyone affirms the value of peace, it is not surprising—although sometimes we forget—that all the main theories of foreign policy recognize peace as a goal. Yet for people and theories alike, peace has been a rather secondary goal, yielding in deference to the belief that war was necessary to preserve security, freedom, prosperity, national honor, or "the American way of life."

Peace also is the professed goal of most foreign-policy critics. Pacifists, for example, contend that peace can be realized if people—and nations—refuse to fight. Marxists claim that peace will be achieved through worldwide solidarity and the eventual triumph of the working classes. Many religious groups, following "theologies of liberation," pin their hopes for peace on achieving justice and community (shalom), which in turn will erode the motivation to violence.

These approaches to peace through pacifism, revolution, and shalom—approaches that guide a great deal of the American peace movement—will not be presented in this chapter. This is not to deny their moral legitimacy but rather to focus on perspectives and choices that actually could guide the U.S. foreign policy during the rest of the twentieth century. Since it is unlikely that a majority of Americans or American policymakers will become pacifists or Marxists or will come to believe in the perfectability of human community during this period, it seems appropriate to omit consideration of these points of view. Moreover, people motivated by these commitments to take foreign policy stands usually accept some form of the isolationist theory, believing that the less the United States does in world affairs the better.

This essay concludes with an exploration of how peace might become an essential goal of U.S. foreign policy—a goal that does not readily give way when other values are at stake. This is not an attempt to describe an ideal world in which weapons are completely eliminated and war no longer is a threat. Rather, it is an attempt, starting with the world as it really is, to see how the United States can act to minimize reliance on war in the short run and to generate conditions hospitable to a more durable peace in the long run.

This is not an essay about "peace at any price." It proceeds from the assumption that all of the values set forth in the opening pages—security, prosperity, governmental accountability, freedom, ecology, community, and peace—are legitimate, that none should be sacrificed in favor of the others. Moreover, we will explore only policy choices that reasonably could be expected to command public support: an essential prerequisite of a viable policy in the United States. For this reason, if for no other, an effective "peace policy" must show how it would advance the other values Americans generally believe in.

Finally, this exploration of how peace can be an essential goal of policy must present its own theoretical basis—its explanation of why, given the world situation in the 1980s, the proposed actions by the United States should have the desired consequences. While this exploration does not accept any of the main theories completely, it will respectfully borrow from each of them because they reflect the actual experience and traditional values of the United States in world affairs.

From this point, I am going to write in the first person—"I think, I believe, I propose"—to emphasize the personal judgment and responsibility at the heart of ethical choices about public policy.

I believe that during the next few years the United States should attempt to achieve its goals and exercise power by being more faithful to the liberal democratic values it has consistently professed throughout its 200-year history. While this does not mean it should be hostile—certainly not militarily—to totalitarian and authoritarian governments, it means that the U.S. should seek to enhance the security, freedom, and material well-being of individuals, whether or not their own governments approve. American military power should be maintained in the short run, but its use, if any, would be strictly defensive, and the active burden of policy would be shifted to economic and political instruments of power. While such a policy will seem naively idealistic to some (especially political realists) and chauvinistic to others (especially isolationists), I believe this is actually a way that the power to secure American interests can be enhanced. Let me set forth briefly what I think should be done and then explain why I think it would work.

The Ten Commandments of U.S. Foreign Policy

1. *Reward good behavior*. The United States should redefine its relationships with other countries, especially with developing and nonaligned countries. It should be clear that the countries to benefit most from relations with the United States will be those (a) whose governments are accountable to their citizens, (b) that have good or improving records of internationally recognized human rights, and (c) that have a reasonably equitable or improving distribution of income.

Although most Communist countries would not qualify, this policy would not imply a change in U.S. relations with them, except where liberalization programs are under way (such as Poland's Solidarity movement in 1980-1981). These countries do not, on balance, benefit from U.S. relations anyway. The big change would be felt in countries like Argentina, Zaire, South Africa, Pakistan, and Panama, where overall military and economic considerations have led to American support in spite of dreadful human-rights violations. Even Israel, itself a democratic country, would jeopardize U.S. assistance if it continued to stand in the way of self-government for and by Palestinians in the territories it has occupied since the 1967 war.

The U.S. would not be hostile to totalitarian and authoritarian states, but it would drastically curtail any benefits such states might otherwise have received or be receiving. And it would be quick to reward liberalization within these countries with hospitable relations, mutually beneficial trade, capital investment, and economic assistance.

2. *Help democratic change agents.* The United States should reinforce the first principle by recognizing and encouraging nongovernmental representatives of the people in authoritarian and totalitarian countries. This is, of course, a sensitive and risky business because it can contribute to the destabilizing of another government. Yet liberal principles hold that people, not governments, have the ultimate claim to political legitimacy, and the United States will need some way of affirming its identification with the world's people. The possibilities include entertaining human-rights leaders (say, from the Soviet Union, South Africa, and Bolivia) at the White House; having open communications with governments in exile and other organizations of nationals opposed to despotic governments or occupying states; and providing financial or technical assistance to trade unions, human-rights organizations, independent news media, and other organizations contributing to a more open and democratic society. It would be absolutely essential that this "intervention" be completely open and nonviolent. Otherwise, it would violate the very principles it sought to advance.

3. *Increase economic assistance.* The U.S. should increase dramatically (at least tenfold) its economic assistance to the developing countries, especially to those that (a) have the greatest need, (b) have viable programs of development, (c) distribute economic benefits equitably, thereby improving the well-being of the poorest, and (d) have good or improving records in international human rights. These criteria do not always go together; some countries will be strong on some and weak on others. U.S. assistance policy therefore would have to make difficult judgments. But overall the policy would be guided by the principle of real benefits to *people* and to governments that do their best to provide for the security, freedom, and

material well-being of their citizens. Although special circumstances would be taken into account, this general standard would not be compromised simply because a government was a good ally in the global power struggles of the United States.

4. *Reform the international economy.* The U.S. should support changes in the international economic system that would generally enhance the openness and competitiveness of the world market but should provide some special protection for developing countries. In particular, it would support programs that would (a) help stabilize the prices of commodities that are the main exports of developing countries, (b) provide low-cost credit for sound economic programs, and (c) encourage developing countries' participation in the exploitation of resources—such as those in the deep-sea bed—that are properly considered the common heritage of humanity, not the possessions of particular countries. These measures, similar to American laws that protect small businesses and limit monopolies, actually would enhance the openness of the world market by limiting the tendency for economic power to be concentrated in a few countries and enterprises.

5. *Expand mutually beneficial trade and investment in developing countries.* The U.S. and enterprises under its jurisdiction should expand commercial relations with developing countries on terms clearly in the best interest of their people as well as ours. This would require U.S. policy that would regulate corporate activity in developing countries: for example, to prohibit investments that, although beneficial to the upper classes, would dislocate large numbers of peasants or destroy their source of food. To offset the corporate disadvantages of such regulation, the government might need to provide incentives to trade and invest through such existing public agencies as the Export-Import Bank or the Overseas Private Investment Corporation.

6. *Create substitutes for interests that now require military defense.* The United States and its allies should reduce their dependence on interests that require a military defense—especially where that defense might require nuclear weapons and/or collaboration with antidemocratic governments. Probably the most dramatic example of this is the dependence of Western Europe and Japan, and to a lesser extent of the United States, on oil from the Persian Gulf countries. I do not mean to suggest that the Soviet Union is about to commandeer the oil fields of Iran, Iraq, and Saudi Arabia, but the combination of geography and shaky local governments surely makes the oil fields impossible for Western governments to defend. Thus

it would be wise for them to invest in a combination of alternative energy sources—coal, hydro, solar, biomass, and nuclear—and conservation rather than relying so heavily on the military defense of militarily indefensible resources. The alternatives will be expensive. But the West's military commitments in the Middle East are expensive, too, and they entangle us with some of the least democratic governments in the world.

7. *Reduce military sales and assistance to antidemocratic countries.* The U.S. should gradually but substantially reduce military sales and assistance, especially to countries (a) whose military services function primarily to control their own populations and to keep existing governments in power and (b) that seek to dominate neighboring countries or peoples. In the process of establishing new nation-states, many governments attempt to use military repression as a substitute for popular consent. While military assistance usually is justified as necessary to prevent external aggression, it often makes it easier for a government to perpetuate unpopular military rule. While military assistance should not be withdrawn without warning, it also should not continue indefinitely. The threat of a future aid cutoff also should be an incentive to get on with democratization. If the government eventually falls, at least the United States would not be marked as a supporter of the "old guard."

8. *Help reform and strengthen international institutions.* The United States increasingly should use, strengthen, and enhance the legitimacy of international institutions, including the United Nations. However, it should not stop criticizing the United Nations, or the role of other countries in it, in response to violations of its own purposes and principles. Official endorsement of a war, for example, by an institution created to "rid mankind of the scourge of war," need not evoke American support. But as an overall policy, the United States should recognize that its own principles of national sovereignty, self-determination, and the rule of law require a forum where the sovereignty of even weak and poor nations is fully recognized. In brief, this would mean that the United States would (a) use the veto with great restraint, (b) refrain from derogatory remarks about the institution, and (c) use the agencies of the United Nations system as much as possible in efforts to promote human rights, economic development, environmental conservation, and general human well-being.

9. *Maintain military forces but anticipate reductions.* The United States should maintain its current conventional military forces while it begins to implement the economic and political policies described above. Signifi-

cant unilateral reductions before the nonmilitary policies have been put in effect easily could be mistaken as a signal that the United States planned a more isolationist policy before its new nonmilitary, interventionist role became evident. This could encourage aggressive military operations by the Soviet Union and its allies or by anti-American revolutionary forces.

However, United States military planning, research and development, and procurement should anticipate a future reduction in U.S. military presence around the globe. Specifically, it should refrain from investing in future military developments and expansion. The funds saved would be a major source of the economic assistance proposed above.

10. *Move toward a "no first use" nuclear-weapons policy.* The United States should announce that a "no first use" nuclear-weapons policy will go into effect within two years and should immediately redefine both nuclear and conventional strategy to anticipate this change. Wherever this would leave a severe imbalance of power (because opposing conventional forces were greatly superior), the U.S. and its allies could either upgrade their own conventional forces or (preferably) negotiate reductions in their opponents' forces.

The "no first use" policy would reduce U.S. reliance on nuclear weapons so that their only function would be to deter a Soviet nuclear attack. This would require only that the United States be sure it could retaliate if attacked, not that it be able to engage in an extended nuclear war. Accordingly, it could abandon plans for such weapons as the MX missile and the Trident submarine-launched missile and engage in arms-control negotiations with the goal of limiting arms on the basis of parity or rough equivalence. It then would not have to continue the nuclear competition as an extension of the overall power struggle with the Soviet Union. Although the Soviet Union might seek to take advantage of this policy and develop a "first use" capability of its own, it should know the futility of such an effort because of America's obvious ability to re-enter the competition.

This policy of nuclear-weapons restraint should be coupled with a strict nuclear nonproliferation policy. Nuclear-energy technology should be available only to countries that ratify the Nuclear Non-Proliferation Treaty and accept "full-scope safeguards" against the development of nuclear weapons. American willingness to forgo some of the political muscle from its nuclear arsenal (by adopting a "no first use" policy) should make developing countries more willing to forgo the short-term political advantages they might achieve by having a small collection of nuclear weapons.

Social Ethics and the
Theory of Foreign Policy

This decalogue does not, of course, provide a blueprint for a world without war or even a complete map of how to get to such a world. But I believe it does define a kind of national behavior and a set of standards for policy choices that would lead in a peaceful direction. Moreover, it is an approach that would do fully as much as any other known policy to provide for the security, freedom, and material well-being of the United States and the rest of the world. Peace, it will turn out, is good for freedom and prosperity. And the promotion of freedom and well-being abroad is a source of power in the pursuit of peace. Here is why.

1. *Peace is becoming a most compelling value.* The reasons for viewing peace as an essential, rather than expendable, goal are becoming more compelling and are accepted by an increasing percentage of the American public. First, in any military competition, there is danger of nuclear war. This danger increases with the design of nuclear weapons for fighting as well as deterring nuclear wars. Second, the rising costs of the military institutions required to carry out current policies not only compete with the welfare of the poor but undermine the health and vigor of our entire economy. Third, the expanding military institutions and the priority given to national security also cause a concentration of power and a legitimation of secrecy inconsistent with democratic values and limited government. In short, they threaten the ''American way of life.'' Finally, the resort to military power abroad often represents the failure of political power based on consent. Thus even when American military power opposes antidemocratic forces, it also supports antidemocratic governments, thereby losing the fragile justification it otherwise might have had.

The fact that a rapidly increasing part of the American public also is insistent on peace—without claiming to know how to achieve it—is an important factor in itself. None of the traditional theories, or the policies based on them, can now command the public consensus needed for any policy to be effective. Unwilling to lose or appear second best, yet also unwilling to intervene or risk nuclear war, the American public is in a quandary about what the U.S. role in world affairs should be. The possibility of war brings this deep ambivalence to the surface. The possibility of peace without loss of purpose could help rebuild the consensus we need.

2. *U.S. power comes from many sources; it can be enhanced by faithfulness to our own best values.* Everything I have proposed recognizes that military force can have a tremendous impact on the course of events and that sometimes it is decisive. I also have taken into account that the withdrawal or reduction of military power by one country can provide an opportunity for others to use military force. I am, in fact, rather similar to the political realists in my analysis of the way military aggression is prevented: by maintaining a rough "balance of power." Accordingly, I have not proposed significant reductions in the immediate deployment of forces.

I have differed from realist and other traditional theories, however, in the emphasis I place on nonmilitary sources of power. In particular, I have claimed that U.S. power to pursue its legitimate interests and advance its values can be enhanced through a number of nonmilitary measures that will increase the friendship and cooperation of a very large part of the world's people who now see America as an adversary. I have done so for five quite different but mutually reinforcing reasons. First in the U.S.-Soviet competition, the principal stakes are the independence and cooperation of countries not directly allied to either superpower but upon which one or both superpowers depend in a variety of ways. Second, although military force is one means of ensuring that small, weak countries are independent (of the Soviet Union) and cooperative (with the U.S.), this means has limited and diminishing utility. The Vietnam experience should have taught us this.

Third, the attitude of a country's population always is important and often is decisive in determining that country's relations with others. This is primarily because of the population's tremendous capacity, over the long haul, to resist domination either by its own government or by a foreign country. Fourth, since World War II, American power has been spent and is now being eroded by collaboration with governments whose principal military problem is how to control their own populations. Finally, American power will be enhanced if it can be used on the side of popular sentiment or to evoke that sentiment. If we want to use a country's port, buy its bauxite, or sell it its first computer, we will do well to have the support of the country's people, not only of its government.

In proposing a number of "liberal" measures designed to enhance human freedom and well-being, I have attempted to take account of the ways they could serve as a source of power and thus as a substitute for military power. Some of these measures are risky and costly; this is not a proposal for "domestic priorities" but for a "global Marshall Plan." Yet if we consider the cost of the Vietnam War and the risk of another one—not to mention the cost and risk of a nuclear war—a foreign assistance budget of $100 billion may not seem so extravagant.

3. *Liberal values are good and should be promoted nonviolently.* My argument assumes that liberal values are good. They are not the only good values or even the best values, and I have not proposed that they be imposed upon others by force or that they always be implemented in pure form. Like all general principles, these need to be adapted to actual conditions. But the idea that the United States should be engaged in vigorous, nonmilitary ideological competition with the Soviet Union and other totalitarian and authoritarian states around the world is essential to my argument. There are two reasons for this.

First, although liberal values at times are defended by military force, they also severely limit the purposes for which the use of force is justified and the circumstance under which it can be effective. Authoritarian governments that abort the rule of law, deny human rights, defend inequality, and govern without consent—governments that flagrantly deny liberal values—cannot be defended in the name of liberal values. Moreover, while "the will of the people" often is difficult to determine, it is clear that it cannot knowingly be denied by force without contradicting the (liberal) principle of consent. Indeed, force, in and of itself, represents the failure of governance by consent and the denial of freedom. Therefore, while military force might prevent other military force from destroying governments based on consent, it cannot create such governments. It is much more capable of reinforcing governments that are themselves based on force.

Second, liberal values are widely accepted, both in this country and throughout the world. Most opposition to these values is in the form of claims that exceptions are necessary because of extenuating circumstances. For example, the Soviet Union's constitution guarantees the freedoms it regularly denies; Guatemala claims only to torture people when necessary for the survival of the nation. Many socialists are not opposed to liberal values but want to extend them to the economic realm. Because of their wide acceptance, these values can be the basis for a national consensus on foreign policy and for international cooperation in the direction of a more peaceful world.

Both the liberal interventionists and the liberal supranationalists share my affirmation of liberal values and my conviction that actively promoting them can be a source of power for eventually achieving world peace. But I believe that they both fail to appreciate fully the implications of these values for the late-twentieth-century world.

Liberal interventionism is overconfident of the capacity of military power to establish self-government and insufficiently sensitive to the tendency of military power to encourage military dictatorships. It may be possible in principle for the Marines to "teach the Latin Americans to elect good men," but in practice it rarely happens.

The liberal supranationalists, on the other hand, are overconfident about the capacity of international law to control the behavior of nation-states in an age of both nationalism and militarism. In the end, I agree, as every liberal must, that law is the only viable alternative to violence, that international law must be the alternative to war. But the law must be based primarily upon consent, and that in turn depends upon the widely shared judgment that the rule of law is in the common good. This simply has not been the case—even for liberals—and it cannot be wished, any more than it can be forced, into reality.

The ideal of "world peace through world law" may not be more than a generation or two away. Thus the United Nations and other international institutions that anticipate it should be supported, strengthened, and improved. My proposals attempt to do this. But for now, the limitations for these institutions must be recognized, as the political realists do best, and policy should be devoted primarily to adhering scrupulously to liberal principles in relationships among nation-states.

4. *With a little regulation, and a little incentive, private enterprise will be the principal answer to material needs.* Every country has an interest in the health of its economy. This is essential to the well-being—probably to the bare subsistence—of its poorest people and to the prosperity of its elites. I also have tried to take account of the fact that national wealth does not guarantee the well-being of individuals and to assert that liberal values require concern for individuals. While free-enterprise purists (including liberal interventionists and political realists) would oppose the regulations I advocate, the fundamental point about my proposals is their reliance on corporate power and the freedom of the world market. The tangible wealth—the goods and services—created through my approach would be primarily the product of private enterprises. And although many of the

countries involved would have "mixed" economies—partly private and partly governmental—the world economy would continue to be a market economy, regulated only slightly by international agreements.

While liberal values normally are associated with free enterprise, I have proposed a reliance on capitalism rather reluctantly and mainly for other reasons. My reluctance follows from capitalism's relatively poor record at distribution. Yet I believe that, with regulation, capitalism still is the best hope for a prosperous, well-fed world in the late twentieth century. I say this for three reasons. First, at the global level (economic relations among states), a market economy is the only thing possible. A planned economy presupposes a dominant central government, which is impossible at the global level. Therefore, the main dynamics inevitably will be the free market, with enough international agreements to prevent excessive concentration of power and to help small, poor countries become full participants in the world system of production, distribution, and consumption.

Second, at the level of nation-states, where production takes place, it simply is a historical fact that it is the capitalist states that have generated enough wealth to be able to finance development programs in poorer countries. Although the oil-rich countries of the Middle East and the Soviet Union can provide some of the needed funds, the big money is in North America, Western Europe, and Japan. Third, in these big-money countries, the big money is mostly in the hands of private enterprise, and the only way to get it is to offer a profit. Therefore, while foreign assistance can be and should be increased, funds for development will become available primarily through trade and investment.

My proposals are realistic about the preeminence of private enterprise in the world, as well as in national, economies. They also recognize that progress toward economic well-being for the world's poor people and countries not only is good for humanitarian reasons but also is a source of goodwill toward countries that help make the progress possible. Thus I have sought to show how private enterprise as well as public resources could be engaged by U.S. policy in the task of building a more prosperous world.

5. *Although security depends both upon arms and upon good political relations, it is the latter that will produce positive results.* My "10 Commandments" for taking peace seriously are very serious about security—just as serious as any of the main theories, and I believe more likely to be successful. There is, of course, no absolute security; the practical problem is how to get as much security as possible. Although I accept the conven-

tional wisdom—identified mainly with the realists but actually incorporated in all the main theories—that the threat of war can help prevent war, I lean more toward the fact that the threat of war is also a source of insecurity. The tendency of wars to escalate, the possibility that they could reach the nuclear level, the loss of international good will resulting from the appearance of being a bully, the erosion of one's economy from the allocation of scarce resources for military purposes—in all these ways, war and the preparation for war are threats to American national security. While backers of the other theories would not deny this completely, I believe they inadequately take it into account.

Without advocating significant curtailment of our military, I have advocated restraint in its use, coupled with a vigorous increase in nonmilitary ways of pursuing interests and purposes. My proposals rest on certain factors implicit in the foregoing analysis but not yet identified. First, the physical security of the United States is not in jeopardy except for the possibility of a nuclear attack by the Soviet Union. While the capacity to retaliate with a devastating second strike—a capacity the U.S. has and will continue to have—is the only means of "deterring" an attack, my "no first use" policy would further reduce any Soviet incentive to launch an attack. Second, United States security should be understood more broadly to include the resources, relationships, and privileges upon which we depend for the well-being of our country and people. This includes imports of oil and other raw materials, use of shipping lanes and ports around the world, and trade and communication with a variety of countries. Our security in this broader sense cannot be taken for granted. It depends upon the goodwill and cooperation of the governments and people whose ports and oil are needed and upon the noninterference of other great powers, especially the Soviet Union. The assertive nonmilitary policies proposed are designed to do all that is possible to evoke the needed goodwill and cooperation, which in turn would make interference by others more difficult and costly.

My proposals and the assumptions behind them are not completely new, but taken together they constitute a novel approach to national security. The "no first use" policy, at least with respect to Europe, has been proposed by political realists and is not inconsistent with the other theories. It really is just a pure form of nuclear deterrence, in which nuclear weapons are available to deter only nuclear (not conventional) attacks. The need for goodwill and cooperation to secure oil, ports, and communication is recognized by all the other theories except isolationism. The Vietnam War was often described as a struggle for the hearts and minds of the people. However, I believe liberal interventionism and political realism greatly overestimate the capacity of military force to command the needed cooperation and underestimate its tendency to be counterproductive. On the other hand, the liberal supranationalists' confidence in international law and cooperative agencies is premature. Therefore, while the presence of military force is essential for the foreseeable future, the big investment in our security should be in nonmilitary measures to enhance the freedom and well-being of the "wretched of the earth."

"Taking peace seriously" should be read with caution. It is one person's attempt to think through an approach to United States foreign policy that treats peace as an essential goal. It reflects many of that person's commitments—particularly the liberal values that inform the policy proposals—which will not be shared by others engaged in social ethics. Everyone must invest himself or herself in the task and, in the end, take responsibility for its conclusion and recommendations. Since no one can be sure of the way to peace, it will be well if many of us join the search for it.

Annotated Bibliography

Studies of the International System

Koehane, Robert O. *After Hegemony: Cooperation and Discord in the World Political Economy*. Princeton: Princeton University Press, 1984. An important presentation of the theory of "international regimes." This contemporary theory reflects many of the ideas expressed in the foregoing essay as "liberal" and "supranational."

Mische, Patricia and Gerald Mische. *Toward a Human World Order*. New York: Paulist Press, 1977. A highly readable presentation of "supranationalist" ideas and ideals. It sets forth a spiritual concept of humanity as part of the basis for its theory of the state and of international relations.

Morgenthau, Hans J. *Politics among Nations*. New York: Alfred A. Knopf, 1949. A classic textbook representing the "realist" theory of international relations.

Economic Development, Human Rights, and Disarmament

Forsythe, David P. *Human Rights and World Politics*. Lincoln: University of Nebraska Press, 1983. Shows how the United Nations, national governments, and nongovernmental organizations interact on issues of human rights. It is a clearly written overview of human rights and also serves as an example of one form of "liberal supranationalism."

Geyer, Alan. *The Idea of Disarmament*. Elgin IL: Brethren Press, 1982. Presents both a political analysis and an ethical/theological argument for disarmament in language accessible to the lay reader.

Hoffman, Stanley. *Duties beyond Borders*. Syracuse NY: Syracuse University Press, 1981. Explains why both individuals and states have responsibilities for other individuals and states. A very readable set of essays about the foundations of both human rights and development as aims of foreign policy.

Sewell, John W., Richard E. Feinberg, and Valerina Kallab, eds. *U.S. Foreign Policy and the Third World: Agenda 1987-1988*. New Brunswick NJ: Transaction Books, 1988. Presents essays and statistical data about Third World development and the U.S. role as a support and a hindrance. A new edition is published nearly every year.

Shue, Henry. *Basic Rights: Subsistence, Affluence, and U.S. Foreign Policy*. Princeton: Princeton University Press, 1980. Argues that a minimal level of food, shelter, and clothing are fundamental rights and should be aims of U.S. foreign policy. The argument is made primarily in terms of liberal political philosophy.

Perspectives from Religion, Ethics, and Political Theory

Bainton, Roland. *Christian Attitudes toward War and Peace*. Nashville: Abingdon Press, 1980. A historical survey that is virtually a classic in its own right.

Sharp, Gene. *The Politics of Nonviolent Action*. Boston: Porter Sargent, 1977. A three-volume exposition of the theory of effective political struggle by nonviolent means. The argument proceeds from political theory and historical analysis. The general perspective has much in common with the preceding essay.

Walzer, Michael. *Just and Unjust Wars: A Moral Argument with Historical Illustrations*. New York: Basic Books, 1977. A complex argument for the relevance of moral reasoning about wars, including such ''modern'' forms of warfare as nuclear threats and terrorism. Difficult going, but worth the effort.

Further Bibliographical Resources

Woito, Robert. *To End War*. New York: Pilgrim Press, 1982. An extensive and thoroughly annotated bibliography of books and pamphlets dealing with all aspects of international relations, political conflict, and political violence.

Koson Srisang
Ecumenical Coalition
on
Third World Tourism

▪▪

Religious Recovery
and Social Change in Thailand

A lone bamboo
  makes not the fence;
True community depends
  on people's participation.

The Problem

▪▪ The traditional Thai social order was grounded on an ideal of Buddhist kingship. The royal power, which by tradition is identical with the sovereign power of the state, is legitimized in terms of the king's great merit and moral preeminence as a pious religious man, on the one hand, and in terms of his military prowess and organizational genius, on the other. To be sure, the conception of kingship has undergone numerous internal developments since its establishment in A.D. 1238. Yet the identity of the people and the sense of social order did center around the symbol of kingship for seven centuries.

This long continuity of the Thai state as a Buddhist community, perceived and organized in terms of the absolute yet compassionate Buddhist kingship, was finally broken on 24 June 1932 when a revolutionary coup d'état took place. By that revolution, a Western-style democratic order was to have replaced the so-called absolute monarchy. But for a variety of reasons, the new democratic vision has not yet been fulfilled. Furthermore, although the ideal of democracy has been generally accepted, several competing claims regarding the best formula for this democracy have characterized Thai political history in the last fifty years. As a result, Thai politics during this period has been marked by numerous coups, each of which claimed to have brought into being a new and "most appropriate" democratic constitution for the country. All the while, those inspired by the Marxist vision and ideology, championed by the outlawed Communist party of Thailand, have also staked their claim that their way is the only solution. The struggle goes on.

In short, the question of the most viable social order for Thailand in the modern world is far from being settled. At the same time, it is clear that the condition of the Thai people today, especially the situation of the poor and powerless majority, has become increasingly unbearable. The sad experience is that following the West has led to more misery. There exists today a double crisis, of justice and of order. Regarding this fact, everyone from the king to the villager agrees. How to deal with it is the greatest challenge.

Where do we turn for wisdom and power in order to combat the threats of death on the one hand and to recover the power of life on the other? Our own cultural heritage and folk wisdom is the answer, or at least is an indispensable part of it. In this paper I shall pursue this from the perspective of political ethics, understood as the exercise of power for the sake of creating a participatory, and therefore just, society.

Noble efforts have been and are being attempted by generations of Thai leaders. I myself have taken a modest part in the form of a doctoral dissertation, "Dhammocracy in Thailand: A Study in Social Ethics as a Hermeneutic of Dhamma" (University of Chicago, 1973). But most of these efforts have focused on the national level and largely have viewed things from the top down. The voices and views from the bottom have been ignored. This is a pity. This paper is, therefore, a modest attempt to recover some of the folk wisdom as an essential element in the recovery and reconstitution of a viable Thai political vision. In doing this, the focus will be on Isan or Northeast Thailand, the region to which I belong. While a full-blown treatment of the subject will have to await another occasion, my purpose here is simply to explore a new possibility and to introduce another method that I believe merits careful consideration.

What are the causes of this double crisis of justice and order in Thailand today? It seems to me that the root cause of this double crisis has to do with the breakdown of comprehensive fundamental thought, the lack of vision and ethical courage, and the ascendency of the ethic of self-seeking and greed. Distortion, concealment, exploitation, oppression, monopoly, and exclusion—all these have rendered poor people objects without real voice or meaningful participation in the decisions that affect their lives and destinies.

Poverty and Marginalization

To be sure, these things have happened before in our past. Still, their modern expressions in the forms of extreme poverty, the systematic denial or violation of human rights, the denial of human dignity, the concentration of wealth and power in the hands of the few, and the resultant social injustice are all too evident and intolerable. Yet an increasing number of the poor, the voiceless, the alienated, and the marginalized have become more conscious of their plight and power. While they might have accepted their lot without much complaint in the past, people today have begun to struggle. They have begun to organize and to realize their potential. Their movements to say no to oppression and injustice and to say yes to liberation and human dignity have sprung up to mark the contemporary historical vitalities. As a result, contradictions and conflicts have intensified with varying degrees of violence, the most notorious of which was the brutal massacre of students at Thammasat University in October of 1976. The drama is still unfolding, and it is the common people who suffer the most.

Let us dwell on the issue of poverty for a little while. In Thailand, a variety of views persists. For example, many if not most villagers still say that their plight is the result of their own karma, the inevitable consequence of their sins or bad deeds in this life or in previous incarnations. Most government officials are quick to maintain that the villagers are poor because they are lazy. This, of course, is not true, or at least it is not the root cause. The ruling technocratic, aristocratic, military, and business elite say that Thailand and Thai people are poor because we have not yet "caught up" with the West. Furthermore, they say that "communist traitors" have hindered their imported plans for "national development." Political parties—when they are allowed to exist (which has been no more than a few years between military coups)—say that the situation is bad because they are not in power. The underground Communist party says that the foreign imperialists (especially the Americans) and their "runnings dogs" (the Thai rulers) have conspired to rob both Thai national sovereignty and national resources.

While it is easy to dismiss these views as mere rhetoric or propaganda, it is more difficult to nail down the nature and cause of poverty in Thailand. The government-appointed Working Group on Rural Development, having carefully reviewed Thai experience in national development during the last twenty years, concluded:

> From both economic and ethical perspectives, uneven development and poverty are the country's main problems. These problems have accelerated and are extremely dangerous to national security. Uneven development and poverty are structural problems. No stop-gap solutions will work. They are rooted in the national development strategy itself. That is, the strategy which has emphasized economic growth, resulting in fact in creating more gaps between the rich and the poor as well as in making poverty unbearable.

The Working Group therefore has recommended a new strategy for rural development. It should be comprehensive, based on the local reality of the villages, focus on the poorest areas, promote the quality of life, and encourage people's participation—thereby helping villagers learn to solve their own problems and eventually become self-reliant.

The Political Dimension

We are a constitutional monarchy, with the king as the symbolic yet very powerful head. The present constitution provides for both the elected Assembly and the appointed Senate, chosen by the prime minister (who need not be an elected member) and approved by the king. Although the constitution discourages too many political parties, more than ten parties competed in the 1983 general elections.

Nevertheless, the combination of the military, the aristocracy, the Thai business elite, and the foreign business and geopolitical interests effectively controls the power. The students, the workers, and the farmers have been effectively checked. With the Kampuchea crisis, the Communist party seems to be in disarray. Most of the 3,000 students who joined them after the 1976 massacre have left. The army has claimed victory over the guerrillas. Things appear quite calm.

The plight of the poor is worse, though. Extrajudicial executions continue, with more sophistication and effectiveness. Yet the people, in Isan and elsewhere, will not give up. The struggle continues.

This, then, is the context in which we seek to recover the Thai cultural heritage, focusing on Isan as a basis for our political vision.

The Religious Dimension

The problem is not merely economic or political; it is fundamentally religious. Religion refers to the divine dimension of human life. This divine dimension is experienced most fully at the traumatic moments in human life and history. This experience of divinity has both personal and communal dimensions. When it happens, humans become aware of their power and limitations, their freedom and submission, their independence and obedience. This divine experience often defies verbalization. It happens when people meditate, when they suffer together, when they celebrate, when they grieve over death or similar losses.

Human experience—religious or otherwise—always takes place in a particular time and space. Consequently, temporal and spatial factors do provide materials that help to give form to a particular human experience or a series of similar experiences. In time, the divine dimension of human experience becomes symbolized. This religious symbolism then mediates human life in the world.

While experiencing the sacred, people become aware of their power and limitations, their freedom and compassion, their identity and obedience. The fullest possible articulation of the profundity of the divine dimension of human experience—whether in the form of myths, dreams, folk tales, or theology—may be called a religious vision. It is precisely this religious vision that orders the human community. That is, it constitutes the community, unites its members, underlies its history, motivates its historiography, emanates its power and authority, and provides its sense of identity and integrity, honor and destiny.

Everything religious begins and ends with human life. Therefore, the basic necessities for life—such as food, shelter, clothing, and medicine—are essentially religious in character. This is why these necessities are dominant in religious visions.

Also, religion and politics are two sides of the same coin. Each, however, has its own integrity. Politics is not something divorced from religion or the religious vision. In fact, politics refers to the application or translation of the religious vision into concrete realities, mediated by power. As such, the authority of political power is nothing more than the religious vision itself. Power therefore includes knowledge of the religious vision, religious symbolism, and the human capacity to act in order to actualize the religious vision.

This is true in both the Christian and Buddhist traditions. Religion, then, is the most profound dimension of life and history. It is precisely that dimension whereby humans realize the fullness of their humanity in the self-less dedication of themselves for others. In the Thai Buddhist tradition, the ultimate motivation for this selfless dedication is symbolized by the term *compassion*. Compassion is a quality of life where all beings are recognized and respected as they are. When persons or a people develop or attain this state of being—in attitude, thought, and action—they have gained freedom. They have attained what the Buddha calls nirvana, the ultimate goal or eschatology. Thus the Buddhist vision is characterized by freedom and compassion. This vision is the source, foundation, motivation, and criterion for Buddhists in their ideal exercise of power or in Buddhist politics.

Sadly, in contemporary Thailand, this connection between religious vision, the necessities of life, and political power appears in a distorted form. In contemporary Thailand, the Western religious vision has become corrupted into an imperialistic vision based on greed: the love of money (and profit) and the idolatry of the self. This greed leads to the concentration of wealth and power, which has its own dynamics (the law of the market) and ideology (capitalism, both private and state).

When this Western religious vision based on greed conceals, distorts, or debases the community, injustice and oppression prevail. People are overtaxed, their dignity is robbed, their wives and daughters are raped, their sons are taken away, their land is snatched, and their very lives are threatened. In short, the necessities of life are denied to them. This is substantially the human condition in Thailand today. The distortion, concealment, and abuse of the authentic Thai religious vision have brought about massive pain and suffering among the people.

Similarly, this substitution of religious visions poses problems involving political power. Three of the most obvious are: the toleration of transnational corporations that buy off land from poor farmers and exploit their cheap labor; the doctrine of national security, with its concomitant militarism and arms race, which promotes the use of force to safeguard national security and benefits the elite at the expense of the poor; and the growth-oriented economic development with massive government schemes that eventually deprive people of the lands and fatten the checkbooks of the economic and political elite, making the poor even poorer.

Recovering the Cultural Heritage: The Story of Isan

In order to deal creatively with the present societal crisis in Thailand, the repossession of the lost religious and cultural heritage is imperative. Symbols are rooted in the depth of life. Thus they require interpretation in order to unfold their powers and possibilities, particularly as their functions become problematic in the time of crisis. Symbols invite thoughts, provoke feelings, and inspire actions. At the same time, greed or selfishness and their offspring—that is, fear and the sense of insecurity that begets exclusiveness and oppression—distort and abuse symbols.

When symbols are distorted and abused, a people's creativity is repressed. What is more, their very lives—especially those of the poor and the voiceless and those who stand with them—are destroyed. This results in the questioning of the symbols. Since the people's struggles in history gave rise to the particular symbols and their interpretation, when the prevailing symbols are used to oppress them, the people—namely, the poor and the oppressed—will act to do away with such symbols and to create new ones. At the very least, a serious reinterpretation of symbols becomes their priority.

The Emergence of Isan as a Symbol

Isan is one of the four major geographical regions of Thailand: the Central Plains, the North, the South, and Isan or the Northeast. It borders Laos and Kampuchea.

But Isan is more than a name. In the eyes of the Bangkok-based ruling elite, Isan has been a pain in the neck. Compared to other regions of Thailand, Isan is the poorest—blessed and cursed with everything that poverty brings. Yet for the people of Isan, the name has become a symbol. The central significance of Isan as a symbol is threefold. First, it provides for the Isan people (one-third of the Thai population) a much-needed sense of identity. It is distinctive from both the Lao people across the Maekhong River and from the rest of the Thai people. It shares a great deal culturally with the Lao people, yet it belongs politically to greater Thailand. This sense of double identity of the Isan people is real and very important.

Second, Isan is a symbol of possibilities for the recovery of the lost heritage. Isan history is the least known of the Thai regions. The long and persistent imperialist policy of Bangkok has, among other things, robbed the Isan people of their historical and cultural heritage. The emergence of Isan as a new encompassing symbol for the Northeastern world holds promise of a rediscovery and repossession of that lost heritage.

Third, Isan has a role in shaping a new and better world, not only for the Thai people but also for everyone in Southeast Asia. The historic and strategic importance of Isan in the struggle of the Communist party of Thailand, for example, is well recognized. Earlier, after the end of World War II, key Thai leaders of Isan background and inspiration played a major role in the short-lived Southeast Asian League, whose purpose was to create a greater Southeast Asian community for the sake of peace and justice in the sharing of our common humanity in a common world.

A Remark on the History of Isan

As noted above, the history of Isan is the least known among the four Thai regions. But certainly Isan must have a much-richer history than what is known to us today. Whatever the reasons for the loss of this historical heritage, it is the duty of the sons and daughters of Isan to recover that lost heritage.

One of the most curious and painful truths about the history of Isan is that it has been systematically and effectively suppressed. As the people appropriate it today, Isan's historical heritage is at once autonomous and interrelated with its neighbors: the Lao to the north and the east, the Khmer to the south, and the Siamese to the south and the southwest.

In his brief account of the formation of Isan, Charles Keyes concludes:

Although the Thai Northeast (Isan) did not emerge as having distinct geopolitical identity until the beginning of the 20th century, a large portion of the population of the region do share a common historical heritage. . . . In consequence of migrations and assimilation, the vast majority of the northeastern populace is today closely related culturally to the Lao on the opposite bank of the Maekhong. Although there are slight cultural variations in the region due to a long period of local autonomy, . . . in the main the people of Isan can be grouped ethnically with the Lao as differentiated from the Siamese or Central Thai. Politically, however, the region has had a history of division. The areas lying along the Maekhong were integral, but secondary, parts of the Lao kingdom for most of the period between the mid-14th and the early 19th centuries, while much of the interior of the Khorat Plateau [Isan] was politically autonomous. Inclusion of the region as a whole into one or another kingdom has occurred only in the pre-14th century period under Angkor [when the populace was itself Khmer] and since 1827 under the Siamese.[1]

Like the North and the South, Isan was gradually but effectively colonized by Bangkok. Through the methods of administrative reforms, educational policy, and the reform of the sangha (Buddhist polity), the political and religious symbols of Bangkok have been imposed on the Isan people, supplanting the indigenous tradition. In this process, it is generally agreed that the symbolic trilogy of *chat* (nation), *satsana* (religion), and *phra mahakasat* (king) has been accepted by the Isan people.

The Isan Cry of Protest

Isan is not only the poorest region, it also is the most cruelly oppressed. The persistent harassment of members of parliament from Isan is well known. It reached a high point after World War II with the brutal killing by the police of Chamlong Daoruang (Mahasarakham), Tong-in Phuripat (Ubon), Tawin Udon (Roi-et), and Tiang Sirikhan (Sakon Nakorn), together with Thongplaeo Chonlaphum (Nakhon-Nayok) in the Central Plains. The burning to the ground of Nasai Village in Nongkhai by the police in 1974 is a more recent example. Moreover, the Isan people participated strongly in both the 14 October revolt of 1973 and the brutal political killings of 6 October 1976.

These events, on top of poverty and the ever-widening gap between Isan and Bangkok, have forced the Isan people to question the legitimacy of the basic symbols that have been imposed on them.

Witness the theme of this *serng* (song) from the movie *Tongpan:*

Isan is boiling hurt,
  caused by the [Bangkok] masters.

They suppress us
  killing the farmers
  accusing them of being communists.

---

[1]Charles F. Keyes, *Isan: Regionalism in Northeastern Thailand* (Ithaca NY: Cornell University Press, 1967) 12-13. This remains the best single source in English on Isan.

The innocents are imprisoned;
  they kill whoever they dislike,
  and those who try to reason.

The people are silenced
  by the oppressive powers,
  acting as political hooligans.

The rulers are immoral,
  the damned tyrants,
  corrupt and robbing.

They deceive and exploit us,
  while worshipping the Americans,
  allowing them to set up the bases;
  nightclubs spread all over.

Our rice and water they take,
  while our poor go hungry.

Isan is poor;
  the people pick fruits from the forest
  to eat instead of rice.

They take our daughters;
  even our wives they do not spare,
  putting themselves above the law,
  pathetic!

But with the strength of our two arms,
  can we afford not to fight?
Drive away the evil kind,
  kick them out with our feet.

The Isan Struggle and the Thai Future: A Consideration of Political Ethics

The problem of Thai political ethics is, to an extent, analogous to making a pair of shoes for one's own use. It is only right to cut the leather in order to make shoes that fit my feet. At the same time, it is absurd to cut my feet to fit a pair of shoes. It does not matter at all whether that pair of shoes was made in Bangkok or Washington or Moscow or Peking. Besides, dwelling in the Isan land, most people go barefoot anyway!

From the standpoint of Isan, the problem of political ethics is that the Isan people have been forced to wear somebody else's shoes: the Bangkok-based political symbols, whose original formulation was inspired by a foreign influence. This pattern of external control continues at all levels of Thai life. It is absurd. For authentic Thai life, liberation is imperative.

Due to the rich and complex nature of religious insights, myth is a common way of articulating and relating several religious symbols at the same time in a form accessible to most people. In this way, myths can summarize the religious understandings and traditions of a people. Modern people, however, often attempt to express these same understandings and insights through philosophy, theology, or political ideology. These expressions, however, do not necessarily supercede myths in their capacity to express a people's basic understandings and traditions.

The Lao-Isan Foundation Myth

In the *Collections of Thai Chronicles*, part 1, the following myth is recorded.

Three humans—Grandfather Langcherng, Khun Khek, and Khun Khan—happened to live among the Gods in Heaven. One day the three humans went to see Phya Thaen, the Supreme God of Heaven, and said to him: "O Divine Lord, we would like to ask your permission to return to the earth. We have not felt at home here. We don't know how to hold ourselves in this heavenly realm."

Phya Thaen granted according to their wish and instructed them to dwell in "the land." As the three humans returned to the earth, Phya Thaen gave them a buffalo to help them toil the land. That buffalo died of old age, leaving behind numerous offspring.

At the land spot where the original buffalo was buried, a bottle gourd tree grew up, bearing an extraordinarily huge gourd. When the gourd was full-grown, people's voice was heard from within it. The three humans used a pointed iron rod, heated until red like fire, to make two holes into that gourd in order to let people come out. Those who came out through these two holes were called Thai Lom and Thai Li, the ancestors of the peoples known as the Kha, the Khamu, the Khom, the Khmer, and the Mon. These people were a little dark because of the heat from the pointed iron rod.

But there were still a lot more people in the gourd after the first exodus. The three humans made three more holes into the gourd, this time using the chisel, to help the rest of the people come out. They were called Thai Lerng, Thai Lo, and Thai Kwang, the ancestors of the peoples known as the Siamese, the Lao, and the Vietnamese. Not affected by the heat like the first group, these people had a fairer complexion.

The original three humans taught all of the people to farm and to weave. They married among themselves. They lived together quite happily until

*they multiplied so much and began to quarrel and fight among themselves.
The chaotic situation among these peoples was reported to Phya Thaen.
So he sent Khun Khru (the Teacher) and Khun Khrong (the Governor) to
come down and help restore peace and order.*

*But these two new chiefs turned out to be a failure. They became in-
capable, careless, seeking only pleasures, and paid no attention to the
plight of the people. It required Phya Thaen to intervene once more. This
time he sent Khun Buhom or Khun Bulom (known in Thai history as Khun
Borom) with absolute power to save the situation. But the people multiplied even more. They needed "things to eat and things to wear." Eventually it was beyond the capability of Khun Bulom. The original three
humans prayed to Phya Thaen to intervene for the last time.*

*This time Phya Thaen sent Pitsanukam and some assistants to the earth
with this instruction: "Go down and teach them to work and produce. Teach
them how to raise poultry, how to grow rice and vegetables and all other
edible plants. Teach them to weave. Teach them to make medicine from
the herbs. Teach them also the language of songs and poetry. Take along
with you all the tools you may need such as hand-spades, knives, axes."*

*Accompanying the Pitsanukam team, Srikhanthap, the angel of music,
was also sent by the Great Phya Thaen. Srikhanthap taught people to make
the various musical instruments and to play them for their enjoyment.*

*With the help from Pitsanukam and his team of angels, Khun Bulom
was able to govern his people and promote their happiness and well-being.
Peace and prosperity prevailed.*

*It came to pass that six sons were born to Khun Bulom. The father sent
them to start new kingdoms of their own: Khun Lo built the Lan Chang
Kingdom (Lao); Yi Phalan built Sipsong Panna (Vietnam); Sam Jusong
built Huaphan Thang Ha Thang Hok (Shan); Saiphong built Lanna (Chiang
Mai); Ngua In built Ayudhya (Siam); and Lokklom built Raman (Burma).*

This myth is the original source of life and world for the Lao-Isan people. It is evidently archaic, at least pre-Buddhist. Recent archaeological
discoveries in Udorn Province, Northeast Thailand, have shown that the
people who lived there were the first people on earth who learned to plant
rice. This myth seems to correspond to, or at least does not contradict, this
new archaeological discovery.

I have examined the twenty-two "original" ancient texts of the Isan
folktales—most of which I have cherished since childhood, thanks to my
father and my grandmother—and it is very clear that this myth is strongly

evident in these stories. But it is important to note that most of the Isan folktales in their present forms have been, to varying degrees, "Buddhized." It would be most interesting to trace that development and the impact or transformation that took place. Obviously, this requires further research. At this point, however, let us limit ourselves to the interpretive recovery of this lost heritage of the Isan people.

The Isan Conception of the World

From the fundamental myth and from the folktales one notes that the world for Isan people is the unity of all beings: the divine, the human, the nonhuman, and the natural. The divine is the origin, the human is the most important, the natural is needed, and the nonhuman is equally real. According to the myth, the supreme divinity is Phya Thaen. But in some folktales, he is identified with Indra, a sign of Hindu influence. In later development, both Phya Thaen and/or Indra acted in accordance with the Buddhist Dhamma and in the service of the Buddha. Nonetheless, Phya Thaen maintained his independence. Historically and sociologically, this refers to the persisting shamanistic traditions and practices among the Lao-Isan people. In actual situations, syncretism seems a natural thing.

According to the myth, the genesis of people had to do with: (1) Phya Thaen, who is the Great Overseer and Supreme Prime Mover, (2) the Buffalo (representing the animals), from whose grave grew the bottle gourd, (3) the bottle gourd (representing vegetation), where people were "conceived," and (4) the land, which was their home.

But once people were born, they needed "things to wear and things to eat." Competing for these things, people fought each other. The use of absolute power "to restore order and to bring peace" by Khun Bulom did not work. Two other things were needed: productive work and the work of art. Only with the help of Pitsanukam, who brought these two things, could Khun Bulom, the governor, restore peace and order. With these dimensions added, the ruler was able to promote happiness among his people and prosperity in his realm. Nature also was more inclined to cooperate in this new "regime" transformed by labor and art.

In many folktales, however, the conditions for peace and prosperity are the people's return and/or adherence to the Buddhist Dhamma. According to the myth, the three original humans were not themselves the progenitors of the people. Yet their roles were imperative, for they mediated between Phya Thaen and the human situation. Khun Bulon, the ruler, was not given the privilege to intercede with Phya Thaen. It is interesting to note that the three original humans came from heaven in the first place. They seemed part-divine, part-human. According to the myth, they never married. In the folktales, the anchorite (hermit) functions similarly to the three original humans.

Though complex and rich, myth does not contain the whole story of a people. Here the Isan folktales help us to see further dimensions of the world. For example, we can identify these themes and values in the Isan folktales: (a) love and compassion as the joy of life and community; (b) the jungle and the courage to die as symbols of freedom from oppression and power to recreate and to reconcile; (c) language as power; (d) truth as freedom and deliverance; (e) meditation as the source of spirituality and power; (f) force and power as worthless by themselves; (g) people—poor, little, neglected, voiceless, and oppressed people—as the source of new life; (h) the power elite as arrogant and demonic; (i) merit that accrues from selfless giving as power and goodness.

Repossessing the Lost Heritage

In the context of the Thai story, the prevailing political vision or ideology has always centered around the encompassing symbol of kingship. This was particularly the case prior to the impact of the Western liberal democratic ideology beginning in the 1850s. In my earlier work, cited above, I drew these conclusions about the significance of kingship in the Thai tradition:

1. Kingship was and has been identified with the Thai nationhood. Without kingship and what it symbolizes, Thailand would lose her historical identity.

2. The religious ground of the Thai kingship has interwoven the three religious elements, namely, the *phii* or spirit, the Brahmanic, and the Buddhist. The last element is all-inclusive and all-encompassing.

3. Thai kingship is the spatial center and temporal prime mover of the Thai order. In other words, the king is both the source and the context of national unity and order and the primary power and authority that moves the Thai order toward national prosperity and the people's happiness, that is, toward destiny and fulfillment.

4. This charismatic quality (the integration of the spatial center and temporal prime mover) of the Thai kingship is accomplished only if and when the king rules in accordance with the Buddhist Dhamma (or Bud-

dhist religious vision). That is to say, the ideal Thai king is both religiously devout and politically wise. (See my thesis, "Dhammocracy in Thailand," 256-57.)

In modern Thai history, particularly since the reign of King Rama the Sixth (Wachirawut) (1910-1925), kingship as a political symbol has been interpreted or ideologized as the most important member of what has come to be the trilogy of Thai national symbols. As noted, this trilogy consists of *chat* (nation), *satsana* (religion, primarily Buddhism), and *phra mahakasat* (king). As a matter of fact, this trilogy originally was formulated by King Wachirawut, who had adapted it from the British model, having spent much of his youth in English schools. When political change was brought about in June 1932 by a coup d'état on the part of a group of government officials, a constitutional monarchy was brought into being. Thus, after 1932, another member, *ratthathammanun* (constitution) was added to the trilogy, making a quartet. For a while, the newest member seemed to have become the darling of the ruling powers. But unlike the youngest child of the Thai tradition, particularly of Isan, who receives the most love and attention, the constitution has been not only persecuted but also rendered virtually meaningless by the multitude of military takeovers.

Whatever the adequacy of this triadic ideology for Thailand, it has been the only official ideology imposed on all levels of Thai society. Today a significant portion of the Thai people have questioned this official ideology—some because it is not effective enough, others because it has become too rightist and exclusive, still others because it not only is inadequate but it also has become an oppressive tool in the hands of the ruling elite. My concern in this connection is to reinterpret the Thai religious vision as a more adequate basis from which to criticize the present Thai ideology and to begin to articulate a more adequate political vision.

In order to deal creatively with the present societal crisis in Thailand, the lost religious and cultural heritage must be repossessed. From the Isan perspective, guided by the interpretation of folktales, the task of repossession consists of three dimensions:

1. Rediscovering the genius of the people (the original religious vision) by interpreting symbols and myths as we are doing here in this project.

2. Critiquing and rejecting the distorted interpretations of symbols, the external imposition of symbols, and the suppression of the authentic tradition. This is what liberation is all about. For the people of Isan, the Bangkok-based elitist interpretations of religion and politics must be crit-

ically assessed; and when they are found to be distorted or oppressive, they must be rejected. Furthermore, negative foreign influence, usually mediated by Bangkok, must be checked. At the same time, these distorted interpretations by the people themselves must be disclosed and rejected: a fatalistic conception of *kam* (inevitable consequence of one's past actions), a male-dominated worldview and ethos, submission to authority without real, critical awareness, low self-esteem, low esteem for land and labor, and a sense of shame regarding one's own roots.

3. Actively appropriating the genius of the people. These values should become the guiding lights of the life and history of our people once more: freedom and compassion; local autonomy; participatory democracy; common humanity; the fundamental unity of the divine, the human, the non-human, and the natural; selfless giving, submission, and obedience to the Ultimate, Divine Power; and forgiveness and reconciliation. All these can be recovered from the Isan cultural heritage.

Conclusion

In the Thai context, we must ask whether the national symbols are still valid. Do they still serve to free and unite the Thai people? Is the present interpretation adequate?

How does one interpret symbols, particularly religious and political symbols? An appropriate interpretation of symbols deals with the societal problem at the root level. Therefore, it takes into account the societal process in its totality. In short, it takes seriously the fundamental struggle of the people in the total context of time and space. As such, there are three dimensions to the task of interpreting the people's struggle.

1. The interpreter seeks to comprehend the character and the cause of the present societal crisis and the basic conflicts therein. Such a comprehension is the result of:

a. the organic participation of the interpreter in the societal crisis and in the people's struggle, partaking with them the cup of suffering and hope.

b. a critical analysis of the genesis and development of the societal crisis.

c. a critical analysis of the cultural, sociopolitical, economic, and motivational forces at work and the resultant power structures that, together, oppress the people, which is the root cause of societal conflicts and crisis.

2. The interpreter of symbols seeks to retrieve the religious heritage and salvage an authentic politics of the people. Three guidelines are basic to this dimension of the interpreter's task:

a. a grasp of the legacy of symbols, the disclosure of the sacred in the historical and cultural process of the people.

b. a critical retrieval of the tradition or the story of the people, fully aware that their symbolization involves distortions as well as liberating possibilities. In order for it to be liberating, the retrieval must be done from the perspective of the silenced, unheard, and voiceless people who have been oppressed.

c. for parabolic as well as for inspirational value, the telling of contemporary stories of people struggling in suffering and hope for their liberation, dignity, and justice.

As a result of this kind of participation and involvement, the interpreter is transformed. If he is not the hired hand of the ruling, oppressive elite, he either "converts" or deepens his commitment to participate in the people's struggle for a fuller humanity. In my view, such a personal transformation, the genesis of a qualitatively different motivation, is guided by the following considerations:

a. The people's struggle and movement ultimately rest on the faith in common humanity and the commitment to mutual respect, both within humanity and between humanity and the cosmos. This faith and commitment is the real source of the poor people's struggle; such qualities have been lost by the ruling elite. This is why the poor and the little people are indeed the seed of tomorrow.

b. The search for a fuller humanity essentially takes the form of dialogue, which presupposes freedom and dignity. However, in certain situations dialogue is not permitted or proves to be an ineffective method for qualitative transformation. In such situations, conflicts often take a violent form.

c. Moral or ethical courage, particularly in the face of massive demonic powers, is required in order to effect qualitative transformation. Ethical courage is motivated by freedom and compassion, human submission and obedience to the ultimate power of peace and justice, truth and beauty—whether such ultimate power is symbolized as God, Dhamma, Allah, or even as Land and People.

What, then, are the implications of all this for the comprehensive and authentic development of the Isan people in the context of modern Thailand?

It seems clear that in order to regain their humanity, the people who have been marginalized will have to take history into their own hands. They have to become conscious of their plight and their power, to accept their responsibility to act and to shape their own life and destiny. That is what people's participation is all about. But the question is how to do this, especially in the face of the overwhelming odds against them. What is the source of their power, other than their sheer numbers?

Here the ecumenical experience, especially in the area of urban-rural mission and the churches' participation in development, is instructive. People's power comes from their consciousness and organization. The essential part of this power is rooted in the people's own wisdom and symbols. It is along this line that I have emphasized recovering the people's cultural heritage.

But more important, following the Isan wisdom, the source of life and community lies in the plight and suffering of the poor. Their cry is the cry of heaven. Their renewal and liberation are the renewal and liberation of humanity. In their suffering and hope, struggle and liberation, lie the beginnings of authentic spirituality.

In the context of Thailand, this means, among other things, that the present Bangkok-dominated social structure and "top-down" strategy of national development will have to be radically modified. People's participation will need to be the hallmark. Poor people need to be helped to regain their identity, dignity, and power to be and to act in order to liberate themselves from all forms of bondage and oppression and to re-create a just and participatory society.

The interpretation of symbols is like an excavation in search of precious treasure. In the light of the present crisis, in Thailand or elsewhere, such an interpretation seems imperative. As shown above, an interpretation of religious and political symbols involves three basic things simultaneously: (1) an examination, an analysis, a diagnosis, and a critique of the societal crisis; (2) a search for a viable alternative such as recovering the original and traditional genius of people that is embedded in their religious and political symbols; and (3) a process of personal conversion and social transformation, resulting in a resolute program of action. All of these constitute a search for a participatory and just society. As such, it is a matter of political ethics.

The starting point for doing political ethics in this way is an option in favor of poor and oppressed people. Therefore, it is bound to be costly. An ethical courage is demanded, for no one should underestimate the massive and well-organized power of the oppressors of people. In spite of this risk, however, men and women of ethical courage have emerged to grace history. Their actions have greatly contributed to the reconstitution of a just world and a new history.

Warren R. Copeland
Wittenberg University

■■

Domestic Poverty

The Historical Context

■ ■ Poverty was discovered as a public issue in the United States in 1904 by Robert Hunter and the Progressives, in 1929 by Harry Hopkins and the New Deal, and in 1962 by Michael Harrington and the Great Society.[1] It probably will be discovered once again in the years ahead by a representative of a new era of reform. Sadly, each time poverty has been discovered, it has been new to the public at large and even a significant proportion of the activists. This is too bad, because we have much to learn from our history of reform.

Before the Twentieth Century

Clearly, poverty existed in the United States prior to the twentieth century. However, it was considered primarily a personal problem rather than a public issue. From colonial times, the widely accepted ideology was that people must work and that people were poor because of flaws in their character. Yet the actual practice was a much more humanitarian concern for neighbors and family who could not make it economically.

The ideology of self-sufficiency reached its high watermark in the Charity Organization Societies that developed great momentum in the last

---

[1] For a further expansion of these historical themes see the first chapter of Warren R. Copeland, "The Politics of Welfare Reform" (Ph.D. dissertation, University of Chicago, 1977).

quarter of the nineteenth century. Based on the survival-of-the-fittest beliefs of social Darwinism, the COS approach sought to prevent indiscriminate charity and to stress moral education over financial assistance. However, by the end of the nineteenth century, America had become an increasingly urban society marked by low industrial wages and periodic massive industrial unemployment. The old ideology was increasingly less persuasive.

Three Eras of Reform

Robert Hunter's *Poverty* appeared in 1904.[2] By defining poverty to include not just those receiving charity, Hunter argued that it was a widespread phenomenon involving more than ten million Americans. More important, he contended that poverty resulted more from social forces than from personal weakness. Therefore, he called for broad social change. He was joined in this appeal by his fellow settlement-house workers and, in a weaker form, by the progressive movement generally. But then came World War I, the Red scare, and the desire for normalcy.

Harry Hopkins took over relief efforts in the state of New York in late 1929.[3] When Governor Roosevelt became president, Hopkins migrated to Washington, where he headed the major New Deal relief efforts. Having begun his career as a settlement-house worker, he shared in the belief that the poor were not simply weak individuals but were people of dignity. What he and the New Deal added to the earlier era of reform was the conviction that the federal government had a responsibility for doing something about poverty. The lasting result is the framework of federal social programs still existing today, in forms like the Social Security Act of 1935. But then came World War II, McCarthyism, and the desire for normalcy.

Michael Harrington's book, *The Other America,* was brought to President Kennedy's attention and thus became a primary source for designing a program to combat poverty.[4] It merged well with the desire to develop domestic programs to make use of new revenues expected because of an expanding economy and with trends among professional reformers toward an emphasis upon organizing poor communities. They all shared the belief

---

[2]Robert Hunter, *Poverty* (New York: Macmillan, 1904).

[3]Searle F. Charles, *Minister of Relief: Harry Hopkins and the Depression* (Syracuse NY: Syracuse University Press, 1963).

[4]Michael Harrington, *The Other America* (New York: Macmillan, 1962).

that many Americans were not participating in the growing affluence of the society at large. The most obvious result was the War on Poverty, with its initial emphasis upon community action, organizing the poor so they could advance their own interests. But then came the Vietnam War, the backlash against demonstrators, and the desire for normalcy.

Three times in this century, poverty has been discovered, described, and attacked. Each generation of reformers has learned important lessons from the struggle. The settlement-house workers developed most effectively the link between local associations and political action. Never since have we found such a sound basis for both research and political strategizing as that provided by the neighborhood democracy of those settlement houses. The New Deal established the necessity of national action to address the systematic basis of poverty. Since that time, all reformers have recognized that the federal government must be the primary actor in alleviating poverty. The War on Poverty made clear that poverty could not be addressed short of fundamental social and economic change and that such change would not come without conflict.

Since the Great Society

That the Great Society ended with the election of Richard Nixon in 1968 is clear from the manner in which the Office of Economic Opportunity was systematically dismantled soon thereafter. Since 1968, inasmuch as the issue of poverty has arisen, it has been in terms of income maintenance—best represented by welfare reform—or in terms of employment—best represented by the Humphrey-Hawkins Full Employment Bill.

While the Nixon administration was quietly killing the Office of Economic Opportunity, it was trumpeting welfare reform. As originally announced, the Family Assistance Plan would have had little effect upon recipients in most of the country, while providing quite significant federal assistance to recipients in the poorer (especially Southern) states. After several revisions, it even would have reduced benefits in many of the more generous states. Its liberal supporters argued that it at least established the principle that the federal government should assure a minimum level of income. It died primarily because some liberals felt this was not enough and some conservatives thought this was far too much. Nixon's advisers also decided they would rather have it as a campaign issue against George McGovern in the 1972 election than as a legislative achievement. Jimmy Carter's attempts to revive the issue raised little enthusiasm in Congress, finally getting lost in the more general crisis of the economy.

The Humphrey-Hawkins Full Employment Bill was first conceived and advanced as the completion of the Full Employment Act of 1946. That act established full employment as a national goal. Humphrey-Hawkins was intended to make it a fact by setting up procedures for stimulating employment generally and ultimately by establishing the federal government as the employer of last resort. Over a period of years, it was continually watered down so that by the time it was passed and signed by President Carter, all it required were regular reports on the status of employment. Thus, the cries of jobs or income have resulted in little new policy.

Nevertheless, the sheer reality of poverty will not go away. While the relative standing of the poorest quarter of our population improved during the 1960s, it has deteriorated since. As a result, the proportion of Americans who are poor, and the gap between them and those who are not, is about the same as in 1960—before the most recent era of reform began. Yet some believe we dealt with poverty in the 1960s, others that we tried and found it impossible, while still others believe that as times get tough, we can not afford generosity. There remains little interest in the issue of poverty itself. Rather, the issue arises only as an aspect of other issues like inflation, homelessness, hunger, unemployment, energy, or taxes. However, this disparity between the persistent reality of poverty and the public ignorance or apathy cries out for further analysis and action.

Some Representative Analyses

How, then, are we to understand poverty as an issue that is both religiously significant and politically actionable? As a first step in addressing that question, I want to look at some descriptions of poverty that are representative of the range of views abroad in the land. Specifically, I want to examine Milton Friedman, Daniel Moynihan, Frances Fox Piven and Richard Cloward, and Michael Harrington. While no list so short can be complete, these four analyses represent relatively developed schools of thought that include many others; they all have significant influence among public actors; and they pretty well cover the range of options that have arisen from recent descriptions of poverty in America.

Milton Friedman

Milton Friedman is the outstanding twentieth-century spokesman for classical liberalism (what we now usually call conservatism) in political economy. More specifically, his analysis of the nature of poverty as a personal problem strikes a responsive chord in the hearts of the American conservative community. His proposal for dealing with poverty (the negative income tax) has directly influenced policy considerations since the early 1960s and was most fully expressed in the Family Assistance Plan of Richard Nixon. In the 1980s his influence, if anything, grew through the popularity of his book and television series, ''Free to Choose,'' and the effect of his ideas upon the makers of Republican economic policy.

Friedman takes up inequality of income both in principle and in practice. For Friedman, poverty is essentially an individual matter. The only social factor he takes seriously is government interference with the market. People are poor primarily because of taste or because of endowment. On the basis of taste, the poor choose a lower-paying job because it allows shorter hours or requires less responsibility. As far as endowment is concerned, he insists that it is impossible to draw a line between natural ability and inherited advantage. Is a person intelligent because of native ability or parental stimulation? Furthermore, he believes that any attempt to draw this line would be an infringement upon the parents' right to help their children.

Not only does Friedman defend the freedom to choose (either an easy job or education for your children), but he also believes that America is enough of a free market that such freedom of choice is the rule. He recognizes that some inequality results from such as racial prejudice, but he sees this as minor. The most significant cause of inappropriate inequality is government interference in the free market with such measures as minimum-wage laws, which eliminate low-wage jobs as the first rung on the ladder of success, or building codes, which eliminate low-cost slum housing. If wages are too low, no one will take the job; if housing conditions are poor, there will be no renters. Let the market decide. When government interferes, it only makes it more difficult for the poor to take the first step toward escaping poverty. In sum, Friedman is committed in principle to freedom of choice and to the free market as the best vehicle for assuring such freedom.

In practice, Friedman argues that capitalism has minimized poverty and, specifically, that there is less inequality in the capitalistic West than in the rest of the world. Moreover, he contends that statistics show a narrowing of differences between rich and poor. However, he concludes that, in any event, the general affluence brought by capitalism has freed the poor from sheer toil with no comparable benefit to the wealthy. Today's American poor typically have automobiles, kitchen appliances, TVs, utilities, indoor plumbing, and so forth. In other words, there is no place better to be poor than under capitalism. The free market allows freedom of choice and provides relative luxury even if one chooses poverty.

Daniel Patrick Moynihan

Daniel Patrick Moynihan has been a constant in poverty politics since 1960. As one of the Harvard-based advisers to Kennedy and Johnson, he urged more emphasis on employment, rather than community action, in the War on Poverty. He also produced a controversial study of the black family, which argued that it was deteriorating seriously and becoming a cause, as well as a result, of poverty and dependency. He brought these emphases on work and family together as Nixon's chief domestic adviser by assisting in the formulation of the Family Assistance Plan. After making a name for himself at the United Nations, Moynihan returned as a Democratic senator to Washington, where he chaired the Finance Committee's Welfare Subcommittee. He is now poised in anticipation of higher calling. Throughout he has written prolifically and broadly, but with a particular focus on poverty.

Unlike Friedman, Moynihan believes poverty is primarily a social, rather than personal, problem. However, he does not emphasize the societywide character of it so much as the role of middle-range institutions. Specifically, he sees employment and family as key factors in poverty.

Poor people tend to have few job skills. Our economy continues to expand its use of technology. This technology replaces many old jobs that required few skills with new ones that call for skills the poor do not have. The wages of the skilled go up; the wages of the unskilled lag behind. This economic reality is compounded by the political fact that for decades the United States has tolerated much higher levels of unemployment than any other industrialized nation. The price—especially for those chronically unemployed, such as blacks, other minorities, and Southern whites—has been paid in crime, drug and alcohol abuse, family breakup, and poverty in the next generation.

The family is what Moynihan views with the most alarm. The poor tend to have large families, producing children who are more likely to grow up to be poor themselves. Even more threatening, poor families are unstable. Divorce, desertion, and illegitimacy rates are much higher for the poor. For black families, the corrosive effects of unemployment and poor education are reinforced by the racist tradition of greater job opportunity for women than men. Unable to support his family and believing they can get welfare more easily without him, the father abandons his family. The result is a permanent class of dependent poor, whose children are even less likely to escape poverty.

Poverty, then, is tied to the failure of two social institutions that stand between the individual and society as a whole: work and family. Sadly, as far as Moynihan is concerned, this is compounded by the failure of American social policy to reinforce these institutions. Rather, he believes Americans have typically emphasized either the individual or the economic and social system as a whole. He believes this tragically ignores the crucial role work and family play in integrating the individual into society, providing a sense of identity and worth for the individual, and stability for the society. He concludes that any effective program to combat poverty must address the middle-range institutions of work and family, which are not now functioning for the poor.

Frances Fox Piven
and Richard Cloward

Along with Lloyd Ohlin, Richard Cloward authored an influential book on juvenile delinquency, *Delinquency and Opportunity,* which argued that the poor must be organized to fight for their place in society.[5] One result was Mobilization for Youth, which sought to test this theory in New York City. A number of articles and books flowed from this experiment, many authored by Frances Fox Piven and Cloward individually and jointly. At the same time, Piven and Cloward became the intellectual apologists and theoretical strategists for the National Welfare Rights Organization. Under the leadership of George Wiley, NWRO put Piven's and Cloward's theories to work with considerable success. Through their writings and personal involvement, they remain widely influential among what remains of poverty activists from the 1960s and 1970s.

Central to Piven's and Cloward's understanding of poverty is that it is not an individual matter, but rather is characteristic of a whole social class. Whereas Friedman locates the cause of poverty in individual choice and Moynihan in the weakening of intermediate institutions, Piven and Clo-

---

[5]Richard A. Cloward and Lloyd E. Ohlin, *Delinquency and Opportunity* (Glencoe IL: Free Press, 1960).

ward believe it is the result of massive social forces. This situation is made worse by the efforts of the privileged to protect and even improve their position in the face of these forces.

Piven and Cloward identify mechanization, especially in Southern agriculture, as the primary social force producing poverty in contemporary America. Great numbers of the poor, and especially the black poor, were forced off the land as tractors and harvesters replaced field hands. Those in power in the South did not respond to the human misery created. This push, plus the lure of jobs, led to a great migration to the cities, primarily in the North.

But the cities did not absorb these migrants. Racism, coupled with a decline in low-skill jobs, left many of them either underemployed or employed at very low wages. Under the pressure of failure, traditional authority patterns—including the family—deteriorated, all of which led to a general disruption. Yet urban officials responded little better than had the Southern power structure. Old alignments remained. As always, the privileged defended their privilege. In this case, the most threatened people were white workers, so antagonism grew between the white working class and the poor, especially the black poor.

For Piven and Cloward, probably the most critical characteristic of the poor is their lack of political power. As victims of social forces beyond their control and of attacks by those whose position they threaten, the poor must turn to politics for help. In the long run, this means the poor must develop institutions that can wield political influence: labor unions, community organizations, churches, and finally political machines. In the short run, the likely way for the poor to provoke political response is by causing trouble. After basic upheavals in the economy, such as mechanization, the second significant cause of poverty is docility among the poor themselves.

Michael Harrington

As I suggested earlier, Michael Harrington generally is given credit for the most-recent discovery of poverty in the 1960s. He followed his book to Washington as a consultant in the formulation of the War on Poverty. While he was disappointed in the result, he defended it as a valuable, if too small, step forward. Although he has remained a recognized expert on poverty, most of his subsequent writing and action has been directed at trying to generate a strong democratic socialist voice within a coalition of the Left. This led to the formulation of the Democratic Socialist Organizing Committee in 1973 (now the Democratic Socialists of America), to which he has devoted most of his energies since.

Central to Harrington's understanding of poverty is the distinction between the *old* poor and the *new* poor. The old poor suffered just as much as the new poor, but they were a part of the general expansion of the capitalist economy. Since that economy needed unskilled and semiskilled labor for its factories, the old poor had good reason to hope that they (and especially their children) would escape poverty. Fueled by the solidarity gained from shared ethnic cultures and shared workplaces, the old poor developed their own institutions—churches, clubs, political machines and, preeminently, labor unions. These organizations provided both political power and reinforced hope.

But today's poor are a hereditary underclass. Blue-collar jobs are declining, leaving the poor in low-paying service jobs requiring simple muscle power such as janitorial work or dish washing. These jobs promise no better future. Indeed, they are part of an economy that is almost separate from the general economy. Wages go up only when the minimum wage is raised. Worse yet, bad schools and high youth unemployment promise another generation of poverty rather than escape. For very good reason, hope dies.

According to Harrington, this pessimism is complicated by the separation of the new poor. The poor are divided between black and white, old and young, working and nonworking. Even the working poor are not centered in large factories. As a result, the new poor are unable to form the organizations that proved so valuable to the old poor. Harrington believes that those researchers, such as Piven and Cloward, who see the poor as a source of social change are ignoring the disorganized and hopeless character of the new poverty. It is more likely to drive the poor, in despair, to the usual social ills—violence, crime, alcohol and drugs, and broken families—than to social action.

Clearly, Harrington understands the new poverty to be primarily a social, rather than a personal, problem. But unlike Piven and Cloward, he also sees it as a political problem: it keeps the poor from organizing themselves politically. Yet he concludes that the effect of poverty is so corrosive of the personal, social, and political life of the poor that they are unable to rise above it on their own. Two things are required as far as Harrington is concerned. First, the poor need opportunities to develop the institutions necessary to become hopeful and powerful. Second, a serious program of social change requires a broader coalition of the Left—one that includes the poor but also extends to labor and the conscience constituency.

Ethical Principles

These, then, are four representative and influential views of poverty. Especially as we begin to consider how each turns to action, we can see some basic ethical principles informing them. Quite simply, Milton Friedman believes personal freedom is the highest public good. He assumes that individuals can be autonomous if they are freed from outside coercion. The only public interests are national survival and the maximization of the private interests of individual citizens. Daniel Patrick Moynihan's primary concern is social integration, not personal freedom. He thinks it is long past the time that liberals should recognize the need for a stable society. Family and work are essential to this stability and weakened dangerously among the poor.

Generally, the public debate over poverty in the U.S. has gone back and forth between the notion of personal freedom espoused by Friedman and the notion of social integration espoused by Moynihan. In an attempt to move beyond the limits of this dialogue, Piven and Cloward fall back upon the freedom of the poor to disrupt social peace. They assume those in power want stability enough that they will pay off the troublemakers to shut them up. The poor would then end up ahead. In principle, this position is very close to the freedom advocated by Friedman. Piven and Cloward also believe there is no public interest, just private interests, some of which have been too long unorganized and unrecognized.

Harrington would also like to see the poor develop into an organized social class. But he merges this concern with Moynihan's interest in the society as a whole. The difference is that society provides a conservative principle for Moynihan while Harrington seeks to change that society. He is convinced that such social change need not limit personal freedom, as Moynihan suggests, but rather can free people—for example, poor people—from the limitations imposed upon them by the present social arrangements.

Evaluating the Debate

The differences among these four positions must be evaluated from at least two perspectives. They contain varying views of the realities of American society. Are Americans basically free except for government interference, as Friedman suggests? Is this society on the verge of disintegration, as Moynihan believes, or in need of disruption, as Piven and Cloward propose? Are the poor capable of organizing themselves, as Piven and Cloward want, or are they so damaged by generations of poverty that this is romantic mythology, as Harrington suggests? Is capitalism a vibrant force for lifting the poor, as Friedman suggests, or a dying structure locking the poor into its basement? All these questions deserve a lot of research. However, the debate also comes from another angle. In what sense does poverty raise the basic religious question of the meaning of human life? And how might we judge these views of the issue on the basis of that question?

Poverty as a Human Problem

"Darkness rather than want is the curse of poverty."[6] So does Hannah Arendt identify the peculiarly human form of poverty. Surely poverty does produce very immediate suffering and misery, yet the deeper meaning of poverty is that the poor are seldom able to develop and to exercise uniquely human characteristics. What sets humans apart from other animals is our capacity for creative individuality and pluralistic community, what Arendt calls natality and plurality. Poor people, though, must be concerned with day-to-day survival. Thus they are reduced to the lowest common denominator of existence. As Arendt puts it: "Poverty is more than deprivation, it is a state of constant want and acute misery whose ignominy consists in its dehumanizing force; poverty is abject because it puts men under the absolute dictate of their bodies, that is, under the absolute dictate of necessity."[7]

On the personal level, poverty robs people of property. Property here does not refer simply to wealth, although money alone could ease many of the problems of the poor. Property, however, refers to the economic security that land once provided—the confidence that I have some economic base to fall back on that is mine. Traditionally, such property was the product of individual labor. Such property is humanly important because it provides the cushion that frees people to take the risks necessary to be creative. It is insensitive to expect such creativity from a poor person who must concentrate on daily survival.

---

[6]Hannah Arendt, *On Revolution* (New York: Viking Press, 1965) 64.

[7]Ibid., 54.

On the social level, poverty robs people of the opportunity to belong. The poor lack organizations that they control, that can express and guard their interests. It is within such associations that people have been able to express themselves honestly and interact with other people doing the same. In this process we learn who we are as well as grow by taking into account who others are. These associations also provide a way to relate to groups with different interests so as to assert ourselves and respond to others. Unorganized, the poor are handicapped. They have no chance to express themselves, to appear as creative human beings.

On the religious level, poverty robs people of value. If the only clear measure of human worth in a society is wealth, the poor do not measure up. Yet few of us would agree that wealth is of basic human value in itself. Moreover, we generally recognize that the single-minded pursuit of wealth does not leave time for being truly human. As Arendt puts it, "The bonds of necessity need not be of iron, they can be made of silk."[8] We are drawn back to the realization that the central value of human life is to actualize our capacities for creativity and community. This realization is the basic religious insight into the human meaning of poverty. At the same time, it establishes the grounds for a common interest in extending freedom from necessity and freedom of association. This is an interest that all human beings, poor or not, share.

Judging the Options

On the basis of this analysis of the human meaning of poverty, some judgments about the four descriptions of poverty are possible. Not only does Friedman's description of poverty stress personal freedom, but he also would be very comfortable with an emphasis on property; this is his strength. However, in playing to this strength, he grossly underestimates the role of social forces rather than personal choice in causing poverty. He similarly overestimates the capacity of private power. Large corporations, as well as government, act to distort the market. Moreover, it is unlikely that more than a few overachievers will escape poverty, except as the poor become organized. Only freedom is acceptable to Friedman as a social value; all else is private. As a result, it is impossible to pursue any public purpose other than allowing individuals to maximize their personal pur-

---

[8]Ibid., 136.

poses. For Friedman, the value of human life is an interesting personal issue but is irrelevant to public action.

Much the opposite of Friedman, Moynihan's strong suit is social integration. It leads him to assume that deviation from the norm is pathology. However, at least some marriages may be breaking up because women refuse to take as much abuse as they used to. Similarly, some people may refuse a dead-end job in hopes of escaping to something better. In either case, deviation might be a sign of individual creativity rather than social pathology. When Moynihan moves to action, he is prepared to force people through incentives and penalties to conform in ways Friedman would reject. So, on the social level, while Moynihan recognizes the importance of institutions, he wants them to fit people into society rather than to challenge the social structure. Finally, at the level of value, stability is the final measure of any other values. Thus it is impossible for Moynihan seriously to consider any understanding of human meaning other than that of the present society.

Piven and Cloward clearly recognize the need for personal freedom. Poverty is a problem for them precisely because it keeps the poor from doing what they want to do. They are champions of the rights of the poor. Piven and Cloward just as clearly affirm the power of social forces and the need for association. Poverty is primarily the result of social forces crushing those too unorganized to fight back. The poor must organize if they are to get anything from the dominant classes. However, at the value level, Piven and Cloward share all too much with Friedman. If anything, they go beyond Friedman to suggest that all statements of public purpose are but rationalizations for the private interests of the speaker. The only value they affirm is the maximization of the interests of the poor.

Obviously, Harrington shares much of the analysis of Piven and Cloward. He wants to preserve individual choice much more than Moynihan, sees poverty as primarily the result of social forces, and believes that the poor must become organized. Indeed, he extends their analysis by recognizing the corrosive effect of poverty on the individual. Not only is this in direct contradiction to Friedman's image of the poor individual able to compete in the free market, but it also serves as a challenge to the faith of Piven and Cloward that the organized poor can challenge the system. In practice, this leads Harrington to call for a coalition of the Left to include the poor but to extend beyond them so as to generate more political power and finally to create a majority. Since this is a broad coalition (as opposed to the narrow activists represented by Piven and Cloward) and a coalition for change (as opposed to the status quo represented by Moynihan), it must be based on some vision of the good society. Thus Harrington does try to outline some terms of human meaning along the lines I have. They turn out to be as general as those I have proposed, leaving plenty of room for debate. Moreover, they are just as dynamic as mine, both demanding and protecting such debate.

The Future

Piven's and Cloward's theory that disruption by the poor would force generous social policy out of politicians who naturally want peace at whatever price[9] worked as long as Moynihan was advising Lyndon Johnson, a compulsive seeker after consensus. But when Moynihan's memos ended up on Richard Nixon's desk, disruption brought reactionary law and order. Nixon built support for that response precisely by reasserting the self-interest of the middle and upper classes. Piven and Cloward could object to this policy shift, but they were vulnerable on the level of principle. If public life is simply the battleground of self-interests, why should not the interests of the majority prevail? They did, and they still do.

In fact, the record of the Nixon administration on welfare policy was not all that conservative. Since basic grant levels for AFDC are set by the states, they continued to rise. The Nixon welfare specialists did continue a series of changes begun by the Democrats to aid those on welfare to move to work. This assistance to the ''working poor'' was justified on the solidly Republican principle of rewarding work effort. It was these very programs that allowed former welfare recipients in low-paying jobs to continue to receive some cash benefits—as well as food stamps, health care, and housing in many cases—that were then cut deeply in the first set of Reagan budget cuts in 1981. The formerly noble ''working poor'' were then portrayed as the ''not truly needy.'' These cuts, plus the deep recession of the first Reagan term, produced a dramatic increase in those officially defined as poor.

On the welfare-reform front, Reagan first proposed that welfare programs be turned back to the states. After considerable negotiations with the governors, the proposal for a new federalism was revised so that the

---

[9]Frances Fox Piven and Richard A. Cloward, *The New Class War* (New York: Pantheon Books, 1982).

states would get AFDC and the federal government would take Medicaid. That proposal never received any serious consideration by Congress. What remains is a stalemate, except for periodic skirmishes over specific programs as a part of the budget debates.

In their latest book, Piven and Cloward characterize the Reagan cuts in domestic spending and the tax cuts that accompanied them as a new class war. They see them as the predictable final stage of the typical cycle they described in *Regulating the Poor* in which disruption by the poor brings government assistance, followed first by social peace and then by the withdrawal of welfare. Once again the capitalist class has reasserted its control of society and has acted to increase its profits. Interestingly, Piven and Cloward speculate that the cycle may not be played out to its usual conservative conclusion this time. Since so many now receive some form of assistance, the rich cannot put the poor back in their place without hurting a much broader group of working people. This creates the possibility that a coalition may be formed to fight these cuts: shades of Harrington.

In the midst of these policy conflicts there appeared an intellectual challenge to welfare itself. By 1980 a shift in popular opinion indicated that the programs of the Great Society had not worked. Along came Charles Murray to argue that they actually had made things worse for the poor.[10] In fact, statistics show that those who are poor are considerably better off now after they receive government assistance. However, Murray assumes that work is always better than government assistance. On that basis he marshals statistics to show a significant increase in those who get help from various government programs. He then links this to rising levels of long-term unemployment, single-parent families, and illegitimacy. He concludes that increases in welfare have caused an increase in the dependency and a decline in the morality of the poor.

If this sounds like an update of the data used by Moynihan, it is. Moreover, the trends first identified by Moynihan have only accelerated since he first discussed them twenty years ago. Trying not to focus on the racial dimension of the issue this time, Moynihan recently pointed out that the number of children living in single-parent families doubled between 1960 and 1982, only noting parenthetically that this means a jump from thirty

---

[10]Charles Murray, *Losing Ground* (New York: Basic Books, 1984).

to sixty percent for blacks and seven to fifteen percent for whites.[11] However, instead of using these data to justify cuts in social programs, Moynihan reaffirmed his advocacy of more government support of families and children.

In the meantime, Harrington has added his own updated analysis of poverty.[12] Besides new data and his reactions to Reagan's program, he contrasts the situations of the early 1960s and early 1980s. Not only has the gap between high-paying, high-skill jobs and low-paying, low-skill ones grown, but now the middle range of blue-collar industrial jobs is declining because of foreign competition. Thus, instead of taking up poverty as an aberration amid a still-expanding industrial economy, as in the 1960s, we now approach it as a symptom of general economic decline. Negatively, this forces us to consider all of the complexities of the international economy. Positively, it means that a coalition for change can reach out to all of those people potentially endangered by industrial decline. Harrington's solutions remain constant: a planned full-employment program and national minimum income for those unable to work.

The debate goes on. The emerging concerns for homelessness, hunger, and family instability may signal the beginnings of a new interest in the underlying issue of poverty. When the next era of reform does come, our history of reform suggests that we could do much worse than to listen to Michael Harrington. In many ways, he hearkens back to the thoroughgoing democracy of the settlement houses. Yet their idealism is tempered in him by the harsh reality that, while vital local communities are essential, poverty is a national problem that calls for a national solution. He has learned that lesson of the New Deal. Moreover, he clearly sees that a creative vision of the public good must be joined to the power of the self-interests of various segments of the population if democratic social change is to happen. We are left with an understanding of poverty and what must be done to end it that recognizes the value of individual creativity, pluralistic association, and human purpose, as well as tough social and political realities.

---

[11]Daniel Patrick Moynihan, *Family and Nation* (New York: Harcourt Brace Jovanovich, 1986) 146.

[12]Michael Harrington, *The New American Poverty* (New York: Holt, Rinehart and Winston, 1984).

Annotated Bibliography

Historical Background

Bremner, Robert. *From the Depths: The Discovery of Poverty in the United States*. New York: New York University Press, 1956. This is the classic study of the discovery of poverty in the industrial United States, covering the period 1830-1925.

Coll, Blanche D. *Perspectives in Public Welfare: A History*. Washington: U.S. Department of Health, Education, and Welfare, 1969. This is a brief history of the English roots and the early practice of welfare in the United States.

Patterson, James T. *America's Struggle against Poverty: 1900-1980*. Cambridge: Harvard University Press, 1981. Patterson picks up where Bremner leaves off and traces the issue of poverty through the Carter administration.

Alternative Approaches

Friedman, Milton and Rose Friedman. *Capitalism and Freedom*. Chicago: University of Chicago Press, 1962.

_____. *Free to Choose*. New York: Avon, 1979. These are the two most direct statements of Friedman's general principles and contain specific discussions of poverty, equality, and income maintenance.

Harrington, Michael. *The New American Poverty*. New York: Holt, Rinehart and Winston, 1984.

_____. *The Other America*. New York: Macmillan, 1962. The latter is Harrington's classic study of poverty in the United States. The former both deals with contemporary evidence and more clearly argues the case for structural change in the economy.

Moynihan, Daniel Patrick. *Family and Nation*. New York: Harcourt Brace Jovanovich, 1986.

_____. *The Politics of a Guaranteed Income*. New York: Random House, 1973. The latter lays out Moynihan's basic analysis and applies it to the battle over welfare reform during the Nixon administration. The former updates the analysis to the present.

Piven, Frances Fox and Richard A. Cloward. *The New Class War*. New York: Pantheon Books, 1982.

_____. *Regulating the Poor: The Function of Public Welfare*. New York: Random House, 1971. The latter is their fundamental analysis of poverty and welfare. The former is their response to Reagan's attack on the welfare state.

Analytic Resources

Arendt, Hannah. *The Human Condition*. Garden City NY: Doubleday, 1959.

_____. *On Revolution*. New York: Viking Press, 1965. The former lays out Arendt's basic description of human action. The latter develops the relation between economics and action and especially her concept of property.

Copeland, Warren R. "The Ethics of Welfare Reform." *Selected Papers*. American Society of Christian Ethics, 1978.

Wogaman, Philip. *Guaranteed Annual Income: The Moral Issues*. Nashville: Abingdon Press, 1968. This remains the best book-length ethical analysis of poverty and welfare since the New Deal.

J. Ronald Engel
Meadville/Lombard
Theological School

■ ■

Ecology and Social Justice:
The Search for a
Public Environmental Ethic

■ ■ One reason the search for an environmental ethic has failed in the
United States is that the two most prominent sorts of environmental ethic
so far proposed—ecocentric ethics and resource-conservation ethics—do
not take sufficiently public moral high ground. They fail to address adequately the actual public character of the environmental issue, which is best
understood as the *issue of ecojustice*. As the present global situation indicates, our failure to respect the natural environment is a function of our
social relationships as well as our relationships to the rest of nature. It is a
part of our ecosocial system as a whole. Thus it is necessarily a public issue in the broadest sense and involves not merely an additive relationship
but an integration of the principles of social justice and environmental ethics. Nature and humanity will be liberated together or not at all.

Both ecocentric ethics and resource-conservation ethics attempt to
counter the destructive system of modern development. This system, based
on "the idea that nature and its resources exist solely to be used for the
material benefit of humans and for the particular profit of those who own
them," has thoroughly characterized the modern American experience.[1]

---

[1] Joseph Petulla, *American Environmental History* (San Francisco: Boyd and Fraser
Publishing Company, 1977) 9.

Ecocentric ethics addresses many of the inherent environmental values at stake in this process, while resource-conservation ethics addresses the use values of the environment and the importance of their sustainable and equitable management. Yet neither speaks to the full range of environmental and social-justice values involved or to their internal systemic interdependence. Thus neither is able to pose the choice of an alternative ecosocial order that is just toward persons and nature.

To say that social justice and environmental protection belong together is to fly in the face of one of the most ingrained ideologies of modern society. Almost everyone accepts that we must choose between jobs or the environment, between racial justice for the oppressed in the cities or environmental amenities for the rich in the suburbs, or between preservation of biological diversity or alleviation of absolute poverty in the developing nations. Unfortunately, this mistaken ideology is frequently enforced by antagonisms and misunderstandings between environmental and social-justice advocates.[2]

A further reason why these positions have failed to create a viable public ethic is that, while each is rooted in the Western democratic experience and bears a loose historical connection to democratic values, neither is interpreted in a way that makes environmental concerns a matter of principle in the struggle for a democratic public order. While critical of the prevailing understanding of modern development, they fail to provide an alternative modern ideal. The normative understanding of democracy assumed here is that freedom and equality in community are of the essence of the nature of things.

A foundation for a viable public ethic of ecojustice may be found if the values identified by ecocentric and resource-conservation ethics are recast in terms of an inclusive ideal of world loyalty and a democratic worldview. A democratic vision of ecojustice is one in which the relations of human beings are free, equal, and participatory with one another and with the rest of nature. On these terms, the struggle for justice in society and the struggle for justice to the natural environment may be seen as mutually complementary and reinforcing ethical imperatives. Ultimately, the ground for such an ethic is a matter of religious faith.

------

[2]See James Noel Smith, *Environmental Quality and Social Justice in Urban America* (Washington: The Conservation Foundation, 1974).

Ecocentric Ethics

Ecocentric, or life-centered, ethics embraces those forms of ethics associated with the wilderness, ecological, and animal-rights movements in American history. While these perspectives lift up different kinds of natural value, and while their political consequences have been different—the first leads to the preservation of natural areas, the second to the maintenance of ecological cycles and species diversity, and the third to the humane treatment of domestic livestock and experimental animals—they all share these characteristics:

1. a worldview that places the human being uniquely but fully within nature
2. an affirmation of inherent value in some aspect of the nonhuman environment
3. a historic affiliation with broadly democratic values

They also share a vigorous rejection of anthropocentric or human-centered ethical traditions that restrict inherent value to human beings exclusively. In the course of the last century, it has been primarily these positions that have formed the ethical backbone of the environmental (as contrasted to the conservation) movement.

The values affirmed by the ecocentric traditions are of several kinds. The wilderness movement is concerned with the transcending values immanent within the whole of nature itself: the everlasting values of evolutionary and cosmic continuity, concentrated in particular places, organisms, and relationships, unmodified by human activity or where human activity is closely identified with natural rhythms. Such values are perceived as independent of human volition yet accessible to human experience through aesthetic appreciation, moral insight, and scientific investigation. Wild nature, as the primal and ultimate ground of value within the nature of being itself, judges all human ambition while providing the ultimate source of human creativity. It ought, therefore, to be preserved.

John Muir, founder of the Sierra Club in the 1890s, asked: "Why should man value himself as more than a small part of the one great unit of creation?" An earlier wilderness enthusiast, Henry David Thoreau, declared that "in wildness is the preservation of the world."

In the American experience, the wilderness tradition has been associated with fundamental motifs of the democratic ideal, especially the right to dissent and the essential equality of every person. Thoreau exemplifies these associations. Writing in *The Atlantic Monthly* in 1856 he argued: "The kings of England had their forests to hold the king's game. Why should not we who have renounced the king's authority have our national preserves, in which the bear and panther . . . may still exist [in] . . . our forests, not to hold the king's game merely, but to hold and preserve the king himself?" The king is the people in a democracy, and Thoreau's idea bore fruit in 1872 when the United States set aside Yellowstone as the first national park in the world "for the benefit and enjoyment of all the people." It is impossible to understand Thoreau's essay "Civil Disobedience"—the most seminal essay in the movement of nonviolent resistance—or his historic plea on behalf of John Brown apart from his experience of the transcendent moral law at Walden Pond.

Landmark political achievements of the wilderness movement in American history, significant more for the principles articulated than for their actual capacity to preserve the American wilderness, have been the formation of the National Park Service in 1916 and the Wilderness Act of 1964.

The ecological movement finds value inherent in nature as humans come to participatory knowledge of the way in which natural ecosystems work and they fit into them. Aldo Leopold, a wildlife biologist, wrote the bible of contemporary ecological ethics, *A Sand County Almanac,* out of his observations of the plant and animal communities near his farm in Wisconsin. He was struck by how processes of cooperation incorporate and transcend the competitive conflicts between organisms within the communities of life. Although Leopold's perspective involved existential components and was not reducible to the conclusions of science, it was nonetheless built upon a long history of scientific research concerned to understand nature as an interdependent, self-regulating system. One of his predecessors was George Perkins Marsh, who posited an inherent "balance of nature." One of his successors was Rachel Carson, who described the disruption of the biological food chain by DDT in *Silent Spring* and launched the environmental movement of the 1960s.

In his conclusion to *A Sand County Almanac,* in a chapter entitled "A Land Ethic," Leopold proposed the following ethical norm: "A thing is right when it tends to preserve the integrity, stability and beauty of the biotic community. It is wrong when it tends otherwise.''[3] The objective value that Leopold sought to affirm, Holmes Rolston III calls "systemic value"— the value of the collective systemic processes that are prior to and productive of the intrinsic values of individual organisms. Since we, along with all plants and animals, only live and achieve our autonomous ends by virtue of our participation in such loose communal systems, ethicists such as Rolston follow Leopold in affirming duties to these systems, moral obligations entailing the maintenance of their fundamental integrity, stability, and beauty.

As a teacher at the progressive University of Wisconsin in the 1930s, Leopold had a greater appreciation for the social dimension of the democratic experience than Thoreau and sought to make the family farm socially as well as environmentally stable. It is possible to speculate that his notion of the "land ethic" drew from an ideal of "citizenship." In *A Sand County Almanac* he writes that "the land ethic changes the role of *Homo sapiens* from conqueror of the land-community to plain member and citizen of it.''[4] In fact, this ideal was frequently appealed to by the science of ecology, or "science of communities," in the early twentieth century. One place its implications are to be found today is in the bioregional ideal of local cooperation and "living in place."

The greatest political victories of the ecological movement of the 1960s were the National Environmental Policy Act of 1969 and the Endangered Species Act of 1973.

Of the ecocentric traditions under discussion, the third, animal rights and liberation, most clearly bears the marks of its beginnings in the age of democratic revolutions. Advocates of animal rights and animal liberation argue that they seek to expand the domain of human rights and the struggle for human liberation to include those forms of life that share with us presumed attributes of inherent worth—for example, the capacity to feel, to be aware. Indicative of the underlying ethical commitment of the movement is the fact that one of its first leaders was William Wilberforce, an English reformer who, after successfully leading the struggle to abolish slavery from the British empire, sponsored the first bill in the British parliament to protect animals.

---

[3] Aldo Leopold, *A Sand County Almanac* (New York: Oxford University Press, 1949) 117.
[4] Ibid., 115.

Both forms of ethical argumentation that typify the movement today, utilitarianism and natural-rights theory, take the individual organism as the exclusive locus of inherent value. This radical individualism has antagonized ecological ethicists while attracting adherents of process philosophy, a perspective that limits duties to subjects only. Both kinds of animal-liberation advocates rely on scientific data and evolutionary theory to underpin their argument that a continuity exists between the higher animals and humans. Both positions, too, posit a hierarchy of inherent value roughly coinciding with the movement from simple to complex forms of life, with human beings on top.

For animal-liberation protagonists such as Peter Singer, the critical physical attribute of inherent worth is "sentience," the capacity of living organisms to feel pleasure and pain. Singer argues for equal moral consideration of all beings who, having this capacity, have interests in their own welfare. For animal-rights protagonists such as Tom Regan, it is the capacity of higher animals to initiate action with a view to satisfying preferences, and therefore to be the "subject of a life," that gives them inherent value and rights comparable (but not the same as) human individuals.

Resource Conservation

Resource conservation is far and away the most dominant environmental ethic in the United States. It is the underlying perspective of almost all work on environmental policy in the social and natural sciences. It is also the "official" ethic embodied in most environmentally enlightened government and corporate programs. Although resource conservation extends into the beginnings of the modern democratic era—at least back to the Physiocrats of eighteenth-century France, who made political economy a moral as well as a quantitative science—and is closely associated with philosophical utilitarianism, its first explicit articulation as an environmental ethic came in the late nineteenth century as part of the progressive movement in American politics. Influenced by several intellectual developments since that time, the basic model has remained substantially the same.

The pivotal figure in the emergence of resource conservation as a viable political ethic in the United States was Gifford Pinchot, head of the Division of Forestry under Theodore Roosevelt. Pinchot was impressed with a fact then only dawning on most Americans, that the frontier was closed. Whatever remained was all that would ever be available for future development. Schooled in European methods of "sustained yield" scientific forest management, he was concerned with how to maximize efficiently the variety of economic benefits (timber, minerals, grazing) of the forests. While at first assuming that private corporations would see the ultimate wisdom of such an approach, he found it increasingly necessary to use government regulatory power and ownership for its achievement. This fit the progressive program as a whole and institutionalized the association of conservation with federal regulation, scientific management, social democracy, economic prosperity, and resource economics that has continued throughout the century.

Pinchot articulated the ethics of resource conservation in the following statement:

> The first great fact about conservation is that it stands for development . . . (not just) husbanding of resources for future generations . . . but the use of natural resources now existing on this continent for the benefit of the people who live here now. . . . In the second place, conservation stands for the prevention of waste. . . . The third principle is this: the natural resources must be developed and preserved for the benefit of the many, and not merely for the few. . . . Conservation means the greatest good for the greatest number for the longest time.[5]

Note the key elements of this idea. First, implicit but clear, the notion of limits ("the resources now existing"). Second, the affirmation of the use value of the environment ("conservation . . . stands for development"). This notion is embodied in the very language of nature as a "resource"— as something with the capacity to be refashioned into something else. Like cosmic, systemic, and intrinsic values, this is a distinct kind of environmental value. Third, the notion of efficiency and restraint ("prevention of waste"). Fourth, the highest or "greatest good." Fifth, the fair distribution of natural resources among present and future populations.

The underlying assumption of resource-conservation ethics is that the nonhuman world has chiefly instrumental value for human beings, and therefore the ethical reason for conserving it is prudential, a matter of enlightened self- or social interest.

---

[5]Gifford Pinchot, *The Fight for Conservation* (New York: Doubleday, Page & Company, 1910) 42-48; also quoted in *The American Environment: Readings in the History of Conservation*, ed. R. Nash (Reading MA: Addison-Wesley, 1968) 59-61.

It is evident that this model is open to expansion in several directions. What constitutes, for example, the limits of the resource is open to empirical definition, as is the best technological and social means to achieve efficiency and restraint. Similarly, the "greatest good" is open for redefinition; it could range from mere economic prosperity to higher aesthetic or scientific values. Fair distribution is also open for redefinition and need not be limited to a utilitarian formulation of the "greatest number." (It is understandable why social-justice advocates, especially those concerned for economic justice, would find the model attractive as well as useful in forming coalitions with those motivated by enlightened self-interest.) Finally, at a high level of generality, the model can even expand the locus of inherent value beyond human organisms, as long as the basic instrumental relationship between means and ends, things of lesser value serving things of higher value, remains.

Each of these expansions is evident in the work of one of the most sophisticated contemporary resource-conservation ethicist-economists, Herman Daly. In *Economics, Ecology and Ethics,* Daly expands the Pinchot model in each of these directions as a way of arguing for the physical and ethical necessity of a steady state economy. For Daly, conservation is part of the solution to the fundamental economic problem, which is how to use ultimate natural means rationally in the service of ultimate moral ends.

Daly employs the systems theory of physics to describe the dynamics of the steady-state open environmental system within which all natural-resource extraction and development must take place. This is the ultimate means on top of which all sustainable ultimate ends must be built. Daly finds the error in twentieth-century Keynesian growth economics to lie in the attempt to maximize material and energy-resource utilization without attention to the constraints this physical system imposes. The false assumption of the modern economic-development model is that technology can substitute new resources for old without limit. While Daly frequently speaks of "ecological" systems, it is the environment as described by the law of entropy that informs his model.

From the perspective of ultimate moral ends, Daly is concerned with the welfare of future generations, respect for "subhuman" life, and inequities in wealth distribution—all ethical values historically associated with, or easily adapted to, the classic utilitarian resource-conservation model. In his view, recognition of the restraints imposed by environmental means leads to a greater social awareness of the ethical problems of distribution and, conversely, moral concern for economic inequity leads to an increased concern for resource conservation.

On the basis of these considerations, Daly proposes the conservation ethics of a steady-state economy, with physical flows of production and consumption minimized, and a style of life that maximizes time-intensive activities, finite wants, and equality of opportunities and benefits within and between generations. A steady-state world economy does not mean a "no-growth" economy. Rather, it means a policy of selective growth governed by ethical considerations: for example, augmented economic growth for the poor and diminished growth for the rich.

A Contemporary Issue of Ecojustice:
Tropical Deforestation

In order to understand why and how environmental problems are issues of ecojustice and why it is necessary that ecocentric and resource-conservation ethics be judged in these terms, it is instructive to look closely at a major global environmental problem. Most American citizens perceive the destruction of the tropical rain forest as a remote problem. In fact, it is environmentally and socially close to home.

The tropical rain forest is the most exuberant expression of nature in the world. Age-old, uniquely adapted to poor soils and high rainfall, it thrives by means of a diversity of plant and animal life without peer. Yet with present trends, most of the tropical lowland rain forest in Latin America and Asia will be destroyed by the turn of the century, and a majority of the remaining highland rain forest will be lost as well.[6]

The consequences are great. It will be the end of the most ecologically complex and evolutionarily successful biomes on earth and will mean the greatest wave of planetary extinctions since the Pleistocene epoch. The number and character of species lost, much less the number of individual

---

[6]Regarding the problem of tropical deforestation as an ecojustice issue see: Gerald O. Barney, *The Global 2000 Report to the President: Entering the 21st Century* (New York: Pergamon Press, 1980); Noam Chomsky and E. S. Herman, *The Political Economy of Human Rights* (Montreal: Black Rose Books, 1979); Shelton H. Davis, *Victims of the Miracle* (Cambridge: Cambridge University Press, 1977); R. J. Goodland and H. S. Irwin, *Green Hell to Red Desert?* (New York: Elsevier, 1975); Norman Myers, *The Primary Source: Tropical Forests and Our Future* (New York: W. W. Norton and Co., 1984); L. J. Webb, "Ecological Values of the Tropical Rainforest Resource," *Proceedings of the Linnean Society of New South Wales* 106 (1983): 263-74; and Catherine Caufield, *In the Rainforest* (Chicago: University of Chicago Press, 1984).

animals and plants lost, will never be known. It also means considerable loss of biospheric integrity. The ecological interdependencies of the tropical forests with other parts of the world, through such relationships as migrating wildlife, atmospheric CO_2 levels, and river, ocean, and watershed protection, are vast and little understood. For people throughout the world, including the United States, it means the loss of unique forest products, genetic resources for agricultural and medical purposes, sources for the enjoyment and knowledge of natural and cultural systems, and vital life-support systems. For those indigenous to the region, it means, in addition, increased soil erosion and siltation, loss of local industries and food supplies, poverty from the failure of intensive farming on cleared land, increase in social, economic, and political inequality, and the virtual extinction of local tribal and hunting cultures.

While the pressure of overpopulation in the tropics is an important factor in this development, it is less important than such factors as highway building, cattle ranching, and logging, which in the Amazon account for at least sixty percent of the total destruction. The much-publicized slash-and-burn peasant cultivators account for only about seventeen percent of the destruction in the Amazon.

What drives the engine of this unparalleled transformation in the ecology of the biosphere? The best analyses indicate that it is a set of mutually reinforcing technological, social, economic, political, and cultural factors.

On the economic side, lopsided international markets, industrial technology, and an expanding appetite for a higher standard of living by affluent populations create needs entirely out of balance with the ecological and social welfare of the countries with the resources to supply those needs. It is economically advantageous in the short run for commercial interests within and outside these countries to join hands in the exploitation of these resources. Therefore, technology and capital from the north are used to turn the rain forests into exportable commodities for foreign exchange and private capital accumulation, to pay debts and to buy military hardware. (Seventy percent of the lumber and beef go to Europe and North America; U.S. corporations are among the major landowners and loggers; the U.S. government and military supported the development of the Amazon highway; and the Amazon Basin hydropower dam, the largest deliberate act of environmental destruction in world history, is a plan of the Hudson Institute.)

It is politically and socially advantageous for elites in less-developed countries to promote this process. Their power is linked with corporate and governmental centers of power in the developed world. The opening of new land to settlement, however doomed it may be in the long run, helps maintain the vastly unequal systems of land ownership. If the existing cultivated land in Brazil were fairly divided, each family would have ten acres. Repressive political regimes create—often deliberately, for greater "internal security"—migrating peasant cultivators. Racial and ethnic prejudice toward the indigenous peoples of the forest is sometimes added to the mix.

Is the issue of the rain forests an environmental or social issue? Clearly it is both. It is an issue of ecojustice. Every step in environmental destruction has the effect of increasing social injustice, and every strengthening of social injustice has the effect of increasing environmental destruction.

One reason this is so is because people and natural environments are never separated in fact, however much they may be in our ideas about them. Our choices and actions always affect both. We do not choose between the nonhuman environment and people but between different "mixed communities" or ecosocial systems of people, animals, and plants. Thus one ecojustice choice at stake in deforestation is the survival of the mixed community of indigenous peoples and the rain forest. Another is the expansion of environmentally and socially repressive regimes.

The key motivational factor that guarantees continued destruction of rain forests' native peoples is the ideology of modernization: the widely shared public ideal of increasing material abundance and consumption through increased technological and social control by corporations and the state. This ideology rationalizes both the unequal distribution of wealth and power and the destruction of the environment. According to this ideology, human creativity is understood as world mastery. Other values include progress understood as colonization, nature as valueless and culture as rational, growth as increase in size, competitive individualism, and nationalism. It is often surprising for Americans, who have left behind their frontier ideology, to discover that the peoples of "developing countries" see themselves necessarily passing through a process of frontier development—requiring the conquest of nature and indigenous peoples—en route to modern nationhood and material affluence.

Australian ethicists Plumwood and Routley summarize the situation as follows:

It is common to encounter the view, associated with the ideology of conquest of nature and expressed frequently and forcefully by technocrats and other powerful figures in places such as Brazil and Indonesia, that the natural ecosystems concerned are really of little or no value, and that their destruction will involve no loss and even a gain because it will permit the development of man-made replacements. . . . *There is the unshakable conviction that the world is being improved, amounting in some quarters to a conception of the goal as an almost sacred mission.* . . . This aggressive technocratic ideology appears to precede the opening of remaining large tracts of land and forest to the markets and influence of the advanced industrial nations.[7]

The Adequacy of Ecocentric and Resource-Conservation Ethics

It is apparent that any ethic that seeks to address adequately the issue of the rain forests must be prepared to speak critically to the issue of ecojustice—the full complement of environmental and social values at stake and their mutual dependence—and to the fundamental character of the regnant system of development through world mastery that negates those values. It must also be prepared to offer an alternative positive vision of ecojustice that can inform various national traditions of public ethics.

The ecocentric ethical traditions are richly present in the story of life that is present in the rain forest wilderness. A genetic language two billion years old, within which we evolved and upon which we in so many known and unknown ways remain dependent, should not be destroyed. Generations of explorers, naturalists, artists, and travelers have attested to the profound contact with the power of being that the rain forest occasions. The values of biological diversity and ecosystemic integrity regionally and globally are obvious. Perhaps less frequently noticed, but not for that reason less important, is the value inherent in each of the incalculable number of individual organisms and the suffering that forest destruction brings for many of them.

Furthermore, of all contemporary ethical positions, the ecocentric traditions have mounted the most radical challenge to the process of modern development: the drive toward technological mastery of the Earth. The im-

---

[7]Val Plumwood and Richard Routley, "World Rainforest Destruction—The Social Factors," *The Ecologist* 12 (1982): 20. Italics mine.

perative to *let being be*—to preserve inherent value in nature—is a powerful motivation to question all forms of personal and social domination.

Resource-conservation ethics now informs most government and nongovernmental organizations' rationales for saving the rain forests. This ethical perspective underlies, for example, the United Nations-sponsored *World Conservation Strategy*.[8] The potential usefulness of the genetic pool is a major argument, as is the potential effect upon human survival of the loss of biospheric integrity. Resource-conservation ethics is also the basic perspective informing most initiatives by national and international agencies to regulate resource extraction and to find the technical and scientific means for sustainable development so that present resources can be used indefinitely.

Resource-conservation ethics also motivates efforts for more just distribution of tropical resources, including a concern for the landless poor and for native populations. Typically persons who see the role of unequal economic conditions in environmental destruction will also hold a resource-conservation viewpoint, arguing that until these injustices are changed, sustainable development will not be possible.[9]

While these strengths are clear, it is also evident that neither ecocentric nor resource-conservation ethics constitutes an adequate public environmental ethic. In the first place, neither adequately addresses the full range of environmental values at issue. Ecocentric ethics does not go very far in defining the right use of the rain forests. It is best in providing grounds for limiting human action. Resource-conservation ethics does not seriously address the inherent wilderness and ecological values of the forests. Theoretically, it could reduce all values in the environment to "resources" for human—or, in revisionist versions, "higher animal"—consumption. If it were sustainable, there would be nothing wrong in principle with turning the entire rain forest into a tropical tree farm.

But equally serious is the fact that neither ecocentric nor resource-conservation ethics is able to deal adequately with the social-justice aspect of the issue or the relationship between environmental and social justice. Ecocentric ethics assumes a worldview that consists of two realities: in-

---

[8]*World Conservation Strategy* (Morges, Switzerland: International Union for the Conservation of Nature and Natural Resources and the World, 1980).

[9]See, for example, Samuel S. Kim, *The Quest for a Just World Order* (Boulder CO: Westview Press, 1984) esp. ch. 7.

dividuals and the whole. Intermediate human groups are omitted. Thus wilderness ethics is rooted in the experience of the human subject confronting the universe, ecological ethics in the awareness of the systemic value of the biotic community as a whole, and animal rights and liberation in the appreciation of the individual organism as a repository of inherent value. In its utilitarian outlook, resource-conservation ethics assumes much the same worldview: private individuals and public collectivities (''the greatest number'').

Neither kind of ethics treats the political associations of human society, the way men and women more or less voluntarily associate in order to live together more justly in freedom, equality, and community. In short, their basic models of human action seem to eschew politics, that is, free moral agents deliberating together about issues in the public realm. This is especially clear in the case of conservation ethics because of its political dependency upon the role of experts. Both forms of ethics are limited in their capacity to address the complexity of the actual motivations and relationships that characterize political life, especially the power relationships involved. They therefore are unable to judge political repression, to name it as the ethical core of the ecojustice issue, or to say what role political parties and social movements must play if it is to be challenged. They are ill-prepared to offer an environmental social ethic and, without one, environmental ethics can become the tool of the very system it purportedly seeks to change. Ecocentric ethics can become the rationalization for withdrawal from social conflict. Conservation can become a rationalization for improving the efficiency of an exploitive economy. It is not surprising that no enduring alliance between environmental movements and movements for human liberation has yet taken place in America.

This danger is evident in the way the American environmental movement in recent years has excluded political and economic analysis from its environmental concerns—an omission apparent in two influential policy statements, *The Global 2000 Report* and *An Environmental Agenda for the Future*.[10]

Although *Global 2000* assesses the long-term ecological and human consequences of modern economic development, it fails to address the role

---

[10]Barney, *The Global 2000 Report; An Environmental Agenda for the Future* (Washington: Island Press, 1985). The former was written for the Carter administration; the latter is the result of a collaborative project by the leadership of the ten major American environmental organizations.

of political and economic structures and makes no systematic assessment of the responsibility of the U.S. government or corporations in causing these changes. While documenting the negative environmental consequences of economic and population growth in the United States, *An Environmental Agenda for the Future* does not question the basic legitimacy of the American political economy. In fact, it explicitly favors economic growth, without any discrimination among different kinds and their differing consequences for different classes of persons.

The failure of the environmental movement to see that our real choices are between different kinds of ecosocial systems—different "mixed communities" or ways of organizing the basic relationships of animals, plants, and humans—shows the power of the modern developmental worldview. The great contemporary dichotomies of our culture—the natural environment as value-filled (ecocentric ethics) and the natural environment as inherently valueless (resource-conservation ethics)—are two sides of the same coin. Both are social constructions of reality by urban populations prone to see the world in terms of people versus environment because this is how their state-capitalist society organizes it and how they experience it.

It may seem unfair to blame environmental ethics for not doing what other ethics ought to do, which is to articulate the social-ethical dimension of public issues. But the same critique could and should be made of most forms of social-justice ethics from the other direction: they fail to attend to the values of the nonhuman environment. The crucial point is that we cannot get away from the fact that environmental and social-justice issues are ecojustice issues; and this realization will eventually have to change our way of thinking about every ethical question—social, environmental, and personal.[11]

Toward a Democratic Environmental Ethic

Where do we look for the sources of an ethic that is adequate to encompass both environmental and social-justice issues? How are we to think ethically about environmental and social responsibility together? What alternative public ideal to the regnant modern-development model can be offered to American society? What positive understanding of ecojustice can

---

[11] Feminist ethics and theology are especially helpful here. See Rosemary Reuther, *Sexism and God-Talk* (Boston: Beacon Press, 1984).

speak to the authentic human aspirations for liberation that lie at the center of the modern project? Much constructive work needs to be done.

This much is clear: an adequate and effective vision of ecojustice in American society must be linked to a re-envisagement of the democratic ideal. This has been the ethical basis for founding much of public worth in our society, and this is the spur to new perfections.

Are there grounds to believe that latent within Western culture (as indeed within other cultures as well) there is a democratic ideal of world loyalty with the potential to lure persons to seek justice for all human and nonhuman existence?

Historical sources for such an alternative public ideal lie neglected within the Western democratic experience. Contemporary environmental and social-justice concern overlooks the holistic thrust of some of the most creative advocates of public justice in the modern period, thinkers such as Wilberforce and Thoreau. Their holistic concern is by no means unique. In American history it was also present in Jefferson's vision of an agrarian republic,[12] in late-nineteenth-century populism and Progressivism, and in the urban social-democratic vision of pragmatists such as John Dewey, who conceived of modernity as the opportunity for each individual to participate in the evolution of the world conceived as a shared work of art.[13]

What would be the character of a reconstructed democratic ideal rooted in such sources? Let us speculate for a moment. In the first place, at its core there would be an ecological worldview, one that conceived all values as members of a series of interconnected ecosocial systems or contexts and as reciprocally related to all other values.[14] This would seem to be a necessary starting place for a truly holistic ecojustice ideal.

Within such a worldview, the relationships between the one and the many are open to interpretation by a "democratic" root metaphor. Wil-

---

[12]For a contemporary exposition, see Wendell Berry, *The Unsettling of America* (San Francisco: Sierra Club Books, 1977).

[13]For the latter, see J. Ronald Engel, *Sacred Sands: The Struggle for Community in the Indiana Dunes* (Middletown CT: Wesleyan University Press, 1983); for Dewey, see Gibson Winter, *Liberating Creation: Foundations of Religious Social Ethics* (New York: Crossroads, 1981).

[14]Gregory Bateson's grounding of mind in ecological relationships is very suggestive for a metaphysics of the ecosocial order that supports principles of ecojustice. For a recent exposition of his ideas, see Morris Berman, *The Reenchantment of the World* (New York: Bantam Books, 1984).

liam James suggested such a metaphor when he asked in *The Will to Believe:* "Why may not the world be a sort of republican banquet . . . where all the qualities of being respect one another's personal sacredness, yet sit at the common table of space and time?"[15] The metaphor of the democratic republic was frequently used by James as a model for a savable world and fit well with his notion of a pluralistic yet internally related universe. Like the metaphors of the Kingdom or the covenant from the biblical tradition, it has an imaginative capacity to include the distinct values of non-human and human societies alike. As Henry Beston wrote in *The Outermost House:* "For the animal shall not be measured by man. In a world older and more complete than ours they move finished and complete, gifted with extensions of the senses we have lost or never attained, living by voices we shall never hear. They are not brethren, they are not underlings; they are other nations, caught with ourselves in the net of life and time, fellow prisoners of the splendour and travail of the earth."[16]

What would such a democratic ontology mean for an ethic of ecojustice? First, it would mean that each of the fundamental ethical principles of social justice in a democracy—freedom, equality, and community—are principles inherent in the ecosocial order as a whole (ultimately, the cosmos; penultimately, the biosphere) and in varying ways in each of its member societies. Thus each individual organism would be understood as being in some unique way a "self" or creative agent (freedom) in relationship with other individuals, each of whom has a similar right to the fulfillment of its unique individuality (equality), and a productive participant in the shared existence of the system as a whole and at least one of its member societies (community).[17]

None of these principles would be absolute or univocal. Rather, the ultimate moral maxim would be thoroughly pluralistic: act so as to maximize the richness of flora, fauna, and human experience through maximizing the freedom, equality, and community of all forms of life. This would be in keeping with the democratic observation that there are many different ways in which organisms and societies of organisms may be free, equal,

---

[15]William James, *The Will to Believe* (New York: Dover Publications, 1956) 270.

[16]Henry Beston, *The Outermost House* (New York: Penguin Books, 1928, 1977) 25.

[17]I am indebted here to Douglas Sturm, "The Prism of Justice: E Pluribus Unum?" *Society for Christian Ethics Annual* (1981): 19. Sturm does not expand these principles beyond human nature, although he speaks of their grounding in "the nature of things."

and communal, many different ways in which life struggles to maximize richness, many different ways in which persons may engage in that struggle.

In fact, much of the richness of social and ecological existence on Earth today is due to the variety of kinds of mixed communities, landscapes, and ways of life that humankind has preserved or helped create in the course of its evolution. This variety was probably essential to the evolution of complex human consciousness and the maximal richness of the biosphere itself, yet it is a variety that is everywhere today being replaced by the monoculture of modern industrial society.[18]

An important implication of this model for the concerns of this essay should be apparent. The distinctive ethical relationships of human beings to one another (social justice) and the distinctive ethical relationships of human beings to nature (environmental ethics) are distinguishable but reinforcing activities, for these are reciprocal values within ecosocial wholes.

This is illuminating because the great ignored fact in ecojustice discussions to date is that social justice and environmental justice in *all* their forms seem necessary for the achievement of a flourishing and sustainable world. Human freedom seems to be as important to the preservation of the environment as the free unfolding of the evolutionary adventure is to the actualization of human freedom; the pursuit of economic, political, and social equality seems to be as important to the sustenance of the natural world as the opportunity of each species and organism to continue in the struggle for life is to the realization of human equality; the full participation of each person in political, social, and economic institutions seems to be as important to the future of the environment as the continuing integrity of ecosystemic processes is to the future of democratic institutions. That these elusive but fundamental reciprocal relationships are not only observed historical tendencies but are in fact true to the nature of things is what the environmental ethical traditions have been clumsily trying to assert for some time. Moreover, this accounts for their vague but stubborn association with democratic social values.

---

[18]See Raymond F. Dasmann, *A Different Kind of Country* (London: Collier-Macmillan Ltd., 1968). This suggests another way of thinking ethically about social and environmental values that cannot be pursued here—one based on the virtues appropriate to various ecosocial contexts.

Given this reading of the nature of our shared political and ecological struggle, it is no coincidence that a repressive political regime will try to eliminate wilderness areas as well as human rights. Wilderness has repeatedly provided refuge for political oppositions as well as nourished ideas of political dissent. The rain forest wilderness supports peoples of different races and cultures, peoples with free and novel purposes of their own. It is in the wilderness, history attests, that countless prophets and revolutionaries have found the moral foundation to support their radical stands for human dignity. Thoreau inherited the mantle of Elijah and St. Francis. Conversely, wilderness will not be long protected in societies that do not respect human rights, as most environmentalists familiar with international conservation issues understand.

Given this reading, too, many kinds of human environmental relationships previously considered ethically required because they serve the cause of social justice may now be judged right for reasons of ecological value as well. For example, resource-conservation ethics has long argued for "material sufficiency" as an instrumental ethical norm. By only using as much as we need, we have more to share with other human beings. But within the context of an ecojustice ethic, sufficiency is also a primary ecological good. One notion of justice now includes giving the human body its due and the values of other natural things, including their "use values," their due as well. Simply stated, eating "enough" is a good for the individual who eats, for other human consumers, and for the natural environment. Both social ethics and environmental ethics become stronger because of the presence of the other. Further, the various meanings of the principles of freedom, equality, and community are expanded in the process.

In a pluralistic and democratic universe, there is neither complete identity nor separation of values; instead, there is overlap. Thus we should not expect that, under all historical conditions, environmental justice and social justice will be mutually supporting. What can be said is that in the long run these relationships are supported by the nature of things and their truth will be borne out. Furthermore, because the same three basic ethical principles of freedom, equality, and community apply to both social and environmental spheres does not mean an absence of conflict in their theoretical development, any more than there is an absence of conflict among these principles in normative social ethics. One of the greatest needs today in the development of an ethics of ecojustice is for the precise nature of ethical and policy conflicts to be made explicit.

To speak of "in the long run" and in "the nature of things" sounds close to speaking of faith. As Roberto Unger has said, "Religion starts with the notion that the realm of values is somehow grounded in the reality of things."[19]

No data within the reach of human knowledge will ever prove for certain that ecojustice is in the reality of things or that a democratic root metaphor illuminates human moral relationships to nature and society. But experience is cumulative and of many kinds, and it points more or less well toward different conclusions. There are good reasons—scientific, historical, logical, existential—to believe that the world is an interdependent reality morally as well as physically. I believe the recognition of this truth is now luring the evolution of human religious consciousness. The symbolic impact upon people throughout the world of the picture of Earth from space attests to it.

This is not to say that we must leave the faith of our fathers and mothers behind. In fact, the opposite is more likely the case if by faith we mean more than literal creedal beliefs. The fundamental worldview of the biblical writers, beginning with Genesis 1, is that of a Creator who loves and cares for *all* creation as a unit:

The Sovereign God is good to all,
 and has compassion over all creation. . . .
The Lord upholds all who are falling,
 and raises up all who are bowed down.
The eyes of all look to you,
 and you give them their food in due season.
You open your hand,
 and satisfy the desire of every living thing.
(Psalm 145:9, 14-16 as paraphrased by William Gibson)

The dualism of society and environment, social justice and environmental ethics, history and nature that has plagued Christian thought is in this respect thoroughly unbiblical—as is any kind of anthropocentrism that would place humankind above or apart from creation rather than uniquely and specially within it. The most sensitive insights into the meaning of ecojustice are now coming from Jewish and Christian social ethicists. In

---

[19]Roberto Maugabiera Unger, *Knowledge and Politics* (New York: Free Press, 1975) 93; also quoted in Sturm, "The Prism of Justice," 20.

this respect, they stand firmly in the prophetic tradition and declare the meaning of God's sovereignty for our time.

Of course, there is a plurality of religious sources for faith in the fundamental unity and goodness of life. What is essential for a public environmental ethic is that faith in that unity be affirmed. Perhaps for this reason, among others, the enlightened founders of the American Republic cast their language large and insisted that the inalienable rights of free persons are grounded not in any particular bible but in the "laws of nature and Nature's God."

264 ■ ■ ISSUES OF JUSTICE

Annotated Bibliography

The Global Situation

Brown, Lester R. *State of the World—1988*. New York: W. W. Norton, 1988.

Kim, Samuel S. *The Quest for a Just World Order*. Boulder CO: Westview Press, 1984.

Myers, Norman, ed. *Gaia: An Atlas of Planet Management*. New York: Anchor Press/ Doubleday and Company, 1984.

Each of these books provides well-documented and comprehensive understanding of the full range of global environmental problems. *State of the World—1988*, a publication of Worldwatch Institute, is updated each year. Kim and Myers are both concerned for the interrelationships of environmental and social problems. Myers graphically presents a wealth of data on the issues facing human and natural evolution. Kim analyzes this data from the perspective of its consequences for the four "world-order values" of security, human rights, economic equity, and environmental integrity, and the legitimacy of the Western model of modern development.

Environmental Ethics

Daly, Herman E. *Economics, Ecology, Ethics: Essays toward a Steady State Economy*. San Francisco: W. H. Freeman and Company, 1980.

Nash, Roderick. *Wilderness and the American Mind*. New Haven: Yale University Press, 1982.

Petulla, Joseph M. *American Environmentalism: Values, Tactics, Priorities*. College Station TX: Texas A & M University Press, 1980.

Regan, Tom. *The Case for Animal Rights*. Berkeley: University of California Press, 1983.

Rolston, Holmes, III. *Philosophy Gone Wild*. Buffalo: Prometheus Books, 1986.

Singer, Peter. *Animal Liberation: A New Ethics for Our Treatment of Animals*. New York: Avon Books, 1979.

Worster, Donald. *Nature's Economy: The Roots of Ecology*. New York: Anchor Books, 1979.

It is difficult to limit this list since there is no good general introduction to the major perspectives in environmental ethics. Petulla comes closest to the approach taken in this essay in his discussion of how the perspectives of biocentrism, ecology, and conservation are rooted in American social traditions and must be judged in terms of their consequences for a democratic ideal. Nash's work is the standard account of the struggle to preserve wilderness values in the United States, and Worster's is the best history of the science of ecology and its development as an ethical position. Rolston is one of the best ecological ethicists at work in the United States, and this collection of essays suggests how rich are the values to be discovered in nature by a discriminating mind. The other works are discussed in the text.

Toward an Ethic of Ecojustice

Barbour, Ian G. *Technology, Environment, and Human Values.* New York: Praeger Publishers, 1980.

Hessel, Dieter, ed. *For Creation's Sake: Preaching, Ecology, and Justice.* Philadelphia: Geneva Press, 1985.

Shinn, Roger Lincoln. *Forced Options: Social Decisions for the 21st Century.* San Francisco: Harper & Row, 1982.

There is a growing literature on the new kind of policy issues that arise when both environmental integrity and social justice are taken seriously. Barbour and Shinn each provide in-depth accounts of the technical and moral dimensions of these issues from a basic ethical perspective of resource conservation. While they, for the most part, equate environmental issues with the problem of limits, they have a good grasp of how the diverse values of human freedom, equality, and community must be taken into account when responding to environmental constraints. Hessel's collection is a nice introduction to current ecojustice discussions among Christian ethicists. Several essays point toward the possibility of an ecojustice ethic that does justice to the full range of environmental and social values.

Warren R. Copeland
Wittenberg University

..

Energy

■ ■ The American public discovered the energy issue in 1973. Actually, we had it thrust upon us by Arabs unhappy with our support of Israel. The energy problem we discovered in 1973 was the oil problem, more specifically, the imported-oil problem. As might be expected, this imported-oil problem is part of a broader energy problem that had developed over a number of years.

Prior to the Civil War, wood, waterwheels, and windmills supplied almost all of the energy used in the U.S. Wood alone supplied more than ninety percent of the fuel consumed in 1850. However, the industrialization that swept across the U.S. and especially the urban North was fueled by coal. Technological advances in the mining, transport, and burning of coal made it more economical to use, even though major resources of wood, water, and wind energy remained. By 1880 there was almost as much coal burned as wood; by 1910 coal provided nearly eighty percent of the fuel burned. The U.S. had undergone its first major transition in fuels.

Yet the proportion of coal burned declined fairly quickly after 1910, and especially after 1920. By 1950 oil and natural gas had replaced coal as the leading fuel. By 1970 oil and natural gas provided nearly eighty percent of the fuel burned in the U.S. The second major fuel transition was complete; oil and natural gas were our basic energy sources.

As in the case of the change from wood to coal, this transition was the result of technological advance rather than resource limitation since immense deposits of coal remained. More efficient means of producing, refining, distributing, and burning oil and natural gas made it cheaper, cleaner, and much easier to handle than coal. The automobile probably was the most important technological development related to the use of oil. The comparable development for natural gas was the transcontinental pipeline, which soon turned a former by-product of oil production into the predominant fuel for home heating and often the fuel of choice for industry and electric utilities.

Many believe we now are beginning the next fuel transition. However, there is much controversy, which we shall consider in some detail later, about the direction of that transition. One candidate for the basic fuel to replace oil and natural gas is nuclear power; the other is solar energy.

In December 1963 the Jersey Central Power and Light Company announced that it would build a nuclear power plant at Oyster Creek. This was the first commercial nuclear power plant built without a direct subsidy from the government. It was the result of years of developmental work on the peaceful use of the atom to produce electricity, much of it financed by the government. The most visible part of this government support was the Power Reactor Demonstration Project launched in 1954 by the Atomic Energy Commission, which built fourteen reactors on a demonstration basis.

In the late 1960s there was an explosion in orders for commercial nuclear plants. In 1966 there were only twelve reactors in operation. Since most of them were small by later standards, these twelve had a total generating capacity of only 945 MWe. By 1970 there still were only eighteen reactors in operation, but fifty-three were under construction. By 1974 there were fifty-five reactors producing commercial power, sixty-three under construction, seventy-three applications under review, and another forty-two for which plans had been announced. It is significant to note not only the numbers but also the size of these new reactors. Many of them had greater generating capacity on their own than the total capacity of all the reactors operating in 1966.

It might appear that the nuclear-power age had arrived by 1974, that the transition from oil and natural gas had begun. Actually, the boom was over, at least for the time being. In fact, most of the reactors that came into operation in the 1970s had been ordered in the late 1960s. The 1974-1975 recession, a decline in projections of demand for electricity, and the growing controversy over the safety of nuclear power brought a halt to expansion after 1974. Many orders were cancelled or postponed; only one new plant was ordered in 1979. High interest rates and the political fallout from the Three Mile Island incident in March 1979 reinforced this lull. As the

1980s began, the U.S. had either reached the threshold of dependence on nuclear power or its end as a major energy source. We shall return to this question later to consider further which it will, or should, be.

The solar story is much more brief. In some ways it is one of the oldest sources of energy; however, the development on a significant scale of active solar heating systems and solar cells for generating electricity is much more recent. Solar heating expanded significantly in some areas of the country, especially since the Federal Energy Act of 1978 and similar acts in some states provided tax incentives for its use. Developed primarily for the space program, solar electricity remains too expensive for broad applications. In sum, solar energy remains primarily a hope for many—especially as an alternative to nuclear power—rather than a large present source of energy.

Parallel to these transitions in the basic fuels, and complicating the present transition, has been the rapid growth of energy consumption in the U.S. Between 1950 and 1970 U.S. energy consumption increased at an average rate of 3.5 percent for a total increase of ninety-eight percent during that twenty-year period. Clearly much of this increase was linked to economic growth since the gross national product increased 102 percent during the same period.

Just as clearly, the economy grew with relatively little concern for the cost of energy. It was cheap, very cheap. Adjusted for inflation, the cost of energy declined by twenty-eight percent between 1950 and 1970. The result was a nation designed to use cheap energy and characterized by an abundance of cars, air-conditioning, plastics, sprawling cities, relatively little insulation, and inadequate public transportation. By and large, government policy served to reinforce this growth in consumption. Tax breaks to producers and price regulation kept prices down. Interstate highways increased auto use and helped spread out cities.

The Crises of the 1970s

All of which brings us back to 1973 or, perhaps better, to 1970. In 1970 domestic oil production peaked and began to decline. While new Alaskan oil slowed the decline somewhat, experts unanimously expected, and continue to expect, U.S. production to decline. However, U.S. energy consumption did not begin to decline in 1970. It continued to grow, if at a somewhat reduced rate.

The solution to this problem was to expand the process begun in 1948. In that year the U.S. imported more oil, primarily from Venezuela, than it exported. The Middle East, especially Iran and Saudia Arabia, gradually replaced Venezuela as the largest source of foreign oil. In each case, the foreign oil simply was much cheaper than U.S.-produced oil. During the 1950s and 1960s, the U.S. government attempted to stem this tide somewhat with tax breaks for U.S. production and import restrictions. The result may well have been simply to accelerate the decline in U.S. supplies. After the peak in domestic production in 1970, imports increased dramatically.

At the same time, the politics of oil heated up. During the thirty years between the mid-1920s and the mid-1950s, U.S. oil companies took over control of the world oil supply. Often with the help of U.S. foreign policy, they replaced the British and French, especially in the Middle East. During the 1960s these oil companies flaunted their consolidated power, especially in holding down prices. Partially in response, the Organization of Petroleum Exporting Countries (OPEC) was formed in 1960. Throughout the 1960s the oil companies and OPEC argued over price, but the excess of oil-producing capacity generally led to victory for the companies. With the decline in U.S. production after 1970, however, the stage was set for a reversal.

1973 was the year OPEC struck. World oil demand was at record levels, in part because the U.S. had just eliminated import quotas. Saudi Arabia sought to use this leverage to discourage U.S. support of Israel by reducing production and embargoing exports to the U.S. and a few other countries. The result was a short-term crisis, especially for the U.S. Yet when the embargo was lifted some six months later, the long-term problem remained. In the meantime, OPEC took control of prices. The result was that by the end of 1974, oil was selling for eight times more than five years earlier. The time of cheap and secure oil was over for a while.

That lesson, however, did not immediately change the level of U.S. energy consumption. Slowed only somewhat by recession, U.S. consumption and importation of oil continued to rise, with imports nearly doubling between 1973 and 1979. Then the Iranian revolution brought new political uncertainty to the Middle East and a second oil shock. With the decline in Iranian production due to the revolution, the world lost ten percent of its production, the U.S. developed lines at gasoline stations, and prices rose again.

With the peaking of domestic oil production, the U.S. became vulnerable in two ways. First, we faced the possibility of supply interruption at
any time due to conscious choice, as in 1973, or due to the accidents of
events, as in 1979. Second, we could look forward to constantly increasing prices for the oil we did get. Already this had caused both inflation and
recession in our economy. It promised to continue to do so. With the expected peaking of world oil production sometime before 2000, the potential for either or both to occur seemed sure to increase. It was in response
to these two dangers that U.S. energy policy after 1973 was formulated.

U.S. Energy Policy after 1973

Politicians must respond to crises, and Richard Nixon surely was a politician. Nixon's response to the 1973-1974 oil embargo was "Project Independence." Its goal was to achieve energy independence by 1985. In
fact, imports doubled over the next four years. The basic strategy of
"Project Independence" was to increase domestic energy supplies. In oil
and natural gas, this was to be accomplished by allowing prices to rise in
order to stimulate production and by speeding up the leasing of drilling sites,
especially offshore. The easing of "unreasonable environmental restrictions" was to facilitate more mining and burning of coal. Some funds were
designated for research and development, primarily in high-technology
solar and synthetic fuels. Very little emphasis was placed on solar energy
or energy conservation.

The largest single source of new energy that "Project Independence"
envisioned was the rapid expansion of nuclear power. The 1980s were to
be the decade of the atom. Plans called for streamlining the licensing and
construction process in order to get reactors into production more quickly.
As a result, nuclear power was to provide thirty to forty percent of our
electricity by the end of the 1980s and half by 2000. As we already have
seen, this did not happen. It also turned out that the predictions for other
energy sources were overestimated, although not so dramatically.

That this was going to be the case was clear by the time Gerald Ford
became president in 1974, so he dropped the goal of immediate independence while basically continuing Nixon's policy. During this period of time,
the heavily Democratic Congress was a major block to the full implementation of the policies of these Republican presidents, both in terms of oil
and natural-gas pricing and of environmental standards.

The Nixon-Ford policy was predominantly, although not exclusively, concerned with the danger of supply interruption. This is the primary reason independence was so important. One specific program aimed at supply interruption that survived was the establishment of a strategic oil reserve in the U.S. from which recoverable oil could be pumped if foreign supplies were cut. In a sense, it was symbolic of the basic thrust of the whole program.

Jimmy Carter's program shifted this basic thrust into a more long-term concern for the relation between energy and the economy. As a part of this shift, Carter's original energy program placed much more emphasis on solar energy and particularly on conservation. The Carter program also envisaged much greater government leadership in energy decisions through various controls and incentives.

Specifically, the Carter plan proposed conservation and fuel efficiency as its cornerstone. Tax incentives and subsidies were to be established to encourage home insulation. Low-mileage cars were to be taxed. Conservation measures for industry and public agencies were to be mandated. In order to encourage such conservation and to stimulate development of new energy sources, the plan also called for increasing energy prices as necessary in order to find replacement energy. Carter planners did not believe, however, that energy companies needed all of the new revenue these price increases would bring. Therefore, they wanted to return a portion to middle- and lower-income consumers for investment in alternative energy sources.

There were two other major features of the original Carter plan. The first was to require a shift in consumption from scarce to abundant fuels. A primary element in this was the requirement that utilities shift from oil and natural gas to coal for generating electricity. Another element was a continued commitment to nuclear power while slowing the commercial development of breeder reactors. The second feature was federal support for research and development. While the majority of this money was targeted for synthetic fuels, more money than ever before was designated for the various solar technologies.

The original Carter proposal was attacked by many as too pessimistic, as too obsessed with conservation. While some of the tax incentives and subsidies were enacted, the energy companies won major congressional victories, especially on pricing. Pressure built in Congress and elsewhere for a return to a supply strategy. In response, Carter proposed a second series of energy proposals. The two most significant elements in this new program were the staged decontrol of oil and natural-gas prices and a program of major government subsidies for the development of synthetic fuels. Both were adopted with some revisions.

Reagan's energy policy essentially was a return to the Nixon-Ford supply strategy. Practically, this meant continued support for the decontrol of oil and natural-gas prices, encouragement of nuclear power, and relaxation of environmental standards. At the same time, Reagan moved to reduce the government's role in energy policy. Subsidies to consumers were cut; conservation and solar programs were nearly eliminated. Even the synthetic-fuel program, popular with Congress and energy companies, was reduced. The basic strategy was to use market forces, mostly prices, to encourage conservation and increase production and to free business from regulations that impeded energy production. By his second term, Reagan claimed success for his energy policy. Imports and prices both were down. The question was whether this was a permanent or temporary situation.

The Ethical Issues

In energy, ethical issues are integrally related to, and often confused with, a whole series of technical issues. Learning to think ethically about energy requires developing the capacities both to distinguish the ethical issues from the technical issues and to recognize how deeply the ethical and technical issues influence one another. There are quite different interpretations of much of the energy data based upon differences in the interpreters' ethical frameworks. There are quite different visions of the most ethical energy future based upon quite different readings of the facts.

We shall consider two different but closely intertwined ethical issues raised by our problems with energy. The first draws heavily upon political and social philosophy. It has to do with the relative value of different images of the good society that our energy policy might serve. Specifically, it deals with the choice between industrial and pastoral views of the ideal society and the overlapping choice in emphasis between personal freedom and social equity. The question is just what sort of society we want. The second ethical issue sometimes is discussed in terms of the traditional conflict in ethical theory between consequential and rule ethics. In this case, it is the clash between the cost-benefit analyses of various energy technologies and the dignity and value of those affected by these technologies.

This is a conflict between two understandings of fairness—one that stresses utility and one that stresses rights and equal protection.

Hard or Soft, Me or Us?

As soon as one enters the energy debate by attending a conference or two or by reading broadly on the subject, it becomes clear that there are two sides. Indeed, considerable effort has been expended to draw the lines between these two sides as clearly and as exclusively as possible. One side is hard and big, or—as Robert Stobaugh and Daniel Yergin have dubbed them—the industrial romantics. This side seeks to support continued industrial expansion. The industrial romantics propose to do so by drilling more oil and natural-gas wells, mining and burning more coal, developing synthetic fuels, and rapidly expanding nuclear power. The soft and small side—called pastoral romantics by Stobaugh and Yergin—envision an energy future marked by conservation and solar energy. They raise questions not only about how efficiently we use energy but also about whether we really need all the economic growth that would require more and more energy.

Industrial Romantics

The big and hard school of thought has been dominated by the energy industries. Mobil Oil has taken the lead in promoting this view in public. Mobil advocates more exploration for oil and gas, more coal mining, more nuclear power, and the development of oil shale and synthetic fuels. In order to make all this possible, they wanted prices deregulated so that energy companies would have more money to finance the above-listed ventures and they wanted relaxation of environmental standards on offshore drilling, mining and burning coal, nuclear safety, and so forth. This was justified in the name of keeping our industrial society growing. While they contended that this economic growth would help the poor by providing jobs, their primary ethical concern is personal freedom. "When there is a conflict between human freedom or the conservation ethic, there is no 'right' or 'wrong' choice. It should be up to the individual to choose what he wants."[1] In fact, what Mobil promises those who support its position is consumptive freedom, the right to do and buy what one wants.

---

[1] "The Real Challenge: Increasing Energy Supply" (New York: Mobil Corporation, 1977) 7.

Within the nuclear debate, David Rossin represents a similar point of view. Rossin believes that oil and gas supplies will decline and that solar energy cannot make a major contribution soon. If energy supplies are to be maintained or to grow, the choice then is between nuclear power and coal. He thinks nuclear power is far preferable in terms of cost, long-term availability, health, and safety. Rossin concludes that the economic growth made possible by more energy supports pluralism, democracy, and equity, but the final appeal remains personal freedom. ''The dearest asset we have in the United States is our personal freedom. . . . Success and growth of nuclear power means enough to go around. It preserves a society in which each person decides for himself how much energy he wishes to use.''[2] Like Mobil, it is this basic consumptive freedom that Rossin fears we shall lose if energy supplies shrink.

The dominant voices in the industrial-romantic school of thought have stressed personal freedom. The Reagan administration adopted this point of view both in program and in principle. Yet there have been other voices advocating similar energy policy for a quite different reason. The NAACP sounds like Mobil regarding developing energy supplies for a strong economy, but it is for the sake of social equity, not personal freedom. ''As long as fourteen percent of our people are unemployed, as long as the earnings gap between Black and White Americans continues to widen and as long as a majority of Black Americans continue to face a constant struggle to attain even the basic necessities of life, our first priority must be the attainment of economic parity for Black Americans.''[3] However, the NAACP does not see the economic growth more energy would make possible as leading inevitably to greater social equity. Therefore, it seeks a much more active role for government in advancing equity than does Mobil.

George Pickering holds a position much like the NAACP in the nuclear-power debate. Pickering contends that energy is a basic human need in an advanced industrial society. While relatively abundant and inexpensive energy does not assure social equity, shortages make it unlikely. Pickering fears that having made it themselves, the U.S. middle class (led by the antinuclear movement) will deny a reasonable standard of living to others by

---

[2]A. David Rossin, ''Centralization, Decentralization and Polarization,'' in Warren R. Copeland, ed., *Energy: the Ethical Issues* (Springfield OH: Ohio Institute for Appropriate Technology, 1979) 7.

[3]NAACP policy statement, 21 December 1977.

rejecting the relatively safe source of energy in nuclear power. He concludes: "It is not right for people who have got theirs suddenly to decide that it's not 'responsible' for other people to want it."[4] Like Rossin, Pickering supports nuclear power, but like the NAACP he does it in the name of social equity, not personal freedom.

Pastoral Romantics

E. F. Schumacher may have founded the "small is beautiful" school of thought, but Amory Lovins is easily its most influential advocate in relation to energy policy. Much of Lovins's argument is technological. Lovins believes nuclear power is inherently dangerous, especially because it dramatically increases the possibility of nuclear-weapons proliferation. Positively, he believes soft technologies, especially solar and conservation, are much more promising than greater and greater dependence upon the complex, hard technologies. During the transition he sees a wide range of technical fixes increasing the efficiency with which we use current fuels. While Lovins advocates government policies that ban nuclear power, protect the environment, and stimulate the development of solar technologies, he depends upon the free market to reject the hard technologies, especially nuclear, as simply too expensive. In the long run, Lovins envisions a society in which the major portion of our energy is produced locally on a decentralized basis.

Instrumental to the emergence of such a Jeffersonian democracy is the reaffirmation of traditional values, which boil down to a form of personal freedom he often calls self-sufficiency: "Underlying energy choices are real but tacit choices of personal values. . . . Those that could sustain lifestyles of elegant frugality are not new; they are in the attic and could be dusted off and recycled. Such values as thrift, simplicity, diversity, neighborliness, humility and craftsmanship—perhaps most closely preserved in politically conservative communities—are already . . . embodied in a substantial social movement."[5]

All in all, Lovins calls for a return to rugged individualism, neighborliness, and decentralized democracy as the value basis for a solar, rather

---

[4]George W. Pickering, "Energy and Well-Being: Whose?" *Electric Perspectives* 79:1 (January–February 1979): 7.

[5]Amory Lovins, *Soft Energy Paths: Toward a Durable Peace* (Cambridge MA: Ballinger, 1977) 57.

than nuclear, energy future. Perhaps in part because of the personal vitality of Lovins, his view dominates the public statements of the pastoral-romantic school of thought.

Other than a difference of opinion over which fossil fuel will provide the bridge to the solar future, Barry Commoner shares in great part Amory Lovins's views on energy technology. Where they differ in policy is with the role of government; this is a tip-off to their value differences. Commoner argues that the government must become very active in promoting the transition to a solar society. Like Lovins, he believes nuclear power should be banned, environmental regulations strengthened, and incentives for nuclear development instituted. However, he also wants government to buy solar technology itself to help create a market for it, and he foresees a time when most traditional energy companies will have to be nationalized or converted into regulated utilities. For him, the alternative is that the energy corporations will take us down the economically and socially disastrous hard path simply because it advances their short-term economic interests.

He calls this larger role of government "social governance." Unlike Lovins, who expects the governmental role to decline over time, Commoner considers this social governance a relatively permanent necessity. This is because it embodies the commitment of the mass of citizens to social equity and the common interest as opposed to the private interests of the energy companies. "It will be difficult . . . to learn how to merge economic justice with economic progress, and personal freedom with social governance. . . . But if we firmly embrace economic democracy as a national goal . . . , it can guide us through the historic passage that is mandated by the energy crisis."[6] Clearly, Commoner's commitment to social equity is at least as important as his support of personal freedom. This fact alone distinguishes him from Lovins.

At the level of guiding ethical principles, energy analyses tend in at least four directions rather than just two, as is often suggested. Images of small-town America do slip into the industrial-romantic vision at times, and pastoral romantics do seem to promise the continuance of industrial society in a more efficient form now and then. (Commoner promises this more than Lovins.) Yet the distinction remains at least as emphases and tendencies. Similarly, Mobil and Rossin mention that the poor will be bet-

---

[6]Barry Commoner, *The Politics of Energy* (New York: Knopf, 1979) 82.

ter off in a growing economy, and Lovins suggests that they too can be self-sufficient. The NAACP, Pickering, and Commoner all support personal freedom as well as social equity. Yet this distinction also persists as a matter of priority and focus. Thus, we are left with this understanding of basic social purposes that underlie the energy debate:

	Industrial Romantic	**Pastoral Romantic**
Personal Freedom	Mobil Rossin	Lovins
Social Equity	NAACP Pickering	Commoner

Within the context of this disagreement over the basic purpose of energy policy, there has been a second related-but-distinct ethical debate raging over just what it means to be fair.

Utility vs. Rights

The view of fairness as utility has been developed into what approaches a science of cost-benefit analysis—so much so that scientists and engineers often do not recognize it as an essentially moral analysis. Deeply imbedded in cost-benefit analyses is the assumption that the good consists in providing the greatest satisfaction to the largest number of people. While many utilitarians attempt to broaden the criteria for judging satisfaction, these criteria are usually reduced to the sum of individual preferences. Satisfaction basically equals what people want.

Since it is impractical always to ask people what they want, most cost-benefit analyses assume that market costs, legal standards, and everyday practices reflect preferences fairly well. For example, in calculating the utility of a coal-fired electrical-generating plant versus a nuclear one, the costs of the fuels, the wages at which employees will work, and the price of land are assumed to reflect the preferences of fuel-producing areas, utility workers, and local land owners. If, for instance, a nuclear plant requires more heavily trained personnel willing to run whatever additional risks are involved, that should be reflected in wage rates. The society's preferences for clean air and water are assumed to be reflected in environmental laws. One cost of each kind of plant would be meeting those legal standards. Finally, most such calculations attempt to estimate people's preferences in everyday life. Owning and operating an automobile represents a certain risk. Of more direct reference to nuclear power, flying in an airplane exposes one to a certain level of radiation. If the same or greater benefit can be supplied by a nuclear-power plant than that of auto or air travel, can we not assume that people will be willing to run a similar risk?

Perhaps the supreme test of this utilitarian approach is the suggestion that people's lives can be factored into a risk-benefit calculation. In other words, do we not act every day as though a certain number of lives is not too high a price to pay for the benefits derived? We could cut auto fatalities dramatically by strictly enforcing a thirty-mile-per-hour speed limit on our highways, but we act as though getting where we want to go more quickly is worth those extra lives. Similarly, we know we could cut down on deaths from lung disorders if we imposed stricter clean-air standards, yet we have made a judgment through our elected representatives that the lives saved would not be worth the cost. In each case human lives themselves become part of our cost-benefit analysis.

There are at least three contemporary challenges to a straightforward utilitarian ethic in recent literature. The first is an egalitarian critique most commonly associated with the work of John Rawls. Rawls articulates two basic principles of justice. The first is a principle of equal liberty: "First: each person is to have an equal right to the most extensive basic liberty compatible with a similar liberty for others."[7] Rawls's second principle stresses the claims of the disadvantaged. A later reformulation of it is probably more helpful for our purposes: "Social and economic inequalities are to be arranged so that they are both (1) to the greatest benefit of the least advantaged and (2) attached to offices and positions open to all under conditions of fair equality of opportunity."[8] Rawls shifts attention away from the greatest good for the greatest number to the greatest good for the least advantaged within the condition of equality of liberty.

Concretely, this suggests two questions to be raised of utilitarian cost-benefit analyses. First, are the costs and benefits freely available to all? Does everyone have an equal opportunity to enjoy the benefits and an equal risk of paying the costs? If the benefits are enjoyed by a select group of people or if the risks are borne by a group of people with limited freedom to escape those risks, then equality of liberty is in jeopardy. Applying

---

[7]John Rawls, *A Theory of Justice* (Cambridge MA: Harvard University Press, 1971) 66.

[8]Ibid., 83.

Rawls's second principle, if the benefits go primarily to those who already are advantaged or if the costs fall most heavily upon the disadvantaged, the act would be suspect *even if* the benefits generally outweighed the costs.

A second challenge to utilitarian analysis arises from the libertarianism of Robert Nozick. It is based in the sacredness of the individual. Individuals must not be forced into any act. Individuals are free to pursue any purposes they choose as long as others are not forced to share those purposes or pay the costs of them without consent. According to Nozick, this is a restatement of "the underlying Kantian principle that individuals are ends and not merely means; they may not be sacrificed or used for achieving the others' ends without their consent. Individuals are inviolable."[9]

From this perspective, the basic problem with utilitarian calculation of the good is that it assumes there is some whole for whom there is a greatest good. In fact, there is not. There are only individuals who make up the whole. Thus anything supposed good for the greatest number is in fact good for some at the expense of others. These others must decide for themselves what is good for them. No good for the whole can be sought except with the consent of all the individuals who make up that whole. If it sounds as if this system of thought makes it hard to govern, that is because it does. Nozick believes in a very minimal state that seeks primarily to protect citizens from coercion by other states or their fellow citizens. He does allow that individuals may also be willing to give up some of their rights in return for what they consider just compensation. In the final analysis the individual must decide, and coercion is unethical.

Obviously, an approach such as Nozick's raises serious problems with most utilitarian cost-benefit analyses. Even if an act can be shown to promise benefits that justify the costs, each individual affected must consent to the act or agree to some form of compensation as the price of consent. This approach also rejects the equalitarianism of Rawls, which is willing to coerce the advantaged for the sake of the disadvantaged.

A third approach, which emerged out of the Third World (and especially Latin American) churches in the 1970s, is liberation theology. In a sense it merges Rawls's concern with the disadvantaged with Nozick's rejection of coercion around the terms "oppression of the poor." If the poor are oppressed, there must be oppressors. Liberation theology borrows from Marxist thought to identify the oppressors as the ruling classes and insti-

---

[9]Robert Nozick, *Anarchy, State, and Utopia* (New York: Basic Books, 1974) 30-31.

tutions and from Christian theology to proclaim the need and hope for liberation from oppression. The oppressors, while powerful, are few. The need is to identify them and how they carry out their oppression and to help the masses organize to overthrow them.

For Richard Shaull, who attempts to relate liberation theology to the situation of the United States, we are faced with a coming apocalypse in which "we will soon be an island of relative affluence surrounded by millions of starving people."[10] The institutions of advanced industrial society are the institutions of oppression, and we, especially those in power in those institutions, are the oppressors. However, the exhaustion of natural resources will bring the threat home to us also and, quite possibly, occasion a re-examination of our basic values in order to survive ourselves.

In Shaull's view, all corporate structures are suspect. The first step toward liberation is to find ways to limit and break corporate power. As he puts it: "The question will be whether we will allow [the current] process to continue . . . toward increasing domination by our major corporations and their servants. Or will we decide that the time has come to use our economic resources to meet the basic and urgent needs of our society: rebuilding our cities, overcoming poverty, providing employment for all, etc."[11] The former threatens even greater oppression; the latter promises liberation.

From a point of view such as Shaull's, utilitarian cost-benefit calculations are but rationalizations for the continued dominance of the ruling class. On the one hand they reflect the power imbalances of the present society, while on the other hand they fail to recognize the changes in power necessary to bring about a liberated, humane future. Thus they are but one more tool of domination.

We are left with the most common means of ethical analysis in our culture, utilitarianism, under serious criticism from at least three directions. This essentially is a conflict over standards of fairness. The utilitarian standard of fairness is the greatest good for the greatest number. Rawls responds with an emphasis on providing additional advantage to those presently least advantaged. Nozick contends that fairness requires either

---

[10]Richard Shaull, "Death and Resurrrection of the American Dream," in Gustavo Gutierrez and Richard Shaull, *Liberation and Change,* ed. Ronald H. Stone (Atlanta: John Knox Press, 1977) 113.

[11]Ibid., 117-18.

uncoerced consent or agreement upon compensation before any individual is asked to pay the price for someone else's action. Finally, liberationists believe fairness requires a radical redistribution of power.

Fairness and Nuclear Power

While this conflict in understandings of fairness can be seen clearly in the debates over offshore drilling for oil, clean-air standards for burning coal, natural-gas pricing, tax breaks for solar collectors, or energy subsidies for the poor, it probably is most dramatically present in the debate over nuclear power.

Before proceeding much further, it is important to clarify just what this nuclear power is that is under debate. We refer here only to the civilian use of nuclear fission to generate electricity. While a few supporters of nuclear power link it to military needs for weapons material, weapons material traditionally has been produced by military reactors in the United States, and the civilian nuclear-power industry prefers to keep it that way. Some opponents of nuclear power argue that it inevitably leads to greater risk of nuclear war. While this is a point well worth debating, opponents agree this is not a conscious goal of civilian nuclear power.

Fission reactors also must be distinguished from fusion reactors. As with the atomic bomb, fission reactors split atoms, only at a much slower rate, to produce heat, and from that heat, electricity. Fusion reactors, none of which is presently in operation or expected soon, would use the same process as the hydrogen bombs—the uniting of atoms—to produce heat and, ultimately, electricity. While fission reactors cannot explode, they potentially can get very hot. Civilian United States reactors do not use fuel that is weapons grade, that is, from which bombs could be directly assembled.

U.S. reactors are called light-water reactors to distinguish them from the kind of reactor popular primarily with the Canadians, which uses water that contains unusually high concentrations of a rare form of hydrogen called deuterium. Since deuterium-rich water is heavier, these reactors are called heavy-water reactors. Light-water reactors also come in basically two types: pressurized-water reactors and boiling-water reactors. They differ according to whether the water that passes through the extremely hot radioactive core of the reactor is allowed to change immediately to steam (boiling water) or is held under pressure and used to turn water in another circulating water system into steam later in the process (pressurized-water reactor).

Both the boiling-water and pressurized-water reactors use enriched radioactive uranium as their fuel. They also produce radioactive wastes. Uranium is a rare metal in limited supply. Therefore, some scientists have proposed that with some design changes a reactor could be developed that would produce radioactive material, largely plutonium. This plutonium could be used as a fuel, thus extending significantly the supply of uranium. Since such a reactor would produce more fuel than it uses, it is called a breeder reactor. While breeder reactors have been built on an experimental basis, they are not presently in use on a commercial basis in the U.S.

The nuclear-power debate in the United States primarily is about whether to continue and/or expand our present light-water reactor capacity and, secondarily, about whether to proceed with the commercial development of breeder reactors. The debate has focused heavily upon issues such as radiation danger, reactor safety, nuclear-waste disposal, and the adequacy of the institutions managing and regulating the industry.

Hans Bethe and David Rossin are good representatives of the supporters of nuclear power. Both men use forms of a utilitarian argument for nuclear power and in the process make certain assumptions that they are prepared to defend. The first is that economic growth is good for a society; it makes life better for ever-greater numbers of citizens. They are industrial romantics. While efficiency can reduce the amount of growth in energy needed to support such economic growth, there remains a need for more energy. Second, both Bethe and Rossin assume that the supplies of oil and natural gas are limited. If we are not running out now, supplies will level off and decline sometime relatively soon. Last, both Bethe and Rossin assume that neither fusion, which is a long way off, nor solar, which can make a growing but limited contribution in the near run, can take up the slack between the need for energy and the end of growing supplies of oil and natural gas.

That leaves coal and nuclear power. Bethe and Rossin proceed to compare the relative costs of coal and nuclear power in fueling the benefits of economic growth. They conclude that nuclear power requires less cost to fewer people. Uranium is less dangerous to mine than coal. A properly operating nuclear plant presents much less of a health hazard than a coal plant. They minimize the risks of a nuclear accident and the dangers of nuclear-waste storage.

Bethe and Rossin contend that the chance of a major accident, a meltdown of the core of a reactor resulting in a large release of radiation into the atmosphere, is extremely small. Similarly, the possibility of a significant release of radiation into the environment from the escape of radioactive waste from storage is very remote. Balancing these distant risks against the known benefits of more energy and the almost-certain deaths to come from more mining and burning of coal, they conclude that nuclear power creates the greatest good for the greatest number and the least harm to the smallest number.

A good example of the intermixture of arguments against nuclear power is the energy statement of the National Council of Churches of Christ in the United States, along with its supporting materials. This statement alternately uses the understandings of fairness we saw in Rawls, Nozick, and liberation theology to reject nuclear power and to project an alternative energy policy.

The National Council restates Rawls in the following terms: "The survival needs of those who are below the minimum material standard of living should be met before the wants of those above that standard."[12] This principle of fairness is used somewhat to justify the populism of solar power, which anyone can create, instead of the centralization of nuclear power, which is controlled by the wealthy. Primarily, however, it is used to justify government intervention to guarantee needed energy for the poor. Nuclear proponents such as Bethe and Rossin are vulnerable on this point in Rawls's term. They only argue that economic growth is as important to the poor as to the rest of the society, not that it will help overcome inequity. There is no reason in principle, however, why someone cannot argue both for nuclear power and for redistribution of income. One might even argue that economic growth is a necessary economic or political prerequisite for redistribution. Few proponents of nuclear power do, but Pickering and the NAACP do.

It is with arguments like those of Nozick that the National Council's specific critique of nuclear power picks up momentum. Beyond asserting that the actual risk of a major reactor accident or release from a waste-storage area is greater than Bethe and Rossin suggest, the statement takes a more-principled position: even if the risks are somewhat remote and the benefits significant, do government officials or utility executives have the right to put the health and even the lives of those living near a reactor or

---

[12]National Council of Churches, "The Ethical Implications of Energy Production and Use" (New York: National Council of Churches, 1979) 4.

waste-storage area at risk without their consent? The National Council suggests not. On a broader time scale, it also asks whether we of this generation have the right to endanger future generations with genetic and radiation dangers without their consent. Once again the Council suggests not.

Finally, the statement uses principles of fairness like those of liberation theology to raise questions of power about energy. There is an anti-corporate tone running through the statement, articulated even better in Beverly Harrison's article, ''The Politics of Energy Policy.''[13] Energy policy generally, and nuclear power specifically, is dominated by the powerful corporations and their political allies. In part, solar energy is better than nuclear power because it is participatory. The *masses* can build and control solar power; the *ruling elite* builds and controls nuclear power. Moreover, this is not just a matter of direct economic control. The ruling elite also heavily influences the control of information about energy both to government officials and to the public at large. Good energy policy requires both the recognition of this corporate control and informational and organizational efforts to confront and defeat it.

As a citizen attempts to think through the controversy over nuclear energy, the abundance of data—much of it contradictory—can be confusing. It helps to recognize that many of the differences in interpretation of data flow from differences in understandings of fairness. It remains to think through this difference in principles before returning to the facts one more time.

Evaluative Comments

We have identified at least two general ways in which the energy debate is in part a debate over basic value assumptions. In the process we have distinguished sharply between utilitarians and liberation theologians, between industrial romantics committed to social equity and pastoral romantics committed to personal freedom. This analytic task is a basic requirement for being morally serious. The purpose of such ethical analysis is to make possible more responsible action, not to reduce us to moral relativists who think that all positions sound equally good.

One way of resolving this moral conflict in order to act is to develop some good reasons for holding one of the moral positions and simply reject

---

[13]Beverly Harrison, ''The Politics of Energy Policy,'' in Dieter Hessel, ed., *Energy Ethics* (New York: Friendship, 1979) 56-71.

the others. For instance, one might conclude that the Judeo-Christian tradition's constant support for the claims of the poor is good grounds for concluding that Rawls is basically right and the alternatives are basically wrong. This is certainly a legitimate moral process, one many ethicists use. Moreover, it would be a major advance over advocating energy policy with no recognition of its value dimension and no rationale for one's position.

We shall proceed in another way for reasons having to do with the very nature of reality and human meaning. The world in which we live is essentially plural and simultaneously essentially social.[14] It consists of a multiplicity of beings and entities, each with its own integrity. The Judeo-Christian tradition has attempted to express that reality on the human level by saying that we are all created in God's image. This concept implies both that we are all centers of creativity and that we all have ultimate integrity. There may well be some situations in which someone has so distorted the image of God, is so evil, that a simple denunciation is appropriate. In that case, the evil one has totally ignored the integrity of others. In most situations, however, we should act so as to respect, protect, and even expand the richness of our differences.

At the same time the world does not consist of separate, isolated individuals. Rather, from our birth we are included in an intricate web of relations with other humans and other entities. We are shaped by these relationships, and we shape those to whom we are related. The Judeo-Christian tradition has always been a tradition of a people, not of individuals alone. Furthermore, it has always stressed relationship with others, including God, as the central religious activity.

This dual character of reality in general and human experience in particular has two implications for this study of energy. First, it suggests that we proceed with our attempt to make ethically informed choices by seeking to respect the integrity of each participant in the debate. We shall do this by trying to discover what basic insights we can glean from each position in the debate. Then we shall attempt to relate these insights to one another. Second, the plural-yet-social character of reality provides guidance for thinking about what constitutes the good society, for thinking about which sort of energy policy we should choose.

With these considerations in mind, let us take a look at the debate between the industrial romantics and the pastoral romantics and between per-

---

[14]See Warren R. Copeland, *Economic Justice* (Nashville: Abingdon Press, 1988) 103-23.

sonal freedom and social equity. Does not each of the four positions have its points to make? Those like Mobil and Rossin can be credited with a realistic view of human beings. They say that we like to consume and that we are much more likely to share from a growing economic pie than a constant or shrinking one. They see the free market as a way of coordinating self-interests so that the most people get served. Anyone who recognizes the power of self-interest—or sin, speaking theologically—cannot dismiss this insight out of hand. However, one can recognize the power of sin without dignifying it; one can appreciate the role of self-interest without concluding that it defines the good. Similarly, a growing economic pie does not lead automatically to more sharing; it may just lead some to gorge themselves. Finally, we can agree that the market is effective as a tool or distributor of goods but very inadequate as a judge of human values. The market delivers to whomever can pay the price; we know a wide range of personal and social needs for which no one can, or will, pay the price just now.

One basic strength of the position represented by Amory Lovins is its critique of our consumer society. We do consume a lot of junk, and clearly consumption alone does not provide meaning in our lives. Lovins's attack on organizations, especially large corporations, also hits home. They do develop a life of their own that they seek to preserve and expand by controlling our economy and politics. Finally, Lovins rightfully celebrates the creativity of individuals and small groups. Yet considerable caution is in order on all three counts. While affluent Americans may well consume too much, a good number of Americans and a far-greater number of people in the world do not. Many people need to consume more, not less. In addition, the belief that the evils of large organizations, especially corporations, can be ended by a return to a more decentralized, pastoral society probably is naive. Moreover, such a society probably would bring evils of its own. Decentralized public schools are segregated; decentralized transportation produced our overdependence on the automobile; decentralized social-welfare programs usually are cheap and mean. In an age when research and development have become an accepted part of almost all large corporations, invention may no longer be in the hands of individuals. Even if it is, inventions must be mass-produced in order to have a significant impact on our society. We had better learn to live with and control the necessary productive process rather than try to escape it by embracing pastoral decentralization.

Mobil's and Rossin's view of the individual human as essentially a self-interested consumer probably sells us short. Lovins's image of the self-sufficient, inventive individual probably overestimates us. Both, however, seek to affirm the basic integrity of the person. We dare not ignore that. What both lack is sufficient recognition that we are social beings. The NAACP and Pickering recognize that it will take conscious political choices by our society to assure that economic growth benefits the disadvantaged. Furthermore, they recognize the power of corporations in our economic and political life but believe that the power of government, not a return to small-town America, will be required to limit that power. Commoner develops this latter point even more fully. He believes it will take powerful government intervention even to get some decentralization, but he also sees a continuing role for a populist government in controlling corporate power and redistributing income and opportunity. In no case is this emphasis on social equity intended to restrict personal freedom. Indeed, it is supposed to increase the personal freedom of the disadvantaged. However, in every case some limits are placed on the right of some people to do what they want precisely in recognition of the social reality that if they do, the action will be at a price to others. In conclusion, those who emphasize social equity seem to do a much-better job of recognizing the importance of both the integrity of the individual and the social character of experience.

The conflict between the industrial romantic and pastoral romantic positions is not so easily resolved, but there are grounds for enough consensus to proceed, if haltingly. The more-thoughtful advocates of an energy-production strategy still recognize that the era of cheap energy probably is over, which means it is highly unlikely that economic growth can continue as it has in the past. Moreover, they are quite willing to admit that some of the trappings of affluence are unnecessary, even trivial. Therefore, they advocate serious conservation efforts as a part of their energy program. At the same time, the more socially conscious of the pastoral romantics recognize that less economic growth will make social equity more difficult. While they contend that economic growth can be sustained primarily by solar energy and conservation, they do allow for the continuance of hard technologies during a transition period. One can envision an energy policy that proceeds to develop solar power and institute conservation just as quickly as possible while continuing hard technologies for the time being. This would allow judgments later on as to just how much energy each source can actually supply. We are left with the immediate question of the safety of certain technologies, especially nuclear power, which we shall consider separately under our discussion of understandings of fairness.

Fairness

Within the context of this basic disagreement over the purpose of energy policy rages the second debate over fairness. The two clearly overlap and influence one another. In weighing the costs and benefits of a nuclear-reactor project, it makes an immense difference whether you share the industrial-romantic commitment to the preservation of industrial society. It is much easier to reject corporations totally if one has the confidence of a pastoral romantic in the productive and equity capacities of a decentralized society. Yet basic purpose and fairness are not the same and should not be confused. Even the most adamant industrial romantic is vulnerable to the charge from such as Nozick of trampling on individual rights. Even your neighborly solar-energy freak must calculate costs and benefits.

How then do we settle the question of fairness? Probably we cannot do it once and for all or absolutely. Moreover, given a commitment to the creative possibilities of the future and a pluralistic world, we would not want to do so. Rather, we shall once again look for the strength of each approach based on the question of fairness.

Cost-benefit analyses focus on the basic need to be productive, to produce the most good for the most people. While its practitioners may allow that concern to run roughshod over other legitimate interests, production certainly is important. There are clear examples in our affluent society of having and wanting more material possessions than are necessary and perhaps good. However, there are many examples in our society—and even more in others—of having far too little. Even the relatively minor suffering caused by a long recession in the United States reminds us that production is of value. On a global basis, having too little is altogether more stark and tragic.

A second strength of the utilitarian understanding of fairness is a greater possibility for comprehensiveness. This has not usually been the case in practice, and one function of the critiques we have examined is to press for consideration of some of the interests typically left out. However, there remains within the search for the greatest good for the greatest number an expansiveness that is a step toward the good for the society as a whole.

If the utilitarians are concerned that there be enough, the Rawlsians want to know enough for whom? Lester Thurow points out that while the energy problem may hurt most citizens of the United States, it is a disaster for the poorest ten percent who spend 34.1 percent of their income on energy and may even benefit the wealthiest ten percent since they only spend 5.2 percent of their income on energy and are more likely to own energy stock.[15] A truly fair energy policy must recognize this reality. How is less clear. For instance, it probably is better to raise the poor's income directly rather than attempt to hold down energy prices. What Rawls affirms is that in some way the total policy must close, not widen, the gap between rich and poor if it is to be fair. In this way Rawls reminds us that the poor are also created in the image of God and must be included in the human community.

Nozick believes in the integrity of the individual. Of that there can be no doubt. That there is doubt from time to time that the cost-benefit analyses of the utilitarians take sufficient account of the rights of individuals indicates the value of Nozick's position. His is the most stark affirmation of the rights claims of the individuals affected by utilitarian calculations. As such, it affirms absolutely the integrity of the individual, but in so doing largely ignores, or rather denies, the social character of reality. In a civilized world, the rights claims of individuals must be recognized and protected by the community. The good society will do so in order to defend the values of individualism and pluralism, but these claims cannot be seen as absolute if reality is social, relational. Therefore, society will require some evidence of significant harm to individuals before concluding that their rights have been taken away, especially if protecting those rights involves some price to society.

A critique based on principles such as those of Nozick makes it clear that utilitarian arguments for nuclear power are morally deficient. In order to make an informed decision between the social utility of nuclear power and the real or potential harm to individuals, the value of the economic activity to be fueled by nuclear power must be argued, not assumed. Some no longer agree that economic growth is automatically good. A case can be made that it is at least a precondition for some major social goods; Bethe and Rossin have not made that case.

If it is established that economic growth is of considerable value, then the question becomes whether the damage to individual rights involved in using nuclear power makes it unacceptable or at least less acceptable than

---

[15]Lester Thurow, *The Zero-Sum Society* (New York: Basic Books, 1980) 29-31.

alternative means of securing the energy the economy needs. That oil production will level off and then decline over the next two or three decades
seems certain. That energy efficiency and alternate technologies such as
solar energy will not be able to make up the loss in oil in the long run seems
very likely. Our choices for the next twenty or thirty years probably come
down to less economic growth, more coal, or more nuclear power. At this
point, technical information about harm produced by nuclear power is
needed. There is much of it, and there is majority agreement about it, but
there also is a significant amount of dissent. Most experts conclude that the
radiation released to the public by a properly operating nuclear reactor is
so small as to create little harm; that the chance of a major reactor accident
harming thousands of people is so slight as to be negligible; and that the
possibility of the release of radioactivity from properly stored nuclear waste
is so small as to present no real danger. Critics, a minority to be sure, argue
that any increased exposure to radiation increases the likelihood of cancer
and genetic damage; that the possibility of a reactor accident is greater than
advocates say (and real, in any event); and that we cannot be certain that
nuclear wastes will remain isolated for thousands of years.

How then shall we proceed? Through some democratic process we shall
attempt to weigh the social utility of nuclear power against its real or potential harm to individuals. While rejecting Nozick's absolute individuals,
it is possible to get some real help for this process from his emphasis upon
consent and compensation. There always is the temptation once one has
concluded that a project serves a good purpose to proceed without convincing others of that fact. The nuclear industry should not be relieved of
the responsibility of being open to scrutiny by its critics and of responding
to them. In particular, it should be required continually to convince those
who live near a power plant or waste-disposal site or who are employed in
the industry that the risk of harm is minimal and justified. With an issue
as controversial as nuclear power, consent will not mean unanimity. Neither can it mean simply majority rule over minority rights. Certainly it does
not mean that a majority must be harmed, but rather only convinced that
the harm to some is sufficient to outweigh the value to others. Moreover,
in a democracy it does not take a majority to make a course of action so
divisive as to be unacceptable. Consent must be sought just as broadly as
possible, and this is as it should be.

Second, in cases where harm can be identified, compensation is in order. A particularly clear example of this has to do with the radiation ex-

posure of employees in the nuclear industry. While the evidence is overwhelming that the exposure to radiation from a properly functioning nuclear plant is negligible for the general public, it is equally clear that those who work in the industry—from miners to operators to maintenance workers—are at much greater risk. That those workers should be compensated for this risk and especially for any actual harm that occurs seems inarguable. Similarly, society must be prepared to compensate those of the public harmed by an accident or a leak of nuclear waste should nuclear critics prove more right than most experts expect. If not, then we should not proceed.

In sum, arguments for the rights of individuals require utilitarian cost-benefit analyses of nuclear power to be much more articulate about the supposed benefits of actions that threaten harm to people. They also demand a continual effort to acquire consent and a willingness to compensate those put at risk. It is good that those making such calculations have their feet kept to the fire in this way. Moreover, these analyses must always be seen as temporary, requiring revision in light of new information and events. Minority critiques of nuclear safety or the hazards of waste disposal must be heard and taken seriously. However, the fact that there are some risks involved in nuclear power and that some people will be harmed is but further proof that we are related, that reality is social. If the benefits outweigh the costs and consent and compensation are taken seriously, it can be fair to proceed with the development of nuclear power.

From a liberation-theology approach such as Richard Shaull's, the utilitarian cost-benefit analyses are but one more tool of the ruling elite. One can hear the ring of truth in this position without charging the analysts with conscious duplicity. The tendency to confuse the interest of one's self or organization with the public interest is a common human weakness, which theologians usually call sin. It is always a problem, but it becomes much more serious when mixed with power, whether economic or political.

We live in a society where private corporations have a lot of power; nowhere is this more clear than in energy. Energy corporations employ many of the scientific experts and fund much of the research in energy. They control much of the technical and economic information about energy. Through indirect contacts and direct lobbying they exert great influence over political decisions, whether legislative, regulatory, or administrative. In each of these areas there is a tendency to assume that the interests of the corporation are the public interest and to use the power of the corporation to further those interests. Consciously or not, most utilitarian analyses have advanced the interests of the energy industries. It is unlikely that this was the conscious purpose of such analyses in most cases, but they have been used this way. A liberationist approach draws our attention to this reality, and it is a reality we dare not ignore.

One response is to reject industrial society in favor of horse-drawn plows, bicycles, home gardens, and windmills. While there is no lack of such pastoral-romantic literature, most of us see this as an unrealistic solution for most people most of the time. Yet it carries a grain of truth in it, for it recognizes that industrial society requires corporate activity of some sort. Large-scale production requires that the resources be organized on a large scale. For example, if solar energy is to be widely used, it will have to be mass-produced; large-scale corporate activity will be required. Industrial society means corporations.

What kind of corporation is not clear. Many socialist countries organize a large part of their corporate activity in government-owned corporations. Many corporations, including most U.S. utilities, are heavily regulated. In some countries, including the United States, private corporations predominate, influenced to varying degrees by government regulations. In some instances, private corporations act almost completely on their own. In all of these cases, however, production is carried out corporately. In sum, unless we are prepared to give up industrial society, the question is not whether we shall have corporations but rather how we shall choose to govern them. Liberation thought reminds us that we have yet to come to terms with that question.

In fact there is a significant difference between oil and natural gas and electricity in this regard. Oil and gas companies are essentially private corporations. Not coincidentally, their prices are being deregulated; government agencies have difficulty getting information about oil and gas supplies and reserves; the companies are required to take responsibility neither for the efficiency of energy use nor for the equity needs of their customers. Utilities are regulated corporations. Their prices are set, usually by a state commission; most information about their present and future generating capacity is public; they must provide home-energy audits and follow stated procedures before cutting off service. The oil and gas companies are rich and their power is expanding; the electric utilities face both economic and political problems.

Unless one believes that what is good for Exxon is good for America, the liberation approach reminds us to be constantly vigilant for abuses of corporate power in our economy and even more in our politics. For this vigilance to result in anything more than a few lone voices crying in the wilderness requires political movements composed of people with various interests who are organized strongly and broadly enough to generate political counterforces. Finally, it means that we must make the political and intellectual commitment to take a serious look at what legitimate role corporations should play in our public life and how best to govern their power in line with that legitimate role.

There are some immediate steps that can be taken in energy policy in support of these long-term concerns. When action was first taken to deregulate oil and gas prices, part of the new money generated by higher prices was to stay with the oil and gas companies so they could find more supplies. However, in recognition that they could use only so much money efficiently for exploration and new production, the "excess" was to be taxed for use in subsidizing middle- and low-income consumers and in developing other kinds of energy. In the meantime, consumer subsidies have been cut, and the oil and gas companies have been buying up alternate energy sources. It is appropriate continually to ask whether oil and gas profits are excessive when these corporations are extending their power both in other energy areas and in our economy generally. Another proposal given some consideration in the late 1970s was for a national oil and gas corporation. This corporation would develop and produce oil and gas supplies from national lands. It would not only provide invaluable information about the internal workings of the industry but also provide a neutral training ground for the experts needed if the oil and gas industry is to be regulated or even nationalized sometime in the future.

For the utilities, the primary problem is effective regulation. Regulatory agencies lack the expertise and independence necessary to develop their own analyses. Even the usual utilitarian studies are suspect if carried out by those being regulated, let alone investigations expanded to include the issues raised in our discussions of Rawls, Nozick, and liberation thought. Our unwillingness to look seriously at how to govern corporations has left our regulatory procedures underfunded, understaffed, and vulnerable to outside pressures. Given this situation, proposals designed to "streamline" the regulatory process, the licensing of nuclear facilities in particular, must be viewed with suspicion. The absence of a competent and independent regulatory process makes delay the primary weapon of those who challenge corporate power.

As practiced in the past, simple utilitarian cost-benefit analyses are morally deficient and subject to critique from egalitarians such as Rawls, libertarians such as Nozick, and liberationists such as Shaull. However, if these critics are seen not simply as enemies to be dismissed but as legitimate points of view, helpful changes in the utilitarian analyses are possible. The result should be much more morally adequate. Nevertheless, it must be recognized that these are not engineering problems, although they are based significantly on scientific and technological data and can be influenced profoundly by new technological and scientific developments. Rather, they are predominantly political issues raising basic questions of human purpose and social organization. As such, they inevitably involve conflict and argument and allow no simple or final solutions. So it must and should be.

Returning to the Debate

At this writing, President Reagan claims that both his economic and his energy policies have been great successes. In fact, Reagan's success in energy is primarily a result of energy price decontrol enacted under Carter. Higher prices did prove very effective at cutting demand; they did much less to increase supply. The increased use of insulation, wood-burning stoves, and high-mileage cars indicates the more-general trend toward energy conservation in our society. But this conservation initially went hand in hand with economic stagnation worldwide. With economic recovery, energy demand in the United States began to grow once more. If the world economy sustains significant growth over a number of years, conservation will not be enough. For now, however, there is an oil glut. Utilities have adjusted their predictions for electricity demand downward. Energy prices have moderated generally, and oil prices have dropped dramatically.

It would seem like an ideal time to act to forestall future energy problems. Instead, we seem to be making no headway on the serious problems of nuclear power, and that industry is dead in the water. Funding has been cut for alternative energy, especially solar. The Reagan administration has moved, or attempted to move, to cut back on regulatory competence and on programs intended to limit the suffering caused by higher energy prices. The primary battle seems to be over whether to drill for oil and gas offshore and in wilderness areas. The president continues to express confidence that the oil and gas companies will find new supplies.

It appears inevitable that the energy problem will return, sooner if the world economy continues to recover, or later if stagnation returns. In either event, geology seems destined to catch up to us, if unrest in the Middle East does not get us first. When the oil glut is gone, it now seems likely we shall be without a nuclear-power industry, with little room left for easy conservation, and with a solar program still starved for research and development funds.

The resulting shortages likely will make critiques of more-pessimistic utilitarian calculations all the more difficult and important. The longer we put off dealing with the moral dimensions of the energy debate, the less hospitable will be the context in which we confront them. Egalitarian, libertarian, or liberation concerns will probably get lost in a crisis of shortages. The longer we put off changing the political and social climate within which these decisions must be made, the greater the danger that energy will severely limit and seriously threaten our social and political institutions.

Annotated Bibliography

Historical Background

Schurr, Sam H., et al. *Energy in the American Economy, 1950-1975*. Baltimore: Johns Hopkins University Press, 1980.

——————. *Energy in America's Future*. Baltimore: Johns Hopkins University Press, 1979. While not particularly readable, these two volumes constitute a comprehensive history of energy use and policy.

Stobaugh, Robert and Daniel Yergin, eds. *Energy Future: Report of the Energy Project of the Harvard Business School*. New York: Random House, 1979. While readers must be careful to note the influence of the conclusions on the analysis, this volume does provide a very good summary of energy-use patterns and of the history of public policy.

Hard or Soft

Commoner, Barry. *The Politics of Energy*. New York: Knopf, 1979. While others, such as Michael Harrington, share Commoner's views, his remains the most fully developed statement of this view.

Copeland, Warren R. "Ethical Dimensions of the Policy Debate: The Place of Equity." *Soundings* 62:2 (Summer 1980): 159-77. This article spells out the analysis in this section in greater detail.

Lovins, Amory. *Soft Energy Paths: Toward a Durable Peace*. Cambridge MA: Ballinger, 1977. This remains the best single statement of the soft-path alternative. Stobaugh and Yergin, cited above, stress conservation more and solar energy less than Lovins and emphasize economic more than value justification.

Mobil Corporation. *The Real Challenge: Increasing Energy Supply*. New York: Mobil Corporation, 1977. This is one of a series of publications that are merely collections of Mobil's advertisements.

Pickering, George. "Energy and Well-Being: Whose?" *Electrical Perspectives* 79:1 (January–February 1979): 1-7.

Pickering, George, and Margaret Maxey. "The Road Not Taken and Wisely So." In *Soft vs. Hard Energy Paths*. Edited by Charles Yulish. New York: Charles Yulish Associates, 1977. Pickering offers the most sustained case against the social naiveté of the soft-path advocates and for the social-equity rationale for nuclear power.

Rossin, A. David. "Economics of Nuclear Power." *Science* 201 (18 August 1978): 582-89.

——————. "Nuclear Power: A Necessary Option." *Journal of Current Social Issues* 14:4 (Fall 1977): 43-48.

——————. "The Soft Energy Path: Where Does It Really Lead?" *The Futurist* 14:3 (June 1980): 57-63. The first article basically makes the economic argument, the second the technical, and the last the ethical.

Utility vs. Rights

Bethe, H. A. "The Necessity of Fission Power." *Scientific American* 234:1 (January 1976): 21-31. This is a clear and straightforward statement of the utilitarian analysis of energy options.

Gutierrez, Gustavo. *A Theology of Liberation*. Mary Knoll NY: Orbis, 1973. This remains the classic statement of Latin American liberation thought.

Hessel, Dieter T. *Energy Ethics*. New York: Friendship, 1979. This includes a revised form of the National Council of Churches' statement (see below) and a group of articles that support that position.

Kaku, Michio and Jennifer Trainer, eds. *Nuclear Power: Both Sides*. New York: W. W. Norton, 1981. This is the best single collection of articles covering the full range of issues related to nuclear power and energy.

National Council of Churches. *The Ethical Implications of Energy Production and Use*. New York: National Council of Churches, 11 May 1979.

Nozick, Robert. *Anarchy, State, and Utopia*. New York: Basic Books, 1974. This has become the standard philosophical source for contemporary libertarians.

Rawls, John. *A Theory of Justice*. Cambridge MA: Harvard University Press, 1971. This has become the standard philosophical source for contemporary equalitarians.

Shaull, Richard. "Death and Resurrection of the American Dream." In Gustavo Gutierrez and Richard Shaull, *Liberation and Change*. Edited by Ronald H. Stone. Atlanta: John Knox Press, 1977. This is Shaull's effort to bring home to the United States the insights of liberation thought.

James A. Capo
Fordham University

..

Television News

■ ■ Americans regularly encounter information about social issues through mass-mediated news. Whether they browse the Sunday paper over coffee, awaken to a clock radio's headlines, listen to updated bulletins during car rides, or faithfully watch "Sixty Minutes" after dinner, Americans integrate the news experience into their busy lives. They value news sufficiently to raise anchorpersons Tom Brokaw or Dan Rather to heroic status in real life and to use top stories as the focus of conversations for friendships or business.

Besides being popular and pervasive, the news habit also helps shape the way decision makers and the general public ultimately respond to social issues and policy. Many observers acknowledge, for example, that the emergence of television network news set a stage and script for national efforts to confront racism in the 1950s and 1960s; to deal with war in the 1960s and 1970s; and to address sexism, energy, ecology, and the economy in the 1970s and 1980s.[1] Political life in the era of the electronic news media would be unrecognizable to its turn-of-the-century practitioners.[2]

As they present information about contemporary events, however, newspersons observe codes of responsible reporting and editing that differ in important respects from the ethical principles and practices at stake in

---

[1] See Marvin Barrett, ed., *The Alfred I. du Pont-Columbia University Survey of Broadcast Journalism*, vols. 1-7 (New York: various publishers, 1970-1980).

[2] Edward W. Chester, *Radio, Television, and American Politics* (New York: Sheed and Ward, 1969) 283-312.

the event reported. Graphic depictions of the horrors of the Vietnam War, the Iranian revolution, or the latest hostage crisis did not necessarily get aired to promote principles such as peace or international justice; nor in the interest of ethical systems in such religious traditions as Christianity, Judaism, Islam, or Buddhism; nor because news professionals uphold the ideology of liberalism or that of communism. Since news people's codes of responsibility differ in important respects, anyone concerned about these or other important ethical approaches to social issues would do well to understand the distinctive tenets of news responsibility and to analyze their implementation in coverage of social issues.

The Principles of Responsible Journalism

During the last three decades, journalism codes in America have upheld objectivity, truth, freedom, and social responsibility as the key principles of a reporting ethics.[3] Working journalists see objectivity as "the use of certain procedures discernible to the news consumer" to gather and structure " 'facts' in a detached, unbiased, impersonal manner."[4] According to this principle, journalists resemble clear pipes that facilitate efficient flow of observable data rather than qualitatively evaluate the data's content.[5] They neutralize their own "wants, tastes, and moral or religious beliefs" to provide information "based on first-hand comparison of reports by credible witnesses," commonly called "sources."[6] The principle of objectivity, in other words, upholds various reporting *techniques* that convey impartiality.

The principle of truth, on the other hand, mandates the faithful representation of *facts in context*. As the American Society of News Editors declared in its 1975 "Statement of Principles," "Every effort must be made

---

[3]Manifestations of each principle have been present in Western journalism for a century or longer. See Anthony Smith, *The Politics of Information* (London: Macmillan Press, Ltd., 1978) 143-56, or Michael Schudson, *Discovering the News* (New York: Basic Books, 1978).

[4]Gaye Tuchman, "Objectivity as Strategic Ritual: An Examination of Newspapermen's Notion of Objectivity," *American Journal of Sociology* 77:4 (January 1972): 660-79.

[5]Harry J. Skornia, *Television and Society* (New York: McGraw-Hill Book Co., 1965) 54.

[6]J. Edward Gerald, *The Social Responsibility of the Press* (Minneapolis: University of Minnesota Press, 1963) 153-55. Also see William L. Rivers and Wilbur Schramm, *Responsibility in Mass Communication*, rev. ed. (New York: Harper & Row, 1969) 150-56.

to assure that the news content is accurate, free from bias and in context."[7] According to the Commission on Freedom of the Press, "Today our society needs, first, a truthful, comprehensive, and intelligent account of the day's events in a context which gives them meaning."[8]

The freedom principle insists on the unfettered right to investigate and report *as journalists see fit.* "It carries with it the freedom and the responsibility to discuss, question, and challenge actions and utterances of our government and of our public and private institutions."[9] Consequently, the news media can operate as a "fourth branch of government" that checks on the other three and insures that the people's business gets done.[10] For many in the news business, freedom outshines all other ethical principles: "If you're going to accept journalists only if they conform to some established norm, you won't have the new blood and vital free flow of new ideas that are absolutely essential to a vital press."[11]

The obligation to a social-responsibility principle stands as the most recent, but least clearly delineated, addition to journalistic codes. Hulteng described the principle this way: "Journalists must observe a responsibility to *the public welfare;* their impressive power should be employed for the general good, not for private advantage."[12] According to the Commission on Freedom of the Press, the new responsibility included providing a forum for the exchange of comment and criticism, projecting the positions of all groups in society to one another, clarifying the goals and values of society, and reaching every member of society.[13] In the view of working journalists, however, social responsibility entails high profes-

---

[7]Article IV from "A Statement of Principles" of the American Society of News Editors (1975), in Bernard Rubin, ed., *Questioning Media Ethics* (New York: Praeger Publishers, 1978) 57.

[8]The Report of the Commission on Freedom of the Press, *A Free and Responsible Press* (Chicago: University of Chicago Press, 1947) 20.

[9]From "Code of Ethics" of Sigma Delta Chi (1973), in Rubin, *Questioning Media Ethics,* 58.

[10]Douglass Cater, *The Fourth Branch of Government* (Boston: Houghton Mifflin, 1959).

[11]"Playboy Interview: Walter Cronkite," *Playboy,* June 1973, 72.

[12]John Hulteng, *The Messenger's Motives* (Englewood Cliffs NJ: Prentice-Hall, Inc., 1976) 23. Italics added.

[13]*Free and Responsible Press,* 20-21. Also see Fred S. Siebert, Theodore Peterson, and Wilbur Schramm, *Four Theories of the Press* (Urbana: University of Illinois Press, 1956) 73-103.

sional standards and training, opportunities for internal criticism and regulation, and machinery for external reviews to insure that citizens obtain the information they require to exercise their political duties.[14]

Taken together, these four principles seem to provide a comprehensive and rooted ethical base for the American news habit. Objectivity deals with the methodological techniques for gathering and presenting the news. Truth mandates the relationship between news and the real-life situation that it claims to "re-present." Freedom delineates the essential right of all news agents, and social responsibility demarcates the primary purpose of news: a well-informed public.

Each principle also rests on traditions of Western civilization that extend well beyond the boundaries of news. Consider, for example, the correspondence between the maxims for press responsibility and the mythologies that undergird American life and belief. The journalist's search for unimpeachable reality parallels the restless quest for the true Kingdom of God on earth by early New England settlers. The impetus for revolution and constitution emerged from the Enlightenment belief that free men can govern themselves when they examine the disparate facts and opinions of their experience in an impartial, rational manner. Finally, the call for *social responsibility* recognizes the Hobbesian view that, since everyone is motivated by self-interest, only strict standards and checks can prevent domination by self-interest.[15]

Besides having roots within the American tradition, these principles seem to be followed by most journalists. One recent volume on press standards observed "a moral flame" in the press that "is responsive to the interests of journalism's ethically sensitive community today."[16] Another study observed: "Those who own and operate American media have no vested interest in our being 'bad.' On balance, they are in their own lives

---

[14]H. Al Anderson, "An Empirical Investigation of What Social Responsibility Theory Means," *Journalism Quarterly* 54:1 (Spring 1977): 33-39. For a view that extends social-responsibility theory to other nations and professions, see Carol M. Thurston, "A Comparison of Attitudes about Social Responsibility among Dutch and American Journalists and Lawmakers," *Gazette* 27 (1981): 123-38.

[15]According to Robert Bellah, the Christian, Enlightenment, and Hobbesian views of society undergird the American experience. See *The Broken Covenant: American Civil Religion in Time of Trial* (New York: Seabury, 1973).

[16]George Gordon, foreword in John C. Merrill and Ralph Barney, eds., *Ethics and the Press* (New York: Hastings House, 1975) xiii.

ethical and moral persons, and would thus, on balance, have a vested interest in that direction. . . . The 'ethic' in our system is the most democratic, the most responsive one yet devised."[17]

Given the inherent attractiveness of these principles, their continuity with the American tradition, and their affirmation by news professionals, current discussions about responsible journalism have focused on their incorporation into the daily routines of newsworkers. Recent books on the subject offer guidelines about reportorial conflicts of interest, relationships with sources, on- and off-the-record interviews, checkbook journalism, and privacy rights.[18]

But does conscientious adherence to these standards insure reporting that enhances enlightened public responses to the events covered? Advocates of responsible journalism assume that observation of the four norms insures adequate coverage. Yet critics complain that news reporting too often obfuscates the "real" events and issues of the day. They cite, for example, the horse-race and celebrity emphases in political campaign coverage that leave debate over election issues in the dust, or at least out of the limelight.[19]

Disagreements among policymakers, journalists, and researchers have raged about the worthiness of coverage during the Vietnam War, the Three Mile Island nuclear incident, and the taking of American hostages in Iran.[20] In each case, weighty evidence suggests that news—especially television news—helped shape public consciousness about and response to the issues involved. Yet the portraits may also have skewed comprehension about what was at stake or blurred important aspects of the event.

Charges about "bad" coverage often have alluded to "irresponsible" journalistic techniques, especially the shortcomings of reporters in the practice of objectivity or social responsibility. Recently, Bennett and oth-

---

[17]Lee Thayer, ed., *Ethics, Morality, and the Media* (New York: Hastings House, 1980) 41.

[18]See, for example, Bruce M. Swain, *Reporters' Ethics* (Ames IA: Iowa State University Press, 1978); or Rubin, *Questioning Media Ethics*, 3-39.

[19]See Paul Weaver, "Is Television News Biased?" *The Public Interest* 26 (Winter 1972): 62-68, or Michael J. Robinson and Margaret A. Sheehan, *Over the Wire and on TV* (New York: Russell Sage Foundation, 1983).

[20]See, for example, Don Oberdorfer, *Tet!* (Garden City NY: Doubleday, 1971), or Dan Nimmo and James E. Combs, *Nightly Horrors* (Knoxville: University of Tennessee Press, 1985).

ers have argued persuasively that conscientious observation of traditional journalistic norms inadvertently leads to a misrepresentation of what is important in current events. Even the best of news too often contains dramatic, personalized, normalizing, ahistorical characteristics.[21] If such is the case, then ethicists need to construct and implement more adequate principles for news, rather than simply blame a few journalists or their parent corporations for irresponsibility.

As part of any reconstruction of principles, it is important to remember that news provides an opportunity for anyone to engage in social-ethical analysis and action this very day. As a form of communication, news can't take place *unless* members in the audience actively respond to the news message via some meaning context.

In a sense, each citizen uses news ethically—as a cultural and political instrument to construct, reinforce, or change personal and shared views of self, societies, and ultimate realities. News, in other words, provides the opportunity on any given day to exercise critical ethical judgment about matters of shared importance in the public world. By flicking a switch, opening a mailbox, or heading for the nearest newsstand, anyone can initiate the enterprise of social ethics by thinking critically about the choices people make when they share mediated messages about their common world and by deciding how best to respond to the news report.

Instead of simply elaborating what is good or bad about the news process, the remainder of this essay exemplifies how this kind of dialogical interaction with journalism might work. Any reader can approximate or develop further this exercise by obtaining news coverage from the period studied.[22] Through comparable analytic steps, readers can also carry out an original and responsible act of ethical inquiry into their news habits. These habits shape public understandings of who we are, what kind of a world we inhabit, and what will endure after the current events fade from the journalistic spotlight.

Do Current Principles of Responsible News Work?
A Case Study of Watergate Coverage

On 17 June 1972, five men were caught breaking into Democratic National Committee headquarters in Washington, D.C. The resulting Water-

---

[21]Lance Bennett, *News: The Politics of Illusion* (New York: Longman, 1983) 7-30.

[22]To ascertain what coverage to order and the ordering process, consult Vanderbilt Television News Archive, *Television News Index and Abstracts* (Nashville: Joint University Libraries, 1972–).

gate affair scandalized the nation, destroyed the second term of the Nixon administration, and led to the first resignation and pardoning of a president. The Watergate experience drastically changed the way Americans viewed themselves by raising fundamental questions about the nation's character, its principles, policies, and institutions. It evolved from an apparently spontaneous, idiosyncratic event to the status of national crisis through ongoing news coverage.[23]

In the fast-paced world of electronic information, Watergate has almost become ancient history—relegated to a few paragraphs in retrospectives about politics during the 1970s. But at the time, public awareness of and concern about Watergate extended from initial reports about the break-in (June 1972) through President Ford's pardon of Richard Nixon (September 1974). Table 1 highlights the major Watergate events making headlines during this period. At times, the coverage became so overwhelming that little else newsworthy seemed to happen.

TABLE 1

Chronology of Key Watergate Events[24]	
1969 20 Jan.	Richard Nixon is inaugurated president.
1970 25 June	Executive branch committee submits a plan to the president for strengthened domestic intelligence.
1971 13 June	*New York Times* begins publishing the "Pentagon Papers." President authorizes secret White House unit to stop security leaks. Unit includes G. Gordon Liddy.
1972 27 Jan.	Liddy proposes to Nixon reelection officials an espionage plan against Democrats.
28 May	Wiretap and photographic team under Liddy breaks into Democratic National Committee offices in Watergate complex.
17 June	Second Watergate break-in to fix phone tap is foiled by police, who arrest the burglars. "Watergate" begins!
20 June	President tells aides Ehrlichman and Haldeman that the Watergate investigation should be contained.

---

[23]Although the discovery of the break-in occurred during June 1972, more than two years passed before enough information and public opinion crystallized to force President Nixon's resignation in August 1974.

[24]Based in part on "Chronology of Watergate-Related Events" by Linda Amster in Gerald Gold, ed., *The White House Transcripts* (New York: Bantam Books, 1974) 813-77.

	22 June	President denies White House involvement in break-in.
	29 June	President's reelection committee begins withdrawing funds, eventually totaling $500,000, for Watergate defendants.
	1 Aug.	Through FBI leaks, *Washington Post* story traces reelection funds to the bank account of a Watergate burglar.
	19 Aug.	House Banking Committee chairman orders a staff investigation of laundered Watergate funds.
	15 Sep.	A federal grand jury indicts the Watergate burglars.
	3 Oct.	House Banking Committee votes against hearings about funds.
	7 Nov.	President Nixon is reelected to a second term.
1973	8 Jan.	Criminal trial of seven Watergate burglars begins.
	30 Jan.	Burglary trial ends with all defendants found guilty.
	7 Feb.	Senate votes to initiate a Watergate investigation.
	19 Mar.	Convicted burglar James McCord writes sentencing Judge John Sirica about perjury and silence at trial and involvement of higher-ups in Watergate. Sirica releases letter to press on 23 Mar.
	2 Apr.	Lawyers for White House counsel John Dean tell Watergate prosecuting attorneys that Dean will talk.
	17 Apr.	President announces that his recently ordered investigation into Watergate has produced "real progress."
	27 Apr.	Pentagon Papers trial judge says that Watergate burglars were involved in burglary related to his case.
	30 Apr.	President accepts resignations of four top aides and responsibility for Watergate, but denies personal involvement.
	11 May	Pentagon Papers case is dismissed due to government misconduct.
	17 May	Televised Senate Watergate hearings begin.
	25 May	Watergate special prosecutor Cox takes office.
	25 June	Dean tells Senate that president, White House, campaign aides, and Justice investigators were involved in cover-up.
	16 July	Presidential taping system is revealed at Senate hearings.
	18 July	Prosecutor Cox requests "Watergate" tapes from president, who on 23 July refuses to comply.
	31 July	Congress gets first impeachment resolution against president.
	10 Oct.	Vice-President Spiro Agnew resigns after pleading "no contest" to a charge of tax evasion.
	12 Oct.	President nominates Gerald Ford as new vice-president.
	20 Oct.	Prosecutor Cox rejects Nixon compromise offer on tapes. He is fired; Attorney General Richardson resigns.
	23 Oct.	President reverses position and promises to surrender tapes.
	30 Oct.	House Judiciary Committee initiates impeachment preparations.
	5 Nov.	Leon Jaworski becomes the new special prosecutor.

	21 Nov.	An 18-minute gap in a tape of the president and Haldeman on 20 June 1972 is announced.
	26 Nov.	White House turns over some tapes to court.
	6 Dec.	Gerald Ford becomes new vice-president.
1974	15 Jan.	Experts conclude that five erasures created 18-minute gap.
	6 Feb.	Judiciary Committee receives subpoena powers for impeachment.
	19 Feb.	Senate Watergate committee votes to end public hearings.
	1 Mar.	Grand jury indicts seven former Nixon aides for cover-up.
	21 Mar.	Appeals court says grand jury can release to Judiciary Committee data on presidential involvement in Watergate.
	2 Apr.	President agrees to pay more than $400,000 in back taxes.
	30 Apr.	President releases edited transcripts of Watergate tapes.
	1 May	Judiciary Committee states that edited transcripts fail to comply with its subpoena of tapes.
	9 May	Judiciary Committee opens impeachment hearings.
	24 July	Supreme Court rules that president must turn over 64 tapes of Watergate conversations to Prosecutor Jaworski.
	27 July	Judiciary Committee recommends impeachment article against president for conspiring to obstruct justice in Watergate.
	29 July	Judiciary Committee recommends second impeachment article for president's repeated failure to carry out oath of office.
	30 July	Judiciary Committee approves third impeachment article for president's unconstitutional defiance of Committee subpoenas.
	5 Aug.	President releases tapes that reveal his political motives for stopping FBI probe of Watergate on 20 June 1972.
	9 Aug.	President Nixon resigns; Gerald Ford becomes 38th president.
	20 Aug.	House accepts the impeachment report of Judiciary Committee.
	8 Sep.	President Ford pardons Nixon unconditionally for federal crimes he committed or may have committed as president.
1975	1 Jan.	Nixon aides are found guilty of Watergate cover-up charges.

Today or tomorrow, readers may be enveloped by an equally intense coverage period (about a natural disaster, revolution, war, hostage crisis, or political scandal). Perhaps the first step in any ethical analysis of such coverage is to remember that today's blockbuster stories eventually will be relegated to mere paragraphs or footnotes in reference books and articles of the future.

But the conventions reporters employ to cover such events, and the habits audience members develop to receive and act on the information, will persist from story to story. These practices and habits ought to be reviewed critically each time any responsible communicator dips into the continuous stream of mediated messages called news.

At the time of Watergate, citizens relied on the news to stay abreast of the implications of these events for the larger issues in American society. How well did the news process work? Did the established principles of responsible journalism enhance or detract from useful deliberations about the issues and values involved in Watergate?

Conventional wisdom credited independent, truth-seeking, responsible news operations with exposing the Watergate scandal.[25] But analysis of early coverage reveals that relatively little of pertinence to Watergate's outcome appeared during the six and a half months of 1972 network reporting.[26] In fact, even though newscasts conscientiously followed the four principles of responsible news reporting during the early period, they offered citizens neither the information nor the interpretations needed to appreciate the depth and breadth of this scandal. Instead of preparing viewers for the massive governmental struggle over extensive White House involvement in Watergate, the networks in 1972 focused on partisan bickering between Republicans and Democrats during an election campaign. Instead of seeking out new information, they mostly reported readily available charges and countercharges offered by party leaders about data first appearing in the *Washington Post*.

Of course, the 40-odd million viewers of a network evening newscast on the Monday after the weekend break-in knew nothing of what was to come. Nonetheless, as social ethicists they might have critically approached that first full reporting day of 19 June 1972. In so doing, they

---

[25]Edward J. Epstein challenged this view and argued that even the premier reporters of Watergate, Woodward and Bernstein from the *Washington Post*, played a minor role in uncovering the Watergate facts. Instead, Epstein argues, the Justice Department, Federal Bureau of Investigation, Judiciary, and Congress provided the information, investigations, and pressure necessary to expose Watergate. See *Between Fact and Fiction: The Problems of Journalism* (New York: Vintage Books/Random House, 1975) 19-32.

[26]This conclusion was reached after examining printed abstracts of all weekday evening network newscasts from 17 June 1972 to 31 December 1972 and after analyzing the actual Watergate coverage aired on key dates during the period. The Vanderbilt Television News Archive has collected videotapes and published summaries of all evening network newscasts since 5 August 1968. Many university libraries now carry these monthly abstracts; the Archive at Vanderbilt can furnish a copy of the actual tape for a nominal rental fee. See Vanderbilt Television News Archive, *Television News Index and Abstracts* (Nashville: Vanderbilt University Library, issued monthly).

could have identified the fundamental plot of that evening's Watergate story and reviewed how the traditional principles of news responsibility operated in the report's structure.

No one should expect that normative criticism of news will develop overnight. Like other virtuous activity, people must cultivate this kind of analysis through regular exercise of the best rational, aesthetic, emotional, and inspirational judgments they can muster.[27] But news analysis represents an essential activity for *social* ethics since it helps make news users better coparticipants in the shaping of messages that constitute their public realm.

If you are not yet interested in attempting a critical stance toward mediated messages like news, you may as well postpone further venturing into the ethical enterprise until this interest is cultivated. For print and electronic media so infiltrate the social life of Americans that most interaction with others now depends on input from the mediated "pictures in our heads" that such messages offer about sex (gender and eroticism), conflict (from internal psychologizing to universal warfare), class (in both economic and pedagogical senses), family, race, even religion, and many other aspects of our lives.

Although critical readings of electronic messages initially may appear difficult to decipher, one can turn to audio or video cassette recorders for practice. Electronically transmitted mass-messages employ repetitious (parsimony), easily recognizable images (stereotyping), and familiar forms of presentation (conventions).[28] Finally, they usually structure their messages dramatically. First, they establish the situation that threatens the established order and depict the major characters who generate or will respond to this disorder.[29] Then they delineate the purposeful responses of the characters to the situation via rising and falling action.[30] They conclude with a

---

[27]See Plato, *Phaedrus and the Seventh and Eighth Letters,* trans. Walter Hamilton (New York: Penguin Books, 1973), and Richard Weaver, "The *Phaedrus* and the Nature of Rhetoric," in *Language Is Sermonic,* ed. Richard L. Johannesen, Rennard Strickland, and Ralph T. Eubanks (Baton Rouge: Louisiana State University Press, 1970) 57-83. Published earlier in Richard Weaver, *The Ethics of Rhetoric* (Chicago: Henry Regnery, 1953).

[28]See Walter Lippmann, *Public Opinion* (1922; rpt., New York: Free Press, 1965) 53-100, or John Fiske and John Hartley, *Reading Television* (London: Methuen, 1978) 13-67.

[29]See Herbert Gans, *Deciding What's News* (New York: Random House, 1979) 8-77.

[30]See Todd Gitlin, *The Whole World Is Watching* (Berkeley: University of California Press, 1980) 205-32, or Lippmann, *Public Opinion,* 125-58.

satisfactory resolution of the situation or a projection of further developments in the action in the not-too-distant future (stay tuned).

If audience members had looked critically at the first weekday newscast reporting after the break-in, they would have uncovered a structure for the Watergate report similar to the ones appearing in table 2.

Critical examination of each network's version of the story reveals that all three incorporated objectivity, truth, freedom, and social responsibility into their coverage. To insure objectivity, for example, all provided information "based on first-hand comparison of reports of credible witnesses."[31] On this day, sources included: law officers investigating the break-in, Democratic political leaders and presidential hopefuls, Republican political leaders and presidential spokesmen. To insure further impartiality, the reports offered videotape from the crime scene and videotaped or verbatim quotes from the sources. Correspondents employed qualifiers such as "seemingly" and "apparently" to avoid making personal judgments about the actions of the intruders.

In the interest of truth, all networks accurately portrayed specific details of empirically observable events. They only presented information verified firsthand by two or more sources. Yet each network chose different accuracies to report, devoted different amounts of attention to the facts, and structured their presentations in different ways. Compare ABC's ninety seconds about the Democratic spokesman "waxing righteously indignant" about the "campaign caper" during "standard political oratory" with forty seconds of less-ironic and -playful coverage from CBS about the same spokesman. NBC made only passing reference to this person's reaction, but chose one of his more-ironic and -pointed observations as a quote. Meanwhile, CBS featured 118 seconds of grave charges raised by Democratic presidential candidates whom the other networks excluded.

Nothing presented by any network could be described as false. Yet each network's selection and structure of "facts" and "truths" implied different interpretations about Watergate, political leaders, the political process and, implicitly at least, the appropriate response of viewers. All began with the same situation: a televised recreation of the bungled break-in attempt. Each network then put forward different agents and acts at the dramatic core of its individual narrative. All presented data that could be empiri-

---

[31]Gerald, *Social Responsibility*, 153.

TABLE 2

ABC: 240 Seconds	CBS: 300 Seconds	NBC: 145 Seconds
1. Intro: 5 nabbed seemingly preparing to tap or bug. (9″)	1. Intro: Illegal bugging was apparently aim; political backgrounds of men kick up a storm. (15″)	1. Intro: Fascinating and exotic story about men trying to install eavesdropping equipment. Connection with presidential reelection efforts. Republicans scandalized and fit to be tied. (30″)
2. Video walkthrough of break-in with narrative. (52″)	2. Video walkthrough of break-in with narrative. (44″)	2. Reactions of Democrats: will try to tighten security. (12″)
3. Info on suspects. (59″)	3. Info on suspects connected with presidential re-election efforts. (18″)	3. Video walkthrough of break-in with narrative. (22″)
4. Reaction of Democratic spokesman to campaign caper, with emphasis on irony and joy at Republicans seemingly with their hands in the cookie jar. (91″)	4. Reaction of Democratic spokesman: How many more are there? (40″)	4. Info on suspects connected with presidential re-election efforts. (12″)
5. Reactions of Republicans: denial of any connection. (14″)	5. Reaction of Republican spokesman: despicable, incomprehensible, fruitless, irrational act. (32″)	5. Reaction of Republican spokesman: surprised and dismayed about a deplorable act that should be fully investigated. (31″)
6. Reaction of presidential spokesmen: no involvement in this third-rate burglary attempt. (15″)	6. Reaction of Democratic candidates against Nixon administration: incredible act of political surveillance that poisons political process; danger to privacy of all citizens; free use of wiretaps leading to quasi-fascism. (118″)	6. Reaction of Democrats: file a lawsuit. (13″)
	7. Info on suspects. (33″)	7. Reaction of presidential spokesman: no comment on a third-rate burglary attempt nor condoning of second-rate activity. (13″)
		8. Reaction of Democratic spokesman: irony and legal action. (12″)

cally verified. Yet the most likely audience responses to each would be quite different.

Should viewers laugh or become angry at the partisan embarrassment portrayed by ABC? Or should they be alarmed by Democratic charges of invasion of privacy and quasifascism chronicled by CBS? Or can they be relieved by the dismayed Republicans who, according to NBC, seek a full investigation of the facts? Time and again in early Watergate reports, networks provided contrasting versions of comparable partisan reactions to Watergate. Which of the three outlined above is really the correct one? Was it ultimately appropriate to set Watergate in the context of partisanship? Did this sort of coverage prepare or distract viewers from the later, persistent view that Watergate transcended partisanship and threatened the roots of the American political process?

Even if the "true" version of Watergate was available in 1972, any efforts to eliminate reporting slants and require strict adherence to a single version of the facts would fly directly in the face of the freedom principle. As it is legally interpreted today, press freedom protects even false reports about matters of public importance as long as journalists have conscientiously observed practices that are professionally acceptable.[32] Besides affirming freedom by offering different slants, the networks also exercised freedom by continuing coverage of Watergate despite threats, pressure, and vindictive reprisals against those publicizing Watergate revelations.[33]

The freedom to transmit anything or everything about Watergate to Americans raises real questions about the usefulness and relevance of what the networks did present in their necessarily compact coverage. For example, although they were visually interesting, how relevant were the video walkthroughs of stairways and offices provided by all three networks? When NBC anchorperson John Chancellor introduced the "exotic" Watergate story as the "talk of the Capital today" and classified a subsequent twenty-second report about delegate-selection rules as more important, he exercised freedom. But what correlation did his disarming, freely offered observations provide for his own newscast's interview with a Republican spokesman who was "surprised and dismayed" by a break-in that he could

---

[32]The Supreme Court's 1964 decision, *New York Times v. Sullivan*, overturned centuries of libel law by affirming press freedom to report defamatory words about the public acts of public officials, even when these words turn out to be false. The press simply had to show that it had not acted with malice but had instead conscientiously followed recognized professional practices when it reported the incorrect information. See Harold I. Nelson and Dwight L. Teeter, *Law of Mass Communications*, 2d ed. (Mineola NY: Foundation Press, 1973) 99-138.

[33]Known steps taken against the press by powers in government range from obscene telephone threats to broadcast-license renewal challenges. See Carl Bernstein and Bob Woodward, *All the President's Men* (New York: Simon and Schuster, 1974) 105 and 220-21, and Timothy Crouse, *The Boys on the Bus* (New York: Random House, 1973) 172-75.

only "deplore" and to which he could not find words to respond? In a society continuously bombarded by data, how relevant is the presentation of constantly diverse, novel fragments of information that are as likely to narcotize or frustrate the viewer as to inform?[34]

The specter of a passive audience held captive by a few centralized news outlets has turned attention to standards for social responsibility. Journalists view this principle as calling for professionally established limits to the exercise of freedom in order to meet the information needs of citizens.[35] Such phenomena as codes of network-news practices, minimal professional training requirements, affirmative-action employment policies, ombudsmen, journalism reviews, and the national-press council help establish general guidelines for the principle. Each network organization affirms at least some of these strategies.

Perhaps the most clearly developed standard of social responsibility in broadcast news is the fairness doctrine. The Federal Communications Commission established the fairness obligation to prevent "powerful broadcasters from using a scarce resource—the airwaves—to control the data received by the public" and to provide "general access for airing the views of various groups and individuals."[36] As "the single most important requirement of operation in the public interest,"[37] this maxim contains two major provisions: "The first . . . demands that broadcast licensees devote a reasonable amount of their programming to controversial issues of public importance; the second . . . requires that when such issues are presented, contrasting views on them be aired."[38]

During their 1972 Watergate coverage, the networks went out of their way to treat the break-in as a controversial issue and to obtain reactions from all interested groups and individuals. On the 19 June reports, for ex-

---

[34]Jacques Ellul, *The Political Illusion* (New York: Alfred Knopf, 1967) 53-67, and *Propaganda* (New York: Random House, 1965) 202-57.

[35]John W. C. Johnstone, Edward J. Slawski, and William W. Bowman, *The News People: A Sociological Portrait of American Journalists and Their Work* (Urbana: University of Illinois Press, 1976) 113-32.

[36]Steven J. Simmons, *The Fairness Doctrine and the Media* (Berkeley: University of California Press, 1978) 11.

[37]Committee for Fair Broadcasting of Controversial Issues, 25 *F.C.C. 2d* 283, 292 (1970).

[38]Simmons, *Fairness Doctrine*, 9.

ample, a total of twelve viewpoints was named: six on ABC (the Republican National Committee, the Committee to Reelect the President, Republican National Chairman Robert Dole, Democratic National Chairman Lawrence O'Brien, Nixon campaign manager John Mitchell, and presidential press secretary Ronald Ziegler); eight on CBS (Dole, O'Brien, Democratic presidential candidates Hubert Humphrey, Edmund Muskie, and George McGovern, Democratic party officials, defense lawyers for the alleged burglars, and bail bondsmen); and six on NBC (the Republican National Committee, the Committee to Reelect the President, Dole, O'Brien, Ziegler, and Democratic officials). The relative time devoted to viewpoints differed for each network on this particular date: ABC and CBS paid more attention to Democrats, NBC more to Republicans. On balance, however, each network provided sufficient time for major partisan viewpoints during 1972.

In the case of Watergate, conscientious observance of fairness did not lead to distinguished coverage. When "reliable" Democratic sources commented, they usually offered negative viewpoints about their partisan and campaign rivals. Republican spokespersons denied involvement and returned the favor. The resulting coverage resembled a classic example of the engineering of public opinion, as outlined by Walter Lippman in the 1920s, long before radio or television became forces in the dissemination of news.[39] By stereotyping, personalizing, and opposing "two sides" of the Watergate incident in standard partisan terms, the newscasts made the report easily recognizable to audiences.

This approach channels all idiosyncratic or threatening aspects of the event out of the mainstream story, thereby creating the illusion that audience members can respond to this event effectively by continuing to act as partisan Republicans or Democrats. Meanwhile, official investigators revealed very little in order to ensure the burglars a fair trial in early 1973. Consequently, the networks in 1972 framed Watergate as a series of conventional partisan accusations, denials, and counteraccusations. Faithful adherence to objectivity and social responsibility, in other words, produced little light but lots of partisan heat about the whole affair.

Early Watergate coverage discloses other shortcomings of the fairness standard. Since the general public knew little and thought even less about the break-in during 1972 and since many other important issues faced

---

[39]Lippmann, *Public Opinion*, 23-49.

America, perhaps social responsibility required that the networks attend less to partisan reactions to Watergate and more to interest-group concerns such as the Indochina war, racism, urban problems, or poverty.[40] Is it more socially responsible to devote a precious twenty-two and a half minutes to issues with clear regional, minority, or advocacy impact than to another rhubarb in Washington, D.C.? Would the full Watergate story ever have emerged if no attention had been paid during those early months?

Careful adherence to fairness also can lead to irresponsible manipulation by news sources. Following a strategy of "no comment" to Watergate developments, the White House, for example, placed the networks in the awkward position of receiving more antiadministration viewpoints than proadministration. The potential threat of grievances under the fairness doctrine forced newscasters who lacked White House statements to downplay opposition comments and to make controversy about the issue seem evenly balanced when it actually wasn't. Viewers could come away from such coverage with wrong impressions about the issue's importance, about the degree of concern on a particular side of the issue, and about the response they ought to form.[41]

Finally, some argue that the social-responsibility principle presumes the social health and vitality of the American social order *as long as* its institutions and their interests enjoy media access and political representation proportionate to their power. These critics maintain that faith in current American institutions and processes—and not the degree of access—constitutes the most serious national problem. They would classify network delineations of Watergate in partisan terms as an instance of the "hegemony" they criticize.[42] In their view, the scandal exposed the serious infiltration of private, capitalistic techniques and values into the American system, which requires radical reorganization to regain its health. The

[40]Fred Friendly, *The Good Guys, the Bad Guys, and the First Amendment* (New York: Random House, 1976) 99.

[41]Michael J. Robinson, "American Political Legitimacy in an Era of Electronic Journalism: Reflections on the Evening News," in *Television as a Social Force: New Approaches to TV Criticism*, ed. Richard Adler (New York: Praeger, 1975) 97-139.

[42]Hegemony "is the name given to a ruling class's domination through ideology, through the shaping of popular" consent. It points to "a whole body of practices and expectations which constitutes a sense of reality for most people in society." See Gitlin, *The Whole World Is Watching*, 1-18, and Raymond Williams, "Base and Superstructure in Marxist Cultural Theory," *New Left Review* 82 (1973): 3-16.

social-responsibility principle, in this view, may help cover up the "real" problems of America rather than make them discussable.

The preceding analysis of an early Watergate report typifies the kind of coverage offered by the networks in 1972. It appears that newscasters conscientiously followed the major principles of responsible journalism. Nonetheless, their observance of these principles did not raise ultimately important or salient issues involved in the scandal.[43] Whatever else it entailed, Watergate did not represent normal partisan bickering between the Republican and Democratic parties. Nonetheless, typical network coverage depicted the scandal as mere partisanship and, in the process, obfuscated viewer understanding of other issues involved in Watergate. The analysis discovered that objective presentation of sources raises but does not resolve serious questions of source reliability. It found that adherence to the principle of truth does not overcome bias. And the exercise of journalistic freedom may exacerbate the dilemma of relevance in today's informationally overloaded society. Social responsibility, on the other hand, seems vulnerable to manipulation and hegemony.

In the case of early Watergate coverage, at least, the institution of network news did not simply portray an issue. Instead, conscientious news coverage seems itself to constitute a pertinent social issue that needs further ethical study. Standard news practices do not sufficiently ensure legitimate portraits of important events nor enhance useful responses to enduring problems in society. Instead, current journalistic methods of conscientiously applying objectivity, truth, freedom, and social responsibility actually may contribute to the persistence of those problems.

A Constructive Alternative for Responsible News

Upon first hearing, a call to reformulate or even reject the principles of responsible journalism sounds heretical. Not only does such a proposal question the daily news rituals of most Americans, it also raises doubts about the efficacy of the journalistic profession. Have journalists misappropriated the objectivity approach of the scientific method and the belief in truth affirmed by the Christian traditions? Do their codes improperly in-

---

[43]Debate about Watergate in 1973 and 1974 revolved around questions of balance of power in government, the unique attitude toward the presidency held by the Nixon White House, runaway campaign financing, a new morality (or lack thereof) in politics, and the eclipse of the public.

corporate the Enlightenment's enthusiasm for freedom and the calculated formulas of social accountability intended to keep in check Hobbesian realism?[44]

Nonetheless, the practical shortcomings of early Watergate coverage demand a reconsideration of the notion of journalistic responsibility. Other scholars of media ethics have reached similar conclusions. Some argue that the standard codes of responsibility have become "devoid of solid theoretical foundations"[45] and leave professional communicators "unsure how to proceed" at a time when "ethical matters have never been more paramount for communicators."[46] Yet many current critiques of the bankrupt situation for journalistic principles end up "destructive . . . because they are not followed by ethics; that is, they describe moral ambiguities that involve journalists but provide little constructive theory for concerned journalists to use to discern the moral among the vile. . . . The mass media still need an ethic from which principles can be drawn to be applied to most every situation that journalists encounter."[47] This section plants some seeds to generate a viable constructive approach to responsible news.

Historical examination of journalism reveals that the definitions, principles, and practices of news have changed over the decades. Schudson outlines six approaches to news, each of which has enjoyed a period of currency since the American Revolution: ideological treatises (after the Revolution), egalitarian commercialism (mid-nineteenth century), entertaining narrative (late 1800s), factual journalism (turn of the century), objective representation (after World War I), and investigative reporting (since World War II).[48] Apparently the nation alters its understanding of news and of journalistic standards as society changes. In the face of still-another

[44]Although he does not discuss journalism, Robert Bellah in *The Broken Covenant* argues that the communal aspects of the Christian and Enlightenment myths have been abandoned in contemporary America; consequently the nation faces the third "identity crisis" of its history.

[45]Clifford G. Christians, "Fifty Years of Scholarship in Media Ethics," *Journal of Communication* 27:4 (Autumn 1977): 24.

[46]Clifford G. Christians, Quentin J. Schultze, and Norman H. Sims, "Community, Epistemology and Mass Media Ethics," *Journalism History* 5:2 (Summer 1978): 38.

[47]John P. Ferre, "Contemporary Approaches to Journalistic Ethics," *Communication Quarterly* 28:2 (Spring 1980): 45.

[48]Schudson, *Discovering the News*. Also see Christians, "Fifty Years of Scholarship," 20-22, and Smith, *Politics of Information*, 143-56.

period of tumultuous change, ethical standards again must be reformulated. But how should this be done?

One scholar of media responsibility recommended the development of a more systematic theory that bases itself on great philosophical and theological traditions; views humans in symbolic, creative, and moral terms; restores discussions of absolute "oughts"; attends to systems grounded in covenant fraternity or spiritual community; and develops value-centered theories of communication.[49] Each of these areas of genuine ethical consideration often remains unexamined by those who simply apply accepted news standards to current reportorial practices.

As a consequence, the most widely circulated models of media responsibility seem realistic and pragmatic (because they readily can be applied) but do not engage in the hard work of systematic ethical considerations about what ultimately matters in life. Because news professionals and audiences dedicate themselves to the here and now during a journalistic report, they have little use for disciplines concerned with enduring or transcendent principles. Unless they can be shown meaningful relationships between the immediate and the truly permanent, the prevalent instrumental approaches to responsible journalism will continue to dominate.

A number of American traditions of philosophical and religious thought have argued that the daily changes and activities of experience interconnect with more enduring ideals in important ways. The philosopher John Dewey thought extensively about religion and values in terms of the mundane and the American democratic experience. In *A Common Faith* Dewey rejects allegiance to any principle that requires a leap of sheer faith and grounds enduring values in the active relation between the projections of human imagination and the conditions of experience.[50] He points to the "actual connections of human beings one with another" as the reservoir for a universal creed that "will change and grow, but . . . cannot be shaken."[51] Our shared communications about experience hold "all the material that gives verifiable support to our ideal faiths." "The Community of causes and consequences in which we, together with those not born, are enmeshed is the widest and deepest symbol of the mysterious totality

---

[49]Clifford G. Christians, "Mass Media Ethics: An Analysis of the Academic Literature." Paper presented at annual meeting of the Association for Education in Journalism, August 1976.

[50]John Dewey, *A Common Faith* (New Haven: Yale University Press, 1934) 52.

[51]Ibid., 80, 85.

of being what the imagination calls the universe. . . . It is the matrix within which our ideal aspirations are born and bred. It is the source of the values that the moral imagination projects as directive criteria and as shaping purposes."[52] Any ethical system that emerges from this "Community" or "matrix" must be critically analyzed to determine whether it contributes to "the significant achievement of men in science and art and all the kindly offices of intercourse and communication" and whether it nurtures and expands "the values of natural human intercourse and mutual dependence."[53]

Journalistically speaking, whenever news workers, newsmakers, and members of the news audience engage in the news habit, they carry out some degree of interchange about their experiences of the current environment. In the process they share their imaginative projections of what these experiences may mean for past, present, and future. Such communicative activity invariably reformulates the character and relative importance of the principles required for good living, for a good society, and for good journalism. Long-standing ethical principles can and do undergo change in the experience. Consider the 1972 airing of charges about bugging or dirty tricks, countercharges about irresponsible reporting and partisanship, and "no comments" about third-rate burglary attempts. Regular broadcast of such events (experience) and interpretations (imaginative projections) eventually raise serious questions about the worth of politics and the worth of the enterprise that reports incessant, self-interested acts of partisanship as though they were important events to share. This sort of early Watergate reporting demoralizes and paralyzes participants in the news habit.

As a modern form of public communication, news plays important religious and political roles. According to Randall, Dewey's religious theory considered

> "shared experience" as the greatest of human goods. . . . "Communication," in the deeper sense of learning from joint experience with others

---

[52]Ibid., 85.

[53]Ibid., 72-73, 85-87. For Dewey, the Christian creeds failed those tests because they preferred unilateral, unexamined dependence on an unverifiable, supernatural existent over natural human intercourse and experience. Some critics have charged that Dewey dogmatically stereotyped and excluded all systems of Christian thought and belief without carefully applying his own tests to their theologies. See John Blewett, S.J., "Democracy as Religion: Unity in Human Relations," in John Blewett, S.J., ed., *John Dewey: His Thought and Influence* (New York: Fordham University Press, 1960) 51-56.

how to enrich one's own understanding of things and to increase one's insight into the values to be found in living together in the human scene, is that perfected activity, that highest possible functioning of human powers, toward the achievement of which all human action should aim. . . . [Politically speaking, the] conscious interplay of finding out each others' interests and views that attends a community of purpose [undergirds democracy].[54]

According to Dewey, "Democracy is belief in the ability of human *experience* to generate aims and methods by which further *experience* will grow in ordered richness. . . . *Experience* . . . is that free interaction of individual human beings with surrounding conditions, especially the human surroundings, which develops and satisfies need and desire by increasing knowledge."[55] Public communication, therefore, in the form of democratic interchange, serves as a ruling metaphor for Dewey's thought.

The religious and political principle of democratic interchange idealizes the face-to-face group relationships of nineteenth-century agrarian America. Times have changed. Nonetheless, it points to an ideal too precious to let slip away in the media-oriented society of today. For it highlights the capacity of persons to give fully human responses to communications instead of engaging in sheerly mechanistic or mass-oriented behavior.

Dewey recognized the dangers that would accompany the explosion of information and the growth of the news business in the twentieth century. Despite great strides in "the physical and external means of collecting information," Dewey warned that the growth in communication services had not enhanced society's capacity to become an "organized, articulate public."[56] Instead of displaying or encouraging democratic interchange, mass-media news too often "limits the contacts, the exchanges, the communications, the interactions by which experience is steadied while it is also enlarged and enriched."[57]

---

[54]Randall, "The Religion of Shared Experience," 109.

[55]John Dewey, "Creative Democracy—The Task before Us," in *The Philosopher of the Common Man* (New York: G. P. Putnam's Sons, 1940) 227. Italics added.

[56]John Dewey, *The Public and Its Problems* (Chicago: Swallow Press, 1954) 179-84.

[57]Dewey, "Creative Democracy," 228.

Applying Dewey's religious and political theories to newsmaking means that the principles of objectivity, truth, freedom, and social responsibility are not to be taken for granted unless they enhance democratic interchange in a practical way. On this basis, then, the manifestation of these principles in news insures responsible journalism to the extent that they facilitate "learning from joint experience with others how to enrich one's own understanding of things and to increase one's insight into the values to be found in living together in the human scene."[58] Both source reporting (objectivity) and accurate re-presentation of the actual environment (truth) are valuable to the degree that they provide joint experiences that are mutually enhancing. Freedom and social responsibility should be affirmed to the extent that they enrich and increase the values worth experiencing individually and sharing collectively.

In addition to helping reformulate the other principles of responsible journalism, democratic interchange also should become a fifth and paramount principle. In *The Public and Its Problems,* Dewey argued that social-scientific interpretation should be incorporated into the news habit and that local communities should be revitalized so that practical discussion and action may once again be the public response to the news. In both instances, the recommendations aim at improving interchange by enhancing "the methods and conditions of debate, discussion, and persuasion."[59] If these suggestions seem unworkable to some professionals in broadcasting, then they had better tune in more often. In the 1970s and 1980s, programs that incorporated Dewey's principle of interchange included public radio's "All Things Considered"; public television's "MacNeil/Lehrer Report" and "The Week in Review"; and commercial television's "Today," "The Phil Donahue Show," "Nightline," and "Sixty Minutes." Special news coverage of national political conventions and social issues are still other examples. As for citizen discussion of and response to the news as a "pub-

---

[58]"For everything which bars freedom and fulness of communication sets up barriers that divide human beings into sets and cliques, into antagonistic sects and factions, and thereby undermines the democratic way of life. . . . Democracy is the belief that even when needs and ends or consequences are different for each individual, the habit of amicable cooperation—which may include, as in sport, rivalry and competition—is itself a priceless addition to life." Ibid., 225-26.

[59]Dewey, *The Public,* 208. For a more complete discussion of this perspective, see ibid., 185-219. Its philosophical underpinnings are found in John Dewey, *Experience and Nature* (La Salle IL: Open Court, 1929) 138-70.

lic,'' many people now devote coffee breaks, lunch hours, and leisure time to the sorts of exchange that Dewey maintained should be more formally revitalized on the local level. To the degree that people analyze individual news reports more critically, these sorts of interchange will better emulate Dewey's paramount principle.

Reflecting on these programs and the viewer response to them helps us to understand that the news can be more than just the transmission and distribution of information. Rather, viewers can begin sharing and participating in—even jointly creating—a common world. Some of this occurs by viewers imagining themselves in the places of other human beings. This can lead us to share and create with other viewers a common faith about what constitutes meaningful human actions. At their best, then, these news programs become what Dewey refers to as communication, "the establishment of cooperation in an activity in which there are partners, and in which the activity of each is modified and regulated by the partnership (empathy)."[60] Unless the news habit generates participation in these activities, it is reduced to either transmission of data or a propagandistic appeal to the emotions. Then it fails to celebrate what for Dewey was the highest form of human experience: sharing in democratic community.

Application

When we reviewed the current principles of responsible journalism, we found them to be high-minded and affirmative of the American tradition. But when we examined whether objectivity, truth, freedom, and social responsibility worked during early coverage of Watergate, we found them inadequate. Although newscasters followed the professionally recognized guidelines of responsibility, their 1972 reports for the most part neither alerted citizens to the scandal that would dominate 1973 and 1974 headlines nor interpreted Watergate in a sustainable manner. Instead of helping to clarify social issues, news coverage seemed to become a social issue in its own right. The responsibilities connected with the news habit require more theoretical and practical analysis than they have been given so far.

For philosopher John Dewey, mass-media news constitutes *the* social issue when its coverage stifles the emergence and celebration of an articulate public. His religious and political notion of democratic interchange

---

[60]Dewey, *Experience and Nature*, 179.

provides a way to evaluate the other standards of journalistic responsibility. It also offers itself as a paramount ethical principle for the news habit. But how would it have worked in the instance of early Watergate news? And what can be done to make it a regular part of the news habit?

Objectivity. If they had applied Dewey's approach to early Watergate news, network journalists would have relied less on partisan sources eager to use each revelation as a publicity device. On 19 June 1972, for example, ABC's ninety-second report on the anti-Republican quips delivered by Democratic Party Chairman O'Brien strains objectivity at the expense of democratic interchange. ABC described O'Brien's speech as "standard political oratory." Yet it devoted five percent of its entire newscast to the seasoned orator's ironic barbs deliberately served up for media attention.[61] CBS and NBC, on the other hand, presented just O'Brien's main charges about the administration's violation of its law-and-order policy. But all three networks often treated Watergate in terms of the personalities of sources readily available to correspondents and most likely to offer provocative, "made-for-television" responses.[62] The qualitative impact their ideas could have had on deliberations about values and choices for public life should have been given greater weight.

Truth. When they presented Watergate in terms of the election campaign, newscasts certainly didn't violate accuracy. However, they did ignore the larger context of Watergate's importance for American life. Given the constraints that govern story selection, newscasters incorporate the factor of long-term importance among their reasons for airing a particular story. Dewey's notion of democratic interchange recommends that those judgments about larger importance be made explicit. The 19 June charges on CBS of candidates Humphrey, Muskie, and McGovern provide one way to raise the possibility of long-term issues involved in Watergate. To be sure, these charges were issued by presidential hopefuls in the heat of a partisan campaign. But in another sense, they pointed to the important is-

---

[61]Edward J. Epstein explains why the machinery of network news favors preplanned statements by national figures in locations convenient to television news crews in *News from Nowhere* (New York: Vintage Books/Random House, 1974).

[62]As reporters on the *Washington Post*'s metropolitan desk, Woodward and Bernstein didn't know and couldn't use widely recognized political sources readily available to journalists assigned to national beats. With their own sources unwilling to appear in public, these young reporters employed different news-gathering techniques and established a different version of what Watergate entailed. See *All the President's Men.*

sues of a poisoned political process, loss of privacy, and executive privilege vs. authoritarian fiat—all of which would be debated for some months to come in the courts, in Congress, and among citizens. Journalists should explicitly offer connections between the immediate event and the longer history of the nation. Then deliberation about the truth and worth of each interpretation can begin.

Freedom. Given its own spirit of open deliberation and experience sharing, the principle of democratic interchange should not be used to curtail newscaster freedom. Still, journalists must weigh their exercise of that freedom against the report's relevance for citizen debate about the major values and choices facing the national community. The video reenactment of the burglary crime by all three networks or NBC's stress on the exotic aspects of Watergate overstepped freedom when they encouraged the audience to respond as spectators rather than as deliberative participants in the news habit.

Social Responsibility. In a similar fashion, the obligation to fairness should not be used to block the possibility of informed responses to events. The 19 June NBC report, for example, included four segments of less than fifteen seconds each about various partisan reactions to Watergate along with a fifth thirty-second reaction. No single issue of contention emerged from the reactions. Although this sort of staccato sequencing insured the inclusion of most major "sides," it did not permit full exposition of any viewpoint or encourage thoughtful audience response to it. Legally speaking, the fairness doctrine does not require the inclusion of every side or a perfect balancing of sides in each newscast. When broadcaster convenience or source satisfaction becomes more important than viewer understanding of and engagement with any single view, the newscasters have subverted the notion of democratic interchange.

Full incorporation of democratic interchange as an additional principle of responsible news would ultimately require new forms of journalistic presentation in addition to these instances of modification. Changes also would have to take place in the way newsmakers and audiences approach the news habit. At the core of these changes would be the realization that news consists not only of factual data but also entails communal celebration. Under the principle of democratic interchange, responsible journalists would seek to replace an authoritative, uncompromising attitude of "that's the way it is" with a more curious, experimental, open-ended model. News would acknowledge and invite participation in what it has been for some time: the expression of thoughtful, democratic judgments about what is important for the contemporary community and why citizens should become publicly involved in deliberations about the community's future.

Annotated Bibliography

Resources for a Media Ethics

Christians, Clifford G. "Fifty Years of Scholarship in Media Ethics." *Journal of Communication* 27 (Autumn 1977): 19-29. A survey of academic attention to media ethics from the 1920s to the present. The author traces the transition from the earlier emphasis on objectivity as the fundamental principle of journalistic morality to the more contemporary concern for social responsibility.

Christians, Clifford G., Kim B. Rotzoll, and Mark Fackler. *Media Ethics: Cases and Moral Reasoning.* New York: Longman, 1983. The application of a systematic framework from social ethics to evaluate the ethical implications of decisions made by media professionals. The book uses the "Potter Box" to dissect four dimensions of moral analysis found in media decisions: definition, values, principles, and loyalties. It employs five different ethical principles: Aristotle's golden mean, Kant's categorical imperative, Mill's utilitarian principle, Rawls's veil of ignorance, and the Judeo-Christian norm of love. The authors deal with such situations as those involving children, deception, sex, media self-criticism, minorities, violence, sensationalism, stereotyping, and the elderly.

Hulteng, John L. *The Messenger's Motives: Ethical Problems of the News Media.* Second edition. Englewood Cliffs NJ: Prentice-Hall, 1985. A review of contemporary principles of media responsibility and analysis of how these principles are practiced by journalistic professionals through their codes of behavior and day-to-day problems in presenting news.

——————. *Playing It Straight: A Practical Discussion of the Ethical Principles of the American Society of Newspaper Editors.* Chester CT: American Society of Newspaper Editors, 1981. An examination of the professional code of behavior approved by the American Society of Newspaper Editors. Special attention is given to the meaning of freedom, fairness, impartiality, and responsibility.

Lambeth, Edmund. *Committed Journalism: An Ethic for the Profession.* Bloomington: Indiana University Press, 1986. A professional journalist turned academician develops a theory of journalistic responsibility based on moral philosophy and political theory. At the core of his framework for proper behavior via the media are such enduring principles as truth, justice, stewardship, humanity, and freedom.

Phelan, John M. *Disenchantment: Meaning and Morality in the Media.* New York: Hastings House, 1980. A humanistic examination of ethical issues at stake in television. Phelan demonstrates that neither media-reform movements nor promises of technological evolution remedy the impoverishments in the quality of life and culture experienced during the era of electronic media. On the contrary, beliefs in reform or technology reinforce the transcendent meaning at the core of any culture.

Interpretations of Media

Adler, Richard P., ed. *Understanding Television: Essays on Television as a Social and Cultural Force.* New York: Praeger, 1981. This sampling from television criticism is organized according to overviews, critical approaches, drama, news, and the future. All essays take television seriously—as society's primary source for information, entertainment, and imaginative forms for perceiving self and world. One critic argues that television shapes the soul by building up a psychic structure of expectations (Novak). Others focus on television as a projection of our collective subconscious (Wood), a ritualized presentation and celebration of national events and myths (Littlejohn and Sperry), and a mediator of morality (Arlen, Modleski, and Alley).

Boorstin, Daniel. *The Image: A Guide to Pseudo-Events in America.* 1961; reprint, New York: Atheneum, 1978. An examination of how Americans through media substitute the artificial for the real in their lives. Chapters deal with substitutions of pseudoevents for news, celebrities for heroes, tourism for travel, shadows for aesthetic forms, and images for ideals. Comparably structured arguments in each chapter define the terms used, examine the origin of the substitution tendency, delineate the present situation, and examine effects on individuals and society. This book applies Platonic thought to contemporary America where much experience is either interpreted or dominated by media.

Enzensberger, Hans Magnus. *The Consciousness Industry: On Literature, Politics and the Media.* Selected by Michael Roloff. New York: Seabury Press, 1974. Essays dealing with the condition of elite art and culture after the rise of the "consciousness" industry. Subjects include the relationship between new media and the avant garde, the availability of media for social change or revolution, the status of literature in the face of media, and the implications of modern media for socialism. For Enzensberger, neither a communications technology nor its institutionalization neutrally transmits information. Instead, each technology favors certain social outcomes, interactions, and values over others. The industrialization of communication expropriates messages for purposes different than those intended. This situation leads to subversion, desacralization, and suppression of value formation.

Frank, Ronald E., and Marshall G. Greenberg. *The Public's Use of Television: Who Watches and Why.* Beverly Hills: Sage, 1980. An analysis of audience behavior in relation to "individual patterns of leisure interests and activities and the psychological needs they satisfy." The findings suggest that enduring interests of persons can shed light on their program choices as well as on their involvement, behavior, and viewing context adopted during TV watching. These findings have implications not only for program advertising; they may also be important for those concerned about developing new religious or ethical strategies regarding TV communication.

Lowery, Sharon and Melvin L. Defleur. *Milestones in Mass Communication Research: Media Effects.* New York: Longman, 1983. A review of eleven studies of media effects on Americans from the 1920s to the present. These research classics investigate movies, radio, television, and comics to ascertain their impact on children, violence, political behavior, and military morale. The authors argue that the so-called "magic bullet" theory of effects does not explain how audiences respond to media messages. No simple cause-effect or stimulus-response relationship operates at the core of media effects. Some of the research examined directly addresses matters of value formation and moral behavior; all of it should be reviewed by anyone interested in constructing a current study into media effects.

Meyrowitz, Joshua. *No Sense of Place: The Impact of Electronic Media on Social Behavior*. New York: Oxford University Press, 1985. An examination of ways that media operate as mechanisms of change in social behavior, as well as differences between print and electronic situations, the new social landscape, and changes in sexual identity, childhood, and political heroes. Meyrowitz argues that electronic media have greatly affected Americans' sense of place. Television disintegrates "distinctions between here and there, live and mediated, and personal and public." Private behaviors are transformed: "Miss and Mrs." into "Ms.," deferential Negroes into proud blacks, children into humans "with natural rights," doctors and presidents into fallible people, and so forth. For Meyrowitz, the electronic age ushers in a new order, not simply a variation of the old system.

Real, Michael R. *Mass Mediated Culture*. Englewood Cliffs NJ: Prentice-Hall, 1977. A look at the cultural assumptions conveyed by American media. Six case studies use different methods of exegesis to flesh out the symbol structure under study. Cases also focus on different elements in the communication process: source, message, medium, and receiver. After examining the Super Bowl, Disney productions, "Marcus Welby," the 1972 Nixon reelection campaign, and a Billy Graham television crusade, Real contrasts their common cultural assumptions with the communicative structures found in a Peruvian Indian fiesta. He finds North American mediated messages oriented to action, measurable achievement, materialism, property, progress, optimism, competition, and individualism.

Williams, Raymond. *Television: Technology and Cultural Form*. New York: Schocken, 1975. An analysis of how television as a technology and cultural form has "altered our world." Chapters explore the developments that created television, the institutions that control it, its forms, and its effects. Williams argues that television meets the growing social need for a continuously updated orientation to the mobility, novelty, and change of advanced urban societies. (Traditional institutions approach new relationships from positions formulated during earlier times and perceptions of space.) Broadcasting attracts persons seeking the paradoxical life-style of simultaneous mobility and privatization offered in contemporary industrial orders. Among cultural forms of television, Williams highlights mediation, dramatization, commodities, intrusion into public and private spheres of life, and planned (yet miscellaneous) flow of images rather than the presentation of discrete events.

Analyses of News

Bennett, W. Lance. *News: The Politics of Illusion*. New York: Longman, 1983. An argument that contemporary news requires dramatized, personalized, fragmented, and ahistorical presentations and reporting. These features make journalists prey to manipulation by sources, particularly those in political power, and lull audiences into uncritical acceptance of the manipulated news product as if it were social reality. Bennett demonstrates that traditional standards of responsible news (such as objectivity, documentary reporting, and so forth) inadvertently make journalists and audiences susceptible to manipulation. He argues that professionals and citizens alike must develop historical acumen, become sophisticated about how media operate, and commit themselves to some system of enduring values so that they can stand against and critically understand the news message.

Dewey, John. *The Public and Its Problems*. Chicago: Swallow Press, 1954. An examination of the challenge to modern democracies posed by mass media. For Dewey, media images and information do not facilitate creation of "publics" to respond to issues facing the social order. New media technologies interconnect large numbers of people in a way that transforms them into inarticulate publics, overwhelmed by the flow of data received and incapable of formulating a socially responsible political response. Dewey recommends strategies for regenerating face-to-face communication about political issues to resolve the challenge.

Epstein, Edward J. *News from Nowhere*. New York: Random House, 1973. An examination of how network organizations gather and present news on their nightly programs. The author argues that the values in the finished news product reflect the economic and political pressures facing commercial television much more than they mirror reality, codes of professional reporting, journalistic consensus about what should be news, or subjective judgments of individual reporters. For Epstein, network television news is presented in terms of dramatic conflict, vivid and recognizable personalities, visually interesting filmed sequences, and the nation as a whole.

Fiske, John and John Hartley. *Reading Television*. London: Methuen, 1978. A semiotic method in the "cultural studies" tradition applied to television. After laying out the signs, codes, and functions relevant to communication, the authors document that television operates as a social ritual, as a modern-day "bard" for the "culture at large and all the individually differentiated people who live in it." In its role as bard, television articulates the established cultural consensus about the nature of reality, locates persons in that culture's dominant value system, celebrates and justifies those representing the culture, assures the culture of its practical adequacy, exposes inadequacies in the culture's sense of itself, convinces audiences that status and identity are guaranteed by the culture, and transmits a sense of cultural membership.

Gans, Herbert J. *Deciding What's News*. New York: Pantheon, 1979. An examination of recurring patterns in national journalism. Gans argues that news highlights how the accepted order is threatened by various forms of disorder and is then restored through recognizable governmental elites and the political system. Gans maintains that news repeatedly favors certain American values: leadership, order, ethnocentrism, freedom, small-town pastoralism, moderation, responsible capitalism, and altruistic democracy. He shows how these values emerge from the rooting of professional journalism in the progressive movement.

Goethals, Gregor T. *The TV Ritual: Worship at the Video Altar*. Boston: Beacon Press, 1981. An exploration of how televised images mediate, reinforce, or challenge the belief systems of Americans. For Goethals, ritualistic dramatization of significant news and sporting events on television offers a religiously deprived population the opportunity to relate to a secular version of transcendent order.

Graber, Doris A. *Processing the News: How People Tame the Information Tide*. New York: Longman, 1984. An analysis of how certain people coped with or reacted to the bombardment of political information received during 1976. The research found that panelists based political judgments on the image qualities and character traits of personages in the news rather than on the policy and issue stories that were also reported. Panelists learned most readily by applying already assimilated interpretive schemata to new information. If cues were absent about which schema to apply, learning became difficult. While media provided factual information, evaluations of meaning originated from personal experience and acculturation.

Nimmo, Dan and James E. Combs. *Nightly Horrors*. Knoxville: University of Tennessee Press, 1985. A comparative analysis of coverage by the three networks of recent crisis events. Employing a dramatistic analysis, the authors discover distinctive patterns of reporting for each network—patterns that persist over time, whenever a crisis occurs.

Schudson, Michael. *Discovering the News*. New York: Basic Books, 1978. A historical review of the different forms journalism has taken over the last two centuries. The study argues that objectivity developed as a response to certain social and cultural conditions rather than as a systematically arrived-at standard for responsible journalism. The analysis traces the evolution of objectivity from stenographic reporting and naive realism to a form of institutional protection from newsmakers and sources of power in the society.

Warren R. Copeland
Wittenberg University

..

Economic Policy

■ ■ Savvy political analysts take pleasure in observing that beneath all the rhetoric over glamour issues, the U.S. electorate votes its pocketbook. The economy nearly always is the issue. That Lyndon Johnson was forced out of office in 1968 by the Vietnam War is the exception in recent years. That Jimmy Carter in 1980, Gerald Ford in 1976, and Richard Nixon in 1960 lost because the economy was in trouble and that Ronald Reagan in 1984, Richard Nixon in 1972, Lyndon Johnson in 1964, and Dwight Eisenhower in 1956 won because the economy seemed relatively under control is the rule. A strong economy reelects incumbents; a weak economy brings new people to office. Surely this rule oversimplifies American electoral politics, but the fact that it is widely believed reflects the importance of economic policy in our national life.

Clearly, this is no less true in the 1980s than in previous decades. In 1980 the United States elected a president who, like John Kennedy and Franklin Roosevelt before him, promised to get the economy moving again. In order to accomplish that end, the Reagan administration set about restricting, if not trying to dismantle, the domestic programs that are the legacy of the New Deal of the 1930s and the Great Society of the 1960s. Indeed, during the first term of that administration, the economy was the issue used to dismiss liberal charges of inequity and social retreat and to postpone conservative cries for an end to busing and abortion and the return of school prayer. The economy was the issue, the only issue.

But what is at stake in this issue for the remainder of this century—economically, politically, and socially? In particular, is anything new in dispute that has not been present during similar past debates? And are there ethical grounds for evaluating what is under debate and for taking a stand in the midst of the controversies?

History of the Issue

In the eighteenth and nineteenth centuries, most of the controversy over the proper role of government in economic affairs in the United States revolved around either trade policy or the printing of money. Protectionism largely lost out to the free traders primarily because of the success of American goods in the world market. If anything, the monetary debate heated up in the latter part of the nineteenth century, its breadth of appeal being represented in William Jennings Bryan's famous "Cross of Gold" address. The cries of some for a loosening up of monetary policy in order to encourage economic growth are signs of the growing industrialization that brought the economic issue to the center stage of American politics. With the rise of capitalistic industrialization came intellectual and political justification of the capitalist economic system.

But industrialization also brought with it some serious social problems that raised fundamental questions about capitalism. One result was a viable socialist party able to generate nearly a million votes for the presidential candidacy of Eugene Debs. Another result was a vast broadening of the ideological spectrum, including not only the socialists, who at this point were not yet dominated by the thought of Marx, but also all sorts of liberals and progressives. Finally, the federal government became deeply involved in the economy not so much through the highly publicized efforts to bust the trusts as through policy shifts such as the passage of the graduated income tax under Woodrow Wilson.

In the aftermath of World War I, partially in reaction to the Bolshevik revolutions in Russia, socialist thought was dismissed as un-American, and capitalists ruled unchallenged both politically and intellectually. Then came the Great Depression, and the economic system once again was an issue. Again, the political viability of socialism was symbolic; Norman Thomas received nearly 800,000 votes in 1932. However, again it was symbolic both of a broader opening of the ideological debate generally and of specific policy changes. The New Deal itself was ideologically complex. Roosevelt himself probably was most comfortable as a patrician capitalist. His advisors and supporters ranged from conservative business people trying to restore capitalism, to rural populists seeking electricity and extensions on their bank loans, to advocates of a conservative form of centralized planning, to socialists who saw Roosevelt as a more realistic, if less pure, alternative to Thomas. And they fought long and hard both about what was wrong with the economy and about what should be done.

The policy result was the framework of the U.S. welfare state, best represented by the Social Security Act of 1935. Perhaps as important was the general public belief that the government, and especially the president, was responsible for the economy. This was reflected in economists and policymakers by the emergence and development of a Keynesian view of the government's role in the economy. According to that view, the government had an ongoing responsibility to oversee the economy and especially to act to stimulate the economy through increasing government spending when private spending declined. One variation on this theme, the war effort, brought an end to the Depression.

Once the war was over, the nation slowly returned to normalcy, which meant a restoration of the reign of capitalist ideology and an end to the practice of Keynesian economics under Eisenhower. With this shift came a series of deepening recessions. By 1960 even a Catholic could get elected on the basis of getting the country moving again. The election did not bring broad-ranging ideological debate. That would wait until the coming of the civil rights and poverty movements and the deepening of the war in Asia in the late 1960s. What the election of Kennedy did bring, however, is what often is heralded as the great test of Keynesian theory: the tax cut of 1962. Kennedy urged it as a means of stimulating the economy; it passed, and the economy grew. Johnson extended the principle, although with some help from war spending after 1967.

So it was that by 1965 we had our ideologies and our policy options pretty well sorted out. While a few crackpots from time to time might get interested in either unbridled capitalism or full socialism, the real discussion was between moderately conservative capitalists and liberal capitalists. Indeed, some even christened this moderate consensus the "end of ideology" and proclaimed us freed from the claims of ideology to the pursuit of realistic political compromise.

On the policy front, our choices were now clear. Republicans wanted sound money, since they had more of it. Inflation was their feared enemy, to be fought by cutting government spending, balancing the budget, and tightening up the money supply. A negative side effect was recession and unemployment. Democrats wanted to put people back to work, since it was their people who were out of work during a recession. Unemployment was their feared enemy, to be fought by increasing government spending, tolerating deficits if necessary, and loosening up the money supply. A negative side effect was higher levels of inflation. The choices seemed reasonable and clear.

By the 1980 election, Jimmy Carter, the Democrat, ran on a Republican economic policy of balancing the budget and controlling inflation. Ronald Reagan, the Republican, advocated a tax cut to get the economy moving again, quoting Democrats Roosevelt and Kennedy in the process. Obviously, somewhere between 1965 and 1980 major ideological confusion took root. Richard Nixon could not decide whether he could gain greater power as his old or new self. As a result, he began as one would expect of a Republican until he was hit by inflation and unemployment at the same time. This convergence generated a new term, *stagflation*. Stagflation converted Nixon to Keynesian economics, or so he claimed. The result, including wage and price controls, shocked orthodox Republicans and dismayed Keynesians because of the half-committed way he went about it.

After the period when the federal government was reduced to a president trying to escape jail, Gerald Ford initiated traditional Republican policies that produced the expected recession. Along with an unpopular pardon, this produced President Jimmy Carter. Carter never could quite decide whether to be a Republican or a Democrat on economic policy. For him, the result was the worst, not the best, of both worlds. While the economic policy positions of Nixon and Carter always were vague, they clearly have proved that it is possible to have higher unemployment and inflation at the same time. How and why is less clear, as we shall see. This brings us to Ronald Reagan and our current confusion.

Ideological Options

There are a number of ways to categorize the various ideological possibilities. For the purposes of this chapter, I have identified three basic options. The first I shall call free-market capitalism. It has variously been called laissez-faire capitalism, nineteenth-century liberalism, or (in contemporary common usage in the United States) conservatism. It stresses limited government and the free market. I shall look further at Milton Friedman as a good representative of this free-market capitalism.[1]

The second option I shall call reformed capitalism. It has variously been called social-market capitalism, reformism, or (in contemporary common usage in the United States) liberalism. It advocates a welfare state and government intervention in the market. I shall take up Lester Thurow as a good representative of this reformed capitalism.[2]

The last ideological possibility I shall call Marxism. It sometimes is called communism, socialism, or radicalism. It boasts no term in contemporary common usage in the United States since it is not considered a viable ideological alternative. It argues that ownership and control of the means of production must become public. I shall examine Paul Baran and Paul Sweezy as representatives of Marxism.[3]

There are some options that I have eliminated in this threefold distinction. There are the ecology-minded proponents of less or no economic growth, such as E. F. Schumacher or Herman Daly.[4] I would contend that they raise an important new issue, resource limitation and environmental quality, which the other contemporary ideological positions must take seriously. However, when pressed on the specifics of economics and political organization, this supposedly new ideological position breaks down as, for instance, Schumacher's socialism or Daly's reformed capitalism come to the surface.

Two other positions also receive short shrift. The aristocratic conservatives who used to dominate political philosophy with their Greek and Roman references, including many of the founders of the U.S., are not active in the present dialogue. The closest representatives are the neoconservatives of the Irving Kristol sort.[5] Yet their final appeal is less to

---

[1]Milton Friedman and Rose Friedman, *Free to Choose* (New York: Harcourt Brace Jovanovich, 1979) is the primary source for my analysis. Milton Friedman, *Capitalism and Freedom* (Chicago: University of Chicago Press, 1962) is a better source on basic principles but not as good on contemporary policy.

[2]Lester C. Thurow, *The Zero-Sum Society* (New York: Basic Books, 1980) and *The Zero-Sum Solution* (New York: Simon and Schuster, 1985).

[3]Paul Baran and Paul Sweezy, *Monopoly Capital* (New York: Monthly Review Press, 1966).

[4]E. F. Schumacher, *Small Is Beautiful* (New York: Harper & Row, 1973); Herman Daly, *Steady-State Economics* (San Francisco: W. H. Freeman and Company, 1977).

[5]Irving Kristol, *Two Cheers for Capitalism* (New York: Basic Books, 1978).

Greece and Rome than to Jewish and Catholic family and community life. When pressed on social structure, this school also seems to break down, generally into either free-market capitalists or reformed capitalists.

Finally, there are the democratic socialists such as Michael Harrington.[6] It is enough at this point to say that I believe they bridge the three alternatives. I shall argue later that they draw upon the strengths of those alternatives in a way that addresses our contemporary historical situation in a particularly powerful way.

Free-Market Capitalism and Milton Friedman

Milton Friedman's ideal world consists of a free-market economy with courts to enforce contracts and an army to defend national borders. Friedman argues that the principles of a free-market economy can be reduced to the same rules of trade that apply to a collection of Robinson Crusoes, each trying to trade what he produces best for what others produce better so that all end up with more. If we add money and the modern corporation, this describes the modern free-market economy well enough to guide policy. The key is that parties to a transaction enter into it willingly; if so, everyone wins.

Friedman recognizes that this does not necessarily describe our present U.S. economy. However, he believes the greatest culprit in this corruption is government intervention. This raises his second basic commitment alongside that of the free market: limited government. Friedman believes that government has some essential functions, but they are few indeed. Specifically, he believes that government must (1) defend the nation from coercion from outside, (2) facilitate the free market by establishing rules for exchange and the medium of exchange (money), and (3) respond to neighborhood effects and the need for paternalism. It is this last category that worries him.

Neighborhood effects are those cases where action by one person inevitably affects another; streets and sewers are a positive example and air pollution a negative one. In such cases government may be involved. However, Friedman excludes many matters that others might consider neighborhood effects, such as highways and parks, arguing that they ought to be operated by private enterprise. Moreover, he often advocates a way

---

[6]Michael Harrington, *Decade of Decision* (New York: Simon and Schuster, 1980) and *The Next Left* (New York: Henry Holt, 1986).

of dealing with neighborhood effects that minimizes government involvement. For instance, he agrees that we all have a stake in an educated citizenry. However, he proposes that we meet that need by providing parents with educational vouchers that they can spend at any school rather than through government's providing a public-school education for all.

In the area of paternalism, he is even more careful. In the final analysis, he believes only children and the mentally incompetent should fall in that category. Otherwise he rejects programs based on paternalism because they force the taxpayers to support someone they may not want to help and they usually limit the freedom of the recipient to act as he or she chooses.

All of this, the free market and limited government, is justified on the basis of maximizing individual freedom. Friedman states this very clearly: "As liberals, we take freedom of the individual . . . as our ultimate goal in judging social arrangements."[7] When Friedman uses the term *freedom*, he means a very simple thing: the absence of outside coercion. I shall call this liberty. He is convinced that people know better than anyone else what they should do. People should be allowed to pursue their own interests, no matter how selfish or generous those interests or how wisely or foolishly they pursue them. The goal of social policy is to allow as many people as possible to exercise their own interests as fully as possible.

Friedman supports the free market and limited government precisely because they maximize such liberty. He believes the free market does this by allowing consumers to buy what they want as long as producers can supply it at a price they are willing to pay. The consumer and producer are free to enter into or reject the transaction. Producers compete for the business of the consumers, choices multiply, and freedom grows.

Limited government keeps government from restricting these choices by forcing people to act as the government orders. If such government coercion is limited to only a few necessary areas, allowing the free market to operate in the others, liberty thrives.

Lester Thurow and Reformed Capitalism

Without fully settling the question of whether or not we have free-market capitalism, Thurow believes it is failing. Americans have suddenly

---

[7]Friedman and Friedman, *Capitalism and Freedom*, 12.

come face to face with their own vulnerability, thanks to oil and international competition. The Arab oil boycott of 1973 and the oil-price rises shook our economy at its core. We now recognize that we must have a secure flow of oil from relatively insecure areas of the world to fuel our economy. Moreover, our economy has yet to recover from the inflation and slow economic growth higher oil prices have brought.

At the same time, we no longer seem to be able to compete with nations such as Japan and West Germany in the industrial goods that have been the mainstay of our economy, such as steel and autos. While there may be considerable disagreement about whose standard of living is actually highest in the world, there can be no doubt that we are falling behind to nations with faster-growing economies.

In case after case, what finally makes a perceived problem an actual problem for Thurow is whether or not it produces inequity. A free-market solution to energy—allowing prices to rise—is a serious problem because it is unfair to the poor, who spend a much larger portion of their income on energy than do the rich. Inflation is not that big a problem because, at least from 1972 through 1978, it seemed to have affected all groups about the same. Recession is a problem because it falls most heavily on the disadvantaged. Inequality defines a social problem for Thurow.

Thurow does not believe our problems can be blamed upon too much government, as Friedman would contend. Nor does he believe they can be blamed on too much welfare or on too great an emphasis on equality. He points out that our primary economic competition, Europe and Japan, have much greater government involvement in their economies and much smaller income differences among their citizens.

Indeed, Thurow's solution is more government and more equality. The most significant proposal he advances on the first front is government direction of investment. In order to restore economic growth, he believes difficult choices must be made to invest in productive sectors of the economy, and even more difficult choices must be made to let less-productive industries die. Since investment in new productive industries involves more risk than private investors usually care to take, and since old industries often are able to hold onto investments long after their productivity fails, governments must take the lead. Specifically, he proposes a central investment board that would direct investment away from the unproductive and into productive areas of the economy. As he puts it most directly, "Japan Incorporated must be met by U.S.A. Incorporated."[8]

On the equality front, Thurow suggests an interim goal of reducing the inequality in the United States to that which exists among fully employed white males. This is based on the assumption that something like fair competition exists among fully employed white males. It is important to recognize that the equality Thurow seeks is not intended to eliminate competition but rather to make it fair, at least as fair as that which presently exists among fully employed white males. This would require a fivefold reduction in the present inequalities in the United States. In order to accomplish such a major reduction in inequality, Thurow advocates a full employment program and a national income floor in order to raise the incomes of those presently at the bottom. In order to bring those at the top down, he supports graduated taxes until the equity goal is reached.

In the final analysis, both of these central goals—greater economic growth and greater income equity—are based on Thurow's commitment to equality. He believes there is a significant amount of "zero sum game" in our present economy. In a zero-sum situation, every time there is a winner, there must be a loser. However, economic growth can minimize the zero-sum aspect of our economy. Enacting greater equity is always difficult; it becomes nearly impossible when there is the same or less to share. When the economy is growing, equality is possible by distributing the growth among those with less. When the economy grows less, equality can be brought about only by taking from those who presently have the most, a practice they can hardly be expected to take lying down. Thus Thurow urges an emphasis on economic growth because it makes efforts to create greater equity more possible.

Yet Thurow realizes that even in the best of circumstances enough of a zero-sum element will remain that hard choices will be necessary. It will take political leadership, party discipline, and a group of citizens committed to the public interest instead of their own private interest to support such a program. In the final analysis, this requires an overriding belief in the principle of equity.

Marxism and Paul Baran and Paul Sweezy

Baran and Sweezy are convinced that capitalism neither can nor should be reformed. Rather, they argue that the very dynamics of capitalism pro-

---

[8]Thurow, *Zero-Sum Society*, 192.

duce basic contradictions that lead to its downfall. Capitalism adds a third factor to the productive process alongside the worker and the product. The result personally and socially is alienation.

Simply stated, surplus value is the difference between what a society produces and the costs of producing it. Under capitalism this difference is retained by the capitalist, leading to a concentration of wealth. Not only do Baran and Sweezy believe that this creates great inequity, but they also contend that it leads inevitably to economic stagnation. Since capitalists continually siphon off the surplus, consumers, who are composed primarily of the workers, cannot afford to buy what they produce. The result is chronic overproduction or shortage of consumption.

The primary purpose of *Monopoly Capital* is to examine how this traditional Marxist concept of surplus value operates in the modern U.S. economy, in which small entrepreneurs have been replaced by large corporations to a great extent. In the modern large corporation, the tycoon has been replaced by the corporate manager. This has brought some significant changes. The manager's primary goal is the growth of the corporation rather than his own wealth. This does not mean, according to Baran and Sweezy, that modern corporations do not seek to maximize profits. Rather, it means that long-term stability and profitability take precedence over short-term returns. Not accidentally, this policy benefits large stockholders, including the managers themselves, at the expense of small stockholders. So the modern corporation continues to seek to maximize profits—that is, increase the surplus—at the expense of both the workers and the small stockholders.

Moreover, Baran and Sweezy argue, the modern corporations are much better able to *increase* the surplus. This is because they operate like a monopoly in that they set prices. Rather than being forced to sell their products at the price consumers will pay, the large corporation cooperates with the other firms in its industry to establish prices that will maximize its profits and thus increase the surplus. Mature corporations do not compete by cutting prices. They instead follow the pricing policy of their competitors, but seek to increase their market share, their portion of total sales of their product. Price competition continues only in industries marked by a great innovation or dispersed ownership, a sign of immaturity.

So surplus merely multiplies under monopoly capitalism, leading inevitably to economic stagnation. Capitalists have traditionally looked to population growth, innovation, and foreign investment to soak up this surplus. However, Baran and Sweezy do not feel any of them works. Increased demand from population growth depends upon economic growth rather than producing economic growth; it can produce greater unemployment and stagnation just as easily as economic expansion. Mature corporations are not threatened by innovative companies. They just buy them out and use them to produce even-greater surplus. Similarly, instead of using up the surplus, foreign investment brings a greater return than domestic investment. Wealth migrates back to the investing corporation, and the surplus grows.

Capitalists do not sit idly by in the face of this ever-expanding surplus, according to Baran's and Sweezy's account. Rather, they identify three primary ways by which monopoly capitalism seeks to stimulate the demand for its products: sales efforts, domestic government spending, and militarism. Under monopoly capitalism, corporations compete through expensive ad campaigns aimed not only at selling more of a particular product but also at convincing consumers to buy more generally. Baran and Sweezy view government spending not as humanitarian effort but rather as an attempt to save capitalism from stagnation. The emphasis on supporting middle-class consumption through highway construction and home-mortgage programs, instead of on basic social problems, illustrates this fact. Finally, monopoly capitalism turns to militarism both to protect its economic imperialism around the world and to create more demand for the products of large corporations.

Since none of these strategies involves a shift in who owns and controls the means of production, they not only result in an irrational use of human and natural resources but also merely expand the surplus by creating greater opportunity for the corporate profit and growth. The inevitable result of this system sooner or later is economic disaster.

In the meantime the monopoly-capitalist system creates personal and social alienation. The fundamental example of this alienation is separation of workers from the result of their work. The product belongs to the corporation; the worker is merely a tool used in producing it. Work is no longer a way of expressing one's full humanity. Now it is but a way to make a living and to finance one's pursuit of human meaning in leisure activity. Baran and Sweezy see this attempt to escape into personal gratification as essentially unhealthy, leading to sexual dysfunction, family breakup, and mental illness.

For Baran and Sweezy, this basic alienation of workers from their work is mirrored in social and political alienation. The result of the rule of profit is a decline in the quality of the society. Poverty and unemployment are constants, housing is out of reach for the average person, education deteriorates, the environment becomes polluted, and the public spirit disintegrates. Society, then, is organized not to meet human needs but to produce profits for the ruling class.

Similarly, the ruling class dominates our politics. Free enterprise becomes an empty concept masking a system in service of monopoly capital. Monopoly capitalists are able to control our supposedly democratic politics to their own ends in part because average citizens are fooled into voting against their own interests, but in greater part because of the power and money of the ruling class.

Since this system is irrational economically and contrary to the interest of the masses, it is doomed. The revolution could come from within as the mass of Americans discover the root of their alienation. However, Baran and Sweezy believe revolutionary change is much more likely to arise from the outside, where the masses have been seduced much less by affluence. In particular, they look with hope to Cuba, China, and other Third World revolutionary societies. By challenging U.S. economic imperialism, revolution in the Third World may bring the irrationality of monopoly capitalism home to Americans.

In the final analysis, the critique Baran and Sweezy level against capitalism arises from a commitment to human community and solidarity. They see capitalism separating individuals from their work and from their fellow human beings. Similarly, the remedies they propose require a reestablishment of this solidarity both as the guiding principle for organizing society and as the common experience of the masses who will bring about the reorganization of society on the basis of that principle. The result, they believe, is both just and economically rational.

In sum, free-market capitalism stresses the liberty of the individual to choose free of coercion. Social policy is judged by whether it advances or limits this individual autonomy. Reformed capitalism argues that all must have an equal opportunity to exercise this freedom. The measure of good social policy is whether it serves to equalize the possibility for the actual exercise of freedom. This generally involves restricting the power and opportunities of the "haves" in order to advance the chances of the "have nots.'' Finally, Marxism advances the claim of human solidarity. It rejects social polity that separates humans.

Criteria for Ethical Evaluation

Liberty, equality, or solidarity, which shall it be? Must we choose? Not necessarily, but probably.

Douglas Sturm has argued for a fourth position, aristocratic conservatism, as the solution to this dilemma.[9] In fact, the appeal of that position for Sturm is its capacity to choose wisely among the strengths of these three. He contends that each expresses a basic dimension of human life: individual freedom, the self as creative agent; social equality, the self as relational; and solidarity, the self as communal. What this suggests is that we need all three. Moreover, if we understand all three in terms of what it means to be fully human, they not only can coexist, but actually support one another.

To be fully human is to be a creative agent. Traditionally, Christians have expressed this reality by saying that humans are created in the image of God. If God is creator, we too are to be creative. Hannah Arendt uses the term *natality* to refer to this same reality.[10] At our most human, we give birth to new words and deeds. It is this human capacity to create that liberty seeks to protect and extend. In the process, however, liberty becomes the rationalization for people doing whatever they want. Maximizing the wants of the few leads to great inequities of money and power; maximizing the wants of the many leads to a mass consumer society marked by sameness, not creativity.

To be fully human is to be related to others. We come to be who we are because of our relations with other people. But if we are all created in the image of God, then these relations should be marked by an equality that allows all to be unique, creative persons. Hannah Arendt uses the term *plurality* to refer to this form of relationship. At their best, human relationships connect while preserving the creative capacities of each participant. The result is not a homogenized mass, but rather a dynamic give-and-take between distinct and unique individuals. This is what equality is

---

[9]Douglas Sturm, "The Prism of Justice: E Pluribus Unum?'' *The Annual of the Society of Christian Ethics* (1981): 15-18.

[10]Hannah Arendt, *The Human Condition* (Chicago: University of Chicago Press, 1958) esp. 175-84.

intended to produce. Instead, it often becomes the rallying cry of competing interests all claiming that equality demands what they want.

To be fully human is to be part of a community. The Jewish and Christian traditions arose from the experience of community. It was the nation of Israel, not the individual Jew, that was key. The early church was marked by a sense of community, of shared destiny. Indeed, Hannah Arendt argues that a common world, a community, provides the necessary context for natality and plurality. This common world includes a shared language and history, but also the products of work. Solidarity is based upon and intended to further such a common world. But solidarity can also be the excuse for excluding those who are different, the occasion for a new tribalism. Furthermore, it can be used as the grounds for rule by the few in the name of the community, as in the Soviet Union.

At their worst, liberty, equality, and community are at war. If we are set free to do what we want, the result is inequality and broken community. The only way to establish equality is to limit some people's liberty. Sooner or later we have got to quit clamoring for equal rights and begin to consider the good of society as a whole. If liberty means doing what I want, equality means getting my fair share of the action, and solidarity means homogeneity, then they are forever at odds.

However, if liberty refers to my capacity to be creative, it requires other humans equally free with whom to share that creativity and a community that provides a place and the means for such sharing to take place. Similarly, true equality can occur only between free people with a sense of shared destiny. Finally, real solidarity is built by free creative people working together. Thus, in principle, liberty, equality, and solidarity recognize what is uniquely human and reinforce one another. They are complementary, not competitive.

In practice, however, we may well conclude that even though we want to reinforce the human meaning of all three, we must place particular emphasis on one or two. For instance, if one were living in the Soviet Union today, liberty might be the most important principle. There, in the name of solidarity, the exercise of liberty brings jail. Indeed, it appears equality also suffers as those who claim to act for the people help themselves and their families to the detriment of others. Interestingly, the result is a tearing apart of solidarity, too, indicating that true solidarity requires liberty and equality.

On the other hand, we in the United States sacrifice equality and community on the altar of liberty. If some of us are to have a right to buy a home in a white middle-class neighborhood and send our children to the neighborhood school, then the children of people who are not white or middle class are not likely to get an equal chance for a good education. If our primary commitments are to our own self-interest, it is difficult to raise questions about the quality of the society. There is no public interest.

The result of this singular pursuit of liberty is that freedom in the human sense is also lost. We are no longer free to create but rather only to win, to manage, to accumulate. This is where we find ourselves in the United States these days. In principle we need liberty, equality, and solidarity. In practice we need much more solidarity and equality in order to have true liberty.

Michael Harrington and Democratic Socialism

This leads us to democratic socialism and Michael Harrington. Harrington begins from Marxism's commitment to solidarity. He argues that our economic ills are structural; that is, they are the natural outgrowth of our economic system. Thus it will take basic changes in the whole system, not just a few minor adjustments to the free market. Specifically, our economic problems result from the centralization of economic power in a few private hands. This corporate elite uses its power to advance the interests of the corporations. They are able to manage markets, set prices, accumulate capital, and finally control politicians to this end. The free-market ideology provides a rational cover for this diversion of the public good to private benefit. In the final analysis this constitutes a denial of solidarity, a destruction of community.

It also produces great inequality. It was as a chronicler of inequality that Harrington first became well known through his unmasking of poverty in the early 1960s.[11] It remains a primary concern of his. He consistently rejects the suggestions of other Marxists that liberal reforms do not deserve support. Rather, he sees efforts to promote greater equality through affirmative action, a guaranteed income, or full employment as supportive of a more fundamental questioning of the capitalist system.

This support for reformist policy coincides with his support for an inclusive, interactive political process. He calls this "coalition politics."

---

[11]Michael Harrington, *The Other America* (New York: Macmillan, 1962).

Much of his work is in search of a coalition of the Left composed of various groups with overlapping but not identical interests, such as workers, minorities, ecologists, the poor, women, consumers, and the conscience constituency. He believes that if the participants in such a coalition can give up some of their particular interests, at least for the short run, it would be possible to enact programs serving some of the interests of all.

This commitment to coalition politics is one aspect of the democratic element in democratic socialism. However, Harrington also recognizes some of the liberty aspects of democracy. He is a firm and consistent advocate of individual freedom. In particular, he constantly criticizes Marxist governments like the Soviet Union that restrict political freedom in the name of solidarity. In fact, he imagines a socialism that is decentralized to minimize bureaucratic control and that protects the private property necessary to sustain liberty.

Harrington and his democratic socialist colleagues are examples of those with thoroughgoing respect for the legitimacy of liberty, equality, and solidarity. However, this respect is matched by the conviction that equality, and particularly solidarity, must be advanced to correct the abuses of liberty in the United States. The result is a balanced, yet forceful, agenda for United States economic policy.

The Current Situation

We return to the twin curses of inflation and unemployment. Only we were not left without counsel. Rather, we were promised the wonders of supply-side economics. We were told that, with the proper incentives and the absence of governmental restraint, the free market could be restored to its vibrant youth. Moreover, we were assured that this was an exciting new solution to our economic problems.

We need only note Milton Friedman's uncontained joy at this prospect to suspect that supply-side economics is not all that new. It calls for less government income, limiting government expenditures, limiting government to the essentials—a position long advocated by free-market capitalists. It proposes to lift the weight of government from the backs of business. This is music to the ears of free-market capitalists. It proposes to cut federal taxes dramatically, especially for the economically successful, in order to reward effort and stimulate investment.

The major break with traditional free-market ideology is the willingness to tolerate the short-term deficit resulting from the tax cut in order to stimulate the economy. However, even this was justified in traditional terms by arguing that the increased revenue resulting from economic growth will produce a balanced budget in the long run. This is an exception people like Friedman could tolerate since they have long believed that the money supply was much more important in controlling inflation than a balanced budget. The greatest convergence is at the level of principle. The argument from expedience is that supply-side economics will bring prosperity—but then free-market capitalists claim it always has. The more fundamentally ethical argument is that supply-side economics will get government off our backs. It will free individuals to produce. It will restore liberty.

Thurow, Harrington, and Sweezy agree that there is a need to renew our basic industrial base in the United States. However, they all believe that simply enriching large corporations and wealthy people is unlikely to produce the desired results. Rather, they suggest that this new wealth will seek its highest profit. At a time of record deficits, the highest profit may be in financing the government's debt. Higher profits may be available from moving production outside of the country rather than from investing in rebuilding U.S. industries. Each, in his own way, argues that these decisions cannot be left simply to private decision making.

Thurow proposes that the public, through the government, establish incentives that encourage investment in productive enterprise. He further argues that liberal programs designed to further equality, such as full employment, can be used to reinforce this process of economic recovery. In the final analysis, he depends upon the market, influenced by these incentives, to work. Equality can be both just and productive.

Sweezy argues for direct government direction of the economy, including nationalization of basic industries such as energy. This would both facilitate public planning to restore the industrial base and place the capital necessary in public hands. By enacting solidarity, we would make possible a rational economy. Sweezy also does not expect this to happen except as it is forced upon us by outside forces such as the collapse of our international economic empire.

Harrington urges both solidarity and equality upon us. He argues that full employment, with the government as employer of last resort, is essential to deal with unemployment. He contends that price controls are the most equitable way to hold inflation down. More fundamentally, he argues for public planning on a variety of fronts—local, regional, and national— and by a variety of techniques. Whether it is national direction of basic investment decisions, worker representation on corporate boards, or neighborhood decision making on how to spend federal funds, the solution is to democratize the economy. The goal is to advance both equality and solidarity while preserving liberty.

Clearly the real choice of specific economic policy requires much more analysis of the actual economic forces at work. The question of what policy can provide the rallying point for political majorities also must be raised. However, it should be clear that a part of the choice of policy depends upon judgments about the importance and possibility of furthering liberty, equality, and solidarity in our economic policy in the years ahead.

Annotated Bibliography

Alternative Approaches

Baran, Paul A. and Paul M. Sweezy. *Monopoly Capital*. New York: Monthly Review Press, 1966. This remains the classic pure Marxist analysis of the U.S. economy. While Sweezy's subsequent books provide considerable updating of what are now some stale data, his articles appearing in nearly every issue of *Monthly Review* are just as good a source for his present views.

Friedman, Milton and Rose Friedman. *Capitalism and Freedom*. Chicago: University of Chicago Press, 1962.

_____. *Free to Choose*. New York: Avon, 1979.

_____. *Tyranny of the Status Quo*. New York: Harcourt Brace Jovanovich, 1983. The first two are Friedman's basic statements on economic policy for a general audience. The first is better on basic principles, while the second deals with more-specific current issues. The third is a less-systematic reaction to the first two years of the Reagan administration.

Harrington, Michael. *The Decade of Decision*. New York: Simon and Schuster, 1980.

_____. *The Next Left*. New York: Henry Holt, 1986. These are Harrington's most recent books addressed particularly to economic policy. The first is now somewhat out of date but gets into the specifics of policy better.

Thurow, Lester C. *The Zero-Sum Society*. New York: Penguin, 1980.

_____. *The Zero-Sum Solution*. New York: Simon and Schuster, 1985. While Thurow's early work on the labor market is quite interesting, his conclusions are well represented in these two books. The former's discussion of the equity goal is better. The latter is better on his various proposals for increased economic growth.

Ethical Analysis

Benne, Robert. *The Ethic of Democratic Capitalism*. Philadelphia: Fortress, 1981.

Finn, Daniel R. and Prentiss L. Pemberton. *Toward a Christian Economic Ethic*. Minneapolis: Winston Press, 1985.

Wogaman, J. Philip. *The Great Economic Debate*. Philadelphia: Westminster, 1977.

_____. *Economics and Ethics*. Philadelphia: Fortress, 1986. In *The Great Economic Debate*, Wogaman establishes some criteria for ethical judgment from the Judeo-Christian tradition and then applies them to five basic ideological positions. In *Economics and Ethics*, he develops quite similar criteria in a similar way and then examines five priorities of the economic order. In each case, Wogaman takes a position somewhere between liberal capitalism and democratic socialism, with significant concerns for the environment. Benne's is the best of the ethical defenses of capitalism. Drawing heavily on Reinhold Niebuhr, he concludes that democratic capitalism sustains a reasonable balance between the demands of justice and the reality of sin. He proposes a series of conservative means to liberal ends as ways of improving this balance even more. Finn and Pemberton give a generally communitarian reading to the biblical and church traditions, emphasizing Roman Catholic resources. While recognizing the contributions of the Reformation and the Enlightenment, they advocate a greater place for community amid current policy discussions.

Constructive Resources

Arendt, Hannah. *The Human Condition.* Garden City NY: Doubleday, 1959.

—————. *On Revolution.* New York: Viking Press, 1965.

Sturm, Douglas. "The Prism of Justice: E Pluribus Unum?" *The Annual of the Society of Christian Ethics,* 1981. The former book by Arendt lays out her basic analysis of human action. The latter one develops the relation between economics and action much more fully. Sturm's analytical framework lies behind the basic structure of this chapter and, with some key revisions, inspires the ethical evaluation carried out herein.